GW00359928

# EXCESS RETURNS

# Excess Returns

## A comparative study of the world's greatest investors

By Frederik Vanhaverbeke

HARRIMAN HOUSE LTD
3A Penns Road
Petersfield
Hampshire
GU32 2EW
GREAT BRITAIN

Tel: +44 (0)1730 233870
Email: enquiries@harriman-house.com
Website: www.harriman-house.com

First published in Great Britain in 2014
Copyright © Harriman House 2014

The right of Frederik Vanhaverbeke to be identified as Author has been asserted in accordance with the Copyright, Design and Patents Act 1988.

ISBN: 978-0857194329

British Library Cataloguing in Publication Data
A CIP catalogue record for this book can be obtained from the British Library.

All rights reserved; no part of this publication may be reproduced, stored in a retrieval system, or transmitted in any form or by any means, electronic, mechanical, photocopying, recording, or otherwise without the prior written permission of the Publisher.

This book may not be lent, resold, hired out or otherwise disposed of by way of trade in any form of binding or cover other than that in which it is published without the prior written consent of the Publisher.

No responsibility for loss occasioned to any person or corporate body acting or refraining to act as a result of reading material in this book can be accepted by the Publisher or by the Author.

# CONTENTS

# FOLLOW US, LIKE US, EMAIL US

**@HarrimanHouse**
**www.linkedin.com/company/harriman-house**
**www.facebook.com/harrimanhouse**
**contact@harriman-house.com**

 Harriman House

# FREE EBOOK VERSION

As a buyer of the print book of *Excess Returns* you can now download the eBook version free of charge to read on an eBook reader, your smartphone or your computer. Simply go to:

**http://ebooks.harriman-house.com/excessreturns**

or point your smartphone at the QRC below.

You can then register and download your free eBook.

# ABOUT THE AUTHOR

FREDERIK VANHAVERBEKE GRADUATED with High Distinction as a Bachelor and Master in Electrical Engineering from the University of Ghent. After graduation he obtained a PhD in Electrical Engineering in 2005. Between 2005 and 2010, he was involved in postdoctoral research projects in Belgium and Singapore in the field of digital telecommunication.

Over the past decade, Frederik has built considerable expertise in the areas of stock investing, company analysis, accounting, etc., through the reading of hundreds of books, articles, shareholders' letters, etc. in his free time. Thanks to his thorough knowledge of best practices in the field of investing he has beaten the market by a substantial margin over the past ten years in his private stock portfolio. Currently, he is employed as a bond portfolio manager at KBC Asset Management, Belgium.

# INTRODUCTION

"The main reason why money is lost in stock speculation is not because Wall Street is dishonest, but because so many people persist in thinking that you can make money without working for it and that the stock exchange is the place where this miracle can be performed."

BERNARD BARUCH (BARUCH, 1957)

THE STOCK MARKET is a place that fires people's imaginations. It is widely believed to be a route to easy riches, where even a person of modest means can become a millionaire through proper stock picking. In reality, very few people know someone who has achieved this. Study after study shows that the vast majority of people who try their chances in the market don't even manage to keep up with stock indexes, never mind beat them. Apparently, making a fortune through stock selection is not as straightforward as most people would like to think.

The fact that few people are able to beat the market is one of the reasons certain academics have posited the idea that markets are so efficient they can only be beaten through luck.[1] These proponents of the so-called Efficient Market Hypothesis (EMH) argue that investors cannot take advantage of price anomalies as every anomaly is eliminated instantaneously by the many smart people that look for bargains in the market.

In addition, the EMH obviously excludes the possibility that the market can be beaten through any particular approach. However, as I show in the following sections, there are plenty of indications that the EMH does not describe market action adequately and that the markets are not always efficient.

## Beating the market

There are different schools of market players who claim that the market can be beaten by means of a particular style. For example, traders try to outsmart the market based on price action. Trend followers or momentum traders, for instance, attempt to sail on the waves of price momentum.

---

[1] See, for example (Malkiel, 2007).

Investors, on the other hand, claim that one can beat the market by focusing on fundamental considerations such as a company's valuation, its management, its financials, the wider economy, etc. Investors analyse these fundamentals and try to buy a stock when it is cheap and sell when it is expensive. Some investors focus exclusively on quantitative data, whereas others include qualitative elements in their stock assessments. Still others, called *macro investors*, believe that one can do better than the market by investing in various assets around the world based on macroeconomic considerations.

To verify the claim that the market can be beaten by means of certain styles I show in Table 1 the annual compound returns of a number of famous market operators with track records of at least ten years.[2]

**Table 1: Annual compound returns (estimates) of a selection of top investors and traders over intervals of at least ten years**

| Name | Compound annual return (years) | Name | Compound annual return (years) | Name | Compound annual return (years) |
|---|---|---|---|---|---|
| **Richard Dennis** | **120% (19)** | *George Soros* | *29% (34)* | Lou Simpson | 20.3% (24) |
| Michael Marcus | 120% (10) | Eddie Lampert | 29% (16) | *W. Schloss* | *20% (49)* |
| Jaffray Woodriff | 118% (10) | P. Tudor Jones | 26% (19) | R. C. Perry | 20.8% (20) |
| Bruce Kovner | 87% (10) | Scott Ramsey | 25.7% (11) | P. Watsa | 20% (15) |
| Randy McKay | ≈ 80% (20) | **Paul Rabar** | **25.5% (23)** | *Tom Knapp* | *20% (16)* |
| V. Sperandeo | 72% (19) | Martin Zweig | 25% (19) | Edward Thorp | 19.8% (29) |
| Ed Seykota | ≈ 60% (30) | *J. Robertson* | *25% (20)* | B. S. Sherman | 19.6% (20) |
| **W. Eckhardt** | **≈ 60% (13)** | M. Steinhardt | 24.7% (28) | D. Einhorn | 19.4% (17) |
| Gil Blake | 45% (12) | C. Munger | 24% (12) | Steve Clark | 19.4% (11) |
| J. Greenblatt | 45% (19) | Joe Vidich | 24% (10) | G. Michaelis | 18.4% (15) |
| William O'Neil | ≈ 40% (25) | **Liz Cheval** | **23.1% (23)** | *Bill Ruane* | *18% (14)* |
| Jim Ruben | 40% (10) | Warren Buffett | 23% (54) | G. Greenberg | 18% (25) |
| *Jim Rogers* | *38% (11)* | Bruce Karsh | 23% (25) | Jack Dreyfus | 17.7% (12) |
| S. Druckenmiller | *37% (12)* | S. Perlmeter | 23% (18) | Daniel Loeb | 17.6% (15) |
| Robert Wilson | 34% (20) | **H. Seidler** | **22.8% (23)** | M. J. Whitman | 17.2% (21) |
| James Simons | 34% (24) | F. G. Paramés | 22.52% (14) | A. Vandenberg | 16.6% (33) |
| Rick Guerin | 33% (19) | **Jerry Parker** | **22.2% (23)** | S. Klarman | 16.5% (25) |
| Jeff Vinik | 32% (12) | Shelby Davis | 22% (45) | T. Rowe Price | 16% (38) |
| Louis Bacon | 31% (15) | Martin Taylor | 22% (11) | Tom Russo | 15.8% (24) |
| David Bonderman | > 30% (20) | **S. Abraham** | **21.7% (19)** | Peter Cundill | 15.2% (33) |
| R. Driehaus | 30% (12) | Tom Claugus | 21% (26) | J. Templeton | 15% (38) |
| **Tom Shanks** | **29.7% (22)** | *B. Graham* | *21% (20)* | John Neff | 14.8% (31) |
| Peter Lynch | 29.2% (13) | A. Bolton | 20.3% (27) | Philip Carret | 13% (55) |

[2] The data was collected from various sources, including: (Covel, 2007), (Faith, 2007), (Greenblatt, 1997), (Train, 2000), (Schwager, 1992), (Schwager, 2006), (Schwager, 2012).

EMH adherents would say these returns are outliers that can be explained by chance; they argue exceptional returns are possible through home runs (e.g., people who invest in a penny stock that increases 100-fold can achieve extremely high returns), and leverage (i.e., the use of debt or derivatives to magnify success). However, when one scratches below the surface of the track records of Table 1, the theory that these people were all lucky falls short.

First of all, it was not home runs and leverage that drove these returns. Virtually all of these returns were achieved through diversified portfolios with significant turnover across periods ranging from 10 to almost 60 years. Although some of the market operators in Table 1 were leveraged, many weren't. Besides, none of those who were leveraged owed their excellent track records to a single lucky strike. In fact, futures traders like Richard Dennis and William Eckhardt probably made hundreds or thousands of trades throughout the considered period.

Second, many of the returns of Table 1 actually understate what these investors or traders could achieve. Various returns shown here are *after* subtraction of sizeable management fees and expenses, so the return before these fees was even greater. Further, some returns were achieved on portfolios that were so large that the market operator's freedom of action and flexibility were seriously impeded. One has to realise that selling and purchasing shares cannot be done as swiftly in large portfolios as in small ones. In addition, large portfolios also restrict the universe in which a portfolio manager can look for a trade since smart portfolio managers don't spend their precious research time on stocks that cannot move the needle of their portfolio. This adds up to mean that these people could not always necessarily act on their best ideas, thus impeding their performance.

A third problem for people who attribute success in the stock market to chance is that some of the returns of Table 1 were achieved consistently and with very low volatility. The most striking example of consistency is Edward Thorp (highlighted in bold and grey) who posted gains in 227 of the 230 months that he ran an investment partnership between 1969 and 1988.

Assuming that the probability of a positive gain in any particular month is about 0.6 (as has been the case historically), the probability that someone can achieve this level of consistency or better is $6.10^{-46}$. This is only a few orders of magnitude higher than the probability that one would find a single specific atom by looking in a random place on earth. It is therefore safe to say that Thorp was not just lucky.

A final and remarkable observation that cannot be explained by the EMH is that many of the people in Table 1 achieved their market-beating performance through a similar style. Names with the same letter type belong to a common school.[3] This kind of structure in the way the market is beaten is, of course, incompatible with EMH.

What is even more unthinkable for EMH adherents is that investment or trading principles can be taught. However, the table shows that some of the famous **Turtle Traders** (highlighted in bold) who were taught momentum trading by Richard Dennis and

---

[3] _Underline + italic_ = quantitative fundamental investing; <u>underline</u> = quantitative-qualitative fundamental investing; **bold** = trend-following trading; *italic* = macro investing.

William Eckhardt were very successful when they struck out on their own. What is more, the legendary trader Jesse Livermore, a pioneer of momentum trading, was the inspiration and mental tutor of the Turtle Traders and many other highly successful momentum traders in Table 1.

Likewise, several of the _Graham disciples_ (highlighted in italics and underlined) who were taught value investing by Benjamin Graham had remarkable success when they applied the value investing principles independently of each other.

Furthermore, the investors highlighted with an underline are a number of so-called Buffett adepts who either openly admitted that they derived their style by following that of Warren Buffett (Eddie Lampert, Joel Greenblatt, Prem Watsa), or who have worked in partnership with Buffett (Rick Guerin and Charlie Munger). Another puzzling achievement is that of George Soros who managed to find a worthy replacement, namely Stanley Druckenmiller, for Jim Rogers to run his hedge fund after the departure of the latter (_all highlighted with italics_).

The implication of EMH that people who beat the market are highly unlikely to be clustered (because they should be random individuals) is also challenged by the so-called Tiger Cubs (not shown in the table). These are highly successful macro investors like Stephen Mandel and Lee Ainslie who used to work in Julian Robertson's Tiger Fund, and who started out on their own after Julian closed his hedge fund down.

As a final challenge to EMH, virtually all of those in Table 1, irrespective of their style or method, refer to the same rare attitudes, habits and mental requirements as being pivotal for success in the stock market (these are discussed in the final chapter of this book).

> "It has been helpful to me to have tens of thousands [of students] turned out of business schools taught that it didn't do any good to think."
>
> **Warren Buffett (Grant, 1991)**

## Renowned investors

The previous section provides pretty convincing material to suggest that the market can indeed be beaten through certain styles of trading and investing. Now that this has been shown, our focus narrows and we turn our attention to how successful _investors_ tend to beat the market. This is the subject that will be discussed in the rest of the book.

Referring to Figure 1, you can see how well the track records of a sample of very successful investors held up against the S&P stock index (with dividends reinvested).[4] The figure shows the average _annual excess_ return of these investors versus the S&P stock market index. Immediately you can see that these investors have been able to beat the market by a considerable margin.

---

[4] The sample consists mainly of the _investors_ in Table 1.

**Figure 1: Approximate excess returns versus the S&P 500 Index (with dividends reinvested) of top investors**

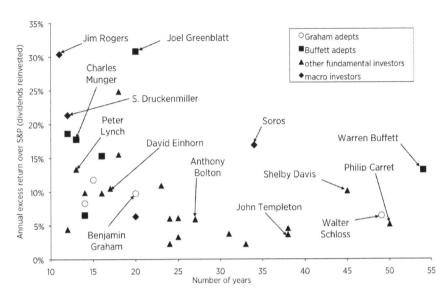

A first observation is that, as one should expect, excess returns tend to decrease when the observation period gets longer. Nevertheless, even over periods of about half a century some investors managed to maintain an excess return of more than 5%. The most astonishing track record is undoubtedly that of Warren Buffett, who managed to beat the market by an amazing 13% per year over a period of 54 years.

In Figure 1, a number of legendary American investors who figure prominently in this book are highlighted:

1. **Benjamin Graham**, generally considered to be the father of value investing, used a style that was mainly quantitative (i.e., based on financial data that can be found in annual reports). He taught value investing to several people who later excelled in the investment industry (e.g., Warren Buffett and Walter Schloss).

2. **Peter Lynch** is one of the best mutual fund managers ever. He managed Fidelity's Magellan Fund between 1977 and 1990. He popularised the growth investment style in the 1990s with his two books *One Up on Wall Street* and *Beating the Street*.

3. **Anthony Bolton** ran the Fidelity Special Situation Fund between 1979 and 2007. In this capacity he was a close colleague of Peter Lynch.

4. **Charles Munger** joined Warren Buffett in the 1970s as a partner in Berkshire Hathaway and has been his right-hand man ever since. Before joining forces with Warren Buffett he built a remarkable track record of his own between 1962 and 1975.

5. **Philip Carret**, who was a good friend of Warren Buffett, had an amazing track record with an annual outperformance of about 5% versus the S&P over the course of half a century (including the Depression years of the 1930s).

6. **John Templeton** managed the Templeton Growth Fund between 1954 and 1992. What sets Templeton apart from the other investors in this list is that he invested regularly in foreign (i.e., non-US) countries.

7. **Walter Schloss** was a colleague of Benjamin Graham until their investment partnership was wound down in the 1950s. After that, he started his own investment firm and racked up an impressive track record over the course of about 49 years with a quantitative investment style.

8. **Shelby Davis** invested primarily in insurance stocks and turned $100,000 into $800 million between the late 1940s and early 1990s.

9. **Joel Greenblatt** compounded his investment partnership at respectively 50% and 40% a year between 1985 and 1995, and between 1985 and 2005. Greenblatt admits that he copied his investment style from Warren Buffett. In recent years he has focused more on quantitatively-driven investing.

10. **Warren Buffett** is probably the investor with the most exceptional track record. Between the early 1950s and 1957, he beat the stock market by an overwhelming degree.[5] Between 1957 and 1968 he managed an investment partnership that returned 31.6% annually before fees. After winding down the partnership in 1968, he focused his efforts exclusively on one particular company that had been in the partnership's portfolio for a number of years, namely Berkshire Hathaway. He turned Berkshire Hathaway into an investment vehicle and managed to grow its book value at an annual compound rate of 20% between 1968 and 2012.

Buffett's track record is not only amazing due to its exceptional length (54 years, not including his early years), but also because of his consistent outperformance even as his assets under management skyrocketed to more than $100 billion. This is illustrated in Figure 2, which shows Buffett's outperformance versus the S&P 500 (dividends included) in each year since 1957 along with the five- and ten-year trailing average annual outperformance. As we can see from this figure, although Buffett trailed behind the S&P 500 in seven of the 54 years, his annual outperformance over intervals of five and ten years was almost invariably higher than 5% a year – even when his assets under management ballooned.

The remarkable track records shown in Figure 1 and Figure 2 give a very strong indication that the market can be beaten through investing. It therefore makes sense to examine how some of the world's greatest investors have managed to beat the market. By observing their approach, we can hope to learn from what they have done and look to apply this to our own investing.

---

[5] It is not clear how much Buffett earned in his early career. But based on his claims that he can easily achieve 50% a year on a stock portfolio of less than $1 million, and that his returns were truly amazing early on in his career, it should probably be north of 50% a year.

As it turns out, the practices and methods of top investors are very different from those of the average market player. What is more, there are eerily striking similarities in their methods. Many of the greatest investors look in the same places for bargains, their due diligence is done along the same lines, their buy and sell disciplines are identical, and they believe that the same set of attitudes, skills and behaviours are critical for success in the market.

**Figure 2: Outperformance of Warren Buffett versus the S&P 500 Index**

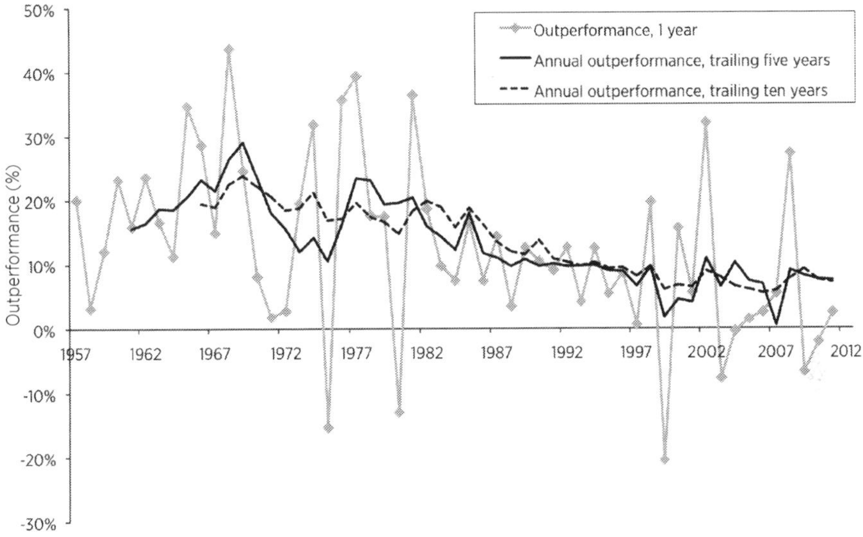

Source: Letters to shareholders of Berkshire Hathaway and letters to the investment partnership of Warren Buffett

## What this book covers

This book focuses exclusively on the quantitative and quantitative-qualitative investment style. The aim is to give a comprehensive overview of the practices applied by the most successful practitioners of these styles. It is very different from other investment books about or written by famous investors as it compiles information from numerous top investors found in hundreds of books, interviews, articles, letters to shareholders/investors, and so on. All of this information is reorganised in a comprehensive and detailed framework. Care is taken to always explain the rationale and logic behind every aspect of the approach of the investors discussed.

As you will see, many of the practices discussed here fit nicely into modern theories about behavioural finance and market efficiency. Also, a recurring theme throughout the book is that beating the market requires effort, focus and discipline. Success in the stock market can be achieved by devoted people who are willing to put in sufficient time and effort, and who adhere to a number of guidelines.

On the other hand, people who take shortcuts, people who can't or don't want to spend much time on their market activities, or people who can't develop the required attitudes and behaviour, stand little chance in the stock market.

This book will help all investors to learn about solid and efficient investment approaches that offer a serious edge in the stock market. They can then look to apply these techniques and habits of successful investors to their own investing, with the aim of improving their returns.

## How this book is structured

In Chapter A I begin with the investment philosophy and its rationale. I explain what investing is all about, how investors think about the stock market, and why they are convinced that this approach offers a competitive advantage. Part I then moves on to look into the investment processes applied by the greatest investors in the world. As they teach us, effective processes consist of three indispensable building blocks:

1. focus of one's attention on stocks that have an above average probability of being mispriced (Chapter B),

2. the fundamental analysis of businesses (Chapter C), and

3. valuation (Chapter D).

In Chapter E a number of process mistakes that many investors make are highlighted and it is shown how these can be remedied.

Part II is devoted to the issue of buying, holding and selling. Chapters F and G discuss the thoughts of top investors on how individual stocks should be bought and sold. Chapter H explains how top investors navigate boom and bust cycles. Finally, in Chapter I a number of common buy and sell errors are discussed.

In Part III (Chapter J) the views of top investors on risk management are examined. Finally, Chapter K gives an overview of the soft skills that top investors deem indispensable for success in the stock market.

# CHAPTER A

## INVESTING PHILOSOPHY AND STYLES

"It is extraordinary to me that the idea of buying dollar bills for 40 cents takes immediately to people or it doesn't take at all. It's like an inoculation. If it doesn't grab a person right away, I find that you can talk to him for years and show him records, and it doesn't make any difference. They just don't seem able to grasp the concept, as simple as it is."

WARREN BUFFETT (GRAHAM, 2003)

BEATING THE MARKET is not easy. Notwithstanding this, Table 1 showed that some people have managed to beat the market over the long term by a significant margin. Virtually all of them have a specific strategy and philosophy (i.e., a view on how inefficiencies are created in the market and how they can be exploited) which puts them into one of a number of schools. This should not come as a surprise. After all, smart market players realise they need a well-articulated strategy based on a sound market philosophy to obtain an edge.

In this chapter (and throughout the rest of this book) the focus is on one particular school: the school of investors. As explained in the Introduction, this is a broad school of market operators that consists of quantitative and quantitative-qualitative investors. This chapter describes the very foundations of the investment school, and therefore serves as a stepping stone to better grasp the logic of the various parts of investing that are discussed in the following chapters.

In the first part of this chapter the basic tenets of the investment school and the rationale behind its investment philosophy are explained. The second section looks at various investment styles that can be employed by members of the school. The third section discusses some mental requirements and attitudes that are indispensable in successful investing.

### A.I The investment philosophy

In general, a market philosophy describes the drivers behind the stock market, and explains how these drivers create pricing inefficiencies. The investment philosophy, which is the market philosophy of investors and which is the focus of our attention here, has as a basic premise that even though price fluctuations are unpredictable over the short run, stock prices constantly fluctuate around their fair value.

Investors refer to this fair value as the stock's *intrinsic value* and they argue that over the long run a stock's price tracks the stock's intrinsic value. According to investors, fluctuations around that intrinsic value can be huge and are caused by emotions, herding behaviour, general misconceptions, imbalances in the attention to different stocks, noneconomic pressures, and the like.

## A.I.1 The intrinsic value concept

Investors argue that every stock has a fair (or intrinsic) value, FF. This is an investor-specific value that depends on the return $\alpha$(%) the investor wants to earn on the stock based on his/her personal risk-reward trade-off with regards to that stock.

Now, as said above, the basic assumption is that stock prices fluctuate around their intrinsic value for many reasons (see below). The opportunity for investors lies in the fact that prices revert to the fair value $FF(\alpha)$ over the long term, when speculation dies down or when the market acknowledges its mistake. As such, investors attempt to beat the market by purchasing stocks that are trading below their intrinsic values and then try to sell them once they are trading close to or above their intrinsic values (see Figure 3).

**Figure 3: Fundamental strategy of investors**

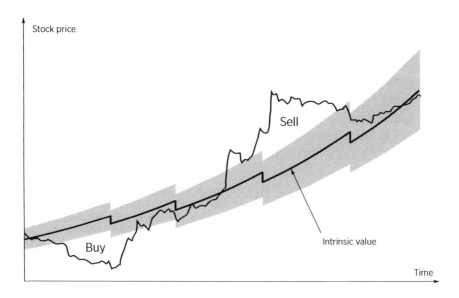

The true challenge for investors is to determine FF. Strictly speaking, the *true* intrinsic value ($FF_{true}$) of a company's stock is the price at which the shareholder would earn an annual return $\alpha$ on its investment up until the stock stops trading on the stock exchange due to an acquisition, a bankruptcy, a going-private transaction, or any other reason, as shown in the following formula:

$$FF_{true}(\alpha) = \frac{P_{fin}}{(1+\alpha)^L} + \sum_{q=1}^{L} \frac{D_q}{(1+\alpha)^q}$$

In this expression, $P_{fin}$ is the stock price shareholders receive for their shares when they are removed from the stock exchange, L is the number of years until the stock is removed from the exchange, and $D_q$ is the dividend per share received by shareholders in year q.

Unfortunately, the model above is of little practical use as it is virtually impossible to predict L, $D_q$ and $P_{fin}$, except maybe for takeover targets. A more practical intrinsic value model is the discounted cash flow (DCF) model.[6] In that model, the intrinsic value is obtained by discounting back to the present the free cash flows generated by the business:

$$FF_{DCF}(\alpha) = C + \sum_{q=0}^{+\infty} \frac{FCFE_q}{(1+\alpha)^q}$$

In this expression, $FCFE_q$ and C are respectively the free cash flow (to equity) per share generated in year q, and the cash per share (cash + cash equivalents).

The DCF model has a clear theoretical foundation that gives true meaning to the concept of intrinsic value. Nevertheless, the discounted cash flow model is not popular in the asset management industry for two major reasons:

1. First of all, finding the inputs for $FCFE_q$ in the model is a daunting task. It requires hard work and expertise. Most people don't come close to putting in the required effort. Even then, many academics are convinced that individuals cannot estimate the intrinsic value better than the stock market itself. This is to say that they don't believe that there is an opportunity for investors to find stocks that are valued incorrectly by the market.

2. A second problem is that, as the quote from Warren Buffett at the beginning of this chapter suggests, many people can't grasp the concept of investing. They see the stock market more like a casino than a place where one can buy "dollar bills for 40 cents" (i.e., buy stocks at a discount of 60% to their intrinsic value).

True investors, on the other hand, fully understand the concept of intrinsic value. They don't buy the argument that investors should resign themselves to the efficiency of the stock market and they see many drivers that can cause incorrect pricing (and therefore investment opportunities).

---

[6] For an excellent and thorough description of the DCF model, refer to (Koller, 2005).

## A.I.2 Stock drivers

Adherents of the Efficient Market Hypothesis (EMH) posit that each stock reflects at all times all public knowledge about the underlying company. Put differently, they believe that a stock price always reflects the market's best estimate of that stock's intrinsic value $FF_{DCF}$. They also find it obvious that no single individual can estimate this value better than the market itself. EMH supporters don't believe in market irrationality or inefficient pricing. They argue that price anomalies caused by irrational market participants are invariably and instantly corrected by rational market players.

Investors debunk the arguments of EMH adepts with two counterarguments. First of all, many market participants pay no attention whatsoever to the fair value concept. In fact, it is probably a minority that is driven by fair value considerations. Numerous market players trade based on momentum, they speculate, they buy or sell on rumours, they try to anticipate the moves of other market players, and so on. Moreover, different people have different objectives. Although the vast majority probably have the common objective of making money, there are definitely people who are only interested in quick gains, and who therefore ignore the long-term potential of stocks.

Second, as we will see in the next section, the actions of people who base their decisions on fair value considerations are driven (unconsciously) to a large extent by instincts and human psychology. So, most investors can't stay rational and detached all of the time even if they want to. Top investors find it inconceivable that the (very) small minority of purely rational investors can always counteract market movements caused by the mass of market players that buy and sell driven by emotions, a trading mentality, or pure speculation. And since human nature is what it is, investors can't believe that these market inefficiencies will ever disappear. To further illustrate this point, below is a discussion of the impact of cognitive biases on the stock market.

### A.I.2.a Cognitive biases

According to modern behavioural finance, the human mind solves problems and answers questions through two types of systems. The first of these, the *reflexive system*, is a kind of intuition that solves problems and answers questions in a split second. This system is driven by instincts and it therefore often takes shortcuts when it tries to solve problems. The reflexive system frequently suggests solutions that seem logical at first sight but that are irrational if one looks more closely. In addition, when the reflexive system is faced with a difficult question it tends to substitute that question with an easier one. The second system is the *reflective system*. This is the rational and conscious system that solves problems through reasoning and thinking. It also keeps the reflexive system in check by questioning the solutions proposed by that system.

People get in trouble when the reflective system does not operate adequately. If that happens, irrational elements can slip unnoticed into decision processes. This can occur, for instance, due to laziness. After all, thinking and reasoning require effort, and it is tempting to accept the answers of the reflexive system without further scrutiny. But even hard-working people regularly let their guard down. Indeed, virtually everyone experiences moments when the reflexive system overwhelms the reflective system. This is typically the case when emotions are running high, or when the reflective system encounters a difficult problem that it can't solve.

Since high-running emotions and difficult problems are part and parcel of stock market operations it should not come as a surprise that most market participants wrestle each and every day with the irrational influences from their reflexive system. This system prompts people to make a number of systematic psychological errors, which are referred to as *cognitive biases*. The most important cognitive biases that tend to drive irrational market behaviour are as follows:[7]

### 1. Overreaction bias

This is the tendency of people to react more fiercely to bad news than to good news. The overreaction bias also gets stronger when expectations are higher. A consequence of the overreaction bias is that people tend to overreact to negative surprises. For instance, many people sell in panic when a company issues a profit warning.

### 2. Pattern and trend seeking

The human brain is wired to look everywhere for patterns and trends, even in noise. For instance, many people *discover* trends when they stare long enough at stock charts, only to find out later that they can't make money on these observations. This pattern seeking bias is supported by the *Law of the small numbers*, which states that people tend to derive patterns and trends from statistically insignificant samples. When a mutual fund manager outperforms his benchmark two years in a row, for example, he is believed to be a genius even though this performance is statistically not that significant.

Common investment errors due to pattern seeking are:

1. acting on too little information,
2. simplistic extrapolation of historical trends in fundamentals and/or price action,
3. attention to illusory correlation patterns, and
4. the idea that one can pick tops and bottoms based on stock price behaviour.

### 3. Overconfidence and the illusion of control

People – men in particular – tend to have too much confidence in their own abilities. A nice example is that the vast majority of people believe that their driving skills are above average (which of course cannot be true). Most people are also convinced that the world is more benign, more understandable, and more predictable than it really is. They frequently have the illusion that they can control or influence processes over which they have no control at all. In coin toss contests, for instance, winners tend to believe that they have a talent for coin tossing.

---

[7] See also (Kahneman, 2011), (Belsky, 1999), (Zweig, 2007), (Dreman, 1998) and (Montier, 2010).

Overconfidence and the illusion of control seem to be present irrespective of a person's level of self-esteem, and typically they are stronger and ubiquitous for complex processes that seem familiar, such as investing. In the stock market, overconfidence and the illusion of control can lead to the following errors:

1. the belief that one can be successful without the proper skills, expertise and effort,

2. trading too much (overtrading) as it is believed to be easy to time one's trades,

3. poor feedback from mistakes (as mistakes are not recognised as such by overconfident people), and

4. inadequate risk management.

## 4. Asymmetric loss aversion

According to research, a financial loss is about two to two and a half times as painful as an equivalent gain is enjoyable. Put another way, the pain of a 10% loss is about as intense as the pleasure of a 20% to 25% gain. This asymmetric loss aversion is probably a result of human evolution as priority to threats and bad news (rather than to opportunities and good news) is indispensable for survival. Common investment mistakes caused by asymmetric loss aversion are:

1. holding on to losing stocks for too long to avoid the realisation of the loss,

2. selling in panic after a loss to make the pain go away, and

3. taking profits on a winning stock too fast to avoid the gains slipping through one's fingers.

## 5. Herding behaviour

People feel comfortable when they follow the crowd, especially when they are confronted with a vague and complex problem about which they feel insecure. Not surprisingly, herding behaviour gets stronger when emotions run high, and when people with authority cheer the crowd on.

An example of this behaviour was what happened when an oil company got into the fertiliser business many years ago. The reaction of all other major oil companies was to acquire fertiliser companies even though there was no strategic and rational reason to do so. The end result was a predictable financial hangover for the companies involved.

One cause of herding behaviour is that people tend to believe that the crowd knows more than they do, and that they are going to be left behind if they stay on the sidelines. So people find comfort in mimicking others, even if those others act foolhardily.

Since investing and trading are vague and complex, and because many people have no clue how to proceed in the stock market, herding behaviour is prevalent among market participants – especially during fits of panic or euphoria. It needs little explanation that blindly following the crowd is a recipe for disaster. It leads to:

1. heavy selling near the bottom of bear markets and heavy buying close to the tops of bull markets (in imitation of other people),

2. chasing popular stocks irrespective of price, and

3. steering clear of unpopular and ignored stocks even if they are attractively valued.

## 6. Biased information filtering

When confronted with a lot of information, people tend to focus on just a few pieces of that information. Most attention usually goes to the most salient (instead of the most useful and relevant) facts. First, the recency bias is the bias that people are inclined to overweight information that is *most recent*. An example is that the expected stock market return over the next six months is two times more dependent on the stock market performance over the last week than over the last few months.[8]

Second, people pay more attention to information when it is *more emotionally charged*. For instance, one is more likely to participate in a lottery when the first prize is extraordinarily high than when it is pedestrian – even if the expected value of the winnings is higher in the latter. Third, framing states that information is more likely to appeal to people when it is *framed in an attractive way*. For example, a service offered at $1 a day seems much more attractive than the same service offered at $365 a year (although both are equally expensive).

In the area of investing, biased information filtering leads to:

1. extrapolation of recent trends (especially when these trends are emotionally charged),

2. poor feedback from past experiences (as only the most impressionable experiences are kept in memory), and

3. investment decisions based on superficial information from appealing stories (and without due diligence).

## 7. Anchoring

When people make a judgment about something, they are apt to build their perspective starting from a piece of information that may be irrelevant to the problem. Anchoring is usually more powerful for problems about which the person has little knowledge. Surprisingly, people continue to use anchors *even when they realise that these anchors are irrelevant and uninformative*. An example of anchoring is that many people create their opinion about an unknown person based on first impressions. Another example is haggling. The price range that is used during the haggling process is usually determined by the first price quoted by one of the two parties involved.

Due to anchoring, investors make the following mistakes:

1. they use the price at which they purchased a stock as an anchor and therefore hang on to losing positions (as they refuse to sell below their purchase price), or sell a winner too soon as it moves above the purchase price, and

2. they believe that a stock is cheap or expensive based on a comparison with historical stock prices (which serve as anchors).

---

[8] Zweig, 2007.

## 8. Consistency bias

This is also called the *confirmation bias* and is the inclination of people to remain loyal to their original opinion by rejecting disconfirming information[9], and by overstressing information that confirms their opinion – even if the former has more credibility than the latter. It also implies that people tend to seek out like-minded people, and avoid confrontation with people who have different opinions.

Two investment errors due to the consistency bias are:

1. the tendency to look for confirming evidence (and dismiss disconfirming evidence) in stock research after a positive or negative story about a stock, and

2. hanging on to losing positions as the investor refuses to listen to the other side of the story.

An extreme example of the confirmation bias was a core of so-called *believers* in the Belgian speech company Lernout & Hauspie. These shareholders refused to accept the bankruptcy of the company and continued to support the company's founders (even years after its demise) in spite of overwhelming evidence of fraud.

## 9. Hindsight bias

This is the tendency to build one's perspective from recently available information to argue that what has happened at a certain point in the past was more predictable than it actually was based on the information that was available at that time. The hindsight bias makes it hard to correctly evaluate past decision-processes and leads to poor feedback. Note that the hindsight bias is stronger when the consequences are worse.[10]

An example of the hindsight bias is the criticism of the credit rating agencies in the aftermath of the credit crisis of 2008 to 2009. People called the rating agencies incompetent because they had given excessively high credit ratings to toxic products. What these critics failed to remember is that very few credit investors or those who rate credit had forewarned people (before the crisis) not to trust the rating agencies.

## 10. Biases caused by sympathy or familiarity

People are favourably disposed toward things related to something they like (this is the *sympathy bias* and the *halo effect*), or to something they are familiar with (*home bias*). The sympathy and home bias have an evolutionary basis as survival requires creatures to be cautious with novel/unfamiliar items, whereas they can afford to feel comfortable with things that are familiar or which they like.

Applied to investing, many people take a liking to companies they are familiar with, companies they feel sympathy for, or stocks about which there exists a fascinating story (this is the so-called narrative fallacy). Therefore, an investor's typical shortlist of purchase candidates consists of companies headquartered close to home (or even the company they work at), companies with nice, easily pronounceable and/or familiar names, companies

---

[9] The consistency bias is often reinforced by the so-called *sunk-cost effect*. This is the tendency of people to stick with decisions in which they have invested considerable money and/or time – even if not changing the decision implies even more costs.

[10] Those responsible for failing to anticipate a catastrophe are often seen as incompetent or negligent.

with excellent products, companies that are often in the media, or even companies that have accidental similarities with the investor (e.g., when the stock ticker is the same as one's initials, or when the company's logo has the same colour as one's eyes).

The problem of these biases is that sympathy for or familiarity with a company may have little to do with the investing merits of that company's stock. In fact, the preconceived ideas due to sympathy and familiarity can lead to:

1. superficial and coloured stock analysis (as investors confuse familiarity with knowledge), and

2. inadequate diversification (e.g., focusing one's portfolio on a particular region or even in one specific firm).

### 11. Endowment effect

This is people's tendency to overvalue one's own belongings. Due to the endowment effect, most homeowners overestimate the value of their house. In the stock market the endowment effect means that investors – especially those who see themselves as long-term shareholders – find it difficult to sell a stock, even when the facts warrant a sale.

### 12. Avoidance of regret

All human beings try to avoid feelings of regret – in particular intense regret. It turns out that regret over a mistake is usually more intense when:

1. there was a wide range of options at the moment the decision was made,

2. the decision involved action rather than inaction,

3. the decision was a departure from the person's usual behaviour, and/or

4. the goal was almost reached before the mistake.

In the stock market, avoidance of regret prompts investors to hang on to losing stocks (out of fear of regretting the sale afterwards), and to sell winning stocks too early (to avoid possible regret over a future decline in price).

### 13. Mental accounting

This is the inclination of people to put their money into separate mental accounts that are treated differently. For instance, people usually find it easier to spend (or waste) money of a holiday allowance, gift money, or casino winnings than money they set aside for retirement. A special case of mental accounting is people's tendency to be more careful about a large amount than a small amount of money (*bigness bias*) – in particular when the small amount is buried in a large amount.[11]

Here are some common investment mistakes caused by mental accounting:

1. excessive trading as the costs of each individual transaction (bid-ask spreads, transaction costs, taxes, management fees) seem small as compared to the amount involved, and

---

[11] That's why smart car salesmen talk about small features (the cost of which seems small as compared to the total cost of the car) only after the client has been convinced to buy a car.

2. holding on to losing stocks as unrealised losses are put in a separate non-cash account that is considered temporary.

### 14. Thirst for excitement

People are predisposed to look for excitement and kicks. This leads to the following problems in the field of investing:

1. people chase the most exciting stocks of the day (e.g., the latest hot IPO), and

2. some people pursue inferior but exciting investment strategies.

## A.I.2.b Inefficiencies caused by cognitive biases

> *"There is nothing new on Wall Street or in stock speculation. What has happened in the past will happen again and again and again. This is because human nature does not change, and it is human emotion that always gets in the way of human intelligence."*
>
> **Jesse Livermore (Livermore, 2001)**

> *"The reason that capital markets are, have always been, and will always be inefficient is not because of a shortage of timely information, the lack of analytical tools, or inadequate capital. The Internet will not make the market efficient, even though it makes far more information available, faster than ever before, right at everyone's fingertips. Markets are inefficient because of human nature – innate, deep-rooted, permanent. People don't consciously choose to invest with emotion – they simply can't help it."*
>
> **Seth Klarman (Heins, 2013)**

Cognitive biases are the source of many investment mistakes and undoubtedly cause a lot of irrational behaviour in the stock market. The law of small numbers, poor feedback (due to overconfidence and the hindsight bias), the recency bias, the consistency bias, and the familiarity or sympathy bias are some of the reasons why many investors don't perform valuable due diligence.

Avoidance of regret, mental accounting, the endowment effect, asymmetric loss aversion and the consistency bias prompt investors to hang on to losing stocks or to sell winning stocks too early against their better judgment. Anchoring, in turn, leads to irrational ideas about the intrinsic value of stocks.

All of these errors are committed by individuals and occur randomly among the universe of investors. It is fair to assume that these errors can be eliminated through arbitrage by rational investors. Therefore, they are unlikely to cause important pricing anomalies.

However, cognitive biases also cause systematic errors that push people in the same direction at about the same time. For instance, the fact that investors jump on upward trends due to extrapolation or herding behaviour can be a very strong force in the markets. Likewise, exaggerated selling pressure in a downtrend due to the overreaction bias, asymmetric loss aversion, herding behaviour and extrapolation can be hard to curb by rational market players. Add to this that trends tend to attract traders and speculators who don't care about intrinsic value, and it becomes clear that it is naïve to expect that rational investors always have enough firepower to bring the market to its senses.

Likewise, rational investors will have serious trouble in keeping an individual stock close to its fair value when emotions around that stock (due to popularity, herding behaviour, thirst for excitement, etc.) are running high. Investors argue that these types of systematic errors cause price inefficiencies that can be taken advantage of. Two direct phenomena that are caused by systematic errors are discussed below.

## 1. The boom-bust cycle

History has demonstrated abundantly that human psychology is a very powerful force that can drive stock prices far beyond their fair value.[12] Basically, individual stocks as well as the entire market are driven by a sentiment cycle, which invariably consists of a boom (bull) phase during which optimism, greed, interest and complacency grow, and a bust (bear) phase with growing pessimism, fear, disinterest and risk aversion. But this is only part of the story. We can actually identify a formidable suite of cognitive biases that drive these boom-bust cycles (see Figure 4).

1. **Pattern seeking and recency bias**: rising and declining markets are reinforced by the inclination of market participants to extrapolate the recent market trend.[13] It is in fact the expectation of *more of the same* that contributes to market excesses around bull/bubble tops, and bear/bust bottoms.

2. **Overconfidence and illusion of control**: the gains in bull/bubble markets bolster confidence among market participants who, after some time, frequently start to believe that they are geniuses.[14] This leads to the growing complacency and risk tolerance that is so inextricably tied to bullish market movements.

3. In bear markets, **asymmetric loss aversion** contributes to waves of panicky selling, and an acceleration of the decline towards the market bottom. Panicked selling together with the overreaction bias and a lower tolerance for risk can explain the phenomenon of capitulation (characterised by heavy selling and steep price drops) around certain bear bottoms.

---

[12] See (Chancellor, 2000), (Kindleberger, 2005), (MacKay, 2008), (Katsenelson, 2007), (Mahar, 2004), (Schiller, 2005), (Smithers, 2009) and (Napier, 2009).

[13] One effect of the recency bias is that during bull markets many people even forget that bear markets are possible.

[14] Warren Buffett warns in his letter to shareholders of 1987: "In a bull market, one must avoid the error of the preening duck that quacks boastfully after a torrential rainstorm, thinking that its paddling skills have caused it to rise in the world. A right-thinking duck would instead compare its position after the downpour to that of the other ducks on the pond."

**Figure 4: Cognitive biases and human nature in the boom-bust cycle**

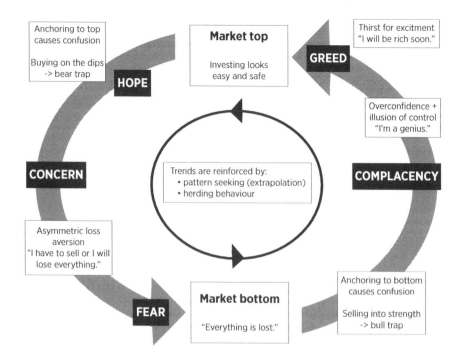

4. **Herding behaviour**: market movements up and down are reinforced by the fact that people tend to follow the crowd. Herding behaviour not only leads to a stronger consensus about market direction, but also draws new herd-following people into bull markets.

5. **Anchoring** is in several ways a powerful force behind bull and bear markets:

    • The fact that market players tend to see previous price levels as references for *cheap* or *expensive* implies that many retracements during bull markets are quickly reversed by people who *buy on the dips*. Likewise, many recoveries during bear markets are sold by people who *sell while they still can*.

    • Movements in certain stocks can cause similar movements in the shares of that company's peers (e.g., companies that are active in the same industry or in the same country). This is so because market participants constantly compare price changes and valuations among stocks. Thus, due to anchoring, movements of individual stocks can drag entire sectors (or even the entire market) along.

6. The **confirmation bias** reinforces the trend of the day. During bullish times, investors want to hear good news, and they want to listen to gurus who proclaim an eternal continuation of the bull or mania. This bolsters confidence among the bulls and sustains the rally. Conversely, at many market bottoms people look for trouble everywhere and they seem to rally around doomsday prophets. This leads to more fear and higher risk aversion.

7. **Thirst for excitement**: addiction to the excitement of the market game can tempt people to pour more and more of their savings into the stock market during upward trends. This reinforces bull markets. Similarly, during bear markets short sellers who are excited by the prospect of huge gains increase their shorts disproportionally, and pull the market lower.

## 2. Inefficiencies related to popularity

> *"People are captivated by exciting new concepts. The lure of hitting a home run on a hot new idea overwhelms caution. The sizzle and glitz of an IPO is just too great."*
>
> **David Dreman (Dreman, 1998)**

Inefficiencies caused by popularity (or lack thereof) are the bread-and-butter of many of the purest value investment styles. Benjamin Graham taught his students that stocks in the doghouse (which typically can be recognised by low valuation multiples) often offer above-average returns, whereas the hot glamour stocks of the moment are better avoided.

Numerous studies have proved Benjamin Graham right.[15] They even found some other surprising facts. First of all, stocks with low Price-to-Book Values (P/BVs) often seem to outperform the market in spite of the fact that many of these stocks suffer from a deteriorating profitability. Popular stocks with continuing strong profitability, by contrast, frequently underperform the market. Second, favoured stocks benefit much less from positive earnings surprises and suffer much more from negative surprises than out-of-favour stocks.[16] All this implies that the market's favourites are much more vulnerable than the market's outcasts.

In summary, popular stocks tend to be overvalued and unpopular stocks tend to be undervalued. Here are some cognitive biases that are responsible for this phenomenon:

1. **Asymmetric loss aversion and overreaction bias**: many unpopular stocks are beaten down due to waves of panicked selling caused by (a string of) disappointing results. Much of this selling is caused by overreaction and the asymmetric loss aversion, so one can reasonably expect that people dump those shares regardless of price during fits of panic. This increases the likelihood that such stocks are punished too hard.

2. **Pattern seeking and the recency bias**: due to extrapolation people expect that stocks that have performed well will stay good, and that stocks with poor price

---

[15] See, for example (Dreman, 1998) and (Damodaran, 2004). Data shows that Graham's notion is a fact of investing in any era. For instance, it is mentioned in (Schwager, 1992) that the stock performance of the most popular stocks between 1901 and 1926 delivered a disastrous return through the end of 1939.

[16] This can be explained by overly positive expectations about the market's favourites and overly negative expectations about the market's pariahs, combined with reversion to the mean in fundamental financial performance.

action will stay bad. In other words, they tend to give too much weight to the past. This leads to price-value mismatches in two ways:

- *Many stocks discount more of the same in terms of financial results.* People (including professionals) often extrapolate financial results in a simplistic way so the market price of poorly performing companies tends to discount a bleak future. This means that when results are bad, the market is not surprised and the stock price does not budge. If results are slightly better than expected, the stock has ample room to rally. Conversely, companies with strong financial performance are expected to continue their extraordinary results. Hence, their stock price discounts a bright future. If these companies can jump over the high bars set by the market, they are unlikely to gain a lot because investors are spoilt and hard to impress. If they fail to live up to the high expectations (not unlikely given the power of reversion to the mean), the market will probably come down hard on them.

- *Many stocks reflect the expectation that the recent stock price performance will continue.* Poor stock price performance in the recent past is enough to scare away people who extrapolate that past into the future. As such, interest in and coverage of unpopular stocks is typically low. This increases the likelihood that the stock is undervalued. Stocks with strong stock price performance, on the other hand, attract the attention of people who expect more of the same. This increases the probability that the stock is fully (or over) valued.

3. **Herding behaviour**: the conviction that the crowd is smart and the feeling of comfort when one follows the crowd contribute to the undervaluation of unpopular stocks and the overvaluation of hot stocks:

- Since the crowd ignores unpopular stocks, most people find it hard to believe that spending their time (let alone their money) on such stocks can pay off. In fact, the hot market darlings of the moment are regarded as the place to be. The consequence is that unpopular stocks receive little coverage and scrutiny, which increases the probability that they are mispriced. The wide coverage of and scrutiny into popular stocks, on the other hand, ensures that undervaluation of these stocks is a remote possibility.

- Stocks go down when the crowd believes that they don't deserve their current price tag. Hence, shareholders of declining stocks who think that the crowd knows more than they do may feel compelled to sell their shares irrespective of price. Conversely, rising stock prices nurture the idea that the stock is undervalued, even in the presence of high valuations. Obviously this selling and buying based on herding behaviour and irrespective of price contributes to irrational pricing.

4. **Distorted risk perception**: unpopular stocks that have been beaten down by the market are frequently believed to be risky (sometimes rightfully so). This means that few people dare to touch them with a ten-foot pole. Buying hot stocks with

strong financials and an excellent track record in the stock market, on the other hand, feels safe. Hence, unpopular stocks tend to trade at low valuations that reflect an overly high level of risk, whereas popular stocks tend to trade at high valuations that reflect an excessively low level of risk.

5. **Thirst for excitement**: the thirst for excitement pushes thrill-seeking market players towards hot and exciting stocks, and away from the stinkers. The chase for hot stocks by speculative investors and traders can cause excessive valuations in these types of stocks.

## A.II Investment styles and strategies

The basic principles of the investment philosophy discussed in A.I (i.e., the intrinsic value concept and the stock drivers) create a framework that investors use to approach the market. Within this framework, practitioners have a lot of leeway to implement the basic concepts of the investment philosophy as they see fit. In fact, one can divide the universe of successful investors into two broad styles, namely the bottom-up and the top-down style.

### A.II.1 Bottom-up style

The bottom-up style is probably the most popular and the most reliable investment approach. Bottom-up investors start out with the analysis of individual companies. They examine financial statements, try to assess the competitive position of companies, and evaluate management. They usually pay scant attention to the economic outlook, as they argue that it is extremely hard to have a clear view on the economic picture. They therefore consider it futile – or even outright dangerous – to give economic predictions a central place in their analysis. In fact, many bottom-up investors try to find companies that should do well irrespective of the economic environment.

There have been plenty of successful bottom-up investors. Pioneers were Benjamin Graham and Philip Fisher. The former adhered to a bottom-up approach based almost exclusively on quantitative (i.e., financial) data.[17] Philip Fisher, on the other hand, stressed the importance of qualitative elements, such as management and a firm's competitive position, in the evaluation of stocks.[18] Many of the great modern bottom-up investors (e.g., Warren Buffett and Joel Greenblatt) derived their investment approach from that of Graham and Fisher.[19]

Within the field of bottom-up investing, there are a wide variety of sub-styles. Top investors do not necessarily limit themselves to one particular sub-style, though. They may opportunistically apply one or another style depending on the market circumstances.

---

[17] Graham, 2003.

[18] Fisher, 1996.

[19] Highly recommended literature on bottom-up investing is: (Rothchild, 2001), (Bolton, 2009), (Cunningham, 2001-A), (Buffett, 1977-present), (Dreman, 1998), (Greenblatt, 1997), (Neff, 1999), (Pabrai, 2007), (Einhorn, 2008), (Cunningham, 2001-B), (Lowenstein, 1995), (Hagstrom, 2005), and (Lynch, 1993).

Or they constantly combine different sub-styles in their market operations. Without trying to be exhaustive, the following sub-styles can be distinguished:

## Value investing

Value investors, like Benjamin Graham and David Dreman, deal with the uncertainty about intrinsic value by limiting their attention to stocks that are *cheap* on a number of valuation multiples such as Price-to-earnings (P/E) or Price-to-Book Value (P/BV).[20] Their focus on low-multiple stocks implies that they often look for value among ignored, unpopular or even outright hated stocks.

Some value investors only buy low-multiple stocks of high quality with the intention to hold on to these stocks for many years. Other value investors pay less attention to the underlying quality and unload their stocks when the gap between price and intrinsic value closes.

## Growth investing

As opposed to pure value investors, growth investors have no problem with high-multiple stocks, provided that they can reasonably project growth rates that are substantially higher than the market's average (e.g., annual earnings growth rates above 15%). They argue that one has to pay up for growth, as above-average growth expectations are usually reflected in stock prices. Given their focus on growth, they also tend to hold on to their stocks for the long haul and they do not sell as quickly as value investors when multiples expand.

One of the most successful growth investing styles– popularised by mutual fund legend Peter Lynch in *One Up on Wall Street* and *Beating the Street* – is Growth At a Reasonable Price (GARP). GARP investors are sceptical of extremely high growth rates. Their favourites are reasonably priced stocks with annual sales and earnings growth in the range of 20% to 30%.

## Risk arbitrage

This is a type of arbitrage where the investor tries to derive a profit from discrepancies between a stock's market value and the value that is expected at the conclusion of a specific transaction. The most common type of risk arbitrage is *merger arbitrage*. This can be applied when a company launches a takeover bid on another publicly listed company. When this happens the stock price of the acquisition target may stay below the price offered by the acquirer due to the lingering uncertainty over the deal. Merger arbitrageurs selectively buy stocks of acquisitions targets with the intention to capitalise on the closing of the price gap when the deal is consummated.

Although merger arbitrage looks easy to the inexperienced, it is a very competitive activity that entails a lot of risk. Indeed, merger arbitrageurs must find deals where the difference between the stock price and the expected transaction price is sufficiently high to compensate for the risk that the acquirer withdraws its offer, that anti-trust authorities do not accept the deal, that the acquirer cannot secure financing for the deal and that the

---

[20] Dreman, 1998.

deal takes much longer than anticipated to conclude. In practice only the most sophisticated arbitrageurs stand a chance in this area of investing.

## Pair trade investing

This is a type of arbitrage applied by many hedge funds, where the investor buys a cheap stock within an industry and sells an expensive stock short within that same industry. The pair trade investor bets that the wide valuation gap between the two stocks is unjustified, and expects to make money when the valuations of the two stocks converge. In this trade, the investor is not exposed to market and industry risk as the combination of a long and a short trade eliminates such risks.

## Vulture investing

This is a very specialised activity that focuses on companies in distress. Vulture investors buy distressed debt instruments (seldom equity) of bankrupt companies or of companies that are on the verge of a collapse. They try to find those companies for which the distressed debt offers compelling value based on their assessment of the business and on what they expect of the workout process (that is the negotiations between all creditors of the business during the bankruptcy proceedings).

Vulture investors embody the basic principles of value investing. They invest exclusively in companies that don't do well and they are genuine bargain hunters as they are looking for debt securities that trade at (very) distressed prices.

Bargain prices for distressed debt are frequently available thanks to selling pressure by investors who are forced to sell (e.g., due to their investment charters), by investors who lack the resources to participate in the bankruptcy proceedings, or by investors who fear that involvement in the bankruptcy process will tarnish their reputation.

To give themselves the best chance of success, vulture investors try to be directly involved in the workout process, they are intimately acquainted with bankruptcy legislation and they painstakingly examine all information about each case they get involved with. Due to its very specific nature, gains and losses in vulture investing are only marginally correlated with the performance of the economy (in particular, interest rates) and the stock market.[21]

## Investing through direct interference

Sometimes investors take stakes in poorly-run businesses with the intention to turn things around. Their favourite companies are intrinsically strong businesses with poor management and/or a poor strategy. In other words, they try to find businesses that can offer substantial upside if management would be replaced and/or if the company would change its strategy. They can try to achieve their goal in two ways:

1. **Activist investing**: in this approach, the activist investor buys a significant stake in a mismanaged business to get on the board of directors, or to rally support from other disgruntled shareholders. Activist investors are an important power to be

---

[21] Excellent reading on vulture investing can be found in (Rosenberg, 2000), (Moyer, 2005) and (Whitman, 2009).

reckoned with because they try to oust management or force it to change its strategy through, for example, proxy fights and public attacks. Three of the most famous activist investors in the US are Jeffrey Ubben, Carl Icahn and Bill Ackman.

2. **Control**: a more radical approach is to take control of the business through a friendly or hostile takeover bid and then impose the necessary changes.

### Private equity

Private equity investors buy stakes in companies with the aim to hold on to their positions for a few years (typically, five to seven years). Over the holding period, they try to maximise the value of these companies, often through direct involvement in management and strategy. There are basically two types of private equity styles:[22]

1. **Venture**: in this style, private equity investors typically take a non-controlling stake in a (usually non-public) early-stage growth company with high potential. Venture investors usually focus on companies that develop a new commercial product in an existing tried-and-tested (and **not** in a new and untried) area.

2. **Buyout**: in a typical buyout, a private equity company takes a controlling stake (possibly together with other partners, e.g., management) in a stable and cash-generating company by buying it out from existing shareholders and by loading it up with a lot of debt.

## A.II.2 Top-down style

Top-down investors start out with the economy and then work their way down to industries, sub-sectors, and individual companies that should do well in the anticipated economic scenario. Although such an approach may seem plausible, top-down investors are faced with more serious challenges than bottom-up investors.

First of all, very few people have a good track record predicting the economy. Hence, every top-down investor has to accept the (high) risk that he or she may end up in all the wrong stocks. Second, even if the expected economic scenario plays out, top-down investors may be wrong about the stocks that benefit the most from that scenario because the market may already have anticipated things.

## A.III Required attitudes and mindset

Investing is not for everyone. As mentioned above, many people don't understand the concept of intrinsic value. Others will find that investing does not fit their personality. Even among those people who wholeheartedly subscribe to the principles of the investment philosophy discussed in A.I, only few can implement it successfully. Genuine investing is a major challenge that requires hard work, expertise, experience, an appropriate mindset and a high level of mental control. If any of these are absent the investor's chances of success are rather slim.

---

[22] Fraser-Sampson, 2007.

First of all, to be successful investors must be better at estimating the fair value of companies than the market. To make this happen, they need unique information that gives them an edge over other market participants. This kind of exclusive information cannot be acquired from others but requires *hard work*. Furthermore, although there are successful investors from all kinds of professional backgrounds, estimating the fair value of businesses can only be done when one has the proper *expertise* to analyse businesses. Many years of *experience* are of course helpful too.

A second requirement is the right mindset. True investors are *independent* and *patient*. Independence, which entails questioning conventional wisdom and being critical of ideas that are unanimously accepted by the crowd, is necessary because little can be gained by following the herd. True investors are also patient because they know that it can take time before the market reflects a stock's true intrinsic value. Successful investors are not in a hurry and they stay disciplined when the markets behave irrationally.

Last but not least, successful investors can detach themselves emotionally from the market. They have the courage to be contrarian and go where other people feel uncomfortable. Their *emotional detachment* enables them to limit the impact of cognitive biases that get so many other investors in trouble. In sum, real investors are the true rational market participants that EMH adepts refer to. However, in contrast to the tenets of the EMH, truly rational investors are scarce. And they cannot keep the market in check.

## A.IV Conclusion

This chapter focused on the market philosophy that is championed by investors. A good understanding of this philosophy is indispensable to see how the subjects of the following chapters fit into the investor's mindset.

First and foremost, everything in investing revolves around the intrinsic value concept. People who adhere to the investing philosophy attempt to beat the market by estimating the intrinsic value of stocks based on fundamental considerations, and by buying or selling when stock prices deviate significantly from their intrinsic value. Valuation and fundamental analysis are the topics of the Chapters D and C, respectively.

Second, according to the investing philosophy, price anomalies are caused by the irrational behaviour of other market players, by market participants with other market approaches (e.g., momentum traders), or by people with other objectives. This insight helps investors to identify stocks that have an above-average probability of being mispriced (see Chapter B). Also, the understanding of irrationalities and the intrinsic value concept are vital to understand how smart investors trade stocks (Chapters F, G and H), and why so many people make process mistakes (see Chapter E) and trading mistakes (see Chapter I).

---

*"What a company's stock sells for today, tomorrow, next week, or next year doesn't matter. What counts is how the company does over a five- or ten-year period."*

**Warren Buffett (Krass, 1999)**

---

# PART I
## THE INVESTMENT PROCESS

# CHAPTER B

## FINDING BARGAINS

"People are always asking me where the outlook is good, but that's the wrong question. The right question is: Where is the outlook most miserable?"

JOHN TEMPLETON (TEMPLETON, 2008)

FROM CHAPTER A we know that fundamentals-based investors want to buy stocks that trade at a significant discount to their intrinsic value (i.e., bargains). Given the efficiency of the stock market, it would be a formidable and extremely time-consuming task to look for undervalued stocks if one lacks a compass that points to potential bargains.

Top investors know that mispricing is more common in some pockets of the market than in other. To avoid wasting their time on stocks that are most probably not worth further scrutiny, they often look for potential bargains in those pockets where they see a good reason for mispricing. And they avoid pockets with stocks that are unlikely to be undervalued.

In this chapter I will give a comprehensive overview of the places that top investors have identified as attractive and unattractive. Due to their inherent differences, a clear distinction is made between stocks in developed and emerging countries. The discussion will cover good ideas, ideas that are probably bad, and good short ideas.

In section B.I top investors' favourite types of stocks in developed countries are discussed. Section B.II gives an overview of the stocks that most top investors shun. In section B.III attractive candidates for short sales in developed markets are summarised. Section B.IV explains how experienced investors hunt for bargains in emerging markets. The practical aspects of screening for bargains are discussed in section B.V. And finally, a concluding section provides a summary of the major lessons of the chapter.

# B.I Good and bad ideas in developed markets

## B.I.1 Good long ideas in developed markets

In developed countries top investors pay special attention to the following types of stocks:

a. ignored stocks,

b. negative-sentiment stocks,

c. specific types of new stocks,

d. opportunities in new trends and events,

e. recommendations from the right people,

f. stocks with catalysts,

g. stocks that are removed from an index, and

h. other miscellaneous opportunities.

Below, there is a thorough discussion of each of these eight categories. The reasons why these stocks tend to be mispriced or undervalued are clearly explained.

### B.I.1.a Ignored stocks

A popular pool top investors like to fish in is stocks that are ignored. These are stocks that people don't talk about, that receive no attention in the media, and that analysts don't cover. Due to widespread disinterest, such stocks tend to be mispriced. There is one caveat, though. The *mis*pricing implies that ignored stocks are equally likely to be undervalued as overvalued. So, the investor has to tread carefully in this area.

To identify stocks that are ignored, one can look for obvious signs of disinterest, such as *lack of analyst coverage*[23] and *low institutional ownership*. In a more targeted search, one can start with companies in one of the four categories of ignored stocks described below, and look for confirmation of disinterest in the form of low analyst coverage and low institutional ownership.

### 1. Dull and unfashionable stocks

Many people believe that nice (or spectacular) gains can be made on glamour stocks. Dull and unfashionable companies, by contrast, elicit a deep yawn. So, the average investor looks for action in glamour stocks and gives boring businesses a miss. This bias creates an opportunity for smart investors. More specifically, five types of stocks that tend to offer opportunities as they are considered dull, woebegone or unfashionable are:

1. **Businesses with a lackluster or unpopular image**: many investors do not pay attention to (and analysts seldom recommend) companies that have an image problem. Here are two types of such businesses:

    - *Companies operating in depressing, disgusting and disagreeable areas*; examples of such businesses according to Peter Lynch and John Neff are:

---

[23] Peter Lynch was excited when he visited a company that no analyst had visited or that no analyst knew.

(i) Companies in the burial business: the burial industry is considered depressing even though it hasn't changed much for centuries, even though it has few new entrants (undertaker is not a popular profession), and even though customers are unlikely to bargain (out of respect for the deceased loved ones). Peter Lynch says in *One Up on Wall Street* that one of his favourite all-time stock picks was the burial service company Service Corporation International which gained about 1000% between 1980 and 1990.

(ii) Companies active in toxic waste and garbage are considered disgusting. When he managed the Magellan Fund, Peter Lynch bought, for instance, Waste Management, Inc., which went up a hundredfold.

(iii) Companies that make things out of disgusting raw materials; an example pointed out by Peter Lynch is the company Envirodyne, which bought a leading producer of intestinal byproducts in 1985. This company turned into a ten bagger within three years after this transaction.

- *Socially irresponsible businesses*: some institutional investors are prohibited to invest in (and many other investors don't want to have a stake in) businesses that produce 'unethical' goods, such as weapons and cigarettes.

2. **Companies in low-growth industries**: few people know that companies in shrinking or low-growth industries can be profitable investments. A study by Jeremy Siegel found that there is significant potential in unpopular low-growth industries. Indeed, many stocks in shrinking industries like energy and railroads have beaten the S&P 500 by a significant margin between 1957 and 2007.[24]

3. **Companies with dull or ridiculous names**: Peter Lynch admitted that whenever he came across a company with a dull or ridiculous name (e.g., Pep Boys), he took a closer look. What tends to make such stocks undervalued is not that it is smart for a company to have a ridiculous name – as a bad name is actually a sign of poor marketing – but the fact that most people (especially professional investors) do not want to be associated with companies that sound ridiculous.

4. **Boring and established businesses**: for instance, Philip Carret liked waterworks and bridge construction businesses.

5. **Cheap stocks with relatively low expected growth**: John Neff believes that companies with low growth expectations are systematically ignored by the market, even when their stock is really cheap. The best risk-return payoff in these types of stocks is often found in companies that combine the following characteristics:

- *Moderate growth*, where earnings are expected to grow about 7% a year in the next five years.

- *Low valuations*, where the PEG ratio of the company is lower than half the PEG ratio of the market.

- *A nice dividend*.

- *A strong track record in growing quarterly earnings*.

---

[24] Siegel, 2005.

## 2. Companies with little or complex information

Most investors and professionals don't bother examining companies that are hard to analyse or companies about which relatively little reliable information exists. Disinterest in such stocks tends to cause mispricing and extra effort to find hidden assets that are overlooked by those who don't have the courage to dig deeper can be very rewarding. Top investors like Seth Klarman and John Templeton deliberately seek out such challenging issues.

For instance, in the 1960s investors tended to avoid Japan due to its opaque accounting rules. John Templeton saw in this a compelling opportunity for those (including himself) who took the trouble to understand the hidden assets and liabilities. Another excellent example is the investment of John Templeton in Teléfonos de Mexico in the mid-1980s, which is described in *Investing the Templeton Way*. Templeton was convinced the company's numbers were unreliable so he undertook the heroic action to count the number of telephones in the country. By multiplying this number with the applicable rate, he found out that the market was vastly understating the value of the company.

## 3. Small companies

> *"It seems clear that there is a greater opportunity to find bargains (and overpriced stocks, for that matter) in the small-cap arena both because there are more stocks to choose from and because smaller stocks are more likely to be lightly analysed and, as a result, more likely to be mispriced."*
>
> **Joel Greenblatt (Greenblatt, 2006)**

Some people argue that the universe of small caps is more appealing than the large cap space as small caps have more room for growth. For instance, small firms are less likely to have products in maturing or declining stages. They are also assumed to have more scope for efficiency gains from learning.

Although this seems plausible at first sight, a critical mind can put serious question marks on the 'more room for growth' argument. Indeed, a large firm can usually be seen as an integrated collection of much smaller business units which each on their own have significant room for growth. As such, there is little reason to believe that a universe of many small caps will grow faster than a set of large caps (which also can be seen as a universe of small caps).

Notwithstanding, it is true that individual small caps with excellent growth prospects can grow much faster than large caps with bright prospects. However, this seldom remains unnoticed by the market. As a matter of fact, the appeal of small caps has more to do with the fact that they tend to be ignored for a number of reasons:

1. **There is little interest in small caps among asset managers**: many asset managers do not invest in small caps because they are difficult to trade (they are illiquid), or because their investment charters prohibit them from owning small stocks.

Professional investors that manage multi-billion stock portfolios (e.g., Warren Buffett) even totally dismiss small caps because it is hard to justify the time and effort needed to analyse them. After all, no small cap will move the needle in their portfolios – not even if it turns out to be a huge winner.

2. **Small caps receive little attention**: small companies are often only known by people who live (geographically) close to those companies. Analysts are unlikely to promote or analyse them, since the low trading volumes in small caps generate little commission income.[25] A nice example of a bargain due to disinterest of the professional investment community in small caps is Haloid. John Templeton was one of the first professional investors to invest in this small photographic company. Although the company had developed a new process, barely any professional was paying attention. Templeton made a gain of 1000% on that company, which later changed its name into the famous photocopier company Xerox Corporation.

3. There is often **much less public information available** about small caps than about large caps. Moreover, the information that is not known is more likely to be bad than good news since firms are quick to bring the good news and hide the bad news. As a result, cautious investors who rely exclusively on public information will think twice before they invest in small caps.

4. **Small caps are (and feel) more risky**: small businesses are usually more risky than large, established firms. In addition, small companies feel less safe (due to higher volatility, less information, etc.) – especially during periods of market turmoil – than the familiar and established names.

Since many small caps are ignored by the average market participant, they are more likely to be mispriced.[26] That's why many top investors like to fish for bargains among the small caps. What makes small caps even more attractive is that the lack of coverage by professionals implies that small caps are often misunderstood by the market.

Value investor Paul D. Sonkin points out yet another advantage of small caps: they are much easier to analyse than big companies because their business models are simpler, they operate in only one (or a few) line(s) of business, and management can more easily be approached. In spite of all these advantages, it is sound advice to avoid companies that are extremely small (such as those with a market cap < $10 million), because such stocks are typically very illiquid. It is also often too hard to find reliable information about such businesses.

## 4. Stocks ignored for formal reasons

Some stocks are ignored because they are perceived as too risky, too marginal or too dangerous for one's reputation. Professionals avoid them or are even not allowed to buy

---

[25] The lack of analyst coverage of small caps has become even more pronounced in recent years as brokers have cut back on sell-side research.

[26] There is even evidence that small caps – and especially micro caps (companies with market caps < $250 million) – are not only mispriced but are more likely to be undervalued than overvalued, since they tend to beat the market (Damodaran, 2004).

them. Private investors may not be aware of their existence, or are not particularly attracted to them. According to Marty Whitman, two types of stocks fit into the category of *ignored for formal reasons*:

1. **Single-digit stocks**: most stocks with a price below $5 to $10 got there after a precipitous drop from much higher prices. Many people see such single-digit stocks as dangerous speculations. As a result, analysts seldom bother to analyse these companies, institutional investors usually don't want to buy them (or may even be prohibited from owning them), brokerage houses will not promote them any more, and banks and brokers will no longer accept them as collateral for margin loans. Marty Whitman acknowledges that single-digit stocks can be risky investments but at the same time he is convinced that the lack of interest by the investment crowd can create bargain valuations for opportunistic investors.

2. **Post-arbitrage stocks**: these are stocks that remain outstanding after the completion of an acquisition offer (i.e., stocks that were not tendered to the acquirer by shareholders). Marty Whitman points out that post-arbitrage stocks can be compelling bargains that sometimes trade at 50% or less of the price at which they were tendered. Such ultra-depressed prices are typically caused by the sales of arbitrageurs who dispose of the stock after the conclusion of the acquisition offer, the lower liquidity of the stock, the risk of a delisting, the risk of a later force-out acquisition at a lower price, and the risk that a new acquisition offer will not occur (so investors get stuck with the stock). Marty Whitman says that the concerns about post-arbitrage stocks are justified to some extent. Nevertheless, he believes that there are opportunities for investors who follow the subsequent guidelines:

   - *Insist on a low price*: one should buy post-arbitrage stocks at prices of at least 33% below the price at which the previous acquisition offer was done. On the other hand, if the acquirer overpaid for the business and/or if the purchased business is basically sick, it best to avoid the stock altogether.

   - *Look for honest management in the acquirer*: to avoid grief caused by a force-out offer at fire-sale prices, Marty Whitman avoids investment in post-arbitrage stocks where management of the acquirer has "predatory predilections."

## B.I.1.b Negative-sentiment stocks

Negative-sentiment stocks are stocks that are out of favour with the investment community. As opposed to ignored stocks, such stocks are usually well-known due to an avalanche of bad news and bad publicity. Owing to the overall negative sentiment, reinforced by cognitive biases like herding behaviour, extrapolation and biased risk tolerance, people tend to overreact vis-à-vis such stocks.[27] Few people buy, and many

---

[27] Herding behaviour is the tendency of people to feel safe and comfortable doing what other people are doing. Extrapolation is the fact that people try to extrapolate recent events into the future. And biased risk tolerance refers to the fact that a person's tolerance for risk is influenced by recent events, especially when they are emotionally charged. See also Chapter A.

existing shareholders sell. Professionals avoid the stock because they fear that association with the company can harm their career and reputation; even if they believe in the stock, they don't want to explain the difficult story to clients. All this causes a steep drop in analyst coverage, and a steady exodus by asset managers.[28] Not surprisingly, the beating that negative-sentiment stocks take frequently leads to bargain prices.

Investing in negative-sentiment stocks is also sometimes called *turnaround investing* because the basic idea is that the company eventually will surprise the market by turning around. It is not an easy strategy, though, because turnaround investors have to deal with three challenges. First, one has to identify stocks that are likely to turn around. In other words, one has to look for stocks that are *out of favour for the wrong reasons*. To minimise the risk of investing in turnarounds, Benjamin Graham recommends focusing on larger companies with proven track records.

Second, to minimise the opportunity cost (i.e., the cost of waiting), one is advised to look for stocks where the *turnaround is imminent* and where the turnaround (if it happens) will be *recognised quickly in the market*. The chances of a quick turnaround are higher in the presence of a *turnaround catalyst* or an indication that the turnaround is near (e.g., insider buying). To avoid the problem of a genuine turnaround going unnoticed by the market, Benjamin Graham and David Dreman suggest limiting one's attention to large companies.

Finally, a third challenge of turnaround investing is to *invest at the right moment*. This is not too early to sidestep excessive risk and not too late in order not to miss the largest gains when the company turns around.

Here are a number of potentially attractive turnaround candidates:

1. **Once popular stocks abandoned by professionals**: these are typically stocks that were once hot and high-growth, but that failed to live up to the market's sky-high expectations. In such stocks, investors tend to move from one extreme (excessive optimism) to another (excessive pessimism).[29] Some value investors, like Benjamin Graham and Paul Sonkin, show(ed) special interest in stocks a few years after their hot IPOs when they had been mercilessly whittled down by investors who expected too much of them.

2. **Fortune's "most despised" companies**: it turns out that stocks that are on the list of Fortune's most despised companies tend to outperform the market significantly.[30]

3. **Sound or great companies that encounter a temporary huge but solvable problem**: Philip Fisher and Shelby Davis pointed out that one can find interesting investment opportunities among *well-run* companies when they suffer due to a big one-time problem that is unlikely to hinder the long-term prospects of the firm. Two types of one-time problems that tend to create bargains are:

---

[28] According to Anthony Bolton, a good sign that a stock is hated is to see the last analyst throw in the towel.
[29] There is some anecdotal evidence that abandoned stocks tend to outperform; stocks that are most sold by institutions tend to outperform the market (Montier, 2010).
[30] (Montier, 2010), (Kahneman, 2011).

- *Operational problems*: Fisher mentions, for instance, that the difficult start-up of a new plant in a manufacturing company often frustrates the market.

- *Bad corporate news*: the stock market often overreacts to bad news such as a prolonged strike, a product recall, an oil spill, or a lawsuit. For instance, the stock of the oil major BP lost more than 50% of its value between April and June 2010 due to the catastrophic Deepwater Horizon oil spill. But by January 2011 the stock had gained more than 60% from its bottom.

4. **Companies in weak industries that are about to turn around**: several top investors believe that compelling bargains can be found in industries where things have gone from bad to worse – provided that there is a reason to believe that the industry will come back. Joe Vidich even believes that the best time to invest in such industries is when all investors (clients) are wondering why one would want to own this type of stock.[31] Top investors approach such bargain situations in two ways:

   - *The opportunity within the opportunity*: investors like Peter Lynch and Richard Rainwater screened selectively for the best companies (or companies in the best sub-sectors) of an industry that was due to bounce back. To minimise risk and maximise returns, Lynch recommends that investors should:

     (i) Wait for signs of a revival in the industry: it is safest to wait until the industry shows signs of coming back to life. This avoids the risk of investing in an industry that is in a terminal decline (e.g., radio tubes never came back).

     (ii) Invest in the greatest companies in that industry: the best companies of that industry are typically able to grab a bigger market share at the expense of weaker competitors (who often drop out). The greatest companies are usually high-growth, low-debt and low-cost penny-pinchers that avoid executive excesses (such as exorbitant executive salaries), treat their (motivated) workers well, and tend to focus on overlooked niches in the market. An example of this type of company that Peter Lynch liked in the 1980s was Southwest Airlines, whose stock price went up 20-fold between 1978 and 1991. The company was the lowest-cost operator in the lousy airlines industry. It didn't leverage itself. It had a unique business model and was excellent in its operations. It had a very competent (and fairly compensated) management team that treated its employees well and it fostered a unique corporate culture.[32]

   - *Buying baskets*: one can also, like Jim Rogers, buy a basket of different stocks in an industry that is going through a deep crisis. In this way, one can benefit fully from a recovery of that industry without bothering about the specifics of individual companies. Jim Rogers likes to buy when a few big companies in that industry are in bankruptcy (or close to it), and when capital expenditures come to a stop.

---

[31] Schwager, 2012.

[32] An excellent description of the nuts and bolts of Southwest Airlines is given in (Freiberg, 1996).

5. **Companies with an idiosyncratic risk**: according to hedge fund star manager Jamie Mai, "Although markets are generally good at estimating the magnitude of a contingent liability, they are often poor at evaluating outcomes probabilistically."[33] He believes that markets generally overestimate the chance that contingent liabilities really will materialise. Therefore, on average it pays off to invest in companies that face litigations, regulatory actions, etc.

6. **Companies in/close to financial distress**: these are companies that are in such deep trouble that many observers believe they will go bankrupt. Due to the fear for bankruptcy (where stockholders are bound to lose virtually all of their investment), most investors steer clear of distressed businesses. Investing in distressed businesses is definitely very risky and should be considered only if the investor is convinced that the chances are stacked in favour of a positive outcome. Especially appealing distressed businesses are those that combine high uncertainty (due to financial problems) with low risk (i.e., the risk of bankruptcy is low), such as:

   - *Distressed businesses with stable cash flows*: Mohnish Pabrai takes a closer look at distressed businesses in industries that throw off stable cash flows and that have low failure rates. Examples are distressed companies in the funeral homes business. This industry has very stable and reliable cash flows and low failure rates thanks to low competitive pressure and due to its low sensitivity to the economy.

   - *Distressed businesses that are likely to be bailed out by government*: it can be very profitable to invest in companies that are in deep distress when the government (or local authorities) can't afford to let the company go bankrupt (e.g., because it would affect the economy or the citizens too much). In such situations, the chances are high that the government will step in with a financial rescue package or, at the very least, be extremely supportive of a rescue operation. Here are two examples:

     (i) Peter Lynch likes utilities in distress.[34] Common causes for distress are external crises (e.g., Consolidated Edison got into a liquidity crisis when oil prices skyrocketed during the 1973 oil embargo), too much leverage (e.g., Entergy Corporation), accidents (e.g., General Public Utilities after the Three Mile Island accident), or inept management (e.g., Long Island Lighting couldn't get a licence for the nuclear plant it had built). The reason why utilities in distress can be interesting investments is that they provide electricity to many families or companies. They cannot be ignored by authorities and they are likely to be bailed out in one way or another.

     To achieve the best risk-adjusted returns in distressed utilities, Peter Lynch recommends investing when the dividend is suspended (or reduced significantly) and selling when the dividend is restored. One caution is in

---

[33] Schwager, 2012.
[34] Lynch, 1993.

order, though. Not all utilities in distress are profitable investments. Sometimes, the challenges faced by the utility can be so huge that the company has to be (partly) nationalised to cope with the problems. This can lead to a permanent loss for shareholders. One notable recent example is Tokyo Electric Power Company (TEPCO). This Japanese utility suffered one of the world's largest nuclear disasters after a huge Japanese earthquake and tsunami in 2011, and had to be nationalised partly to deal with the problems.

(ii) John Templeton was attracted to companies of essential industries that were about to be wiped out by catastrophic events. For instance, he opportunistically invested in a basket of the most heavily beaten-down American airline stocks right after the 9/11 terrorist attacks (which threatened to bring the entire American airline industry down) because he knew that government would have to step in to save the airlines.[35]

## B.I.1.c Specific types of new stocks

### 1. New shares in special situation transactions

The first group of appealing new shares are stocks that are issued (often along with other non-equity securities) in special corporate transactions. Famous fans of such special situation stocks are the legendary investors Joel Greenblatt[36] and Seth Klarman[37]. They explain that these types of stocks tend to be undervalued for two major reasons.

First of all, special situation stocks are often not well understood by the market because they are complex, or because they appear unattractive (e.g., they may be highly leveraged). So interest in these stocks is usually low. Second, these stocks are often distributed to investors who didn't ask for them. Needless to say, these investors show little commitment to the position. In fact, many have incentives to sell the stock, irrespective of its merits. For instance, some (institutional) investors may be forced to sell the stocks because their investment charters prohibit them from holding on to the shares. Others with a trivial position in the new stock sell because they can't justify the time they would need to figure these stocks out. Still others are unfamiliar with the new shares and don't feel comfortable until they get rid of them.

Here are five types of special situation stocks:

---

[35] To make sure that he bought the most beaten-down stocks he gave his broker the order to buy only low P/E stocks that lost at least 50% of their value on the day the market reopened after the attacks (on 17 September 2001).

[36] Joel Greenblatt also mentions that even higher returns can be earned (with higher risk) by investing in derivatives of special situation stocks. This can work wonderfully because most option investors do not take the special situation into account when they value such derivatives. The safest and most attractive derivates are those that allow the special situation to be recognised by the market. They therefore must expire after the catalyst of the price move and/or preferably have a relatively long expiration period of a few years. Examples are LEAPS (long-term options of about 2.5 years) and warrants (Greenblatt, 1997).

[37] Klarman, 1991.

1. **Merger securities**: these are securities – possibly including (preferred) stock, but also bonds, warrants, and rights – that an acquirer offers in exchange for the shares of a company it tries to acquire. The main reason that these securities are often undervalued is that most investors (including sophisticated ones) who receive these securities feel uncomfortable holding them. They want to get out and so they sell these securities indiscriminately. Joel Greenblatt recommends reading the provisions attached to these securities, which are often unusual, and selectively investing in the most attractive ones.

2. **Preferred stock in going-private securities**: the preferred stock that is part of the package offered to shareholders in exchange for shares in a transaction where management tries to take a company private (e.g., in a leveraged buyout) can be very attractive. On the one hand, the preferred stock can be very valuable because it allows investors to invest in the company alongside a well-incentivised and motivated management. On the other hand, the preferred stock is often cheap because many investors ignore it (or dump it), since it is typically only a small part of the exchange package.

3. **New stock of companies that emerge from bankruptcy**: Joel Greenblatt and Anthony Bolton research stocks that are distributed to claimholders (banks, bondholders, trade claim holders, etc.) of bankrupt companies as part of a reorganisation plan. These shares tend to trade at depressed price levels for three reasons. First, there is selling pressure from the many claimholders that just want to be compensated as soon as possible and therefore have no interest in holding the shares for the long term. Second, distressed debt investors (or vultures) also tend to sell rather quickly because they are more interested in moving on to the next distressed debt opportunity than in holding the stock for a long time. A final reason for potential undervaluation is that these stocks are usually not on the professional's radar screens. If they are, they are still unlikely to be promoted by analysts and brokerage houses since they do not generate sufficient commission income. Nevertheless, Joel Greenblatt warns that investors have to be very selective in this area. Chances of success are highest in:

   - *Relatively small companies*: competition from other distressed debt investors is usually lower in small distressed businesses. The reason is that distressed debt investments require considerable due diligence. To be cost effective, professionals therefore tend to focus on the larger deals.

   - *Good businesses*: it is best to avoid businesses of poor quality. The best investments are companies with inherent strengths (e.g., strong brand names, leadership in market niches, competitive advantages, etc.) that failed due to excessive leverage, certain unprofitable business lines (that have been divested before the company emerges from bankruptcy), or due to a product liability (e.g., asbestos claims) that was settled in the bankruptcy proceedings.

4. **Stub stock after recapitalisations**: shares that remain outstanding in the market after a recapitalisation (or recap), are called stub stocks and can be compelling bargains right after the recap. In a recap, a company repurchases a large portion of its stock by offering cash, bonds and preferred stock in exchange for its shares. The result is a company with high leverage that scares many investors away.[38] Provided that the leveraged company tries to sell assets (to reduce its leverage), and has healthy cash flows and improving profit margins, stub stocks can be very profitable investments.

5. **Parent company after the spin-off of a complicated division**: according to Joel Greenblatt, companies that spin off a complicated division (e.g., a regulated business) deserve special attention. Once the parent company is stripped off the division, it may be a much more attractive takeover target.

## 2. Spin-offs

A spin-off is a company that is spun off entirely or partially from its parent company. As such, it is also a special situation stock. Due to their specific characteristics spin-offs deserve a separate discussion. Numerous top investors have said repeatedly that (partial) spin-offs can be very rewarding investments.

Studies confirm that spin-offs (and to a lesser extent also their parent companies) tend to outperform the market substantially in the three first years after their separation. Famous examples of spin-offs that rewarded investors handsomely are the seven Baby Bell companies (Ameritech, Bell Atlantic, Bell South, Nynex, Pacific Telesis, Southwestern Bell, US West) that were spun out of ATT. Peter Lynch mentions in *One Up on Wall Street* that these seven spin-offs together gained about 170% (including dividends) between 1983 and 1988, which was two times better than the market.

One possible reason for the outperformance of spin-offs is that the market often underestimates or fails to acknowledge that many spun-off businesses are set to improve their business performance. There are several reasons why the business performance of spin-offs tends to improve after they gain their independence.

First, managers of spin-offs are usually well motivated. In contrast to the situation before the spin-off, they can run their own show without interference from the parent company. Second, management of the spin-off can usually manage a business that is more sharply focused than before. Thirdly, the parent company usually prepares and structures the spin-off such that it has all it needs to succeed. Indeed, parent companies normally have a vested interest in the success of the spin-off as failure would reflect badly on the parent company whereas success usually benefits shareholders of the parent company (who often are also shareholders of the spin-off).

Another reason for the mispricing of spin-offs is that the documentation relating to them tends to be complex. It is also often hard to understand the pro-forma financial

---

[38] Note that also the distributed securities (bonds and preferred stock) can be interesting investments (though usually less so than the stub stock), because most shareholders want to dispose of them as soon as possible (as they feel uncomfortable when they hold these securities).

statements related to the spin-off. The need to go through hundreds of pages and to spend many hours researching a spin-off investment deters many investors. The resulting lack of interest in complicated spin-offs is more likely to cause pricing inefficiencies. But even then, not all spin-offs are created equal. Therefore, spin-off investors have to be selective and look for:[39]

1. **Confirmation by insiders that the deal is attractive**: according to Joel Greenblatt, significant insider actions can be a genuine tip-off that a spin-off has investment merit. It is especially important to check out whether:

   - *Insiders want shares (or options)* in the spin-off, either by participating in the spin-off operation, by buying stock of the spin-off some time (e.g., a few months) after the transaction, or by receiving stock (options) in the spin-off as part of their compensation package.

   - Management wants to *keep the transaction low-profile*: when management does not promote the stock, it may be an indication that they want to keep the stock price as low as possible (e.g., to buy extra shares at a low price).

   - The *deal is made unattractive* for many (especially institutional) investors. When the deal looks unattractive (e.g., by keeping the spin-off small and illiquid), the stock price may stay low for a while which will enable management to accumulate positions in the shares at low prices (e.g., in a rights offering, see below).

2. **Spin-offs that are structured in a way that benefits shareholders of the parent company**: the best returns are likely to be found in those spin-offs where there are plenty of reasons to believe that management (of the parent company) wants to create an attractive deal for its shareholders. The following two types of spin-offs usually satisfy this criterion:

   - *Spin-offs distributed to shareholders of the parent company*: as a spin-off shrinks the size of a business, it is the opposite of the popular practice of empire building. Therefore, it is fair to assume that a spin-off operation where the parent company distributes shares of the spin-off to its shareholders is done with the sole intention to create value (for the shareholders). Since in such a transaction there is also no reason to bring the spin-off to the stock market at an expensive price, management can see it as appropriate to go for a relatively cheap price that leaves plenty of room for price appreciation (which will please long-term shareholders of the parent company).

   - *Rights offerings*: a rights offering is a spin-off operation where shares of the business unit that is spun out can be purchased by means of (marketable) purchase rights that are distributed (for free) to the shareholders of the parent company. The aim of a rights offering is to sell shares of the business unit to

---

[39] In the US, one can examine public filings like the SEC Form 10 (and especially its first few pages) to find more information on any particular spin-off.

the shareholders of the parent company.[40] As such, management has little incentive to pursue a high price and to keep shareholders happy it will not do so. Note also that the most appealing rights offerings are those with oversubscription privileges (meaning privileges to buy additional shares if the rights offering is not completely subscribed). Such privileges are an indication that management is interested in building up equity stakes beyond the capacity allowed by the rights they received.

An excellent example of an attractive rights offering is given by Joel Greenblatt in *You Can be a Stock Market Genius*. Liberty Media was spun out of Tele-Communications in 1990. Professional investors were discouraged from investing in the spin-off as Liberty Media was small (compared to the parent company), and because the share price was deliberately fixed at a high level (which limited liquidity, as retail investors are less active in stocks with high prices). Everybody who took the trouble to check out the position of the CEO John Malone would have found that he was to become an important shareholder of Liberty Media. As it turned out, Liberty Media returned about 1000% in the two years following its spin-off.

> *"Any time you read about a spinoff being accomplished through a rights offering, stop whatever you're doing and take a look."*
>
> **Joel Greenblatt (Greenblatt, 1997)**

3. **Spin-offs where selling pressure is to be expected**: selling pressure is usually only to be expected in spin-off transactions where a parent company distributes shares to its shareholders. When that happens, shareholders of the parent company receive shares they didn't ask for so some are tempted to sell. Institutional investors may even be forced to sell due to restrictions in their investment charters (e.g., the market cap of the spin-off may be too low). More selling can be caused by investors who are not interested in analysing the merits of the spin-off because they are unfamiliar with the business, or because the position is too small to warrant research time. Finally, some spin-offs may look like toxic waste (e.g., when the parent company loads the spin-off with liabilities) and scare shareholders away. A nice example of the latter is the spin-off operation of Marriott in the early 1990s.[41] Due to the real estate crisis, Marriott decided to spin off the attractive part of the business into Marriott International, and leave the unsalable hotel

---

[40] This has to be contrasted with equity carve-outs, which are spin-offs where shares are sold to the public without rights. Equity carve-outs are basically plain IPOs and are usually not that attractive (see also IPOs) – except when they are done under duress (e.g., when a company in distress spins off a unit to alleviate its financial problems) or under difficult market conditions.

[41] Greenblatt, 1997.

properties and low-growth concession hotels in the highly leveraged Host Marriot. Joel Greenblatt was attracted to Host Marriott as he expected tremendous selling pressure for three reasons:

- Host Marriott was the toxic waste of the original company due to its (apparently) unattractive assets and high liabilities,

- Host Marriott was small and was active in another type of business than the original business (so institutional investors would feel uneasy holding on to it), and

- Little information was released about the operation, so institutional investors felt uncomfortable about it. What also made the deal attractive was that the architect of the plan was to become the CEO of Host Marriott (so he had a vested interest in its success), that the Marriott family would still own about 25% of Host Marriott (so they were not trying to get out), that Marriott International would support Host Marriott financially (through loans), and that Host Marriott was highly leveraged (which would magnify returns if things worked out well).

As far as timing is concerned, the best moment to buy a spin-off would be about one year after the transaction. At that point the selling pressure has worn off and the superior business performance of the spin-off becomes clear to the market place.

### 3. IPOs where the issuers have the incentive to settle with a bargain price

Although the average IPO is usually *not* an attractive investment (see below), if one has a good reason to believe that the issuer will bring the company to the market at a cheap price it may be worth a closer look. Here are some examples of potentially attractive IPOs:

1. **IPOs in privatisations of government-controlled companies**: Peter Lynch states that the shares of government-owned companies that are sold to the public in privatisation operations can be cheap due to political reasons. This is so because a major concern of many politicians is to please citizens (who are, after all, voters). Therefore, many politicians would rather sell such shares at bargain prices than rip their citizens off. What can also make such shares compelling investments is that government-owned companies are often mismanaged. Hence, entrepreneurial forces and motivation may be unleashed when government-owned companies are privatised. An example of a once in a lifetime gift of the British government to its citizens was the IPO of British Telecom. Nevertheless, one must be aware that not all stocks in this area are bargains, because not all governments sell shares with political considerations in mind. For instance, in the 1980s the Japanese government brought a number of government-owned companies to the market at insane valuations amidst a serious market bubble.

2. **Demutualisations**: according to David Einhorn and Seth Klarman, investors can make a killing in operations where companies with a mutual structure (e.g.,

insurance companies that are owned by their policyholders) go public. In demutualisations the new shareholders typically end up with the company as well as the proceeds of the IPO. In other words, the new shareholders get the company for free (irrespective of the IPO price). If, in addition to this, management of the company is incentivised by stock options at the IPO price there is good reason to believe that the IPO price will be attractive. There is also academic evidence that the operating performance improves after demutualisation of, for instance, insurance companies.

## B.I.1.d Opportunities in new trends and events

Some people believe that trends and specific important events are always discounted in stock prices. That makes sense. Whenever there is a hot new trend or evolution in an industry and/or technology, investors typically gravitate towards a number of high-profile beneficiaries of this trend or evolution. Hence, it is unlikely bargains will be found among those stocks.

Nevertheless, top investors have identified several potential opportunities among companies that are impacted by new trends or sudden events. For instance, in its rush the crowd often overlooks a number of less obvious beneficiaries. At the other end of the spectrum, investors often penalise too harshly those companies that are expected to suffer from the new trend or event. And third, investors regularly fail to take certain trends or events into account as they are focused on the short term.

### 1. Stocks that are penalised too much

Some companies that are expected to suffer from a trend are penalised too much. For instance, when a new technology emerges it is common that companies of old competing industries are bid down. Although it is undeniable that new trends can hurt old industries a lot, sometimes the crowd overestimates the harm the new industry will inflict on the Old Guard. The opportunity for investors lies in companies that are incorrectly assumed to suffer (a lot) from the new trend.

For instance, in the mid-1990s the idea prevailed that the new satellite TV would wipe out cable TV. This put serious pressure on the stocks of cable companies. Although star investor Glenn Greenberg acknowledged the merits of satellite TV, he was not convinced that it would replace cable TV entirely, due to technological problems in the implementation of satellite TV. Moreover, he correctly envisioned a bright future for cable companies thanks to new services and deregulation (with more freedom about price increases). He put about 40% of his assets in cable companies by the end of 1998 at very attractive prices. Needless to say, the bet paid off excellently.

### 2. Indirect beneficiaries of new trends

Some beneficiaries of a trend are not recognised by the market as such because they are not the obvious beneficiaries. In other words, investors often overlook a number of less straightforward and less flashy secondary beneficiaries of a trend. A surprising fact is that some of these secondary beneficiaries often reap the largest rewards from the trend. The result is a significant undervaluation of some of the strongest (secondary) beneficiaries of the trend – at least in the first stages of the trend. Some examples of secondary beneficiaries that can be compelling investments are:

1. **Suppliers to a strong growth industry**: in the Gold Rush in 19th century America, sellers of picks and shovels made decent profits, while a great many gold diggers were left holding the bag. The same principle remains valid nowadays. Legendary investors like Julian Robertson and Ralph Wagner used to look at suppliers to the service providers in booming or transforming industries because these companies often benefit the most from trends. Here are some examples:

   - Suppliers of telecommunication equipment (e.g., Cisco) were better investments during the internet boom of the 1990s than the telecom operators that directly provided the internet service.

   - In the late 1970s investors started to realise that suppliers to the oil industry (e.g., exploration companies) were attractive beneficiaries of the oil boom.

   - When airline demand grew fast in the 1960s, a company like Monogram that supplied chemical toilets for airplanes made solid profits.

   - Peter Lynch points out that when stocks are popular it is often a better idea to invest in the mutual fund companies that supply the funds than to invest in the funds themselves.

2. **Clones of a successful innovator**: Mohnish Pabrai likes companies that lift their business idea from existing innovators. While the market usually pays a lot of attention to the innovator, they seldom show much interest in the cloners. Nevertheless, great cloners often dislodge the innovator they copied. Examples of excellent cloners are Microsoft (cloner of IBM) and Wal-Mart (cloner of the Kmart business model).

3. **Multinationals with high exposure to emerging countries**: many investors are attracted to the high growth rates of emerging countries but they don't realise that investing in pure local emerging market companies is full of dangers. It is often much safer to benefit from the emergence of certain countries through multinationals that have important activities in these emerging countries. The most attractive multinationals are often those with activities in the strongest growth sectors of emerging countries: financials (retail banking, insurance, pension fund management), beverage and consumer products (dairy business, brewers, luxury goods), pharmaceuticals, and infrastructure plays (construction, suppliers to construction, owners of infrastructure).

## 3. Underappreciated beneficiaries of sudden events

During certain catastrophic events, investors sell stocks en masse and indiscriminately. Hereby, they often also sell those companies that stand to benefit from the event. For example, Turkey was hit by an earthquake in 1999 which caused a sell-off across the board. When that happened Jim Leitner purchased the beaten-down shares of glass manufacturers, because he realised that they would benefit enormously from the strong demand for new windows when people would have to repair the damages.[42]

## 4. Beneficiaries of secular trends

Sometimes the market fails to recognise (or ignores) long-term secular trends because investors are too preoccupied by the short term. A nice example of a secular trend that is often overlooked in its early stages is the commodity cycle. As Jim Rogers explains in *Hot Commodities*, commodities move in secular bull and bear markets[43] of about 18 years, driven primarily by imbalances between demand and supply. Even more interestingly, commodities seem to be negatively correlated with stocks, in the sense that commodities tend to be in a secular bull when the stock market is in a range-bound/secular bear, and vice versa. As such, stock investors can actually make a lot of money during secular range-bound markets for stocks by investing in companies that are primary beneficiaries of the commodity bull that is going on at that moment.

Although Jim Rogers prefers direct exposure to commodities through the futures market during secular bulls in commodities, he points out the following two types of companies that are likely to beat the stock market during commodity bull markets:

1. **Commodity-producing companies**: it stands to reason that commodity-producing companies will be primary beneficiaries of a secular bull in commodities. However, selectivity remains important because such companies can have company-specific issues that may depress the stock price.

2. **Businesses in commodity-rich countries**: all businesses whose prosperity is closely connected to the economy of a commodity-rich country (e.g., retailers, hotel chains, restaurants) are potential market beaters. In addition, since the currencies of commodity-rich countries tend to perform well, foreign investors may see their stock investments appreciate even more.

## 5. Companies with new future revenue sources

According to hedge fund market star Tom Claugus, new revenue sources that are still a few years away are often not discounted into a company's stock price.[44] This can be explained by the fact that short-term analyst estimates don't include this new income source, and because current statistics (which are used by many investors) don't reflect them. Hence, investors who take the trouble to examine profit and revenue sources a few

---

[42] Drobny, 2009.

[43] Secular market movements in commodities or stocks typically last between one and two decades. During secular markets, prices usually move up and down in shorter cycles of a few years. In secular bull markets prices move up over the course of the secular movement and valuations get stretched further and further. In secular range-bound markets prices move sideways and valuations fall. In secular bear markets, prices move downwards and valuations fall.

[44] Schwager, 2012.

years into the future may discover from time to time stocks with prices that do not take this new source into account.

## B.I.1.e Recommendations from the right people

In general, the average stock tip is not worth much. Even worse, taking stock tips can be downright dangerous. There are some very specific exceptions, though. Many top investors do take tips seriously provided that they come from reliable and well-informed sources. However, they never take tips at face value – they always do their own due diligence. More specifically, they point out that valuable ideas can come from:

1. **Tips from competitors**: since companies continually monitor the marketplace and closely examine the steps of direct competitors, they accumulate a lot of knowledge about their competitors in terms of strengths, weaknesses, market position, etc. For this reason, top investors try to detect worthwhile investment ideas by sounding executives out about their competitors. This can be done in two ways:

   - *Direct tips from executives*: in interviews with executives Peter Lynch, Shelby Davis, Anthony Bolton and Philip Fisher usually tried to find out which competitor impressed them the most.[45] Then they started analysing that competitor.

   - *Indirect tips*: according to John Templeton, frequent takeovers at high premiums in a particular industry can be a major tip-off that many companies in that industry are undervalued.

2. **Tips from respectable investors**: it is obvious that the investment ideas of the best investment minds in the world – in particular ideas that are shared by many of these minds – can provide starting points for further analysis. It may not always be possible, though, to obtain their best ideas in time:

   - *Some top investors are willing to share their ideas*: there are a very limited number of investment letters that give timely and reliable recommendations about stocks. One example is The Prudent Speculator:
   **www.theprudentspeculator.com**

   - *Some top investors are reluctant to share their ideas*: top investors try to keep their ideas hidden in order not to disrupt their own trades (by actions of those who would mimic their trades). Notwithstanding this, plenty of information about the market operations of many excellent investors is available with some delay:

     (i) In some countries large investors have to disclose their holdings on a regular basis (e.g., quarterly in the US). Two web services that track the holdings of some of the best investors in the US based on publicly filed documents are GuruFocus (**gurufocus.com**) and Stockpickr (**stockpickr.com**).

---

[45] For instance, Shelby Davis frequently asked executives explicitly about the competition and which competitor they feared most through the question: "If you had one silver bullet to shoot a competitor, which competitor would you shoot?" (Rothchild, 2001).

(ii) The letters to shareholders of mutual funds, hedge funds, or other investment vehicles managed by these investors can be publicly available (in particular on the internet).

3. **Tips from insiders**: a third source of valuable investment ideas are the insiders of companies (management, reference shareholders and members of the board of directors), because they should have superior knowledge about the prospects and the fair value of their company. Smart investors know that words are cheap and that the statements of insiders about a stock's valuation have to be taken with a grain of salt. They also know that it is forbidden to act on *material non-public information*, so they are wary of acting on exclusive information that they receive firsthand from insiders. For these reasons smart investors look for actions by insiders as tip-offs to the undervaluation of a stock:

- *Insider buying*: many top investors pay special attention to share purchases by insiders (including shares acquired through options provided that the shares are not sold) as an indicator of a stock's undervaluation. Information about insider transactions can be found in many countries with regulatory instances (e.g., Form 144 and Form 4 with the SEC in the US), in business publications (e.g., the *Wall Street Journal*), or through commercial services (e.g., Bloomberg). Studies confirm that insider buying can indeed be a reliable indicator of future outperformance over the long run[46] – especially in the year that starts six months after the reporting of insider purchases. According to Lakonishok, one of the most reliable metrics to determine the strength of insider purchases is the net purchase ratio (NPR), defined as:

$$\text{NPR} = \frac{(\text{insider purchases}_{6m} - \text{insider sales}_{6m})}{(\text{insider purchases}_{6m} + \text{insider sales}_{6m})}$$

where insider purchases$_{6m}$ and insider sales$_{6m}$ are the number of insider purchases and insider sales over the last six months. However, not all insider buying is equally reliable. For instance, insider buying is a much stronger sign of undervaluation for small companies than for bigger ones.[47] And it is also more reliable when the stock trades at a low multiple. Furthermore, the most reliable insider buys are characterised by:

(i) *Aggressive insider buying*: the larger the scale of the insider buying and the more consistent the insider buying in time, the more reliable the sign that the stock may be undervalued. To determine whether a purchase is significant for a certain insider, one can compare the amount purchased to that insider's entire holding, to his or her overall personal wealth, or to his or her annual remuneration.

---

[46] Note that insiders are prohibited from making short-term round-trip trades in some countries (e.g., the US), which implies that they will only buy with long-term prospects in mind.

[47] According to a study by Lakonishok, there is actually little difference in performance between large cap stocks with high NPRs and those with low NPRs.

(ii) *Insider buying by CEO or CFO*: since the CEO and the CFO are usually best informed about the evolution of their business, insider buying by these top executives is a more reliable sign of undervaluation than purchases by other insiders. Insider buying by CFOs is an even stronger indicator of future outperformance than purchases by the CEO. Insider buying by reference shareholders, on the other hand, seems to be the least reliable.

(iii) *Several insiders are buying*: the larger (and the more diverse) the group of insiders that are buying, the more reliable the signal. In fact, according to a study of Lakonishok, a strong buy signal in small companies comes from insider purchases of sizable amounts by at least three different insiders.

(iv) *Unexpected insider buying*: Anthony Bolton mentions in *Investing Against the Tide* that unexpected insider purchases (e.g., purchases after a significant rise in the stock price) are the most significant.

- *Stock repurchases*: companies often try to create value for their shareholders by repurchasing their shares when they believe they are undervalued. Since stock repurchases are done with corporate money rather than with private money, they are a less reliable indicator for undervaluation than insider buying. Making matters worse, executives can repurchase shares for other reasons than the creation of value. They may, for instance, try to push the share price up, buy shares to cover options issued to employees, etc. For this reason, Warren Buffett complained in 1999 that although repurchases in the 1970s were a reliable indicator of undervaluation, this was no longer the case in 1999. I would not go as far as Buffett but investors must nevertheless always remain sceptical of stock repurchases. At the very least, one should try to ascertain whether repurchases are done for honourable reasons or not.

- *Dividend increases*: a board of directors that raises a company's dividend shows its confidence in the company's future. Although a dividend increase in and of itself is unrelated to a company's valuation, a significant dividend increase at a company with a cheap valuation can be a tip-off that the company is undervalued.

## B.I.1.f Stocks with catalysts

Even if one can find a stock with a price that is significantly below fair value, there is always uncertainty about when the price-value gap will close. Obviously, the faster the gap closes the higher the internal rate of return on the investment. Therefore, it makes sense, as Joel Greenblatt suggests, to insist on a higher discount to fair value for stocks without a catalyst than for stocks with one.[48] On the other hand, one must be aware that catalysts which are generally acknowledged by the market are likely to be priced into the stock price. That's why many top investors don't pay much attention to catalysts that can trigger the closing of the price-value gap when they buy or sell stocks.

---

[48] Heins, 2013.

Another type of catalyst that tends to be more amenable to excess returns are so-called value catalysts. These are events that probably will increase the company's value (i.e., the company's future cash flows), but where the market temporarily fails to take this event into account. Value catalysts come in two kinds:

1. **Internal catalysts**: these are favourable changes within the corporation, such as:

   - *New management*: although a change of management – through discharge, pension, or death – can be a factor of concern,[49] it can also be the beginning of a process of exceptional value creation. The main challenge for the investor is to determine whether the new people in charge are up to the task, and whether one can expect a change of course that will benefit the company. For instance, Mario Gabelli bought shares of Giant Foods when the founder passed away because he expected a sale of the company or new management that would be focused on earnings increases.

   - *New corporate or product strategy*: similar to new management, a new strategy can be a source of wealth creation or a good reason for concern. Investors have to apply their judgment to determine whether the new strategy is likely to pan out or not.

   - *Improved operational efficiencies*: improving profit margins and improving return on capital can create significant value for shareholders if these improvements can be sustained in spite of competitive pressure. The most attractive investments in this area are companies that have low profit margins due to inherent leverage, but where the investor has good reason to expect an improvement.

   - *Liquidation of an unprofitable division*: Joel Greenblatt points out that a restructuring where a company disposes of a big and unprofitable division can be a strong value catalyst because it rids the company of a money-losing business line (such that the hidden profitability of the profitable business can emerge), and because it enables management to focus its attention on the profitable core business. In addition, since shedding a business unit is a difficult step for managers (because it shrinks their empire, just like with spin-offs) one has every reason to believe that the operation is done to benefit the company's shareholders. To minimise the risk and maximise the returns of such investments, Greenblatt recommends focusing on situations with:

     (i) Limited downside thanks to a low valuation, or the presence of valuable assets that are hidden by the unprofitable division;

     (ii) A good remaining core business (after divestment of the division);

     (iii) A management team that has the incentives to create value;

     (iv) Little interest from other professional investors who may drive the price up – competition from other investors will usually be lower in companies with small market caps.

---

[49] A change in leadership creates uncertainty and some top investors argue that it is a good reason to sell the stock. For instance, Frederick Kobrick consistently sold stocks from his portfolio when there was a change of management (Kobrick, 2006).

2. **External catalysts**: there are also a number of catalysts outside the company that can create value:

- *Shareholder activists*: activist shareholders can start a catalytic event (e.g., a change in management, change in strategy, etc.) through proxy fights, their presence in the board of directors, shareholder resolutions, the media, and letter-writing campaigns. Stocks that activist investors target tend to outperform the market by an impressive margin. This is not surprising for two reasons. First, if their actions are successful activists can create a lot of value through the changes they impose. Second, activist investors do their homework much better than the average investor before they commit to a situation. They have to do so because they need to take a stake of at least 5% in a company before they can begin to demand changes. Given the outperformance of *activist stocks* it is good practice to keep close tabs on the transactions of some of the best activist investors around, like Carl Icahn, Bill Ackman, Dan Loeb and Barry Rosenstein.

- *Industry merger and acquisition activity*: M&A activity provides a benchmark for fair values in certain industries and therefore it can expose the undervaluation of companies in these industries. The companies in such industries that are most likely to be acquired with a serious premium are companies that have a low valuation (versus other companies in that industry), a good business, and no insider control.

- *Political or economic events*: an important political or economic event can be a catalyst for stocks that stand to benefit from the event. For instance, in 1939 John Templeton anticipated America's involvement in the Second World War. He reasoned that when the US was dragged into the war, industrial and transportation firms would be pushed so hard to support the war that even the least efficient businesses would prosper. Based on this idea, he purchased the industrials and transportation firms that were beaten down most in the stock market and about which sentiment was most negative (all stocks trading below $1). In this way, he benefited from the resurgence of these businesses when the US entered the war while keeping his risk low (through the wide diversification over many issues).

## B.I.1.g Stocks that are removed from an index

In the previous sections we have seen various types of stocks where shareholders are motivated or forced to sell due to their investment charters, out of ignorance, because a stock doesn't *feel* right, etc. Since motivated/forced selling is basically done for non-economic reasons, it can create bargain situations.[50]

---

[50] Forced or motivated selling is not limited to the equity market. For instance, bonds are usually sold off by professionals when a company files for bankruptcy or when the credit quality falls below a certain threshold. Motivated selling also occurs in the area of real estate, such as when a bank forecloses on a property and is motivated to sell the estate as quickly as possible (because it is not in the business of real estate management).

Another type of stock that suffers from forced selling is a stock that is kicked out of a stock index. Indeed, the removal of a stock from an index usually causes a massive sell-off by all funds that use the index as a benchmark, and by all index funds and ETFs that track the index. As certain indexes are used as benchmarks for billions of dollars, this kind of forced selling can be heavy.

According to Seth Klarman, what makes this forced selling even more compelling is that stock underperformance frequently precedes expulsion from an index. In other words, stocks that are removed from the index are often already undervalued before their removal. An example of an excellent opportunity in this category was Woolworths. When the stock left the S&P 500 it lost 50% of its value in a couple of days. No more than three months later it had more than tripled from its bottom.

## B.I.1.h Other miscellaneous opportunities

Here are a number of other potential bargains:

1. **Pre-merger/acquisition stocks**: according to David Swensen, stocks can be interesting arbitrage investments right after a merger announcement. The reason is that many shareholders sell their shares during merger-induced price rises, which creates opportunities for patient arbitrageurs.

2. **Stocks with asymmetric payoffs**: Anthony Bolton and Mohnish Pabrai like stocks with *asymmetric payoffs*. These are stocks that have excellent upside (if something works out) and limited downside (because if the thing doesn't work out, the company will still be fine). In such stocks, one can sometimes get a free (and implicit) call option on certain very rewarding (but uncertain) projects. In *Investing Against the Tide*, Anthony Bolton gives the example of an oil exploration company with stable cash flows from existing oil wells, and with a number of wildcat wells with potentially huge rewards (that are not reflected in the stock price) if successful.

3. **Great companies**: although the market is usually quite efficient in the evaluation of a company's quantitative data (profits, margins, ROE, etc.), it is often less efficient in discounting qualitative characteristics like corporate culture, management, board of directors, HR policies, branding, etc. For instance, according to some studies, investors can earn impressive above-average returns by investing in companies that belong to Fortune's list of '100 Best Companies to Work For', companies with strong brand names, and companies with the highest quality earnings (i.e., companies with the lowest difference between earnings and operating cash flows).

4. **Parent of a spin-off**: in addition to spin-offs, the parent companies of spin-offs can be interesting investments. For instance, the parent that spins off an undesirable business unit can be attractive because institutional investors may wait until after the spin-off to start buying the parent company. An example of a successful investment in the parent of a spin-off was Joel Greenblatt's investment in American Express. Investors steered cleared of American Express when the company decided to spin off its investment bank Lehman Brothers in 1994. The reason was that the very volatile earnings history of Lehman Brothers made it hard

to determine the future earnings of American Express ex-Lehman Brothers. Joel Greenblatt figured out that the market failed to appreciate that American Express would be very profitable after the spin-off. He was right and the market recognised its mistake as American Express rose by about 40% over the year after the spin-off.

## B.I.2 Bad long ideas in developed markets

As explained above, top stock pickers look for bargains in pockets of the market where stocks tend to be undervalued. They don't waste their time examining stocks that belong to pockets that tend to be fairly or overvalued. Table 2 provides an overview of the types of stocks that top investors give a miss, and contrasts this with the attractive stock ideas discussed in B.I.1. In the subsequent sections the different types of stocks to be avoided are discussed.

**Table 2: Good and bad ideas for scrutiny in stock markets of developed countries**

| Potential bargains | Stocks to avoid |
| --- | --- |
| **Stocks ignored by the crowd**: dull and unfashionable companies; complex companies; small companies; stocks ignored for formal reasons | **Stocks in the spotlight**: stocks with fancy names, in fancy industries; companies with high visibility; blue chips |
| **Negative-sentiment stocks**: despised companies; companies in lousy (turnaround) industries; companies with temporary problems; companies close to financial distress; once popular, now abandoned stocks | **Positive-sentiment stocks**: companies that are widely admired; companies in high-growth industries; companies where everything seems to be perfect |
| **Specific types of new securities**: merger securities; preferred equity in going-private transactions; new stock emerging from bankruptcy; stub stock after recap; parent of complicated division that is divested; spin-offs; special IPOs; demutualisations and privatisations of government-owned companies | **Most IPOs** |
| **Opportunities in new trends/events**: suppliers to growth industry; cloners of successful innovators; underappreciated beneficiaries of sudden (catastrophic) events; multinationals with emerging market activities | **Typical bad ideas in new trends**: hot, direct beneficiaries of new trends; pioneers; companies bound to suffer from new trends |
| **Tip-offs to good ideas from the right people**: companies praised by competitors; purchases/recommendations from respectable investors; tips from insiders: insider buying + stock repurchases | **Red flags from reliable sources**: companies that lack respect from competitors; sales by respectable investors; short selling by respectable investors or indefinite investor pool; Insider selling and seasoned stock offerings |
| **Stocks removed from a market index** | **Stocks added to a market index** |
| **Stocks with catalysts**: internal catalysts: new management, new corporate or product strategy, improved operational efficiencies, liquidation of unprofitable division; stocks with external catalysts: shareholder activists, industry M&A activity, political or economic events | **Speculative stocks**: post-bankruptcy stocks; companies without earnings; companies with insufficient information |
| **Other**: pre-merger stocks; stocks with asymmetric payoffs; great companies; parent of a spin-off | |

## B.I.2.a Stocks that are far from ignored

It was explained in B.I.1.a that many stocks that are ignored by the investment community are priced incorrectly due to a lack of attention. Conversely, stocks that are in the spotlight of the financial community (i.e., stocks that are covered by many analysts, that are tracked closely by numerous other professionals, and that are followed painstakingly in the media) leave much less room for market inefficiencies. As such, well-known stocks are usually priced correctly. They may even be overvalued because investors are willing to pay up for the safety and security that such companies convey. Making matters worse, well-known stocks are typically quite vulnerable to the whims of the (institutional) investors who follow their every move.

As such, it should not be surprising that enthusiasm about household stocks is low among top investors. Although they don't avoid them systematically they are very critical of their mispricing. These stocks often command a higher price than warranted by their fundamentals, so smart investors know that they must do their homework well. Tip-offs that a stock enjoys wide interest in the market (and therefore is less likely to be a bargain) are *heavy analyst coverage* and *high (low-quality[51]) institutional ownership*. Here are some specific types of stocks that typically qualify as far from ignored:

1. **Companies and industries that sound attractive**: companies with a cool or fancy name and businesses in industries that sound attractive or that appeal to people's imaginations usually receive more than their fair share of attention.

2. **Companies with high visibility**: investors that want to limit risk often embrace businesses that are believed to have high visibility. These can be companies in stable industries, companies with a lot of public information, companies about which there is little disagreement among analysts, and so on. Unfortunately, David Dreman found in *Contrarian Investment Strategies* that visibility is usually just a mirage. People who seek visibility often pay too high a price for a false sense of security.

3. **Blue chips**: while many small caps stay under the radar of the investment community, no blue chip[52] can escape market attention. In fact, blue chips tend to be over-researched and over-owned. This tends to push their price up to rather high multiples. What makes blue chips even more dangerous is that many investors fail to realise that the growth of companies that have turned into blue chips tends to stall. The lethal cocktail of exaggerated expectations and high multiples has cost many blue chip investors a bundle. When John Templeton invested in Japan, for instance, he rarely bought stocks of the TOPIX Index as he found the best bargains elsewhere.[53]

---

[51] Institutional ownership of high quality (i.e., heavy ownership by renowned investors) can be a strong indication that a stock is undervalued (see also B.I.1.e).

[52] Blue chips are the stocks with the highest market caps of the market.

[53] Templeton, 2008.

## B.I.2.b Hot stocks

It is natural for people to flock towards hot stocks because they give them the warm fuzzies, because they feel safe, or because they have a great and exciting story to tell. Also a number of cognitive biases draw investors to hot stocks, such as crowd behaviour (it feels safe to buy something that many other people buy or hold), extrapolation (the successful past years are extrapolated into the future), thirst for excitement, etc.

The problem is, of course, that overexcited investors who trample each other to get their hands on hot stocks often lose their sense of rationality. Making matters worse, the excitement and attention for the company's industry tends to attract new competition (within that industry), which puts pressure on the company's profitability. The end result is a hot stock with a sky-high valuation that reflects an overoptimistic view on the future[54], even though prospects are anything but spectacular.

Figure 5 shows an example of a hot stock. The shoemaker Crocs, Inc. came to the market with a new type of shoe that was claimed to offer medical benefits. In 2006 and 2007 sales and earnings steamed ahead at a blistering pace. The stock soon became hot and was bid up by overenthusiastic believers who expected that Crocs would take over the world. As can be seen in the chart, the stock was almost a six-bagger between March 2006 and September 2007. In the summer of 2007, the stock traded at a hefty P/E multiple of about 45.

**Figure 5: The rise and fall of the hot stock Crocs Inc.**

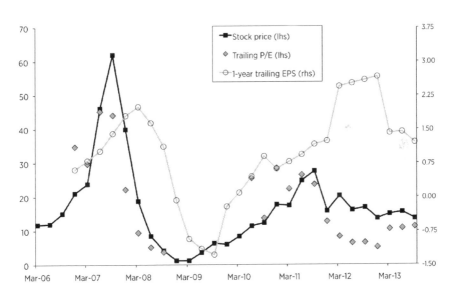

Source data: Bloomberg

---

[54] Note that, more often than not, valuations of hot stocks are so high that even if the overoptimistic expectations of the market materialise the stock is unlikely to offer a decent return.

At that point, a number of critics warned that the stock was far too expensive. They pointed out that the company's business model was too risky to justify such a high valuation because it was too dependent on fashion and taste (many people hated the design of the shoe), and because it lacked a competitive moat (although the shoe was protected by patents, it could easily be copied by other creative shoemakers).

Figure 5 indeed shows that there were problems with the company's business model. In the first half of 2008 the company's sales and earnings growth slowed down considerably. By the summer of 2008 (even before the credit crisis broke out in full force), the stock had already lost 85% of its value. In the midst of the credit crisis in 2008, the stock's fall even accelerated. By December 2008, the stock had lost about 98% of its value compared to September 2007! The tumbling sales and earnings rattled investors who now clearly expected that the company would not survive. Although the company managed to turn earnings and sales around between 2010 and 2013, it couldn't regain its former glory as operating margins remained consistently below about half the operating margins that were common in its heyday.

It is not surprising then that top investors avoid hot stocks. They warn in particular against the *hottest stock in a hot industry* (to be avoided at any price, according to Peter Lynch), *hot stocks of weak or mediocre companies* (because the price-value gap can become astronomical for such companies), and *fundamentally risky hot stocks* (e.g., hot companies without earnings or with a single product).

In any case, apart from excessive valuation multiples, one can recognise hot stocks as follows:

1. **The company is widely admired in the media and by professionals**: whereas companies that are despised tend to be undervalued (see above), companies that are loved by the media and in the executive world tend to be overvalued. Definite red flags are:

   - *Regular hallelujah stories in the media*: when the media is all over a company and praises it as a way to go story, investors should beware.

   - *The company figures on a list of most admired companies*: the stocks of companies on the list of Fortune's 'Most Admired Companies' tend to underperform the stocks of 'America's most spurned' companies significantly in the years after they receive their respective titles.[55] This observation is not only valid for the US, but is probably valid in any country. As an illustration of this, Figure 6 shows the stock performance relative to the Belgian Bel-20 index of 13 publicly traded companies that received the nomination of company of the year (selected by professional business consultants) or for which the CEO received the nomination CEO of the year (selected by readers of a financial magazine) between 1999 and 2007.

     As we can see in the figure, in the first year after their nomination the stocks of these companies underperformed the broader market by about 20%. Four years after their nomination they still trailed the market index by more than

---

[55] Montier, 2010.

30%. When we take a closer look, the poor performance of these stocks can be attributed only partly to the overvaluation of the stock. Surprisingly, the majority of the companies that were used in the sample also showed poor financial results (almost no growth, or a decline in book value per share) in the years subsequent to the award. This raises serious doubts about the ability of professionals and the public to recognise companies that are deserving of admiration.

**Figure 6: Curse of the award**

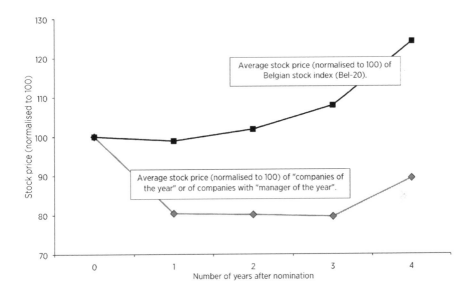

- *Analysts unanimously recommend buying the stock*: when all analysts that cover the stock are convinced that it is a strong buy, and when they project exceptional earnings growth going forward,[56] high expectations are most probably already reflected in the stock price.

2. **High institutional ownership and/or high analyst coverage**: smart investors see high professional activity around a stock as a red flag. Jim Rogers considers a stock as very hot when institutions own about 80% of the stock. Robert Wilson said that a good time to sell a stock is when "elaborate research reports start appearing."[57]

> *"Stocks heavily owned and constantly monitored by institutions have often been among the most inappropriately valued."*
>
> **Warren Buffett, 1985 letter to the shareholders of Berkshire Hathaway**

---

[56] Apparently, stocks where analyst expectations about long-run earnings growth are much higher than recent earnings growth tend to underperform the market significantly.

[57] See (Train, 2000).

3. **Friends or acquaintances** (with no professional background in investing) **own – or worse, recommend – the stock**.

4. **The company's industry is hot**: it is evident that companies in hot industries are likely to be significantly overvalued. Some signs that an industry is hot are wide attention in the media and with friends, high institutional ownership of companies in that industry, or:

    - *New and highly-paid graduates that crowd into the industry*: Jim Rogers warns against companies in industries that are popular and where professionals are highly paid – in particular when these professionals are business school graduates. Massive inflows of new graduates is not only a sign that the industry is hot, but also indicates that competition heats up and that excesses (e.g., high salaries) are about to put pressure on future profitability.

    - *The industry shows high growth*: companies in high-growth industries are often the market's darlings. Many top stock pickers are not enthused about high-growth industries and warn that it is wrong to pay handsomely in advance for high growth. Indeed, study after study has shown that high growth does not equate with high stock returns.[58] One can think of several reasons for this phenomenon:

        (i) One problem of high-growth industries is that they tend to attract a wide range of smart competitors who claim their part of the pie. Due to the cutthroat competition, many of the companies in that industry will not make it. The profitability of those that survive may also be permanently impaired.

        (ii) Another problem is that high growth can temporarily mask a company's weaknesses, such that significant problems may arise once the growth abates.

        (iii) A third problem is that the competitive playing field of high-growth industries is inherently unstable. This has two severe consequences: it is extremely difficult for investors to evaluate the long-term economics of any company in that industry; and companies in high-growth industries are risky because they have to constantly make new and correct strategic decisions to avert the road to oblivion.

        (iv) A fourth problem is that high growth in an industry may not be secular but temporary (e.g., cyclical). Jim Rogers, for instance, is wary of industries with little inventory, low receivables, high profit margins (e.g., 20%), high return on equity (e.g., more than 25% pre-tax), and where capital expenditures grow very rapidly (e.g., 40% to 50% a year).

## B.I.2.c Most IPOs

In B.I.1.c it was explained that certain types of new stock issues can be very attractive investments. This cannot be generalised to the average IPO, though. As opposed to so many investors who seem to be excited by IPOs, top investors have long known what

---

[58] For instance, according to a study by Jeremy Siegel, stocks in some of the fastest-growing industries, such as financials and information technology, have underperformed the S&P 500 between 1957 and 2007 (Siegel, 2005).

recent studies confirm – companies that go public tend to significantly underperform the market in the years after their IPO.[59] The dreadful performance is most outspoken for IPOs of small companies and especially for microcaps (with sales below $50 million).

Equally noteworthy, it is rather unrealistic for the average investor to expect to get shares in the most attractive IPOs because these shares are usually reserved for friends and family of the brokers who bring the company to the market. Hence, investors who sign up for an IPO are likely to get all the stock they asked for in the least attractive IPOs and none (or very little) in the most attractive ones.

The underperformance of IPOs is easy to understand and basically stems from the lethal cocktail of overvaluation and poor prospects:

1. **Probable overvaluation**: one can expect that the stock of most firms going through an IPO is overvalued – or at least, fully valued – for the simple reason that it is not in the owner's interest to offer the stock at a bargain price.[60] Owners of the firm, which can include entrepreneurs, management and venture firms, have plenty of reasons to bring the stock to the market at a high price. The higher the price the lower the number of shares they will have to cede in the IPO for the same proceeds. A problem for IPO investors is that the owners are actually in a good position to get away with a high price. For starters, the owners have a much better view on what their business is really worth than outsiders. Second, management and the brokers who lead the IPO can resort to a number of practices to boost the price at which they can sell the shares to the public, such as:

   - *Overhyping the IPO*: they can push the business to the public by means of exciting stories, overoptimistic cash flow projections, earnings management (e.g., delaying discretionary expenses, freezing hiring) in the period prior to the IPO, and so on.

   - *Timing the IPO*: owners can wait until the market is complacent enough to overpay for their business. Understanding this, the worst time to invest in IPOs is probably during a raging bull market, in a period when many companies go public (i.e., during an IPO boom), or when the public is (over)excited about the company's industry and/or business.

2. **Instability of the new businesses that go public**: a high price is only part of the problem of IPOs. Another problem is that many IPOs are young and inexperienced – they may not even have made a profit before they went public. As a result, the business fundamentals of these businesses – especially the smaller ones – disappoint the market in the months and years after the IPO. This, combined with possibly sky-high expectations built into the IPO price, is bound to lead to disaster for the gullible IPO investor.

---

[59] See, for example (Damodaran, 2004).
[60] One possible exception is stock in a government-owned company, as explained in B.I.1.c.

> "The new issue market is ruled by controlling stockholders and corporations who can usually select the timing of offerings. Understandably, these sellers are not going to offer any bargains. It's rare you'll find X being sold for half-X. Indeed, in the case of common stock offerings, selling shareholders are often motivated to unload only when they feel the market is overpaying."
>
> **Warren Buffett (Cunningham, 2001-A)**

## B.I.2.d Dangers in new trends

As opposed to the beneficiaries of new trends summed up in B.I.1.d, some dangerous investments related with new trends are *direct beneficiaries of the trend* (because they tend to be hot and overvalued), and *pioneering companies* (because they can be displaced by cloners or established firms and/or because they are inexperienced). Another type of risky investment is a company that will probably *suffer irreversibly from a new trend*. An example of the latter would be an expensive cosmetics company at a moment that women start using less make-up.

## B.I.2.e Reliable tips to bad ideas

It was mentioned in B.I.1.e that one should be very sceptical of tips. Tips from neighbours, friends, shoeshine boys, hairdressers, or even from so-called insiders (e.g., employees working at the firm) seldom have value. Even tips from investment professionals like analysts and brokers should be looked upon with extreme caution and suspicion. Notwithstanding, we have also seen that the signals of a company's competitors, respectable investors, and certain insiders can have value. One should therefore be cautious with stocks in the presence of the following red flags:

1.  **Lack of respect and admiration by competitors**: for instance, each time Philip Fisher noticed in conversations with executives that they were not really impressed by a particular competitor, he saved himself the trouble of looking into that competitor.

2.  **Bearish opinions and operations by respectable investors**: when top investors sell shares of a company or express a (very) negative opinion, one should take heed. The signal becomes stronger yet when:

    *   *Various* respectable investors share the bearish stance.

    *   One or more top investors *go short the stock*, or when the *short interest ratio on the stock is high*. Going short is a much clearer message than expressing a negative opinion or selling out of an existing position. The reason is that short sellers do their homework much more thoroughly than long investors.[61] They have to if they want to survive because short sales are riskier than long positions. Hence, it should be taken as a clear warning sign when an excellent

---

[61] Top stock picker Glenn Greenberg even admits that he gets the most valuable research on stocks by talking with professional short sellers. In his experience, the research of short sellers is vastly superior to that of long investors.

investor goes short a stock, or when the short interest ratio is high (indicating that many short sellers are betting against the stock).

3. **Bearish insider signals**: investors are advised to keep track of the following insider signals that can spell trouble for shareholders:

- *Insider selling*: while insider buying is usually an unambiguously bullish sign, insider sales are less easy to interpret. The problem is that insiders can sell shares for various reasons that are unrelated to the stock's merits. They may sell because the company's shares represent too much of their assets (so they try to diversify their portfolio somewhat). They may need money to make a large purchase (e.g., buying a house). Or they sell to cover tax liabilities related to the vesting of shares. Alternatively, insiders may refrain from selling shares when they are instructed to do so from above.[62]

  However, insider selling can be considered a strong bearish sign, in particular for relatively small companies, when the sales occur on a large scale by various insiders, and when the CEO and the CFO are on the selling side. Anthony Bolton adds still another criterion: he considers unexpected insider sales (e.g., insider sales after the stock has fallen a lot, or when the stock looks very cheap on a number of multiples) to be a strong indication that something is seriously wrong with the company.

- *Trading in derivative securities*: Aswath Damodaran explains in *Investment Fables* that stock prices tend to suffer when insiders hedge their stock positions after a run-up in the stock price or before an earnings announcement.

- *Seasoned stock offerings*: companies that issue new shares are often overpriced, because it is in the shareholder's interest to obtain funds with as little dilution as possible. So, the announcement of a secondary stock offering (SSO) can be seen as a potential red flag for investors. The sign is less clear when insiders participate in the SSO, and/or when existing shareholders get first crack at the new shares because in that case overpricing would hurt the insiders and the existing shareholders.

## B.I.2.f Stocks added to an index

Stocks that are added to an index are seldom bargains for two reasons. First of all, such stocks have usually outperformed the market right before they enter the index.[63] In many cases these stocks owe their strong performance to rising popularity and multiple expansion. This implies that they are likely to be expensive prior to their entry into the index.

Second, the addition to the index makes these stocks even more expensive due to forced buying by funds that track the index or that use this index as a benchmark. In *The*

---

[62] For instance, at Lehman Brothers the CEO did not want senior management to sell shares lest this would send an undesirable message to the market (Weiss, 2012).

[63] Indeed, managers of market indexes usually select as members stocks with sufficient liquidity and with the highest market capitalisations. So, if a stock is considered a candidate for an index its market cap must have risen faster than that of other stocks.

*Future For Investors*, Jeremy Siegel confirms the underperformance of stocks that are added to the S&P 500. His studies show that investing in the original S&P 500 of 1957 would have beaten the S&P 500 in the five decades between 1957 and 2005.

## B.I.2.g Speculative stocks

As explained in Chapter A, an investment is a calculated and fundamentals-based bet that a stock will beat the market over the long term. Speculations do not qualify as investments, because speculative bets are not based on fundamentals. According to investors, buying speculative stocks is a Greater Fool's bet, where the speculator hopes to unload his shares on another speculator who is even more foolish than himself. This can be dangerous because it is far from certain that one can find a Greater Fool. Needless to say, top investors avoid speculative stocks such as the following:

1. **Post-bankruptcy stocks**: Joel Greenblatt warns against equity investments in companies that have filed for bankruptcy. In his experience, the shares of bankrupt companies tend to trade for some time (before they really go to zero) at valuations that are hard to justify. One should always remember that there is seldom value left for shareholders in bankruptcy restructurings.

2. **Companies without earnings history**: top investors like Peter Lynch and Marty Whitman believe that common stock investors should avoid companies that haven't made a profit yet – especially when these companies are small and exciting (and thus not cheap at all). Lack of an earnings history makes a company very risky because the business cannot fund itself (i.e., its survival is still dependant on fundraising from external sources), and because it is extremely difficult to predict the outlook for such companies. Investing in unprofitable pioneering companies must be left to professional private equity investors.

3. **Stocks with insufficient information**: according to Marty Whitman and Peter Lynch, it makes little sense to invest in companies about which clear, relevant, reliable and regular information is not available. The whole point of investing is to gain an edge over the market, and such an edge is hard to achieve when basic information is lacking. Making matters worse, the information that is not made public is more likely to be negative than positive because managers of such companies show the good news and try to hide the bad news. Examples of companies that usually disclose insufficient information are:

   - most over-the-counter and pink sheet issues, and
   - companies with inscrutable financial statements.

## B.I.2.h M&A arbitrage stocks

It was mentioned in B.I.1.h that pre-M&A stocks can be bargains *right after* an M&A announcement due to motivated selling by existing shareholders. However, in most situations the valuation gap closes rather quickly as professionals set up arbitrage positions immediately after the M&A announcement. This heavy professional activity leads Joel Greenblatt and Marty Whitman to believe that the average investor has little business in M&A arbitrage operations.[64] They suggest especially avoiding situations where the acquired company is big because there competition with professionals will be toughest.

## B.I.3 Short ideas in developed markets

The pockets in the stock market that top investors avoid (described in B.I.2) are good places to ignore, but they are not necessarily good short ideas. Short selling (or shorting) refers to the practice where an investor borrows shares from another investor to sell them in the market. The short seller bets on the decline of the share price and tries to make money by buying the shares back at a lower price (after which they are returned to the rightful owner).

A major disadvantage of shorting compared to long investing is that shorting has an unfavourable asymmetric profit-loss pattern. Indeed, the downside is theoretically unlimited (as there is no limit to how high a stock can climb), whereas the upside is limited to 100% (which happens when the stock loses all of its value).

Due to this risk and since the stock market can be quite irrational for some time, intelligent short sellers are much more selective than long-only investors. The following sections present the characteristics of interesting short ideas and warnings against common short traps, based on the ideas of legendary short sellers (e.g., Julian Robertson and Jim Chanos) and the extensive description of the art of shorting in Kathryn Staley's *The Art of Short Selling*.

### B.I.3.a Characteristics of good short ideas

To maximise their chances of success, successful short sellers look for three characteristics in short candidates. First of all, the company must have poor fundamentals. Second, it should be possible for the short seller to carry out the short sale with peace of mind. Finally, there should be one or more triggers that indicate trouble for the company is just around the corner.

### 1. Poor fundamentals

By focusing their short sales on stocks with poor fundamentals, short sellers protect themselves against the irrationality of the stock market. Indeed, the market seldom ignores bad news about fundamentals. When the fundamentals are not that bad, however, investors can remain irrational much longer than a short seller can afford to stay short the stock. Here is an overview of the poor fundamentals that short sellers look for:

1. **Management issues**: the ideal short has all of the following four management issues:
   - *Dishonest management*: smart short sellers look for companies with unreliable and deceitful managers and/or with managers who always try to hide (or put

---

[64] This is not to say that M&A arbitrage cannot be profitable for professionals. Warren Buffett, for instance, has been very successful for many years in his arbitrage operations.

a positive spin on) bad news. With dishonest management there is an above-average chance that the company's books are cooked, and that investors are in for unpleasant surprises. Short sellers are especially fond of dishonesty in financial services and insurance companies because in these industries managers can easily boost earnings (and trick the market) for a while through bad loans and poor underwriting policies. Apart from open display of dishonesty, tip-offs that management may not be forthright are: signs of creative and aggressive accounting; complex/confusing/murky financial statements; and acquisition policies with the intention to hide the poor performance of the core business.

- *Greedy management*: insider sleaze indicates that management's interests are put before those of its shareholders, which obviously bodes ill for the stock. To determine whether management is greedy one should look for (e.g., in the company's proxies): excessive management compensation (e.g., exorbitant salaries versus the company's earnings or big bonuses that are not tied to specific efforts or targets); golden parachutes (i.e., excessive retirement or severance packages); and dubious non-arm's length transactions (i.e., transactions with relatives/officers/managers that benefit the latter and that harm the company).

- *Exuberance*: short sellers like managers that throw money out of the window, especially when it happens close to the top of the company's earnings cycle. Signs that management does not understand that thrift is important for survival in a competitive world are excessive management perks (e.g., a plane at management's disposal, lofty company apartments, etc.), the construction of a new and flashy headquarters, and the like.

- *Ineffective board of directors*: a board of directors that behaves like the CEO's lapdog is redundant and a total waste of company resources. Therefore, short sellers like boards that rubberstamp the CEO's decisions, and where dissent (among directors and between the board and the CEO) is discouraged. A tip-off that the board is ineffective is a lack of independent directors.

2. **Poor financial situation**: interesting companies for short sellers are companies with:

- *Poor balance sheets*: good short candidates have ugly balance sheets, preferably with some overvalued and/or illiquid assets. Furthermore, a poor balance sheet is not only a sign of a poor business, but also makes it difficult for the company to raise money.

- *Poor returns on equity*: companies that are unable to achieve decent returns on their equity or capital often have difficulty funding their activities out of their own operations. Hence, they are usually at the mercy (and subject to the whims) of external capital suppliers.

- *Poor cash flows*: companies that do not generate sufficient cash flows risk a liquidity crisis. The most interesting short candidates are those that not only generate little cash but that have at the same time an insatiable appetite for cash.

3. **Flawed business models**: excellent short ideas have unrealistic (e.g., very risky) business models. Tip-offs that a business model is not working are a high cash burn, a hefty buildup of inventory (especially in periods where such buildup should not be expected), or confirmation that the company fails to meet the objectives set out in its strategic plan. An example of a company with a flawed business model was the toy manufacturer Happiness Express Inc. in 1994. The company burnt millions of dollars while inventories piled up. The high inventory levels of toys on December 31 (right after the Christmas season) indicated that the company's business model was flawed.[65]

4. **Growth saturation**: companies where growth saturates after a period of impressive growth can be compelling short candidates if the market fails to anticipate the growth deceleration. Short sellers get excited when they notice that management of such a company is desperate for growth. They know that managers are likely to compound their problem when they announce new growth initiatives like international expansion (in particular to emerging countries such as China and Russia), and expansion in a different line of business. Successfully entering an emerging market or managing a totally new business are very hard to pull off and are bound to lead to disaster if they are started in a hurry and without the proper preparation. Short sellers look for the following two possible types of growth saturation:

   • Growth saturation due to a *peak in popularity*: this can refer to a fad product that is at its peak in popularity and that has nowhere to go but down (e.g., because all possible customers already have the product).

   • Growth saturation due to a *pipeline fill*: this happens when the distribution channel for the company's star product is filled, i.e., when all possible distributors (e.g., stores) are supplied with the product. In that case, future revenue growth drops from high double digits to the (much lower) rate of consumption of existing consumers.

5. **Poor industry**: Julian Robertson points out that there are short opportunities in industries that are misunderstood or in industries in decline (provided that the market does not factor in that decline). Hedge fund manager Joe Vidich suggests yet another industry that is a prime candidate for short sales – namely that which is a supplier to an industry where capital expenditures are deferred. For instance, when mining and natural resource companies postponed capital expenditures in 2007 to 2008 he saw suppliers to those companies as definite short opportunities.

## 2. Attractive stock characteristics

Many smart short sellers only short stocks with poor fundamentals when the stock characteristics are also right. They usually look for stocks with:

1. **Overinflated prices**: although not all short sellers see high multiples as indispensable (e.g., Jim Chanos likes to short value stocks with very poor fundamentals), bubbly

---

[65] Staley, 1997.

valuations make a company with shaky fundamentals even more attractive as a short. Examples were the generic drug companies in the 1990s. These companies commanded earnings multiples of 30 to 40 because the public perceived them as exceptional growth vehicles. In reality, though, they had to operate in a very competitive environment as they produced a commodity product without a decent sales force.

2. **High float**: many short sellers focus their activities exclusively on stocks with sufficiently high floats (e.g., stocks with publicly traded stock outstanding > $500 million) because it is easier to borrow stock for such issues without fear of buy-in.[66] In addition, it is much harder for management of large companies to squeeze out short sellers in a concerted effort with existing shareholders.

3. **High popularity among professionals**: short sellers look for stocks with high institutional ownership and high analyst coverage. First of all, they love the market's favourites because these stocks are frequently overvalued (see also B.I.2.b). Second, when professional followership is high, the stock becomes vulnerable to unpleasant surprises. Indeed, when there is bad news the many analysts that follow the company are likely to downgrade the stock at almost the same time and large professional investors will run for the exit en masse. So, overresearched and overowned companies can collapse spectacularly when something bad happens. Shares of marginal and underresearched companies are often less vulnerable. The lower attention of the market and the slower reaction by the less sophisticated shareholder base (which may be composed of friends of the company's management) can keep such stocks at irrational price levels for a long time.

4. **Middle-sized short interest**: attractive short ideas often have a short interest ratio (that is the number of shares sold short relative to the float) in the range of 5% to 10%.[67] On the one hand, such middle-sized short interest indicates that some (probably clever) short sellers are already betting against the stock, which provides comfort for the short thesis. On the other hand, short interest ratios in that range are not high enough that the short seller should fear a short squeeze (i.e., a sudden price increase caused by panic among short sellers who desperately want to cover their short).

## 3. Short triggers

Since the market can remain irrational for a longer time than short sellers can remain solvent, successful short sellers also try to find shorts where the problems are likely to surface soon. Stated otherwise, they look for short ideas with attractive stock characteristics and poor fundamentals that also have one or more short triggers like:

---

[66] Buy-in occurs when the owner of the stock who lent the stock to the short seller asks for his stock back. When this happens, the short seller is forced to buy the stock back in the market (irrespective of whether he has made a profit on it or not) if he can't find anyone else who is willing to lend the stock. For small stocks replacing the owner with another owner will be harder than for stocks with high floats.

[67] A study found that between 1976 and 1990 stocks with a short interest ratio in excess of 5% underperformed the stock market significantly. Short interest ratios in excess of 15%, on the other hand, appear to be risky due to the above-average danger of a short squeeze.

1. **Insider sales**: managers of companies that are about to collapse will often try to get out before the cave-in. Therefore, short sellers consider insider sales in a stock that they have pegged as a potential disaster a very telling sign. This trigger becomes even more significant when the insider sales are unexpected (e.g., right after a bullish announcement of management) or suspicious (e.g., before the expiration of the lock-up period of an IPO). For instance, in 1988 the founder and president of Medstone started selling shares three months after the company's IPO, even though the lock-up period was six months (sales before lock-up were allowed only upon approval of investment bankers). This turned the company into a potential short.[68]

2. **Resignation of a key person**: the unexpected departure of a key person (e.g., chairman of the board, CEO, CFO, head of sales) in a company with poor fundamentals and good short stock characteristics is often a strong trigger, irrespective of the official reason for the departure. Frequently, the departure of a key person at such a company is caused by turmoil inside the firm, even though it is presented to the outside world as a friendly separation due to 'health reasons', 'personal reasons', 'pursuit of other interests', etc. In the example of Medstone discussed above, the chairman of the board resigned at about the same time that the president was selling shares. This was a second red flag that investors should have heeded.[69]

3. **Audit turnover**: a change in auditor is one of the strongest signs of impending trouble.

4. **Late filings**: accountants and accounting firms are very well aware of the filing rules so when a company is late filing its financial statements there is a considerable chance that management is trying to hide something.

5. **Rumours that are vehemently countered by management**: short sellers like it when rumours about the bad shape of a company finally emerge, while management denies all allegations, stresses that the rumours have no basis, or starts a concerted effort to squeeze the short sellers out.

## B.I.3.b Dangers and traps for short sellers

Figure 7 gives an overview of typical short candidates that successful short sellers look for in the stock market. The figure also shows three types of stocks that, according to top short sellers, are better left alone:

1. **Overvalued but good companies**: Julian Robertson, Joe Feshbach and Jim Chanos warn against the short sale of companies that are not that bad – even if the valuation seems ridiculous. One problem with the short sale of companies that are in decent financial shape and that have smart management is that they can usually finance their growth without external fundraising. So they are unlikely

---

[68] Staley, 1997.
[69] Staley, 1997.

to get into financial problems. Second, as long as the company is not overwhelmed by a very tough problem, the market can keep its confidence and the stock multiple may expand even more.

2. **Technology companies**: experienced short sellers rarely short technology stocks because these companies are much harder to evaluate than other businesses. Fickle inventory changes and receivables, frequent insider trades (irrespective of the stock's merits), volatile profit margins, the existence of spectacular growth stories in technology (which make people dream and which lead to open-ended growth forecasts), and the low credibility of analysts in the sector are just a few reasons why many short sellers avoid technology stocks like the plague. Jim Chanos, for instance, got burnt by America Online in the 1990s due to the fact that people made open-ended growth forecasts about the company. He started shorting the stock in 1996 at $8, and covered his last short two years later at $80.

3. **Beaten-down stocks**: intelligent short sellers know that is not easy to squeeze the last puff out of a cigar butt. In other words, it is usually not worthwhile to open a short position on a stock after it has plummeted. Everybody knows about the company's problems, professionals have given up on it, and analysts have dropped coverage. So what is left for the short seller?

**Figure 7: Features of attractive short candidates**

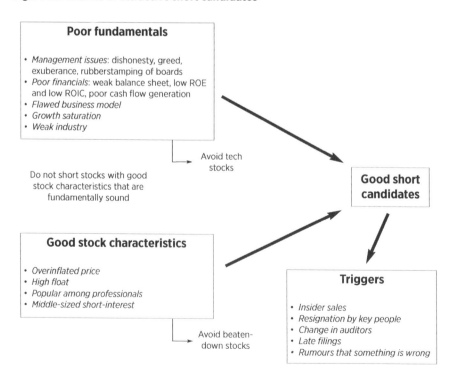

# B.II Good ideas in emerging markets

In section B.I we looked at good and bad investment ideas in the developed markets of the Western World (Western Europe, North America, Japan, and Australia-New Zealand). It is evident that many of these ideas are also likely to be mispriced in emerging markets. Nevertheless, investing in less developed countries deserves a separate discussion because it is fundamentally different from investing in the developed world.

First of all, emerging markets are fraught with dangers and risks. Due diligence should pay special attention to problems such as a lack of (accounting) transparency, fraud, lack of liquidity or restrictions on the trading of securities, economic and political instability[70] (with wars, high dependence on commodities, incompetent leadership, etc.), political interference (including expropriations and nationalisations), corruption, disregard for the interests of shareholders by government and businesses, poorly developed stock markets, and inadequate or no regulatory oversight.

Emerging markets also have another dynamic which developed markets do not. For instance, markets that are dominated by local investors are sometimes driven as much by rumours and conspiracy theories as by fundamentals. In addition, as investors from developed countries often have large stakes in emerging markets, their behaviour can have a very important impact. The limited liquidity of emerging markets combined with the mood swings of investors from developed markets (first a flow to emerging markets when they are hot and then repatriation of money when developed market investors get scared) can cause huge volatility. Furthermore, when investing in emerging countries in other time zones important news can break when the investor is asleep.

Another problem is that many investors perceive emerging markets as an evident and compelling investment case. The economies of emerging countries grow much faster than those of the developed world so that, as the reasoning goes, it is logical to expect higher stock returns. Unfortunately, this perception is not always justified. Although there is a theoretical relationship between corporate sales (earnings) growth and GDP, the relationship between GDP and stock returns is less straightforward. Indeed, high growth commonly leads to high valuations that may discount too much of that growth. In addition, high growth causes cutthroat competition that tends to eliminate numerous companies. This poses two big problems for emerging market investors:

1. stocks in emerging markets may discount very strong future growth[71] and leave little room for disappointment, and

2. many of the real beneficiaries of the economic boom of emerging countries may be companies that are not on the stock market (or may not even exist) yet.

---

[70] As an illustration David Swensen mentions that since the early 20th century the stock markets of more than half of some 36 emerging countries were (temporarily or permanently) closed at some point due to wars or nationalisations, and almost half of them were still *emerging* 100 years later (Swensen, 2005).

[71] Note that stocks in emerging countries **should** trade at a discount to stocks with similar growth rates in developed countries due to the additional risks they entail.

All this illustrates that investors must approach emerging markets differently than developed markets. Below, I first explain how top investors identify compelling growth stocks in emerging countries. Second, I discuss some contrarian opportunities in these countries. Finally, I briefly present a number of other opportunities.

## B.II.1 Growth investing in emerging markets

When top investors look for growth stocks in the emerging world, they usually narrow their search down to attractively priced stock markets of countries with favourable investment prospects. From there on, they try to find those companies that stand to benefit the most from the country's strong expected growth. Following is an overview of this three-step process, mainly based on the ideas of John Templeton, Jim Rogers, David Swensen and Mark Lightbown.

### B.II.1.a Attractive emerging countries

As a protection against unpleasant surprises top investors focus their investments on relatively stable emerging countries with favourable economic prospects and an investor-friendly climate. More specifically, they favour countries with the following characteristics:

1. There must be **economic and political reforms**, with:

   - The *right focus*: the reforms must be aimed at the development of the country and at the creation of new wealth through sustainable competitive advantages. The mere redistribution of income from natural resources (e.g., oil) is definitely not the model top investors are looking for. Usually, reforms that promise durable comparative advantages for the country include:

     (i) Programmes to *increase the level of education*: it goes without saying that education is essential for the development of any country. Hence, massive investment in education is a prerequisite if a country wants to create a sustainable competitive advantage versus other countries. For instance, Japan and South Korea have prospered – in spite of their lack of natural resources – thanks in large part to their focus on excellent education.

     (ii) Focus on the *export of products higher up the value chain as the development progresses*: the ambitions of the political reformers should go beyond manufacturing and the export of commodities (in particular of agricultural products). The final objective must be to turn the country into a developer and exporter of sophisticated industrial goods. This is so important because basic goods – and commodities in particular – compete on price. If the country prospers and salaries rise, the comparative advantage in the production of basic goods versus poorer countries diminishes. If no switch is made to sophisticated goods (which provide a much higher barrier to competition than basic goods) the country's development may stall. An example of a country that moved up the value chain is China. It first was a manufacturer of simple products like buttons, but gradually moved in the direction of products with higher added value like training shoes and clothes, and more recently cars and high-tech products.

- Promise of *pay-off in the medium term*: if the reforms won't lead to an improvement in people's living standards within a couple of years, the reforms may be discontinued before they bear fruit due to dissatisfaction and waning support.

- *Solid political backing*: the change agent (i.e., the political leader who tries to realise the economic reforms) must enjoy political backing:

  (i) The change agent must have sufficient friends in parliament and/or congress.

  (ii) Preferably, the change agent should not be an outsider but must be someone from within the ruling political class who sees the need for change. For instance, Boris Yeltsin and Gorbachev came from within the Communist Party and acknowledged that Communism had brought the Soviet Union to the brink of bankruptcy.

2. A mentality of **saving and reinvesting instead of spending**: top investors like emerging countries with significant trade surpluses and low levels of debt (preferably debt < 25% of GDP) because these indicate that people and the government prefer saving and reinvesting over mindless spending. Preferably, governments of these countries also establish mechanisms to stimulate domestic saving among their citizens. The advantages of a high savings rate are threefold. First of all, countries with high savings rates can finance their growth without the help, interference, and goodwill of foreign countries or foreign investors. Second, in countries with high savings rates national investors and local/national authorities have the means to build the infrastructure (roads, airfields, public transportation, power plants, etc.) that is needed for the country's development. And finally, a high savings rate reduces the currency risk for foreign investors. China, Japan and Korea are all countries that managed to finance their industrial growth through high savings rates and financial reserves.

3. A **hands-off government**: attractive emerging countries have local and national governments that promote free markets and capitalism. Top investors are wary of countries where authorities change business rules at the drop of a hat, or where companies are regularly directed from above to accept unprofitable business. That's why David Herro, for instance, avoids mainland Chinese companies (which often have to put the state interests before the interests of shareholders) and companies in Russia (where the government feels entitled to regularly change the business rules). What investors should look for in emerging countries are actions, measures and policies that unleash the entrepreneurial spirit of people, such as:

- *Privatisations of publicly-owned enterprises*: when publicly-owned companies are sold to private investors, productivity often improves significantly thanks to reduced bureaucracy, the pursuit of more profitable projects, higher motivation (among the workforce and the new owners), and so on. Moreover, privatisations in previously monopolised industries lead to increased competition, which forces managers to focus on the bottom line.

In countries with socialistic tendencies where nationalisations and expropriations are the order of the day, by contrast, entrepreneurship is stifled. The uncertainty and fear for nationalisations or expropriations causes a climate where foreign and domestic investors switch to survival mode, characterised by the deferral of investments and the avoidance of ambitious growth targets. Examples of countries with these tendencies are Argentina and Venezuela. For instance, Argentina seized the Argentine subsidiary YFP of the Spanish oil company Repsol in 2012 after sizable investments of Repsol in a shale gas/oil venture of YFP. The aim of Argentina was clearly to reap the upcoming profits of the business. The result was that other multinationals grew suspicious of Argentina and the country (until very recently) could not find a partner to continue the shale gas/oil venture.

- *Elimination of all kinds of rules* on prices (e.g., price controls), on the acquisition of capital (e.g., thresholds on stakes held by foreigners in certain domestic companies), on labour (e.g., salaries based on privileges instead of productivity), and on business development (e.g., incentives to develop plants at unfavourable locations). The abolition of such rules enables individuals to pursue their own goals.

- *Low and stable tax rates*: these stimulate companies to retain profits or to reinvest in their business. Countries to avoid are those where government feels entitled to a large portion of the wealth created by companies (through high tax rates).

4. **Favourable demographics and geography**: to reduce the risk for quarrel, violence or civil wars that may knock an economic reform off course, one should look for emerging countries with:

- *Ethnic uniformity*: there are usually fewer internal conflicts and there is usually a stronger focus on common goals in countries with a relatively homogeneous population compared with countries that consist of sharply different ethnic groups with different cultures, languages, etc. An example of a vast country with a high degree of ethnic uniformity is China.

- *Normal average family size*: when the average family size in a poor country is out of control (say, five or more children per family), the limited wealth created by the country has to be shared among too many people. The resulting poverty can be a spawning ground for terrorism, tribal violence, revolutions, and the like.

- *Manageable geography*: the country should be as uniform as possible geographically. The problem of a vast country with huge geographic differences is that economic reforms are harder to implement due to complications such as political competition between power centres.

5. **Decent infrastructure**: in an attractive emerging country infrastructure (e.g., roads, airports, ports, power plants) is adequate such that it does not hinder economic growth. Moreover, infrastructure should keep pace with the country's economic development.

6. **Investor-friendly climate**: finally, an emerging country can only be attractive for investors if the investment climate is hospitable:

   - There should be *systems in place that permit capital movement*: this refers to the presence of a stock market with sufficient liquidity, an experienced banking system and a convertible currency.[72]

   - There must be a *culture among politicians and industry leaders to regard investors as business partners* who are entitled to a return on their investment. Signs that the business leaders of a country are not yet ready in this respect are, first, the presence of different voting classes (where foreigners can only buy the shares with the lowest voting class). Second, there may be massive salaries for management that drain profits away from shareholders and into the pockets of this management. Third, watch out for a lack of transparency and communication towards investors. Examples of companies that some top investors are wary of are family-controlled companies in Asian countries. The problems with many of these companies are that they put the interests of the family – which are not that much aligned with the interests of the other shareholders – first. They deliberately avoid transparency and they do not publish information by which investors can identify insider-dealing or conflicts of interest.

## B.II.1.b Attractive stock markets

Too many investors take it for granted that emerging countries with high GDP growth produce high stock returns. In reality, there is little evidence that high GDP growth begets high stock returns. Plenty of studies have shown that over the past decades stocks in emerging markets have **not** outperformed the stocks of developed countries. Even worse, there are indications that there is a negative correlation between the stock returns in a country and its GDP growth.

For instance, China was one of the fastest growing countries in the world in the 1990s but it had one of the world's worst stock returns in that period. One potential reason for this surprising fact was mentioned above – competition can mean that high sales growth does not necessarily translate into high profit growth. However, the main reason is that the stock valuations in promising emerging markets often leave little room for disappointment.

The lesson is that, from a fundamental point of view, one should look for stock markets with *compelling valuations* in attractive emerging countries, and avoid markets where the growth is already (over)discounted in stock prices. Intelligent emerging market

---

[72] Sometimes countries (e.g., Malaysia in 1998) may unexpectedly restrict the convertibility of their currency to avoid an exodus of foreign investors. This illustrates that it is important to examine how the government of an emerging country has handled economic problems in the past.

investors understand that, given the high uncertainty and risks of emerging markets (e.g., political and economic instability), stock valuations in developing countries usually should be lower than in the developed world. In addition, in emerging countries with high inflation (and high interest on fixed income instruments), stocks must be cheap if they want to be attractive versus bonds.

According to Jim Rogers, other technical factors that can play a role in the attractiveness of a stock market are the following: the liberalisation of investment conditions, the permission for pension funds to invest in stocks, and efforts from government to make information more easily available to foreign investors.

## B.II.1.c Attractive growth stocks

An investor who has found a stock market with a compelling valuation in a country that he/she deems attractive could try to earn a decent return with relatively low risk by investing in a wide basket of stocks – or better yet, an index fund or ETF. Higher returns can be earned by the more ambitious and adventurous souls who look for the industries and individual stocks that stand to benefit disproportionately from the country's development. Hereunder is a brief overview of the growth industries and individual growth stocks that top emerging market stock pickers find attractive.

### 1. Attractive industries in emerging countries

Here are some potentially attractive industries in emerging countries:

1. **Financials**: this is usually an interesting growth sector thanks to deregulation and a growing middle class. Examples of attractive subsectors are:

   - *Retail banking*, which typically grows at a strong pace in emerging countries thanks in large part to an increasing savings rate, higher demand for mortgage loans, and the abundance of corporate funding opportunities. Marko Dimitrijevic also mentions that retail banks in emerging countries tend to benefit enormously from exploding demand for consumer and mortgage loans when interest rates decline.[73] It is crucial, though, to avoid poorly-run banks with inept management.

   - *Pension fund management*, which is a growth sector because more and more people and businesses can afford to set something aside for retirement when an emerging country develops.

   - *Insurance*, which can be a strong growth sector in developing countries because a growing number of people will look for (and can afford to take) insurance of all kinds (life insurance, fire and casualty insurance, medical insurance, etc.). John Templeton liked insurance companies (and also banking businesses for that matter) in emerging countries for still another reason: insurance businesses usually invest in the local stock market to avoid currency risk and can therefore be seen to some extent as indirect plays on that country's stock market.

---

[73] Drobny, 2009.

2. **Beverages and consumer products**: in the first phase of a country's development, diet changes and the affordability of products that were previously beyond the reach of most people often lead to a steep increase in the consumption of milk, yoghurt, beer and soft drinks. For this reason, global stock investors must definitely check out industry sectors like soft drinks, bottling, beer brewing, and the dairy business. In a later stage, all kinds of more luxurious consumer goods (e.g., consumer appliances, TVs, cars, luxury goods) may see explosive growth.

3. **Media companies**: John Burbank points out that media companies are typical fast growers in emerging countries.

4. **Pharmaceuticals**: more people can afford medication as a country develops, so manufacturers of branded pharmaceuticals can be compelling investments.

5. **Infrastructure**: there are plenty of infrastructure projects in developing countries and the intensity of the use of the infrastructure often increases exponentially, so there are three kinds of infrastructure plays that deserve special attention:

   - *Infrastructure builders*: companies that are directly involved in the construction of new infrastructure (e.g., construction firms) benefit from the strong demand for their services.
   - *Suppliers to infrastructure builders*: firms that supply the raw materials (e.g., cement, bricks, etc.) or equipment (e.g., concrete mixers) to construction firms can benefit disproportionally from the rapid infrastructure expansion. Note, however, that it is best to focus on those firms that have a strong local competitive advantage which protects them against sophisticated foreign competitors. A nice example would be a local quarry. As transportation costs are an important cost component of stone from quarries, one should not fear foreign competition for this type of business.
   - *Infrastructure owners*: companies that own important infrastructure can profit from the rapid growth in the use of that infrastructure. Examples would be regional airports or companies that own toll roads or toll bridges.

Sectors that top emerging market investors typically shun are cyclical businesses with high fixed costs (e.g., the steel business), businesses where the companies have no control over the yield and/or price of their output (e.g., farming, including poultry), businesses where governments support unprofitable or irrational players (which makes life miserable for even the most efficient company in that sector), or businesses that face cutthroat competition from other emerging countries (e.g., textiles and shoemaking).

## 2. Attractive individual stocks

Attractive economic growth means that competition (from local firms and from sophisticated multinationals[74]) can be fierce in emerging countries – in particular in the

---

[74] A local partner of a multinational (e.g., a local bottler of Coca-Cola) can be a relatively safer play than a purely local company due to the backing of the multinational (with cash and expertise).

industries discussed above. The competitive pressure can result in disappointing profitability and earnings growth, or even outright failure for the middling emerging country firm. This is one of the reasons why the stock market returns of emerging countries are often mediocre or poor. It also serves as a warning against indiscriminate buying of companies in emerging countries.

Notwithstanding, the potential of successful firms in emerging countries can be phenomenal. The point for investors is to focus on those companies that have all it takes to succeed, and to avoid the marginal opportunities. Good places to start looking are attractively priced companies in attractive industries. In addition, the legendary emerging market investor Mark Lightbown looked for companies with:

1. **High profit margins**: these serve as a cushion against unpleasant surprises (which are all too common in emerging countries). Besides, profit margins that are high relative to those of competitors indicate that the company has a competitive advantage, and that it may become a winner in its industry.

2. **Intelligent capital allocation**: good emerging market firms spend their available funds and cash flows intelligently. Less attractive are companies where government can or does impose sacrifices for the sake of the country (i.e., to do unprofitable business). An example of the latter would be the Brazilian government controlled oil company Petrobras. This company has to sell gasoline at prices below international market prices in the Brazilian market, meaning that shareholders of Petrobras are de facto subsidising Brazilian gasoline consumers.

3. **Market control and pricing power**: a company that has control over its market can lead it in the direction that it wants. For instance, a soft drink bottler with a huge market share can capture the market much more easily with new soft drinks than a marginal player.

4. **Medium size and high growth**: the most attractive companies are medium-sized businesses that still have plenty of room for growth.

5. **Business savvy**: to gain confidence in the sustainability of the business, emerging market investors must look for companies that owe their success to energy and business acumen, and not to luck or to the temporary lack of competition.

## B.II.2 Contrarian investing in emerging markets

Growth investing in emerging countries can be very rewarding, and likewise contrarian value investing. Emerging countries are fertile hunting grounds for deep value investors because sentiment about these countries tends to swing from one extreme to another. The reason is that emerging countries are explosive cocktails of danger (a dangerous investing environment) and hope (the often misguided perception of compelling investment opportunities). This, in combination with the typically low liquidity of these markets, leads to a volatile love-hate relationship between investors and emerging markets.

In logical fashion, deep value investors have a special interest in out-of-favour countries with very cheap and broken down stock markets. Provided that the cause for the negative sentiment is isolated, stocks in such markets can offer spectacular returns that are largely uncorrelated with stocks in developed countries. Interestingly, contrarian emerging market investors are not necessarily concerned about the long-term growth prospects of the country. Unlike growth investors, they pull out of the market once the extreme value gap has closed. Here are some examples:

1. In the early 1990s few investors were interested in Brazil due to the political and economic chaos. This lack of interest meant Brazilian stocks were dirt-cheap. In spite of the high inflation and low GDP growth over the 1990s, the Brazilian stock market was one of the best performing markets in the world between the early 1990s and the early 2000s.

2. Macro investor Jim Leitner purchased shares in Zimbabwe when everybody fled the country due to hyperinflation. He invested in Sri Lankan plantation stocks when investors avoided the country due to the civil war. And he picked up cheap stocks in Pakistan after the assassination of the Pakistani president.

3. John Templeton invested through a mutual fund in the depressed Korean stock market during the Asian financial crisis of 1997-1998.

## B.II.3 Short selling in emerging markets

The many dangers that lurk in emerging markets are obviously opportunities for well-informed short sellers. However, hedge fund manager Martin Taylor points out one important problem for short sellers in emerging markets: the fundamentally worst companies are prime takeover targets.[75] Multinationals who try to get a foothold in emerging countries will often try to acquire bad companies. They know that the takeover of excellent companies can spark nationalistic reflexes, such that government and regulatory approval for such deals is hard to obtain.

The acquisition of bad companies, by contrast, is much easier. To avoid acquisition risk, Martin Taylor only shorts bad companies that are unlikely to be taken over due to expected opposition by shareholders against takeover attempts. For instance, takeovers of government-controlled companies or of companies that are owned by the company's pension fund are unlikely due to a fear of *selling out* or headcount cuts after the acquisition.

## B.II.4 Practical aspects of emerging markets investing

It should be clear by now that emerging markets present opportunities for courageous growth and value investors alike. Figure 8 gives a summary of the opportunities discussed above.

In spite of their appeal, many investors will find that direct investment in certain emerging markets is unfeasible because of investment restrictions or because the analysis of emerging market companies is hard. An attractive and easier alternative for direct

---

[75] Schwager, 2012.

investment might be to invest in multinationals with significant emerging market exposure. Investment holdings with large emerging market exposure and emerging market funds are other alternatives.

**Figure 8: Investing in emerging countries**

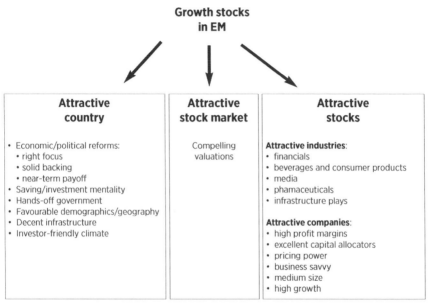

Shorting: be aware that fundamentally-poor companies are popular acquisition targets for foreign companies

Contrarian investing: look for out-of-favour countries

Nevertheless, the very fact that many emerging markets are not easily accessible is also one of their strengths. It discourages other investors and leads to a less crowded investment arena. Hence, plenty of rewards await the investor who is willing to dig deep into emerging markets. For instance, while many investors shy away from certain countries because of murky accounting rules or because the reported numbers are unreliable, investors like Seth Klarman and John Templeton embrace such situations. In the 1960s John Templeton learned that the earnings of subsidiaries were not reported in the financial statements of Japanese companies which gave him the opportunity to discover the tremendous value that was hidden in Japanese companies way before most other professionals even had Japan on their radar screens.

## B.III Finding ideas

This chapter concludes with a sketch of a number of methods that are used by top investors to find interesting investment ideas. In this section the focus is on the generation of ideas in developed countries (the approach to emerging countries is very similar). In

Figure 9 I show the main sources of information that top investors resort to, and indicate what types of investment ideas they are most likely to produce. Each source is then discussed separately.

**Figure 9: Sources of investment ideas**

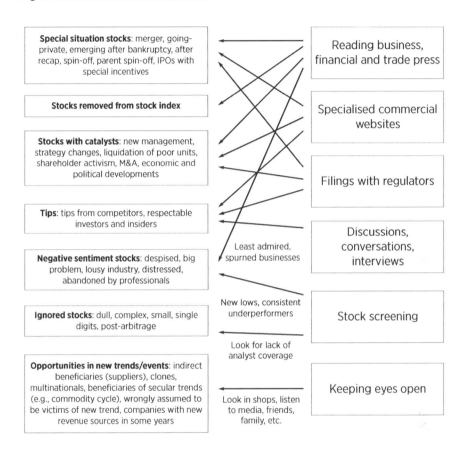

## Reading

Reading is without any doubt the best source of investment ideas. Virtually all top investors are avid readers of the business and financial press. They read newspapers (e.g., Warren Buffett and Michael Price read respectively about seven and three newspapers a day), business literature, broker reports, books, annual reports, etc. In Charlie Munger's opinion, since investing is such a broad field serious investors have no other option than to devour heaps of books, newspapers and articles.

This makes perfect sense. Reading is not only an expression of strong interest in everything that happens in the business and investment world, it is also crucial in order to get early exposure to new investment ideas. Indeed, the business press can point early on to special situation operations, turnarounds, great or despised companies, possible catalysts (e.g., new management or restructurings), new trends, emerging countries, and so on. In addition, the business press can be very helpful in assessing the merits of investment ideas through information about management, corporate strategies, HR policies, and the like.

## Filings with regulators

In well-regulated countries, companies and investors who manage large portfolios have to submit special reports to the regulating authorities with respect to certain types of operations. These regulators usually put these filings at the disposal of investors. For instance, most special situation transactions cannot be done without appropriate filings (e.g., spinoffs have to be filed in the US with the SEC). Insider transactions or investments by large investors[76] must be reported on a regular basis. These filings can be perused by investors when searching for investment ideas.

## Stock screening

Another popular way to find potential bargains is to actively screen for certain types of stocks in one of two ways:

1. **Software screeners**: there are a number of commercial and freely available software screeners that can be used to obtain lists of stocks (out of the entire stock universe) that meet certain fundamental criteria. Although one should never take the lists such screeners produce at face value – because there can be errors in the data and because cheap stocks are usually cheap for a reason – they are excellent as a starting point for further scrutiny. For investors, two types of criteria are useful:

   - *Value criteria*: stocks that are cheap can be stocks that the market ignores or hates. So, one may look for stocks with high dividend yields, or with low multiples like price-to-earnings (P/E), price-to-book value (P/BV), or price-to-cash flow (P/CF). As a variation on this theme, one can look for stocks with low multiples and strong fundamentals. For instance, Joel Greenblatt's *magic formula* looks for non-financial stocks with low P/E combined with high return on invested capital (ROIC).

   - *Price performance*: many investors show special interest in stocks that have performed poorly in the recent past. It is not unusual to find bargain-priced stocks among such companies as they have tested investor's patience, and because they have frustrated and disappointed many others. Moreover, such stocks may have suffered high selling pressure from institutional investors. Some top investors like Mohnish Pabrai look at the lists of stocks that are at their 52-week low. Walter Schloss was especially interested in the stocks that made it into that

---

[76] In the US, investors who manage more than $100 million must file 13-F reports with the SEC each quarter. Note, however, that there can be a serious time lag between the actual transaction and the moment the report is made public.

list after a precipitous decline. Bruce Greenwald, on the other hand, has special interest in stocks that underperformed the market for at least two years in a row. He believes that consistent underperformance (over several years) puts even more pressure on investor sentiment than a single year of underperformance.

2. **Browsing specific stock lists**: another way to discover ignored/unpopular companies is to look into a number of stock lists that are published in the business press. For instance, one can find lists of stocks that hit one-year lows in certain financial newspapers or magazines. Or one can peruse lists of the most despised companies to find valuable investment ideas. Likewise, lists of 'best companies to work for' can be tip-offs to great companies that the stock market may not value as such.

## Specialised services (including websites)

Reading dry and complicated filings submitted to the regulators can be time-consuming and hard. Access to stock lists and effective software screens is also not always straightforward. For those investors who don't want to do the heavy lifting themselves, there are a number of (usually commercial) services and websites that provide information on interesting investment ideas. For instance:

1. The website Magic Formula Investing (**www.magicformulainvesting.com**) shows the American stocks that rank highest on the P/E and ROIC criteria of Joel Greenblatt. Other services provide scores and ranks of companies based on their fundamentals (e.g., Profitcents, **www.profitcents.co.uk**). Among the companies with the worst fundamental ranks one can undoubtedly find a number of stocks that are beaten down excessively by the market.

2. Some services (e.g., the Value Line Survey in the US) publish lists of value stocks.

3. Institutional holdings of stocks can be tracked on certain websites like Vickers Stock Research (**www.vickers-stock.com**).

4. Some services are specialised in insider transactions (e.g., Form4Oracle, **www.form4oracle.com**).

5. There are a number of dedicated websites (e.g., GuruFocus, **www.gurufocus.com**) that track the transactions of top investors.

6. Other websites focus on special situation stocks, such as Spinoff Profiles (**www.spinoffprofiles.com**) and Gemfinder (**gemfinder.com**).

## Discussions, conversations, interviews

Interesting investment ideas can be picked up in letters to shareholders (or similar reports) from excellent asset managers, in interviews of corporate leaders, by tracking the operations of top investors (including activist investors), and in discussions with competent investors.

With respect to the latter, there are a number of websites where excellent investors share investment ideas and explain the background of certain companies. Mohnish Pabrai regularly checks out the ideas presented in *The Value Investors Club*, *Outstanding Investor*

*Digest* (**www.oid.com**) and *Value Investor Insight* (**www.valueinvestorinsight.com**). Kevin Daly reads *The Value Investors Club*, the *Wall Street Transcript*, and *SumZero*. Note that some of these websites are only accessible by members, where membership remains reserved for exceptional individuals.

## Keeping one's eyes open

Peter Lynch and John Neff recommend investors to keep their eyes open when they wander through retail stores and shopping malls,[77] listen attentively when they hear about new products in conversations, stay tuned to the media (e.g., in order to hear about calamities that may offer opportunities), or examine new products of companies that catch the fancy of family members or friends.

By paying attention to what goes on in society, and by learning about what teenagers, friends, family members, and acquaintances like, one can gain exposure to new promising opportunities and trends years before they are noticed by professionals who rely solely on broker reports and theoretical research. In the same vein, Mark Lightbown and Jim Rogers suggest travelling and the reading of newspapers in foreign countries to find interesting investment ideas in emerging countries.

---

[77] The most interesting shops are often situated on the highest floors of malls because mall managers want customers to walk by as many shops as possible on their way to their favourite store.

# CHAPTER C

## FUNDAMENTAL BUSINESS ANALYSIS

"I would rather be certain of a good result than hopeful of a great one. I don't look to jump over 7-foot bars. I look around for 1-foot bars that I can step over."

WARREN BUFFETT, 1996 LETTER TO THE SHAREHOLDERS OF BERKSHIRE HATHAWAY

FUNDAMENTAL BUSINESS ANALYSIS is one of the cornerstone(s) of the investment process. After all, although there may be a disconnection between a company's success and its stock price over the short to medium term, price action over the long term is almost completely determined by a company's business success (or the lack thereof). Business analysis is indispensable to making reliable fair value estimates of companies.

But not all analyses are created equal. Business analysis that makes a difference in the market place is characterised by the right mindset (e.g., a willingness to dig deeper than other investors, a critical mind, objectivity, independence), and requires superior skill to interpret and find relevant information about companies (e.g., by focusing on businesses within one's "circle of competence").[78]

In addition, powerful business analysis hinges on three pillars: quantitative analysis, qualitative analysis, and management analysis. Unlike many professionals who believe that the quantitative analysis of businesses (screening a company's current and past financial statements, and comparing the gathered data with those of competitors) reveals all an investor needs to know, top investors pay at least as much attention to management and qualitative business aspects.

This chapter focuses on the interpretation of company information. Acknowledging that there are countless books on the subject of business analysis, the aim is not to give a comprehensive overview of conventional analysis techniques. Rather the focus is on those

---

[78] A recurring piece of advice among top investors is that people should focus on business areas where they have superior knowledge and expertise. By focusing on their *circle of competence* they have an edge over investors who are not that familiar with such types of businesses. For instance, Peter Lynch says: "The insurance professional ought to take advantage of this edge, and not blow it by shunning the insurance stocks and buying railroads or waste management companies, the workings of which he or she is entirely ignorant." And "Employees at the malls have an insiders' edge, since they see what's going on every day, plus they get the word from their colleagues as to which stores are thriving and which are not." (Lynch, 1993)

aspects that receive special attention by top investors. At the end of this chapter I provide an overview of information sources and I discuss some practical aspects of business analysis.

# C.I Quantitative business evaluation

There is plenty of excellent, in-depth literature on how to analyse financial statements.[79] Interested readers can consult this literature for thorough descriptions of classical quantitative analysis. This section presents those aspects of quantitative analysis that top investors find most important.

Before moving on, a warning is needed to the effect that accounting rules can differ from country to country. As such it may not always be straightforward to interpret and evaluate quantitative data in countries with accounting standards that are very different from the ones the investor is familiar with. To avoid these kinds of problems, some top investors do not invest outside their home country. For instance, Walter Schloss never bought one stock outside of the US. Even Warren Buffett hesitated a long time before he made his first investment overseas.

Equally important to point out is that even among companies with the same accounting standards, the chosen methods can be very different (e.g., depreciation methods can be more or less aggressive). So, investors always have to remain aware that quantitative analysis is more than just *reading the numbers*.

## C.I.1 Analysis of the income statement

A profitability analysis includes an examination of earnings, profit margins, return on invested capital, the sensitivity of profitability to economic cycles, etc. According to numerous top investors, the most attractive long-term investment candidates are companies with:[80]

1. **Solid track records of (positive) earnings**: top investors avoid companies that still need to make their first profit because such companies are inherently speculative. In addition, Benjamin Graham looked for companies with stable earnings trajectories and no earnings deficits over the last five to ten years.

2. **Unblemished track records of dividend payments**: since dividends are a very strong sign to the market, management will usually try everything it can in order not to miss a dividend payment. For this reason, the dividend history is a very important indication about management's competence and about the company's sensitivity to fluctuations in the business cycle. So, if the company pays a dividend, one should preferably see steady increases in dividends per share over the last 10 to 20 years, and no temporary declines or discontinuations.

---

[79] For example (Epstein, 2005), (Friedlob, 2001), (Bernstein, 2000), (Bragg, 2007), (Fridson, 2002), (Heiserman, 2004) and (White, 2003).

[80] Keep in mind that one has to correct for accounting differences (e.g., expensing versus capitalisation of certain expenses), one-time items (e.g., extraordinary profits/income) and specific corporate events (e.g., mergers, postponement of capital expenditures) when comparing financial statements of different companies.

3. **Excellent profit margins**: the greatest companies have gross, operating and/or net profit margins that are consistently higher than those of their peers, and their industry's average.[81] Above-average profit margins are indicative of a strong competitive advantage thanks to a unique strategy, superior operations or products, and the like. What is more, superior profit margins also serve as a safety cushion against business downturns, since companies with the lowest margins are likely to suffer substantially bigger declines in profit when sales are under pressure.[82]

4. **Extraordinary return on invested capital**: companies that earn high returns on the capital they invested in their business (in absolute terms and relative to competitors) typically enjoy a strong competitive position. They also usually have management with superior capital allocation skills. Top shorter Jim Chanos believes that because return on capital is very hard to manipulate, low returns expose a lot of wormy companies. Since return on equity (ROE = net income/book value of equity) can be increased through higher leverage (which is risky), the best return measures are return on invested capital (ROIC = Earnings Before Interest & Taxes/(debt + equity + deferred taxes)) and return on assets (ROA= Earnings Before Interest & Taxes /total assets).

Of course, not only current and past profitability matter. For attractive investments there are good reasons to believe that superior profitability will be maintained or improved in future years thanks to the company's exceptional competitive position, its extraordinary execution, and its efforts to defend and extend its position. Ideally one should see improving profitability metrics over the past few years. Consistently deteriorating profit margins and declining returns on capital – in particular relative to competitors – can be warning signs that the company is losing out to the competition.

> *"If you just stick to buying good companies (ones that have a high return on capital) and to buying those companies only at bargain prices (at prices that give you a high earnings yield), you can end up systematically buying many of the good companies that crazy Mr. Market has decided to literally give away."*
>
> **Joel Greenblatt (Greenblatt, 2006)**

---

[81] Strictly speaking, to evaluate profit margins one should compare companies with identical business models and the same product mixes. This is not always easy because peers may have somewhat different product mixes and may use very different business models and business practices. To avoid being misled by such differences, one should always look at profit margins in conjunction with return on invested capital.

[82] A perverse fact is that low-margin businesses are usually the big winners when the economy recovers, because they can increase their earnings disproportionally through even a small margin improvement. Investors must be aware of the fact, however, that investing in low-margin businesses before a business downturn (i.e., when the economy does very well) is a dangerous proposition.

## C.I.2 Evaluation of the balance sheet

Balance sheets are very important to bond investors, but stock investors cannot afford to ignore a company's financial health either. In fact, many of the best value investors give priority to a stock's potential downside before they contemplate its upside. They therefore look at the balance sheet (and cash flow statement) *before* they check out the income statement. Numerous companies have got themselves in trouble when they have taken on more debt than they could afford. Top investors such as Anthony Bolton and Peter Lynch admit that the biggest mistakes they made in their careers were nearly always in companies with poor and/or deteriorating balance sheets.

When evaluating a balance sheet one first has to examine the company's *liquidity*, i.e., the company's ability to meet its short-term obligations. Classical liquidity metrics to watch are the current or quick ratio, working capital, interest coverage (e.g., earnings before interest, taxes, depreciation & amortisation/net interest expense), etc. As with other metrics, one should see whether these liquidity metrics are adequate for the business. One should also compare them with peers in the same industry. Further liquidity issues that receive the special attention of top investors are the amount of short-term debt and the amount of floating-rate debt. Floating-rate debt can create liquidity problems because it causes fluctuations in interest payments. Short-term debt, on the other hand, is dangerous because it has to be rolled over regularly.

The other aspect of a balance sheet examination is *solvency*, i.e., the company's ability to maintain sufficient liquidity over the long term. One must examine the company's financial leverage (debt ratios), and compare this with industry averages. Appropriate debt levels vary from industry to industry. As a rule of thumb, top investors don't like companies with debt higher than half of common equity. Although a high level of debt increases ROE, it is definitely not necessary to achieve exceptional results. In fact, as pointed out by Warren Buffett, great businesses throw off sufficient cash to fund their projects without leverage.[83] For this and the following reasons, top investors like Marty Whitman, Peter Lynch, Warren Buffett and Alex Roepers avoid overleveraged businesses like the plague[84]:

1. **High debt exposes the company to high risk**: since high levels of debt cause large fixed costs in the form of interest and regular principal payments, they can cause serious problems when the business is going through a difficult period due to internal factors (e.g., when the business loses market share) or external factors (e.g., an economic recession).

2. **High debt can cause funding problems**: all else being equal, the cost of funding is much lower for well-capitalised than for poorly capitalised companies. To make matters worse, highly leveraged companies frequently have to look for funding

---

[83] In his 1987 letter to shareholders Buffett mentions a Fortune study that supports this view. In that study, the 25 companies (out of a sample of 1000) that achieved an average ROE of 20% (and not less than 15% in any single year) between 1977 and 1986 used very little borrowings as compared to their interest-paying capacity.

[84] Some private equity investors specialise in highly leveraged companies, such as leveraged buy-outs (LBOs). But, unlike the average common stock investor, these people are professionals who do a very thorough due diligence. They usually take control of the business and they are only interested in companies with very stable cash flows.

when they suffer a setback (as they have to cover the high fixed interest costs). They also often have to raise capital under unfavourable conditions (e.g., through a secondary stock offering after the stock is beaten down).

3. **High debt ties the hands of management**: whereas a well-capitalised company usually has a lot of freedom to take new initiatives, the priority of a leveraged company is to service its debt. As a result, highly leveraged businesses can have trouble funding new projects and/or fighting off competition. Moreover, when firms have high debt loads creditors may try to interfere in the firm's strategy (in particular in the case of bank debt), and they may block certain initiatives.

## C.I.3 Cash flow analysis

As a final part of a financial statement analysis, one must examine the company's cash flows. Special attention must be given to the evolution of *operating and free cash flows* over the past years, both in absolute terms and compared with competitors. One also has to compare the cash flows with reported earnings as a check against earnings manipulation and to better understand certain accounting choices.

## C.I.4 Further tips and red flags

> *"If you read a financial disclosure three times and cannot understand it, it is intentional."*
>
> **Jim Chanos (Weiss, 2012)**

When scrutinising financial statements, it is important to:

1. **Read the footnotes**: investors must examine the footnotes to better understand the financial statements, and to search for threats like looming debt problems or hidden liabilities (e.g., unfunded pension or healthcare liabilities).

2. **Look for earnings management**: many companies try to manipulate their earnings to paint a brighter picture of themselves.[85] To avoid being taken in by ruses and to increase the comparability of financial statements, investors have to make appropriate adjustments to the presented numbers. They have to be wary especially of the following red flags that are often related to creative accounting:

   - *Auditors that are not independent*: this can be the case, for instance, when the auditing firm also has a consulting relationship with the company.

   - The presented *figures are too good to be true*, e.g., perfect sales and earnings growth.

---

[85] See, for example (Mulford, 2002), (O'Glove, 1987) and (Schilit, 2002).

- *Anomalies between growth rates and balance sheet items*: examples are receivables that are out of line with sales, inventory growth that is much higher than the growth in Cost Of Goods Sold (COGS), rising plant, property and equipment while accumulated depreciation stays behind, etc.

- *Improper capitalisations and overvalued assets* (e.g., assets that are not marked to market).

- Management has a *history of managing earnings*.

- *Complicated and opaque accounting*: a typical ploy of earnings manipulators is to make the financial statements so complex and voluminous that even the most experienced analysts are discouraged from digging any deeper. As investing requires a serious degree of comfort with the financial statements, smart investors steer clear of companies that complicate analysis for investors. Warren Buffett says that he even won't try to figure a company out if he finds it too tough.

3. **Evaluate the risk of distress**: a company's financial health can be analysed through a scrutiny of the balance sheet in combination with the income and cash flow statement. Apart from number crunching, there are some red flags that top investors like Anthony Bolton always check out:

   - Presence of a *going concern warning* in the financial statements: a warning from the auditors that the company may not be able to continue in business as a going concern is very rare and indicates that the risk of distress is high.

   - *The Altman Z-score or H-score*: it is best to avoid companies with Z-scores below 1, and H-scores below 25. According to a study of Morgan Stanley, stocks with a Z-score below 1 underperformed the market by about 5.7% a year between 1991 and 2008.

   - *The opinion of debt investors*: look at the price of the company's bonds, and the credit default swap spreads, as indications for the opinion of credit and bond investors about the company's financial health.

## C.II Qualitative business evaluation

> "If the future could be told from a balance sheet, then mathematicians and accountants would be the richest people in the world by now."
>
> **Peter Lynch (Lynch, 1993)**

Traditionally books on business analysis pay scant attention to the qualitative assessment of businesses. This reflects the belief among many professionals that quantitative analysis is the bedrock of business evaluation. One cannot deny that the numbers are important, and that there have been (and there still are) many investors who are highly successful without looking at anything more than the raw (quantitative) data.[86]

However, when it comes to long-term holdings many top investors warn that a more thorough understanding of the underlying business and management is indispensable. Warren Buffett is a vocal champion of qualitative business assessment. Early on in his investment career he pursued a purely quantitative approach. When several of his *bargain* investments performed poorly, he began to realise (under the influence of Charles Munger and Philip Fisher) that his investment process was incomplete. Later on, he acknowledged the limitations of a purely quantitatively-driven investment strategy.

Apart from Buffett, numerous other top investors have racked up impressive investment returns by incorporating qualitative business elements in their due diligence. This is a strong indication that qualitative business evaluation deserves more attention than it commonly receives in the investment community. One can also make a strong case for qualitative analysis based on a number of other arguments.

First of all, the value of hard (quantitative) data has probably been diluted in recent years by the easier access to such data. The internet has made it possible for individuals to obtain vast amounts of information with the click of a mouse. Professionals with specialised financial services (e.g., Bloomberg) can even see all kinds of data and financial metrics without ever opening a single annual report.[87]

A second argument in support of qualitative analysis is that it constitutes a competitive advantage. Indeed, as mentioned above, we live in a world where most investors do not take the time to check out the qualitative factors, because they are too busy checking out the financials. Few investment professionals (let alone individuals) have received proper training in qualitative business analysis. So, even if they would want to examine the qualitative factors, they don't know how to go about it. This implies that people who combine a quantitative analysis with a thorough qualitative screening can gain knowledge that is vastly superior to what other investors have at their disposal.

In the next sections there is a brief overview of the most important subtleties in the evaluation of qualitative company factors as pointed out by some of the brightest minds in the investment world. The discussion covers industry factors, the company's business model, its competitive position, control over its destiny, and the growth potential of businesses. The evaluation of management is deferred to section C.III.

## C.II.1 The company's industry

The success of an investment is determined to a large extent by the industry in which it operates. According to top investors, the main factors that determine the attractiveness of an industry are:

---

[86] Some investment styles, such as the deep-value styles of Benjamin Graham and Walter Schloss, revolve entirely around the superior and unbiased interpretation of financial statements.

[87] This might open up another opportunity for investors who like to do the digging themselves. When all professionals are looking at the same ready-made data, those who take the trouble to peruse documents themselves can find valuable, unique and hard-to-come-by information that many other people don't know about.

1. **Barriers to entry**: a frequently recurring theme among top investors is the importance of barriers to entry. These barriers are very important factors in a company's *competitive moat*. Barriers to entry deter outsiders from entering an industry, as new entrants can only become successful if they first overcome these barriers. The threat of new entrants in an industry is very much a function of the trade-off between the cost of overcoming entry barriers and the benefits of having a position in that industry. Provided that internal competition among the existing firms is reasonable, industries with huge barriers to entry are usually more stable and more profitable than industries with low barriers. Industries that can easily be entered by existing or new corporations, by contrast, are bound to suffer from fierce competition for market share, and have to accept attendant poor profitability. The most important entry barriers are:[88]

   - *Economies of scale*: if companies that operate at a large scale in that industry have significant cost advantages, new entrants will have to enter the business at large scale or face a cost handicap.

   - *Capital requirements*: if huge financial resources are required to compete in the industry new entrants may be deterred – in particular if the required investments are risky. For instance, in the pharmaceutical industry, R&D budgets can be very high. So, new entrants will have to invest heavily in R&D projects with uncertain payoffs if they want to take on the big pharma players with competing products.

   - *Need for product differentiation*: if companies have to differentiate themselves from other companies to be successful in an industry, new entrants will have to invest heavily (e.g., in advertising) to overcome customer loyalties.

   - *Availability of distribution channels*: if the distribution channels are already used at full capacity by the current players in the industry, new entrants may have a tough time getting their products to the customer. For instance, supermarkets will be reluctant to offer yet another type of soda drink on their already fully occupied store shelves.

   - *Other cost disadvantages*: new entrants may face considerable disadvantages versus established players in terms of proprietary knowledge, patents, available locations, and access to raw materials.

   - *Government regulations*: governments may limit or prohibit entry into a new industry. Limited access is, for instance, common in regulated industries like utilities and telecom.

2. **Competitive pressure**: the intensity of rivalry inside an industry is another important factor that determines the prospects of players in that industry. It is a function of:

   - *Opportunity for differentiation*: when the products that are made in the industry offer little opportunity for differentiation (i.e., the product is a commodity), companies have to compete head-on for market share through

---

[88] Porter, 1980.

price concessions. When the product can be differentiated, players can use more creative strategies to defend their position.

- *Popularity of the industry*: industries that are hot in the investment and/or business world are usually not the most stable places for business. Popular industries draw too much attention and therefore attract a lot of competition. Boring, unpopular, disagreeable, no-growth industries are usually safer.

- *Make-up of major players*: industries where the biggest players are of equal size, where they have comparable resources, and where the strategic motivations of players are diverse and irrational usually suffer from the most intense internal competition.

- *Exit barriers*: when it is difficult for unprofitable players to get out of an industry due to exit barriers, they are likely to stay and make life miserable for everyone through the creation of overcapacity and through desperate price cuts. Sources of exit barriers are expensive specialised assets, high fixed costs, strategic interrelationships with other business units and emotional commitment to the industry.

3. **Threat of substitutes**: the position of the industry versus new entrants and internal rivalry are two of the most important factors that determine the strength of an industry. However, according to Michael Porter's famous competitive model, there are three more powers industries have to cope with: buyers, suppliers and substitutes.[89] The position of individual companies versus buyers and suppliers is discussed below. As far as substitutes are concerned, one has to realise that there is always the threat that customers will replace the industry's offering with a substitute product that can perform a similar function (e.g., fructose instead of sugar) or that satisfies a similar need (e.g., a plane instead of a bus to travel a distance). Therefore, investors must try to identify substitute products and estimate whether and how much these substitute products will affect the industry.

4. **Capital requirements**: Warren Buffett, David Einhorn and Don Yacktman take a liking to industries that can make decent profits on relatively few tangible assets. Companies in such industries can hold their ground without the need to pour a large part of the cash flows they generate back into their business every year. Examples of capital-light industries are computer software (e.g., Microsoft), pharmaceuticals, consumer goods with strong brand power (e.g., Coke), service industries (e.g., consultancy), etc.

One advantage of capital-light businesses is that they can expand more easily and more profitably than businesses that have to invest huge amounts of capital for expansion (e.g., in plants and equipment, such as airlines and companies in the steel industry). Another advantage is that capital-light businesses are less likely to suffer from inflation. Capital-intensive businesses, by contrast, have to make capital investments all the time and therefore are more vulnerable to inflation.

---

[89] Porter, 1980.

5. **Rate of change**: because of their focus on sustainable competitive positions, top investors like Warren Buffett and Peter Lynch shun industries with rapid change and with short or unpredictable product life cycles such as technology[90] and biotech. In such industries competitive advantages can evaporate quickly and leaders have to make a lot of good decisions to maintain their lead. Conversely, they embrace industries with high stability because in these industries it may be hard for a manager of a leading company to spoil its competitive position. An example of a stable industry is the funeral services business. This business hasn't changed much over the last few centuries. In addition, profits are highly predictable as profit margins are stable due to limited competition and because revenue (which is proportional to the number of people that pass away) can be predicted reliably.[91]

> *"A business that constantly encounters major change also encounters many chances for major error. Furthermore, economic terrain that is forever shifting violently is ground on which it is difficult to build a fortress-like business franchise. Such a franchise is usually the key to sustained high returns."*
>
> **Warren Buffett, 1987 letter to the shareholders of Berkshire Hathaway**

## C.II.2 The company's business model

A company's business model describes how the company will make money and beat the competition. It is basically the foundation of the company's success or failure. Serious long-term investors always try to understand an investment's business model, and look for its strengths and weaknesses. They know that one should only buy a stock if one has sufficient confidence in the business model. If not, one is unlikely to keep hold of the stock when the company hits the occasional rough patch (as virtually all businesses do at one time or another).

To maximise their chances of success in the selection of attractive business models, top investors follow two major tenets:

1. **They systematically avoid**:

   - *Complex business models*: top investors like Anthony Bolton, Warren Buffett and Peter Lynch embrace simple and shun complex business models. Their rationale is that although complex business models might work, investing in such businesses basically comes down to a leap of faith. According to Peter Lynch, the litmus test

---

[90] Investors who try their chances in technology anyway are highly recommended to get familiar with the books of Geoffrey A. Moore on competition in the technology sector: (Moore, 2006) and (Moore, 2005).
[91] Mohnish Pabrai made a 100% gain on the funeral services business Stewart Enterprises in a period of only a few months in 2001 to 2002 when he realised that such a predictable business was worth much more than three times cash flows.

is to try to explain a business in as little time as possible. Only businesses that can be explained with a crayon in less than three minutes pass his test.

- *Companies without repeat business*: companies that make products that customers have to buy only once (e.g., fad products) do not lend themselves to long-term investments. Strong business models are based on repeat business that comes from stable and real demand for the company's products, or from service and maintenance tasks. For instance, manufacturers of big-ticket items like elevators and gas turbines can generate a lot of repeat business from post-sale maintenance contracts. Or producers of razors or electric toothbrushes often sell these products at cost (or give them away) in order to generate high-margin repeat sales of blades and toothbrush heads.

2. **They painstakingly examine the track records of business models**. A common theme among top investors is that they avoid companies that lack proven track records over periods that include at least one business cycle. They argue that a solid track record is so important because it shows that the business model works in good and bad times. They liken investment in companies without track records to gambling on an unproven idea. In their opinion, it makes no sense to risk one's assets on ventures when so many great companies with proven business models regularly trade at prices far below their intrinsic value.[92] When evaluating the track record of a business, top stock pickers pay special attention to:

- *Profitability*: Peter Lynch, Warren Buffett and Philip Fisher do not invest in companies that haven't turned a profit in previous years. Even more dangerous than unprofitable businesses are companies that steadily burn through their cash with little prospect of any change in the short term. An example of the latter would be a cash-guzzling biotech business that still needs to get its first medicine to the market.

- *Market share evolution*: a strong indication that a business model works is that the company consistently gained market share vis-à-vis its competitors over the past few years.[93] To make sure that the gains in market share are the result of a strong business and are not due to excessive price concessions or too much risk taking, one must examine whether they come from sustainable competitive advantages, and whether the company has produced higher cash flows in the meantime.

- *Scalability and repeatability*: the best businesses remain successful when they expand. As opposed to so many investors who try to get first into a business that has high growth potential, top investors are patient and stand by the

---

[92] Investing in ventures without track records is so risky and so specialised that it should be left to professional private equity investors (who, by the way, as a group are not particularly successful at it). Common stock investors must also realise that the most promising ventures are seldom accessible to non-professional investors.

[93] A shortcut to see whether a company gains market share is to compare its sales growth with that of its direct competitors, or with the industry's average.

sidelines until they see confirmation that the business model is scalable (i.e., that it keeps working during the company's expansion). Although this implies missing a potential share price run-up in the first stages of the company's life, they stress that most of the money is usually made during the company's stable growth phase. For instance, in the restaurant chain business Peter Lynch would not invest in a new restaurant chain before it had been successful in different geographic locations.

> *"It's only when the tide goes out that you learn who's been swimming naked."*
>
> **Warren Buffett, 1992 letter to the shareholders of Berkshire Hathaway**

## C.II.3 The company's competitive position

A business model and the execution thereof determine a company's place in the competitive landscape. Attractive long-term businesses occupy a stable position from which they cannot be easily dislodged by competitors. Hence, understanding the strength of a company's competitive position is paramount in the assessment of its longevity and prosperity.

Part of the competitive strength is determined by the company's industry, as discussed above. Hereunder we look into the competitive strength of individual businesses. First I present a popular and effective framework to asses a company's competitive advantages. Second, I give an overview of the most important pillars that shore up the company's competitive position. And finally, I discuss the sustainability of competitive advantages.

### C.II.3.a Power versus customers, suppliers, and internal rivals

A company's competitive position, and that of its industry, can be examined effectively through Michael Porter's five forces analysis.[94] Some forces for industries have already been discussed above (barriers to entry, internal rivalry and the threat of substitutes), and these also apply to the competitive strength of companies inside these industries. For instance, some companies in an industry may have a superior position versus new entrants and substitutes thanks to the barriers they have created and thanks to the uniqueness of the product they make. Three other of Porter's forces that have a decisive impact on the company's success within its industry are:

1. **Power versus customers**: a business is made or broken by its customers (consumers, distributors, retailers, corporate clients, etc.), because in the end customers decide whether to do business with the company or not. Some important factors in the power versus customers are:

---

[94] (Porter, 1980) and (Porter, 1985).

- The company's *product*: the more a product appeals to customers, the higher the power the company will have versus its customers. Important elements in a product's appeal are:

  (i) *Need for the product*: ideally, people crave the product, and they need it irrespective of economic conditions. For instance, products like diapers, soap and medicine will be bought under virtually all business conditions, whereas purchases of big-ticket items like cars are usually postponed during harsh economic times. Another example is Coca-Cola; food and drink retailers cannot afford not to have Coca-Cola on their shelves as many customers look for this item when they go on errands.

  (ii) *Price versus product quality*: evidently, the cheaper the product (for a similar quality), the more appealing it is going to be to most customers.

  (iii) *Differentiation of the product*: a powerful product is one that is substantially different from competing products. For instance, Starbucks introduced differentiation to the previously commoditised coffee business through its new store concept and through its relentless focus on coffee quality. Unique product characteristics make customers reluctant to replace the product with that of a competitor. In addition, when the product is differentiated, the company is in a comfortable position to raise prices without fear of major repercussions on sales. Even more, product differentiation reduces the bargaining power of distributors or retailers, as they cannot afford not to supply the product (if they don't their customers will go elsewhere).

    All this has to be contrasted with businesses that make commodity products. Commodity businesses lack all of these strengths and therefore are usually much less appealing.[95] Obvious examples of commodity businesses are raw material producers (e.g., mining companies, companies in the steel industry). But even an industry like airlines is a commodity business, as the majority of customers travelling in economy class will only look for the cheapest price when they book a flight.

- *Service*: excellent service can add another dimension to a product's differentiation. Great companies put their customers first, they listen attentively to their clients' needs, and they constantly try to improve their service.

- *Ease of switching to competing products*: an important factor in the power versus customers is the so-called *switching cost*, i.e., the cost of switching to competing products. For instance, Microsoft has tremendous power versus customers because the cost of switching to other software packages is enormous. Indeed, if a company decided to switch to a competing software

---

[95] As mentioned by Buffett in his annual letter of 1982, success in a commodity business depends on the ratio of supply-tight to supply-ample years. The least attractive commodity businesses are those where periods of oversupply and overcapacity (which are unprofitable to the business) are much longer than periods of undercapacity (during which the business usually prospers).

package it would face enormous retraining costs and it would have to deal with extraordinary compatibility problems (e.g., it would no longer be possible to process documents in Microsoft Word from customers or suppliers).

- *Number of customers*: the power versus customers will usually be higher the more revenue is spread among different customers. When sales are concentrated in one or a handful of customers, bargaining power versus customers will be low as each of these customers will know that it is important to the company. Dependence on a few customers is also risky for another reason: it exposes the company to a substantial revenue loss if one of these customers drops out. An example of a risky business due to customer concentration is a local supplier of specific parts to a particular plant of a car manufacturer. When the plant closes down, the supplier is usually out of business.

- *Other advantages that accrue to the customers*: investors must try to understand all the motivations customers have for doing business with the company – in the case of a business this means those who make the buying decisions for the business – in particular those customers that account for the highest revenues, or those with the highest growth potential need to be understood. It is, for instance, important to realise that the interests of the decision makers are not always perfectly aligned with those of their corporation. Just one example is that someone with a frequent flyer status of a certain airline company will often try to find flights that can give him/her more award miles, even when other airlines might offer cheaper flights.

2. **Power versus suppliers**: a force that is often overlooked but which can play an important role in the competitive position of a company is its relationship with suppliers (including its own workforce as a supplier of labour). Companies which have suppliers that can easily raise prices are obviously in a much weaker competitive position than companies whose suppliers are under pressure to keep prices down. Some conditions that determine the strength of suppliers are:

- *Competition faced by suppliers*: the pricing power of a supplier will be weak if it faces a lot of competition from other suppliers and/or from substitute products, and vice versa. For instance, when the labour market (which can be seen as a supplier to the company) is tight, the firm may experience serious upward pressure on salaries.

- *Importance of the company to the supplier*: a supplier will obviously find it hard to raise prices for a customer that accounts for an important share of its revenues or profits. For instance, a retail giant like Wal-Mart has tremendous bargaining power versus many of its suppliers, as the sales in the Wal-Mart stores typically represent a very sizable portion of these supplier's revenues. Conversely, suppliers have much more bargaining power versus customers that account for an insignificant share of their business.

- *Ease of switching to competing input product*: if it is hard to replace one supplier with another (e.g., due to the differentiation of the input product or due to switching costs), the company will have trouble pitting one supplier against another. This weakens its bargaining power versus the suppliers. For instance, heavily unionised companies cannot easily change their workforce and therefore regularly have to cave into labour union demands.

- *Importance of the input product*: when the input that is purchased from the supplier is a critical component of the product that is manufactured by the company, the bargaining position of the company will be weaker, and vice versa.

3. **Power versus internal competitors**: understanding a company's competitive position inevitably involves sizing up the company's direct competition. Investors must examine how crowded the marketplace is. Furthermore, top investors like Warren Buffett and John Templeton stress that investors must try to understand the strategy, financial situation and market share of all direct competitors of an investment candidate. In this evaluation, it is important to remember the many advantages that accrue to:

- *Market leaders*: top stock pickers like Philip Carret, Philip Fisher and Julian Robertson are fond of industry leaders with dominant market shares. Market leaders are usually the most profitable businesses of their industry and they can smother smaller competitors to death thanks to economies of scale, their strong bond with customers (they are often perceived as making the best product and the product of the leader feels safe), and their powerful position versus suppliers (who cannot afford to ignore them).

  For instance, product leaders like Wrigley, Kellogg, Heinz, Kimberly-Clark and Coca-Cola are inevitable. Their products are very popular as they are believed to be the highest-quality products in their respective categories. As such, they get first crack at shelf space in retail shops. Thanks to the high market share of their killer brand products, they also have huge scale advantages versus peers in terms of production, advertising, etc. In addition, thanks to their strong image they can charge higher prices than competitors. All this implies that these companies are more profitable than competitors and that their market position is nearly impregnable (as long as they don't make very stupid mistakes).

- *Duopolists*: Glenn Greenberg points out that duopolies (where only two companies compete with each other, such as the duopoly of Freddie Mac and Fannie Mae in the US) are attractive. The reason is that competition between the two companies of a duopoly tends to be weak, while government interference is not so likely as it is with monopolies.

## C.II.3.b Pillars of competitive strength

A company's competitive position is determined to a large extent by how the company positions itself against the five forces described above through its business model.

However, good intentions and an excellent strategy are only the start of a strong competitive position. At least as important is execution. Here some essential functions that support the company's position in the market place are briefly discussed.[96]

## Culture

Culture refers to the values, norms, attitudes and beliefs that prevail at the company and that guide the behaviour of employees. An effective culture that is ruthlessly pursued and consistently enforced is the fabric that keeps a business together. It motivates employees to work together towards common goals. In companies with a strong culture, people know what they are supposed to do without directions from above. A strong and inspiring culture that permeates a company is also motivating as it creates a cult-like environment where people feel special (because they feel that they belong to a special organisation).

Many investors and business analysts pay little attention to corporate cultures. Most even totally ignore it in their business analysis. Nevertheless, the managers of numerous highly successful companies believe that this is a big mistake. Many attribute a large part of their success to their corporate culture.

For instance, Kenneth Iverson, who turned the near-bankrupt steel company Nucor into the most successful steel business in the US, said that he owes 80% of his success to the company's corporate culture. Also L. V. Gerstner, who managed the successful turnaround of IBM in the 1990s, stressed in *Who Says Elephants Can't Dance?* the importance of the corporate culture in the resurrection of IBM. In *Pour Your Heart Into It*, the CEO of Starbucks (Howard Schultz) explained how the corporate culture of Starbucks played a crucial role in the company's success during the 1990s.

So what makes a culture so powerful that it constitutes an important competitive advantage? First of all, *effective cultures are strong*. They are pursued with fervour throughout the company. Employees believe in the values, norms and attitudes, and understand their meaning. Companies with strong corporate cultures apply the values and norms consistently, even when it is costly to do so (e.g., no massive layoffs when employees are considered to be the company's most important asset). Managers in companies with strong cultures are *genuine and natural* (i.e., not fake and formal) role models and ambassadors of the corporate values. Companies that take their corporate culture seriously ruthlessly remove all employees (including top performers and senior managers) who are incompatible with the culture. They also rigorously screen new hires to ensure that they are cultural matches.

As far as the nature of the values and norms is concerned, it is obvious that effective cultures have values and norms that inspire people and motivate them to put their best foot forward in everything they do. There is no single *best* corporate culture, but here are a number of cultural elements that tend to be present in many of the greatest companies:

1. **Commitment to excellence** in everything one does (production, design, R&D, operations, etc.).

---

[96] See also (Blanchard, 1998), (Collins, 2002), (Collins, 2001) and (Peters, 2006).

2. **Pursuit of integrity and honesty** inside the company. Integrity creates trust. Integrity means that one can count on others and that promises are kept. Honesty implies that employees show respect for each other, irrespective of their rank in the organisation. It also means that there is nothing to hide and that nobody takes his or her unfair share of the rewards.

3. Genuine **concern for all stakeholders**: being close to customers, employees, shareholders, suppliers and the outside world creates a strong bond with all parties that have an impact on the company's success. It also creates goodwill, which can be helpful in times of need. For instance, customers that have always been treated with respect will be more tolerant of mistakes than customers with poor customer experiences. Suppliers that have always been paid a fair price for their goods are more likely to be less strict (e.g., in terms of price or receivables) when the company is in financial problems. Or journalists and public opinion are more likely to forgive a misstep by a company that has given back a lot to its community.

> *"In large part, companies obtain the shareholder constituency that they seek and deserve. If they focus their thinking and communications on short-term results or short-term stock market consequences they will, in large part, attract shareholders who focus on the same factors. And if they are cynical in their treatment of investors, eventually that cynicism is highly likely to be returned by the investment community."*
>
> **Warren Buffett, 1979 letter to the shareholders of Berkshire Hathaway**

4. **Candid and abundant communication**: in companies with strong communication misunderstandings are less likely, innovation is easier, problems are exposed and solved more quickly, and people feel more involved and motivated (as they have a better view on what's going on in the company). In *Made in America*, Sam Walton, the founder of Wal-Mart, argues that effective communication throughout the company was an important factor in the success of the business. Walton shared business numbers with his employees to give them a feeling of involvement. He organised a merchandising meeting each Friday and a store manager meeting each Saturday morning. In these meetings, people were given information, and ideas were exchanged and discussed. He also made sure that he stayed in close contact with the truck drivers who delivered goods to the stores, which helped him to detect morale and attitude problems early on.

5. A **thirst for innovation** and fear of complacency: companies that do not rest on their laurels, where employees constantly question the status quo, and where managers are not satisfied with the current state of affairs, are less likely to get 'caught asleep at the switch' when a new competitor challenges their position or when a new trend makes their products obsolete. Through constant innovation and improvements, companies can carve out a sustainable position in a changing world.

6. A **bias to action and risk taking**, supported by a tolerance for failure: in companies where action is appreciated and rewarded, ideas are tested quickly, decisions are taken fast, looming problems are tackled instantly, products are brought to the market without delay, and people gain much practical experience and knowledge. Action orientation can be a strong competitive advantage in a world where too many companies look for excuses not to do something, where paperwork is elevated to a higher status than action, and where studies and committees often stand in the way of immediate results. Note that a bias to action is inextricably linked to the encouragement of risk taking and a tolerance of failure.

7. **Trust**: lack of trust leads to fear. It undermines loyalty as people don't feel involved. It makes collaboration harder because people are suspicious of one another. And it stifles innovation as people keep quiet and don't try anything out of the box. Companies that value trust delegate power and spending power down to the lowest levels in the hierarchy. They tend to replace control with peer pressure. And they strictly enforce integrity and honesty.

8. **Informality and fun**: fun and informality create a unique image with customers and in society. They alleviate stress, create better relationships between employees, and lead to more communication. Throwing parties, the absence of privileges and perks for higher management, informal dress codes, and the like also express a high level of recognition for the work of all employees – irrespective of job position. For example, under the highly successful leadership of Herb Kelleher, flight attendants at Southwest Airlines were encouraged to bring fun into their job. They would, for instance, hide themselves in the overhead lockers and pop out when passengers opened the lockers.[97]

9. **Simplicity** in operations, processes, working methods, accounting, etc.: simple procedures prevent bureaucracy from delaying decisions and projects. Simple language makes things understandable to everyone inside the company. Simplicity in operations and strategy also offers a competitive advantage as many companies can't believe that simple procedures are worth imitating (because they believe that complex procedures are more likely to offer a competitive advantage).

10. Many companies try to instil **a sense of ownership** (i.e., the feeling of being a co-owner of the firm) throughout their organisation as this leads to a stronger focus on business results. It creates a sense of involvement and responsibility, which leads to higher motivation. It also leads to attention to detail, shareholder orientation, cost consciousness and so on. After all, nobody washes a rented car. Ownership can be fostered through stock ownership, incentive bonuses, open communication and the delegation of power. Starbucks, for instance, was one of the first companies in the retail world to have a stock option plan.

---

[97] Freiberg, 1996.

> *"Reward excellent failures. Punish mediocre success."*
>
> **Tom Peters (Peters, 1994)**

> *"Oh, screw it, let's do it."*
>
> **Richard Branson (Branson, 1998)**

## Human resource management

In Chapter B it was mentioned that companies that top the lists of best employers tend to beat the market. This suggests that the market underestimates the role of human resource management in a company's success. Smart investors, by contrast, know that a powerful HR policy can contribute enormously to the bottom line through its impact on turnover, access to talent (on the job market), employee motivation/commitment/loyalty, and goodwill in the workforce.

In practice, many companies fail miserably at HR management, even though they claim that they "value their most precious (human) assets."[98] Top investors evaluate the following factors when they examine a company's HR policies:

1. **Turnover and union affiliation**: low turnover and low unionisation usually (though, not always) indicate that people feel well at the firm. Another positive sign is a large list of job applicants. A nice example of a company with happy employees was Nucor under Kenneth Iverson. The company had no unions and there was once even an incident where workers harassed union representatives out of loyalty to Nucor.

2. **Elements of effective HR**: essential elements of effective HR management are:

   - *Respect and consideration for employees at all levels of the company*: some highly effective companies (e.g., the very successful Belgian food retailer Colruyt) try to obtain respect by putting all new hires in a hands-dirty job at the bottom of the hierarchy before they can climb up to a higher position.

   - A *fair and competitive reward* system with above-average wages.

   - *Attention to the needs of employees inside the company*, such as providing the necessary resources and training, listening to the voice of everyone, etc.

   - *Attention to the needs of employees outside the company*, such as providing medical insurance, respect for family quality time, job security, etc. For instance, Paul Galvin, one of the founders of Motorola, helped to pay college tuition for the children of employees who couldn't afford it. Another example was Star Furniture during the Depression years of the 1930s. The company vowed not to lay anyone off. Instead, it reduced salaries, including those of top management.[99]

---

[98] To better understand the power of excellent HR policies useful resources are (Sartain, 2003) and (Harrison, 2007).

[99] Miles, 2002.

- *Quick dealing with grievances and problems.*
- Incentives to participate in the company through share and option programmes, which *create a sense of ownership.*
- *Effective hiring and firing procedures*: this includes, for instance, intensive screening for a match with the corporate culture before hiring someone. Also, hiring policies focused on diversity (in race, gender, religion, educational background, personality and so on) can be effective since diversity facilitates innovation.

## Structure, organisation and processes

Another important pillar of competitive strength is the way the company is organised in terms of:

1. **Rules, processes, and procedures**: the best companies look for a balance between rules, formal systems and informality. On the one hand, they fight bureaucracy vigorously. On the other hand, they introduce rules, formal systems and processes – especially when they grow bigger – to avoid crises, and to enforce compliance from employees on certain criteria. Nevertheless, smart businesses keep procedures as simple as possible. They keep the required paperwork to a minimum. They limit the number (and duration) of meetings. And they give individuals a lot of latitude.

2. **Management structure**: great companies pursue a lean management structure, with as few layers as possible, and with a relatively high span of control (i.e., managers have more subordinates than in the average business). Excellent companies also keep the headcount at corporate headquarters to a minimum. A lean management structure has numerous advantages. It leads to better communication because there are fewer layers to block or distort communication. It is cheaper. It is more transparent. It leads to higher accountability (as it is harder to hide behind others when there are fewer layers). And it leads to a higher speed of execution (as layers slow down decisions and execution). A prerequisite for a lean management structure is of course that managers delegate power to people at lower layers.

3. **Business units**: the optimal organisational structure depends on the type of business, the company's strategy, its culture and its stage of development. As a rule and irrespective of the structure, small business units are preferable over large ones because they are easier to manage and because people work much closer together in small business units.[100] Furthermore, decentralisation of a number of functions (while keeping others like real estate and accounting centralised) with a lot of autonomy for individual units is usually better for businesses as they grow bigger.

---

[100] There seems to be a magic number to division size, namely 153. Below that size, people can work together energetically on an informal basis and without much in the way of hierarchy. Beyond that size, formal rules and hierarchy appear to be necessary to keep the unit together.

## Marketing

Marketing refers to all kinds of activities by which a company tries to facilitate adoption of its products in the marketplace. It consists of the selection of markets, understanding of the needs and expectations of customers, product design, and all activities to win customers over (e.g., advertising and sales efforts). As marketing can be a powerful source of differentiation, good marketers can charge more and generate more business than less successful marketers for a similar product.[101]

Figure 10 gives a summary overview of the various components of effective marketing and how it is interrelated with other functions inside the business. Marketing should be centred around the customers the company has selected. These customers have a number of basic expectations about the company's product, such as its usefulness, accuracy, consistency, quality and availability. The customers can be impressed when the company fulfils some higher expectations by giving advice and by creating a kind of partnership.

**Figure 10: The marketing function**

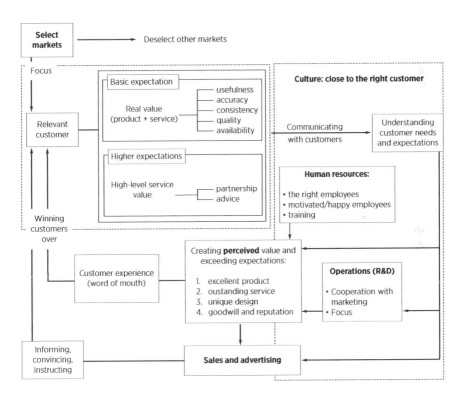

---

[101] Excellent books on effective marketing are (Bedbury, 2002), (Cialdini, 2009), (Godin, 2003) and (Pine, 1999).

To better understand the customer needs and expectations, the company should have a culture where being close to the customer (including abundant communication with the customer) is a core value. Its HR should: be focused on hiring people who put clients first; keep employees happy such that they remain motivated to serve customers well; and provide training where needed to improve customer orientation. R&D departments should stay in close contact with the marketing department and focus on products that are likely to be accepted in the market.

All this should lead to a product offering with a high perceived value (i.e., a product of high quality, outstanding customer service, and an appealing design) that exceeds the expectations of the selected customers. The exceptional product offering creates word of mouth which, together with sales and advertising efforts, helps to win new customers over and keeps existing customers on board.

Hereunder I discuss in more detail some marketing aspects that many great companies pay special attention to:

1. Pursuit of **exceptional customer service**: good marketers try to impress customers by providing a service that is vastly superior to that of their competitors. Exceptional customer service includes (but is not limited to):

   - High *accuracy*: e.g., customers expect correct invoices.

   - Extraordinary *consistency*: credible customer service is the same for each customer and in each location. For instance, all stores of a retail or restaurant chain should give the same amount and type of customer service.

   - A high level of *availability*: exceptional customer service also means that the product should be easily available. For instance, free parking lots, convenient shopping hours and prompt answering of phone calls all increase availability.

   - *Exceptional treatment of customers*: keeping customers informed (e.g., about orders), taking prompt responsibility for failures (without discussion), and surprising actions all contribute to exceptional customer service. An example of the latter is the initiative by Eliot and Barry Tatelman of Jordan's Furniture (owned by Warren Buffett's Berkshire Hathaway) to give out umbrellas to customers of their shop when it rains.[102]

   - *Genuine advice*: for instance, Amazon.com provides customer reviews of books which can help people to decide whether to buy the book or not.

2. **Product consistency and quality**: for instance, McDonald's makes sure that the Big Mac menu has the same taste everywhere around the world (e.g., by centralising the production of French Fries). Another example is Procter & Gamble, which owes its success to a large extent to its unwavering commitment to product quality.

3. **Close contact and confrontation with (the right) customers**: excellent marketers listen attentively to their customers and they reject at the same time customers that are disruptive to their business (e.g., customers that are too demanding,

---

[102] Miles, 2002.

customers that treat employees badly, etc.). A nice example of how a company can get close to its customers is Operation Bear Hug at IBM when Lou Gerstner managed the company's successful turnaround. In that operation, the 50 members of senior management and 200 other executives each had to visit five of IBM's biggest customers. They had to report the feedback they received directly to Lou and take actions to improve the customer relationships based on this feedback.[103]

4. **Focus on the right customer**: successful marketing entails market selection and a razor-sharp focus on the selected customers. This involves turning down or ignoring demands from customers that do not belong to the selected market. For instance, when a bank positions itself as a bank that treats everyone equally (i.e., that gives no privileges to anyone), it should reject rich customers that make special demands.

5. **Brand management**: good marketing means doing everything you can to avoid brand dilution or confusion about what the brand stands for. This means that companies should pay special attention to the impact on their brand of an expansion of their business, of the selection of the points of sale, of the selection of business partners, and so on. Starbucks, for instance, has always been very careful in the selection of companies for its partnerships. Its CEO Howard Schultz wanted to avoid at all cost the possibility that the reputation of Starbuck's high-quality coffee would be affected by a partner with less concern for product quality.

6. **Creativity in product design and advertising**: great marketers try to make a unique product and present it to the world in a creative way. Logitech is an example of a company that became successful thanks to its focus on the functionality and style of electronic devices such as webcams and computer mice. Similarly, the paint manufacturer Dutch Boy connected with customers when it designed a paint jug that was easier to close and easier to pour from.[104] Cleanliness of delivery trucks or easy-to-use forms are also examples of design done right.

7. An **above-average sales organisation**: great companies have an effective (and preferably small) sales force. They also provide excellent training to their sales staff.

## Research and development

For many companies R&D is a critical function that is essential for their survival. At the very least, a flow of new products and patents must enable companies to maintain their relevance and edge in the ever-changing marketplace.[105] Excellent R&D also strengthens a company's position vis-à-vis competitors. When evaluating R&D, one should examine:

---

[103] Gerstner, 2003.

[104] Godin, 2003.

[105] Top investors (e.g., Warren Buffett and Peter Lynch) are reluctant to invest in companies that are too dependent on R&D, because of the inherent risk and uncertainty that this entails. While they see little problem investing in large R&D-dependent firms in stable industries (e.g., large pharmaceuticals), they avoid the most risky types of businesses, such as small companies whose survival depends on the success of one or a few products (e.g., small one-product biotechs) or companies in industries that change very rapidly (e.g., technology).

1. **Amount spent on R&D**: there appears to be a strong correlation between the amount companies invest in R&D and their stock returns.[106]

2. **R&D effectiveness**: one should definitely not limit one's attention to the amount spent on R&D (relative to company size), but one also has to examine R&D effectiveness quantitatively (e.g., the contribution of products released over the last few years compared to overall sales) and qualitatively:

   - *Consistency of investments in R&D*: excellent companies realise that R&D is a priority, no matter what happens. As opposed to so many other companies, they not only invest heavily in R&D during prosperous times, but they keep these investments up when times are tough.

   - *Ambitious R&D*: R&D should seek to disorganise and should not be focused on incremental adjustments to the status quo. In effective R&D departments, researchers work at challenging projects and they try to create new products and new technologies outside the company's traditional lines of business. Note that ambitious R&D projects are not only indispensable to improve one's position in the marketplace – they also tend to attract the most talented researchers.

   - *Communication with other departments*: productive R&D departments do not work in an ivory tower. They maintain close communication with other company departments, in particular with sales, marketing, manufacturing and development.

   - *Team dynamics*: the dynamics among team members of the R&D department is a crucial factor in overall R&D effectiveness.

## Innovation

Closely related to R&D is innovation. As explained by the late management guru Peter Drucker in *Innovation and Entrepreneurship*, innovative companies actively scout for new opportunities through constant examination of demographics, unexpected successes and failures, faulty market perceptions, changing market structures, new knowledge, and so on. As such, innovation is much broader than the common popular idea that it is related to new technologies (based on new knowledge). In fact, many profitable innovations have little to do with new technologies or *bright ideas*.[107]

Here are the typical characteristics of serious innovators:

1. They **focus (and bet) on opportunities** and **are not beholden to the past**. Too many companies try to defend the past because they like to stick with things they are familiar with, due to emotional commitment, out of fear for the short-term cost of abandoning the past, and so on. Innovators, on the other hand, are careful not to fixate on what used to work. Instead, they exploit and invest in new opportunities. They don't waste precious resources (e.g., capital and management time) on activities that are doomed.

---

[106] Koller, 2005.

[107] To better understand the dynamics and requirements of innovation, refer to the following excellent books on this topic: (Drucker, 1993), (Berkun, 2007), (Christensen, 2003), (Kelly, 2001), (Rogers, 2003), (Schrage, 2000), (Gladwell, 2002), (Peters, 2003), (Kim, 2005) and (Utterback, 1994).

2. They pursue **diversity in the workforce**. Effective innovators want to have mavericks, weirdoes, people with different nationalities and backgrounds, and so on in their ranks. They understand that similar people (e.g., people with a similar educational background) tend to think in the same way, often have the same preconceptions, and have a narrow view on the world. Diversity, on the other hand, stimulates innovative ideas. After all, excellent ideas often come from people who think out of the box, who don't have fixed habits in certain areas, or people who look at problems from a unique angle.

3. They constantly **put innovation in the spotlight** (e.g., by featuring and celebrating innovators and heroes). This instils the perception that innovation is important and that innovation can contribute to prestige inside the company. An example of how IBM tried to gain a reputation for innovators was its Fellows system. People in this programme were supposed to shake up the system over a period of five years.[108]

4. They create **special reward and incentive systems** for innovative projects and ventures. Acknowledging the fact that managing innovations is very different from running mature businesses, they use performance benchmarks for ventures that are different from those of typical business units. In the same vein, some excellent innovators build some slack into the organisation that leaves room for champions, mavericks and zealots to try things outside of the mainstream. For instance, McDonald's breakfast menu and GE's aircraft engines are the result of skunk works – as these projects are known – by small groups of zealots.[109]

5. Real innovators are **action-driven** and try to make many **demos and prototypes** as early as possible in the design process.

6. Innovators emphasise the importance of **communication** with virtually everyone (to get new ideas), especially with customers, suppliers, and between employees of different backgrounds and at different levels in the organisation. At one company, engineers tried to solve a problem of removing empty boxes from the production line by means of a sophisticated electronic detection system. First-line workers came up with a far better and cheaper solution: they proposed the use of a ventilator to blow the empty boxes from the conveyor belt.

7. They closely **monitor competitors** and learn from them. For instance, Sam Walton, the founder of Wal-Mart, spent much of his time checking out the competition. He visited other retailers to see what they were doing right in order to learn from them.

### Operations

Operational systems like accounting, information systems, transportation and distribution, and production and manufacturing frequently offer great opportunities to establish sustainable competitive advantages. The reason is that these systems can take years to develop and perfect. Hence, companies who do not pay sufficient attention to these systems may need many years to catch up with competitors.

---

[108] Gerstner, 2003.
[109] Peters, 2006.

In addition, effective and powerful systems ensure the smooth working of the company even when people at the top change. A case in point in the car industry is Toyota, which has built out its operations so brilliantly that even a change of management seems to have little impact on the company's performance.

When building out and maintaining their operations, excellent companies always seek out the best practices, and continually try to improve these systems. Two remarkable facts about top businesses are:

1. They are **wary of new technologies** and try to avoid fads. Contrary to the conviction among so many investors, very few successful companies mention technology as an important driver of their success. Although it is a fact that the greatest companies tend to be pioneers in the use of new and promising technologies, they always remain disciplined when it comes to the integration of technology in their operations. Whereas the average competitor may be quick to embrace the latest fad (for fear of being left behind), great companies are selective and careful in the adoption of new technologies. They only look for technologies that fit perfectly within their strategic focus (e.g., when they can create a new competitive advantage), and which will make their operations *significantly* more efficient. This also means that they have no problem in turning their back on new technologies for which they can see no substantial merit (for their business).

2. They **do things differently from their competitors**. Excellent companies question conventional wisdom. For instance, Southwest Airlines – one of the most successful airline companies in the world in one of the toughest industries around – beat the pants off competitors by avoiding conventional practices that were taken for granted by competitors. As opposed to its competitors, Southwest did not use the hub-and-spoke system. It avoided the more expensive, larger airports. It flew only one type of aircraft to simplify training, to have a better bargaining position versus aircraft makers, and to have cheaper inventory management. It pioneered the use of paperless tickets. It perfected the speed of the turns on the ground. And it applied open seating.[110]

## C.II.3.c Interconnections between the pillars of competitive strength

Each one of the pillars of competitive strength discussed in the previous section can constitute a competitive advantage in its own right. Effective operations, first-class HR management, an inspiring corporate culture, unique marketing, and above-average productivity in R&D and innovation all help a company to stand out among its competitors.

It is important to realise that these pillars do not operate independently of each other. Figure 11 shows the main functions inside a business and their interconnection. For instance, marketing people are dependent on the R&D department (under operations management) for the realisation of their ideas. HR must supply each function with appropriate talent, and should bring the best out of all employees. The way business units

---

[110] See (Freiberg, 1996) for the success story of Southwest.

and the workforce (including management structures) are organised will have an important impact on how operations and marketing are performed. And the corporate culture serves as an overlay to all functions that determines how people think, how they make decisions, how they do things and what priorities they set.

**Figure 11: Pillars of competitive strength and their interconnections**

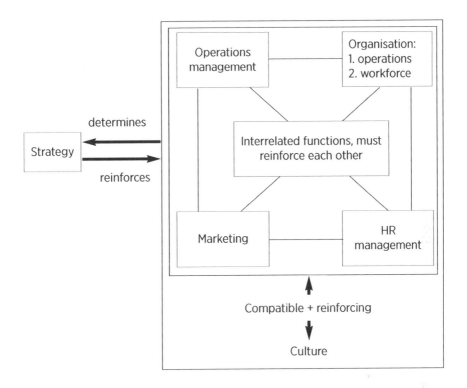

So, it is not only the quality of each separate pillar that matters, but also the degree to which these functions are geared toward each other to help realise the company's strategy and business plan. For instance, a company with R&D that is focused on the development of products that customers crave (as identified by the marketing people) will be at an advantage over a company where R&D people are out of touch with the marketplace.

Similarly, a company where the HR department manages to attract the brightest engineers and scientists is likely to have more productive R&D than companies that can't find qualified researchers. And a company with a corporate culture that reinforces the corporate structure and operations is more likely to have a smooth organisation with invigorated employees. For instance, when responsibility and autonomy are corporate values, it will be easier to establish an effective, simple and non-bureaucratic organisational structure with few management layers than it would be if the corporate culture stressed control of employees.

## C.II.3.d Sustainability of the competitive advantages

From the previous two sections, it should be clear that a company's competitive position is determined to a large extent by its position versus Porter's five forces, and by the way the company performs critical functions like HR, innovation, marketing, operations, etc.

Not only the current competitive advantages matter, though. At least as important is to assess whether the competitive position can be sustained (or better yet, improved), or whether there is a considerable risk that it will be corroded in the future. After all, long-term intelligent investors look for companies with strong and durable competitive advantages. Important factors in the evaluation of the sustainability of a company's competitive position are:

1. **Position in the industry**: the business with the most sustainable competitive position in an industry is a market leader with an impregnable franchise (e.g., thanks to a very strong brand name and/or a powerful distribution system).[111] The way to examine whether a company is a franchise is to carry out a five forces analysis, and to ask "Would the world really miss the company if it disappeared?"

2. The **whole set of pillars and their nature**: the pillars of competitive strength and the way they reinforce each other can be important sources of competitive advantages. However, the most sustainable competitive advantages derive from:

   - Elements that are *hard to emulate* for competitors: for instance, a unique culture and genuine HR management are typically much harder to copy and implement than certain types of operations (such as the automation of a manufacturing activity).

   - Elements that are *hard to detect* or that remain hidden for competitors: elements that many managers dismiss as unimportant (but which matter a lot, such as integrity), or a whole range of small advantages over all pillars are much less likely to be replicated by competitors as they are unlikely to be detected.

3. **Commitment to maintaining/improving the position**: great companies relentlessly try to improve their advantages versus competitors, and never become complacent.

## C.II.4 Control over destiny

Top investors avoid companies that do not have a firm grip on their own destiny. Examples of risk factors that may cause a loss of control over one's future are:

1. **Risk of government interference**: all else being equal, industries that are prone to government intervention and regulations (e.g., utilities, banking, mining) are less attractive than those that are less likely to be regulated. Even more dangerous is the risk of expropriations, which is not illusory in politically unstable developing countries.

---

[111] An additional advantage of franchises is that their power versus Porter's five forces enables them to raise prices more easily than competitors that have a weaker moat.

2. **Reliance on government support**: companies that are very dependent on government support (e.g., subsidies and tax breaks) may face an unviable business model when this support is reduced or eliminated. For instance, certain European renewable energy companies got in serious trouble when European governments decided to scale back the subsidies for renewable energy during the European sovereign crisis of 2010 to 2013.

3. **Strong dependence on R&D**: the outcome of R&D is inherently uncertain. So, companies whose future hinges too much on the output of research (e.g., biotech companies) can lose their position if that research is not sufficiently productive.

4. **Dependence on fashion**: companies whose success depends on getting the latest fashion right always run the risk of falling out of fashion.

5. **Dependence on critical decisions**: Warren Buffett avoids companies that regularly have to make critical bet-the-farm decisions to survive. An example is Boeing, which has to make decisions about the very expensive development of new airplanes with clock-like regularity.

6. **Too much leverage**: all else being equal, the more leveraged a company is the more sensitive it is to a loss of control when business conditions are unfavourable. It has already been explained that financial leverage can work against a company, but financial leverage is hardly the only form of leverage. Some companies have high operational leverage, i.e., they have high fixed costs and a relatively high break-even point in sales. Similar to financial leverage, corporations with high operational leverage have to deal with substantial recurrent expenses (fixed costs) that make them vulnerable when sales fluctuate around their breakeven point. A third type of leverage is industry/geographic leverage, i.e., the strong dependence of a company on a certain industry or region. Whatever the type of leverage, the potential problems are always the same: although leverage works for the company when business conditions are favourable, it can be fatal when they are not. For this reason, David Herro feels very uncomfortable investing in companies with more than one type of leverage.

7. **Heavy reliance on weather conditions**: it is often a good idea to give companies that are too dependent on weather conditions a miss. For example, one reason why Warren Buffett avoids companies in farm-related enterprises is that profits of such companies are too dependent on harvests.

8. **Heavy reliance on macro factors**: companies that depend too much on the following macro influences have limited control over their destinies:
   - The *business or capacity cycle*: cyclical companies (i.e., companies that are very sensitive to the business cycle or to capacity cycles in their industry) are seldom good long-term investments, unless they manage to grow bigger (e.g., by taking more market share) with rising peak profits over every cycle.
   - *Commodity prices*: companies with profits that are too dependent on commodity prices (e.g., mining companies, oil exploration businesses) may take a big hit when these prices drop.

- *Interest rates and currencies*: companies with a lot of floating rate debt, or companies with a currency mismatch between assets and liabilities, are bound to suffer when interest rates or currencies move against them.

- *Inflation*: some firms may suffer from shrinking profit margins (or even failure) if inflation gets out of hand. Primary victims of out-of-control inflation are companies with weak competitive positions (i.e., firms that cannot raise their prices easily), or companies with long-term, non-indexed service contracts. Examples of companies that can cope well with inflation are real estate companies (real estate tends to rise along with inflation), advertising agencies, shopping centres (leases are often linked to inflation), and companies with strong brand names like Coke (as they can easily raise prices to offset inflation).

## C.II.5 Growth

As a rule of thumb, one should avoid companies whose sales are in decline. Even at prices that appear cheap, such businesses often turn out to be so-called *value traps*. No-growth or slow-growth companies can be interesting value plays over the medium term, but juicy long-term returns are unlikely with such companies. Therefore, long-term investors are more interested in companies with growth prospects that can support the stock price for a (very) long time.

Indeed, since earnings are one of the two main drivers of a company's stock price over the long term (the second being multiple expansion/compression), long-term investments should hold the promise of sustained and decent earnings growth. Since earnings can only grow through revenue growth and margin expansion, investors must evaluate profitability as well as revenue growth. After all, when there is little room for further margin expansion, earnings growth will be capped by revenue growth.

This section covers several investment considerations with respect to growth. First of all, investors have to decide in which growth stage they want to invest, keeping in mind the risk-reward trade-offs of different growth stages. Second, to better understand the future, one has to examine the past. A third issue is whether the company manages its growth well. Finally, investors have to be aware of the risk of growth saturation.

### C.II.5.a Growth stage

When people look for companies with good growth prospects they tend to search for promising businesses in new, appealing industries (e.g., new technologies). Or they invest in pioneering companies that may turn into the next big thing. This approach is terribly flawed for two reasons. First, many pioneers in new industries fail due to fierce competition. For instance, the number of internet companies of the late 1990s that are still in existence is a very small minority.

Second, there is no assurance that high sales growth in an industry will lead to high profit growth. Look no further than the very poor value created by car and airplane companies over the past 60 years. The main problem of new growth industries – especially when they are hot and popular – is that they actually may suffer from subpar profitability (and below-average profit growth) when numerous companies compete for leadership.

As mentioned in Chapter B, top investors seldom put their money in pioneering companies or in embryonic industries. They admit that small companies in new industries can be exceptional investments, but they do not believe that the tiny chance for an excellent return outweighs the inherent risks of such investments.[112]

They also focus on earnings and cash flow growth rather than sales growth. Serious entrepreneurial growth investors like Peter Lynch prefer companies in their *fast-growth stage* (see Chapter F) with a track record, a scalable business model, and a strong balance sheet. More conservative top stock pickers, on the other hand, prefer established companies with *strong competitive positions* and plenty of room to expand within their industry.

## C.II.5.b Historic growth evaluation

To get some clues about the growth potential of a business, it is recommended to examine the past. Top investors look at historical earnings and revenue growth over several years (or even decades), including at least one full business cycle, and then evaluate:

1. **The average historical growth rate**: although it is dangerous to extrapolate historical growth rates, past growth can help one to understand a company's future potential. Unless there are clear catalysts to expect much higher growth in the future than in the past or unless there are reasons to expect that growth will level off significantly in future years, the most attractive businesses have grown in sales and earnings at rates above the market's (say, more than 7% a year) and the average for their industry. Some top investors like John Neff avoid companies that have grown too fast in the past (e.g., growth rates > 20%) for fear that such rates are not sustainable, and because stocks of such companies tend to be hot. Other top investors like John Templeton deliberately seek out companies with exceptional growth rates (e.g., earnings growth > 20% a year), but only invest when the price seems reasonable.

2. **Consistency and solidity**: ideally, revenues and profits should have grown consistently over the past few years. One certainly has to examine how sales and profits held up during a business downturn (recession) to get an idea about the cyclicality of the business.

3. **Quality of historic growth**: revenue growth of the highest quality is growth through the sale of more (physical) units, or through price increases. The value of revenue growth through acquisitions, on the other hand, should be discounted.

4. **Revenue versus profit growth**: it stands to reason that intelligent investors are only interested in profitable growth. Growth in sales only benefits shareholders when it is coupled with sufficiently high returns on investment. Smart investors eschew businesses that grow for the sake of growth and they see revenue growth at the expense of earnings growth as a clear sign of weak management.

---

[112] Keep in mind that venture capital investors are in the business of taking these chances. But one has to realise that they are in a much better position to find promising businesses than the average common equity investor (e.g., due to their access to non-public equity).

## C.II.5.c Growth management

The growth path of small businesses (with market caps of smaller than, say, $1 billion) is littered with pitfalls and challenges that can bring the company down if they are not handled and anticipated correctly. For this reason, investors in small and fast-growing companies have to carefully track developments.[113] Here a number of common mistakes in growth management are given:

1. **Clinging on to power and control by the founders**: in many small enterprises, the founders consider the company as their child, and therefore refuse to give up control. They are reluctant to delegate, and they surround themselves with faithful aides. This can be a very costly mistake because entrepreneurs do not typically have the required management expertise and skills to guide the company through a fast growth path. Smart founders put the good of the company first. They are willing to step aside when there is a need for a more professional management team.

2. **Not introducing appropriate processes and systems (on time)**: founders of small enterprises can be slow to introduce processes and systems. They fear that these will introduce bureaucracy that may hamper the entrepreneurial spirit. Or because they were successful without them they believe that they can continue without them. Unfortunately, as companies grow bigger they have to start planning. They must create performance management systems. They need a minimal amount of bureaucracy. And they must build the infrastructure that a big company needs well before it is used at full capacity.

   Lacking processes and systems, the whole company can come down due to fire fighting (permanent crises that are never resolved), inertia (big companies are not as nimble as small ones), and the high dependence on certain individuals. Although it is true that too many processes and systems can smother the entrepreneurial spirit inside a company, smart managers know how to balance the two against each other. Here are some tip-offs that a company is struggling with processes and systems:

   - The company *doesn't seem to get resources in line with the expanding growth*, is unable to handle its payables and inventories, can't make the product fast enough, and experiences an insatiable need for more space, equipment, people, etc. This can be caused by poor resource management and a lack of planning (e.g., for infrastructure and hiring).

   - The company suffers a *sudden loss in profitability that it can't explain*, and it has a *poor understanding of how the company is doing*. A potential culprit for this is the poor development of operational systems, especially in the area of planning and accounting.

   - *Constant fire-fighting* (recurrent crises), overworked and insecure employees – which can lead to morale problems, high absenteeism, and high turnover. These are often caused by a lack of planning and systems.

---

[113] For an excellent and thorough discussion of common growth issues, refer to (Flamholtz, 2007).

3. **Poor HR practices**: common mistakes in the human resource management of small growth businesses are:

- *Skimping on hiring*: successful small growth businesses look for experienced professionals with the right managerial, operational, accounting and legal skills before they are needed. Although such professionals are expensive, hiring these people is necessary to help the company avoid and/or anticipate the many pitfalls and growing pains that befall the typical growth company during its fast-growth stage.

- *No management training*: as companies grow bigger, they must provide in-house or out-of-house management training programmes. Symptoms that the management development programmes are inadequate are: too many and/or ineffective meetings, superiors that focus too much on doing work than on the management of people, no follow-up on plans, and the feeling that managers have to do things themselves if they want to get them done.

- *Vague organisational structure*: many small companies don't think the organisational structure (e.g., management hierarchy, responsibilities, etc.) through, and end up with a structure that consists of too many management layers where people have unclear responsibilities. This can cause frustration, constant bickering about responsibilities, duplication of work (due to poor communication), a slow decision process, and tasks that are left undone.

- *Little performance management*: when the work of people is not evaluated, poor performers stay in the business and good performers are not rewarded correctly (and may leave the company out of frustration). A common phenomenon caused by too little performance management is that the company grows in sales but not in profits.

## C.II.5.d Realistic growth projections

When making sales and earnings projections, it is convenient to expect more of the same. However, naïve extrapolation of historical trends is seldom correct. First of all, reversion to the mean is a powerful force that pulls all companies (over the long term) in the direction of the industry's average growth trend. According to research performed by Jeremy Grantham, financial series tend to mean revert over periods of about seven years.[114]

Second, and even more importantly, as so many investors tend to extrapolate historical growth, it is reasonable to expect that this type of growth is discounted in stock prices. For these reasons, intelligent investors look at the future through a more realistic lens. They try to anticipate disruptions to exceptionally strong growth, or they try to identify catalysts that will propel subpar growth higher.

Basically, growth projections should be based on the overall quantitative and qualitative evaluation of the business as described in previous sections. Nevertheless, hereunder I would like to point attention to two factors that are important in the estimation of future earnings and sales: analyst expectations and the problem of growth saturation.

---

[114] Heins, 2013.

## 1. Use of analyst expectations

One source of information for future growth is analyst expectations. Although such expectations have to be taken with a grain of salt they can be valuable when used in the right way.[115] For instance, one can compare the analyst consensus with one's personal view to identify companies where analysts (and the market, which is typically a reflection of the analyst's expectations) underestimate future growth. David Dreman also uses analyst expectations in another way; since analysts have an optimistic bias, he avoids companies with earnings that analysts expect to be down, because earnings of these businesses often fall even faster than analysts anticipated.

## 2. The issue of growth saturation

For every high-growth company there is a time when the company's growth tops off and the business matures (see Figure 12). A dangerous trap for growth investors is to hold a market darling with a sky-high valuation when growth begins to taper off permanently. Indeed, such investments usually take a dive when the market recognises that the stellar growth rates of the past are history.

**Figure 12: Transition to maturity**

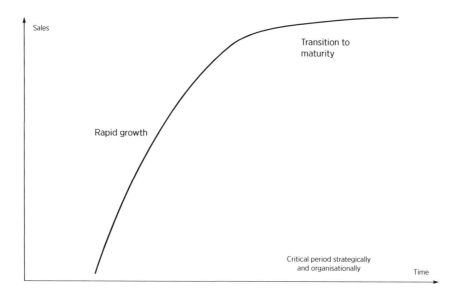

In addition, as if overvaluation were not enough, the stock price can be further depressed due to a number of other problems that maturing companies typically encounter, such as:[116]

---

[115] Dreman, 1998.
[116] Porter, 1980.

1. sloppy strategies, which can be masked by high growth, may get exposed when growth drops,

2. there is a danger of overcapacity if the company did not anticipate the decelerating sales growth,

3. as maturing companies have been around for some time, their customer base may have become more sophisticated and experienced such that customers may turn into tough bargainers, and

4. ambitious employees and top performers may lose their motivation and leave the company as the prospects of promotion shrink.

To anticipate growth saturation, investors must examine the financial statements for signs that growth is levelling off. Even better is to look for indirect clues, such as a peak in the popularity of a product. Another indication is the problem of pipeline fill. In this case, the distribution channel (the pipeline) is full (e.g., every store in the country has the product), and the growth rate drops to the rate of consumer consumption.

Useful tip-offs that growth is saturating and that management is desperate to extend the superior growth path are talk of international expansion (especially to emerging countries), and expansion in unrelated lines of business.

## C.II.6 Red flags

Finally, after a thorough examination of the industry, the company's business model, its competitive position, control over destiny, and growth issues, one has to check whether the company is exposed to significant risks. Although risk factors can be an opportunity for bargain hunters if the market overreacts to them, it is best to steer clear of companies with risks that can be fatal and/or that are not fully appreciated by the market. A separate evaluation of the risk factors must always be part of an intelligent investment approach. Here is what investors should look for to detect risks:

1. **Risks buried in the footnotes**: it is important to screen the footnotes of the financial statements for risks such as lawsuits, or liabilities for environmental or regulatory infringements.

2. **Complexity of the business**: it was mentioned above that top investors embrace simple business models. Their love for simplicity also goes beyond the business model and extends to the business and industry itself. They shun complex industries. For instance, Francisco García Paramés, nicknamed the 'Spanish Warren Buffett', avoids banks and insurance companies as such companies are, in his opinion, black boxes. On the other hand, top investors are fond of simpleminded companies. Peter Lynch says in *Beating the Street* that he dreams of companies that can be run by "any idiot." The rationale is that investing in complex businesses usually implies much higher risk because: complex businesses need geniuses at the top (if not, expect a lot of management mistakes); investors will find it hard and

time-consuming to keep track of what happens at the company; future cash flows are hard to predict (and so intrinsic value is inherently uncertain); and complex businesses may be too dependent on individual top executives.

3. **Customer risk**: customers can pose a serious threat in two cases:

   - *Overreliance on a handful of customers*: Peter Lynch avoids companies with sales that are too concentrated on one or very few customers. A first problem of customer concentration is that it can create high bargaining power with the customers. A second problem is that high reliance on any particular customer can lead to serious loss of business if that customer gets in trouble or stops doing business with the firm.

   - *Little selectivity in the choice of customers*: if a company does (too much) business with customers of questionable creditworthiness or poor integrity, it substantially increases the risk that it will not get paid on its bills.

4. **Suspicious company events**: there are a number of events that are precursors to future trouble:

   - *Insider sales*: one should be especially wary of massive sales by top executives – in particular when these sales are of the irregular kind (e.g., sales before the end of a lock-up period).

   - *Resignation of key people*: the resignation of a key person (often announced as 'resignation for personal reasons') is a definite red flag.

   - *Auditor turnover*: a change in auditors is often caused by disagreements about the financial statements between the auditors and management. As such it is one of the strongest signs that management is trying to manipulate its financial statements.

   - *Late filings*: given the fact that CFOs and accounting departments know very well the deadline for the filing of financial statements, a late filing suggests that management is trying to hide something.

---

> *"You should invest in a business that even a fool can run, because some day a fool will."*
>
> **Warren Buffett (Bolton, 2009)**

---

## C.III Management evaluation

There's little doubt that corporations can benefit enormously from great management. One must realise at the same time that the role of managers in a company's success or failure is often overstated. In reality, the impact of any single individual – be it a CEO or other executive – on a corporation is limited. History has given many examples of managers with exceptional track records who couldn't turn problematic businesses around.

Another issue is that it is not always easy to determine the contribution of a manager in a company's success. In fact, many managers that receive accolades in the media don't deserve their reputation. Some of them are one-hit wonders that by accident headed the right company at the right time. Others owed their success more to the people around them than to their own skills.

> *"When a management with a reputation for brilliance tackles a business with a reputation for poor fundamental economics, it is the reputation of the business that remains intact."*
>
> **Warren Buffett, 1980 letter to the shareholders of Berkshire Hathaway**

Hence, although top stock pickers believe that excellent managers can create tremendous value for corporations with good economics, they are critical of the ability of such managers to turn lousy businesses with bad inherent economics into superstars. For this reason, their first concern is always with the business. Only after they have found a company with a strong franchise and a reasonable valuation, will they take a look into management.

They may not be too demanding of management in businesses with extraordinary franchises, but they are totally intolerant of corporations with bad leadership – irrespective of the business. Investors shouldn't expect any good from stocks (even if they are bargain-priced) with bad leaders that only care about themselves and which disdain common shareholders. In fact, as pointed out by Warren Buffett in his letter to shareholders of 1979, corporate leaders with poor character, style or vision are likely to attract a shareholder constituency of poor quality, which can harm the interests of serious investors.

If one studies literature on the best practices of managers it is striking to find that prominent management gurus and successful managers praise the very same management characteristics that the greatest investors look for.[117] Hereunder the major elements that should be examined in a due diligence process are summarised, namely the personality of the managers, their skills and experience, their focus, their allegiance to the company, and the passion and energy with which they perform their duty.

## C.III.1 Personality

The personality of top executives is extremely important because it determines how they think, how they deal with challenges and problems, what they find important, and what they are likely to pursue in their corporate actions. Essential personality traits that top investors look for in senior management are integrity, modesty (combined with ambition), non-complacency and independence.

---

[117] See (Kouzes, 2007), (Drucker, 2006), (Pfeffer, 2000), (Collins, 2001), (Buckingham, 1999), (Pfeffer, 2006), (Pfeffer, 2007), (Taylor, 2006), (Peters, 1994) and books written by or interviews given by some very successful CEOs (e.g., (George, 2003), (Branson, 1998), (Welch, 2005), (Gerstner, 2003), (Schultz, 1997) and (Walton, 1992). For an excellent book on what Warren Buffett looks for in management, see (Miles, 2002).

## C.III.1.a Integrity

Integrity means being honest, holding your promises, playing by the rules, and holding oneself to high ethical standards. For Warren Buffett, Anthony Bolton and Julian Robertson, integrity tops the list of personality traits they look for in management. Even an almost purely quantitatively-driven investment legend like Walter Schloss came to realise the importance of management integrity, after some bad experiences with managers of questionable reputation. It is worthwhile to remember that many companies trading at low multiples and headed by unreliable managers are value traps.

> *"In evaluating people you look for three qualities: integrity, intelligence and energy. If you don't have the first, the other two will kill you."*
>
> **Warren Buffett, 2001 letter to the shareholders of Berkshire Hathaway**

> *"Integrity is just a ticket to the game. If you don't have it in your bones, you shouldn't be allowed on the field."*
>
> **Jack Welch (Welch, 2005)**

Investors who put their money in companies that are managed by honest people don't need to worry that management will try to take advantage of them and they should not fear that management will try to hide important news. Investors who insist on management integrity understand that integrity builds trust and confidence down to the lowest levels of the corporation and among all of the company's stakeholders. Smart investors look for the following indications of integrity in management communications, the annual report, interviews, feedback from employees, and the like:

1. **Straight talk**: honest leaders are forthright and open. They speak the truth and openly discuss how the business is faring – under good and difficult circumstances equally. They are not scared to discuss important challenges and problems. They don't clam up when things go wrong and they don't try to cover up bad news. Red flags are inconsistencies between the letter to shareholders and other parts of the annual report, or significant issues that are hidden in the footnotes and that are not discussed elsewhere in the annual report.

2. **Clear and unbiased financial statements**: honest managers help investors to understand the business and therefore present the company's financials in a way that is easy to read and easy to understand. They use conservative accounting, they do not manipulate the numbers and they don't use misleading financial measures in their communications to shareholders. Red flags are stress on

irrelevant information (e.g., pro forma results, or adjusted earnings that are of questionable value), the constant recurrence of one-time losses, earnings restatements, suspiciously stable earnings, and the like.

3. **Even-handed view on the future**: honest managers are not overly optimistic and upbeat about future prospects. They remain cautious because they know that the future is always uncertain.

4. **Responsibility**: honourable leaders don't look for excuses or scapegoats when things go wrong. They take responsibility for failures and own up to mistakes. Taking the blame is reassuring because it increases the probability that management will deal with the problems, and do things better next time. In addition, great leaders give credit where credit is due. They don't score off their own people but shower those who deserve it with praise.

5. **Consistency**: managers that value integrity relentlessly remove everyone who lacks integrity. They don't play favourites and they do not tolerate that the rules are broken. Major red flags are conflicts of interest and related-party transactions such as leases to family members, loans to executives and family members on very beneficial terms for the lenders, etc.

## C.III.1.b Modesty, but ambition

Many of the greatest leaders are humble. They don't let their ego go to their head. They don't brag about their achievements and always point to the contributions of so many others in their organisation. This type of mature leadership inspires trust, respect and credibility. But let there be no mistake: in spite of their modesty, great leaders are ambitious and decisive. Put differently, excellent leaders pursue excellence but let the numbers speak for themselves. Here are some indications that management is humble:

1. Modest leaders **acknowledge their own limitations** and know that they don't have all the answers:

   - They *admit mistakes*. Arrogant leaders, by contrast, stick to their decisions at all cost and try to justify them even when all the evidence says that they are wrong. They therefore are less likely to rectify errors and they are more likely to cling to the past.

   - They are *curious and constantly try to learn new things*. Managers that lack modesty, on the other hand, believe that they already know everything they need to know.

   - They *listen to others* (employees, customers, etc.) and embrace healthy dissent and variant opinions. Managers that lack modesty talk a lot and ignore (or consistently fight) the opinions and ideas of others.

   - They *ask for feedback, input and counterarguments* when they have to take a decision. Arrogant managers, by contrast, take difficult decisions with incomplete data and knowledge in less than a trice.

- Whereas managers who think they know better surround themselves with yes-men, humble managers try to compensate their own weaknesses by *hiring the best people they can find* – even if these people are outspoken, smarter, or more experienced than they are.

2. Modest managers **keep their egos in check**: they subordinate their ego to the well-being of their company:

   - They are *willing to change their mind*. This has to be contrasted with arrogant managers who can't accept being wrong, and who stubbornly stick to their own opinion in spite of strong counterevidence.

   - In their communications to shareholders they invariably *use the word "we"* and seldom say "I."

   - They want to *avoid a management cult*: modest leaders shun the media and business press. They don't litter their annual reports with pictures of themselves and they don't feel comfortable when they receive a 'manager of the year' award.

   - They *don't try to put their stamp on the company*: humble managers are not interested in leaving a legacy. For instance, modest managers are not intent on empire building if this is not in the interest of the company. While ego-driven managers stress the connection between the company and themselves in every possible way, modest managers only want to build an enduring company that can keep on prospering when they are no longer on board.

   - They treat everyone in the organisation with *respect and consideration*, irrespective of his or her rank. The former CEO of Southwest Airlines, Herb Kelleher, is an excellent example. He showed the same amount of genuine interest and empathy when he talked to hotel valets, cleaning ladies, flight attendants, members of his board of directors, or judges of the Supreme Court.[118]

3. Managers that are modest are **not promotional**. They don't hype their company. They don't make unrealistic forecasts and promises. They rather make no forecasts at all; they let the results speak for themselves.

4. Humble managers **won't accept more than their fair share of financial compensation**. Here are some of the clearest signs that a manager recognises that performance is the result of a collective effort:

   - Great leaders *do not accept exorbitant compensations* that put the salaries of other employees and executives to shame.[119] According to Philip Fisher, a definite red flag is waving when the salary of the number-one man is much larger than that of the next two or three. Also the difference between the highest and lowest paid employees is an informative metric, because it appears to be negatively correlated with financial performance.[120]

---

[118] Freiberg, 1996.

[119] Note that an extravagant lifestyle is often closely related to an egotistical and ego-driven leadership.

[120] Pfeffer, 2006.

- Great managers *avoid executive perks*, such as special parking lots, apartments, private jets, executive lounges and restaurants, etc. The absence (or limited use) of executive perks sends the message that the contributions of *all* employees are equally appreciated.

## C.III.1.c Non-complacency

Success breeds complacency because most people believe that a winning formula should not be changed. However, if management in a competitive world does not rock the boat, others are likely to do it in its place. Excellent managers never become complacent. They don't take a dominant market position for granted. They relentlessly question the status quo. They look for the obsolescence of winning formulas. And they are willing to abandon the past – regardless of emotional bonds and sunk costs.

Chuck Huggins, CEO of the Warren Buffett-owned See's Candies, is an example of someone who understood the need for non-complacency very well when he said: "We'll still poke at everything we do, because we believe there is no such thing as perfection and we believe we can always do better."[121]

> *"There should be present the greatest possible number of people with the ingenuity and determination not to leave things just at their present, possibly quite satisfactory, state but to build significant further improvements upon them. Management must recognise and be attuned to the fact that the world in which they are operating is changing at an ever increasing rate."*
>
> **Philip Fisher (Fisher, 1996)**

## C.III.1.d Independence

People feel comfortable when they follow the crowd. Hence, it is common for business leaders to do what their competitors are doing. Warren Buffett calls the urge to blindly follow and imitate industry peers – no matter how silly or irrational that behaviour may be – "the institutional imperative."

Examples of the institutional imperative are acquisition sprees at ridiculous valuations in certain industries, and rising leverage throughout a sector. Great leaders don't fall for the institutional imperative. They are independent thinkers. They are sceptical of the latest management fads, they won't follow competitors when their behaviour doesn't make sense and they realise that conventional actions usually lead to conventional (i.e., average) results.

## C.III.2 Experience and skills

Personality is just the start of management evaluation. Logically, excellent managers also have the capacity to execute. To evaluate this management aspect top stock pickers examine management's background and experience (education, business savvy, etc.), the way management allocates capital, and its strategic insights.

---

[121] Miles, 2002.

## C.III.2.a Experience and track record

Top investors prefer management that has proven that it can deliver. As a rule, they like managers that have built successful track records in lines of business that are similar to those of the company they head now. They systematically avoid companies managed by people with spotty track records (e.g., managers that have wrecked a previous company).

John Templeton and Frederick Kobrick point out that one should examine how management handled past failures and difficult times, at the current company or a previous one. Warren Buffett suggests reviewing annual reports from a few years back, paying special attention to what management said then about strategies for the future, and how this has panned out or changed.

## C.III.2.b Capital allocation

Capital allocation is the management skill to allocate capital to functions and projects that maximise shareholder value over the long term. In the business world excellent capital allocators are scarce. A first problem is that many top executives got promoted to the highest management ranks thanks to their operational excellence. Many of them do not have a financial background, and few have received training in capital allocation. Second, the actions of managers are driven by a lot of factors that can be both rational (e.g., value creation) and irrational (e.g., keep pouring money into an unprofitable prestige project).

Since excellent capital allocation is so important for shareholders, intelligent investors closely examine management's capital allocation skills. Top investors provide the following guidelines to determine whether management uses its capital well or not:

1.  Good capital allocators are very **cost-conscious**. They usually run a tight ship and hawkishly monitor all expenses. They abhor excesses, extravagance, frills, corporate overhead (i.e., headquarter expenses), and overstaffing.[122] On the other hand, they won't save on things that really make a difference, such as salaries, hiring experienced (and expensive) people, advertising, important technologies, R&D, and so on. To evaluate the cost consciousness of management, it is imperative to look at management's track record and ignore good intentions.

> *"The manager of an already high-cost operation frequently is uncommonly resourceful in finding new ways to add to overhead, while the manager of a tightly-run operation usually continues to find additional methods to curtail costs, even when his costs are already well below those of his competitors."*
>
> **Warren Buffett, 1978 letter to the shareholders of Berkshire Hathaway**

---

[122] Peter Lynch says: "The extravagance of a company's corporate office is directly proportional to management's reluctance to reward shareholders." (Lynch, 1993)

2. Good capital allocators **focus their resources** (time, financial resources, human resources) on opportunities, not on problems.

3. The best capital allocators **think long term**. They take a short-term pain if this is in the interest of its loyal long-term shareholders and they won't give in to the short-term pressure of impatient and disloyal traders or speculators. For instance, smart managers do not cut R&D expenses in a business downturn to prop up their current earnings, as they know that current R&D is pivotal to the company's success some years hence.

4. Excellent capital allocators **are cautious with leverage**. They avoid excessive debt because they know that it can backfire and they certainly don't buy the popular belief that debt is good as it enforces discipline.

> *"Huge debt, we were told, would cause operating managers to focus their efforts as never before, much as a dagger mounted on the steering wheel of a car would be expected to make its driver proceed with intensified care. But another certain consequence would be a deadly – and unnecessary – accident if the car hit even the tiniest pothole or sliver of ice. The roads of business are riddled with potholes; a plan that requires dodging them all is a plan for disaster."*
>
> **Warren Buffett, 1990 letter to the shareholders of Berkshire Hathaway**

5. Great capital allocators are **wary of acquisitions** because they know that most acquisitions do not create value. All too frequently acquirers overpay, they overestimate the positive synergies (or underestimate the negatives) of a merger, and they have to deal with unexpected and complex problems during the integration process. If the acquirer also has a poor balance sheet (e.g., caused by the use of debt to take over the acquisition target), operating risk from the integration of the newly acquired company will compound the company's financial risk. This is not to say that acquisitions never make sense. Cisco, for instance, was a very successful serial acquirer.[123] To separate the wheat from the chaff, one should keep in mind that smart acquirers:

- Buy companies at *fair to cheap prices*: they only buy a company when they receive at least as much value as they have to yield. For this reason, they often prefer the acquisition of private companies (where pricing tends to be less efficient). They have no problem dropping out when an acquisition attempt escalates into a bidding war with irrational bidders.

- Buy businesses for *strategic reasons*: excellent acquirers do not acquire for the sake of excitement or to build an empire that can boost their ego and their pay. They seldom buy corporations in unrelated businesses (i.e., businesses about which they have little expertise). They look for acquisition targets that

---

[123] Pfeffer, 2006.

can strengthen their position in certain markets or that can help them to quickly acquire specialised skills and expertise in their own field of business.[124] Cisco added still another element. It wanted the acquisition targets to be geographically proximate because it reasoned that this would facilitate collaboration and the integration process.

- Stay *realistic about synergies*: they are sceptical of positive synergies (cost synergies are the most reliable), and realise that acquisitions often create negative synergies such as customer alienation, employee turnover and morale problems. They actually manage the integration process in a way that maximises the positive synergies and minimises the negatives. When Cisco acquired businesses, for instance, it always planned and implemented the integration process quickly to keep the key people (i.e., the brains) on board.

- They look for a *cultural match*, because they know that many acquisitions fail due a misfit between the corporate culture of the acquiring firm and that of the acquired. When Cisco acquired companies, for instance, it was only interested in deals with the requisite cultural fit.

- They prefer the acquisition of *companies that are small compared to their own size*, because this poses less integration problems and risks. Cisco, for instance, was not interested in mergers with companies of its own size because it feared that this would cause struggles about control over the combined entity.

> "When given a choice of working hard to fix a base business or, instead, completing a glamorous acquisition and crowing about its promise on the financial TV stations, too many executives opt for the latter. A good portion of IBM's success was due to all of the deals it didn't do."
>
> **Lou Gerstner (Gerstner, 2003)**

6. Rational capital allocators **shrink their capital base if this is in the interest of shareholders**. Unlike so many corporate leaders who are primarily concerned with expanding their empire, the best capital allocators repurchase shares and shed business units (through spin-offs or sales) when this is the best way to create value. They also increase dividends when they can see no better use for their cash.

7. Conversely, excellent capital allocators **keep earnings inside the firm if they can earn a high return on these earnings**. This means that:

   - Smart managers do not repurchase their company's shares when they are not attractively priced. Share repurchases only benefit shareholders if the shares are bought below their intrinsic value. Managers who repurchase shares to prop up the stock price irrespective of their value are actually squandering valuable shareholder resources.

---

[124] See, for example (Hamel, 1996) and (Ries, 1996).

- Good capital allocators do not consider dividends as some kind of remuneration to shareholders. Higher dividends do not always benefit shareholders. As long as the company can earn a sufficiently high return on its retained earnings shareholders will be better off if they are not given any dividend at all. This is the reason, for instance, that Warren Buffett's Berkshire Hathaway never paid out a dividend. Of course, some companies have a reputation of being steady dividend payers, and therefore have many loyal shareholders that count on regular distributions from the firm. In that case, maintaining and increasing dividend streams makes perfect sense.

8. Thanks to the intelligent management of their capital, excellent capital allocators have fewer financial problems than their less efficient peers. By keeping costs down, by avoiding unnecessary risks (e.g., through low leverage and caution with acquisitions), and by thinking long term, intelligent capital allocators have to resort much less to restructuring initiatives than their peers.

   In addition, they usually **handle financial problems very differently** from their competitors. When they encounter difficult times, they will try to cut away the fat, not the muscle. This means they don't look to the obvious and easy roads (e.g., slashing HR expenses through layoffs, lower salaries, etc.) because this undermines employee loyalty and commitment at the very moment the workforce's contribution is most needed. They also rarely cut back on product quality and service, because this leads to a death spiral where customers leave and more cuts are necessary. Excellent capital allocators are creative and look for other places where they can save money. They would, for instance, eliminate perks, introduce the habit to fly economy, and so on. Or they would simply wait out the hard times. They definitely tread with great caution and restraint in trying to make savings that affect the workforce and product/service quality.

## C.III.2.c Strategic thinking

Strategy explains how the company will maintain and strengthen its position in the marketplace. Management and execution of the strategy are core responsibilities of top management because people at the top are the only ones who can see the business in its entirety, who know the company's strengths and weaknesses, and who are supposed to understand the competitive landscape in its various parts. Managers with an excellent vision pursue a unique strategy that is different from that of their competitors. In this way, they add another dimension to their competitive moat.[125] In addition, they pursue a strategy that builds on their own core competencies and strengths.

---

[125] A company that has exactly the same business model and strategy as one or more of its competitors can only beat those competitors through operational effectiveness. Betting on one's own operational superiority (and the operational inferiority of competitors) is arrogant in a business world where all companies have access to the same tools, the same information, similar equipment, etc. So, although all great managers pursue operational superiority, they also try to have a strategy that is different from that of their competitors.

This also implies that great strategic thinkers don't like to stray outside their area of competence, that is they avoid branching out into unrelated businesses. Numerous companies have made the mistake of investing in companies that were totally different from (and less profitable than) their core business.

Gillette once purchased a digital watches manufacturer and had to write the business off shortly thereafter. Even a stalwart like Coca-Cola made the mistake of getting involved in businesses that had nothing to do with soft drinks. The problems of diversification (which, Peter Lynch refers to as "diworseification") are manifold. Here are some major issues:

1. It **dilutes resources** because management time and financial resources are spent on non-core businesses, leaving fewer resources available for the core business. For instance, Coca-Cola fell on hard times when it was getting into businesses that were unrelated to its core business (i.e., selling syrup). When the new star manager Goizueta took control of Coca-Cola, he realised that the company was wasting resources on businesses that were far less profitable than its core business. As a result, he divested these businesses and reallocated the company's resources on the production and sale of syrup.

2. Diversification can **alienate customers**. When PepsiCo owned Pizza Hut, competing pizza restaurants were unlikely to serve Pepsi's soft drinks. When GM owned the car rental business National, it was hard for GM to sell cars to competitors of National, such as Hertz, Avis and Alamo.[126]

3. It can **dilute the company's image**: diversification can create confusion when people can no longer see what the company stands for.

4. It means entering a business where **competitors are likely to have more knowledge and expertise**. Several years ago the Belgian real estate company Atenor tried private equity as a side activity. It found out the hard way that private equity is a business for pros and that it couldn't get the most profitable deals. Some years later, the company decided to abandon its private equity activities and it returned to its core business.

---

*"Lack of focus is the most common cause of corporate mediocrity. Many companies, when the going gets tough in their base business, decide to try their luck in new industries. Too many executives don't want to fight the tough battles of resurrecting, resuscitating, and strengthening their base business – or they simply give up on their base business too soon."*

**Lou Gerstner (Gerstner, 2003)**

---

[126] Ries, 1996.

## C.III.3 Value promoters

A third important management function is the promotion and defence of a company's values. Value management is extremely important for executives, not only because top managers have the power to impose values on their subordinates (i.e., all employees), but also because top managers have a strong signal function.

As part of their value-promoting attitude, excellent managers take culture management very seriously. They breathe the company's values and norms, and are exemplary role models. They strictly enforce the company's values and norms on employees. They also constantly monitor the strength of the culture throughout the organisation to prevent its degeneration. And they pursue a culture that is appropriate to the company's goals and growth stage.

Furthermore, great managers stimulate innovation. They pursue a culture where people try things out. They motivate their employees to bank on opportunities, and to question current practices and activities. They are tolerant of weird (creative) people, and support champions who try to achieve things by colouring outside the lines. They also create the necessary organisational structures (e.g., autonomy) and incentives (e.g., budgets, other benchmarks) to give new ventures all the chances of success.

Finally, excellent managers communicate relentlessly and unambiguously about their values, vision, strategy, etc. They also talk a lot with employees at all levels of the company and they walk the floors. They are accessible (e.g., they have an open-door policy), and listen to problems and suggestions of everyone inside the firm. For instance, the late founder of Wal-Mart, Sam Walton, returned phone calls personally – there was no secretary that filtered his calls.

## C.III.4 Ownership and allegiance to stakeholders

Intelligent investors want managers that feel morally responsible for the well-being of the company and its stakeholders. If managers have a highly developed sense of ownership for the business, shareholders can rest assured that they will work hard to create value and build an enduring organisation. Top investors look for the following indications of management's commitment to the corporation:

1. Excellent managers **make their organisation self-sustaining**: unlike star managers who try to make their organisation overly dependent on themselves (so that everyone identifies the company with that manager), great managers want to create a company that can prosper in their absence. They launch management education programmes (if these are lacking), maximise the self-reliance of business units and operations, and thoroughly groom the people that will take their place when they leave – many years before they really leave.

2. **High insider holdings**: the amount invested in the company's stock as a share of management's total personal wealth or compared to his or her annual compensation tells a lot about its personal involvement with the company's well-

being. High insider holdings align management's interests with those of the shareholders. They signal management's faith in the business. They keep managers focused on the creation of shareholder value. And they make sure that management thinks twice before it takes a gamble or an unjustified risk.

3. **Long tenures**: as a long tenure signals loyalty and commitment, people who manage a company for many years (or better yet, decades) inspire more trust than CEOs who switch jobs every few years. Closely related to this, excellent managers like to surround themselves with people who have been promoted from within the organisation. After all, these people can be expected to be loyal and usually know the corporation inside out.

4. Great managers look at people's merits and **avoid favouritism**. They are only interested in the best partners and employees. Committed managers will even yield their place if they feel that other people are better suited for their job.

5. **Long-term thinking**: managers that are concerned about their firm's well-being think long term. They don't hesitate to sacrifice short-term results if this benefits the long-term outcome. They show concern for long-term shareholders, and have a disdain for short-term analysts and traders.[127] Although they communicate a lot and even though they are open to investors, they avoid putting too much time in monthly updates or regular appearances in the media that would distract them from their real job.

6. **Fair compensation**: when management is committed to its business, compensation is fair, tied to the (long-term) performance of the company, and tied to the contribution of each employee and manager. A definite red flag that raises serious doubts about management's good intentions is insider sleaze where managers benefit financially at the expense of shareholders. Examples of the latter are golden parachutes, low-interest (or interest-free) loans to management, and related-party transactions (e.g., family members who do business with the company on very attractive terms).

---

*"The mark of authentic leaders is how well their organization does after they are gone."*

**Bill George (George, 2003)**

---

[127] One example of extreme concern for long-term shareholders is Warren Buffett, who is as much bothered by significant overvaluation as by significant undervaluation of Berkshire's stock. The problem he has with over and undervaluation is that it leads to shareholder returns that can be vastly different from the value that is created in Berkshire Hathaway.

## C.III.5 Energy and passion

> *"The first question I always ask myself about somebody in his position is: Do they love the money or do they love the business?"*
>
> **Warren Buffett (Miles, 2002)**

A final aspect that many investors overlook is management's passion and energy. Excellent managers love their company and their job. They are proud of the products they make. And they tackle challenges with energy and realistic optimism.[128] Their passion motivates them to work hard and go the extra mile. It gives them the energy to remain enthusiastic when they encounter setbacks. It makes them curious about everything that relates to the company and its industry. And it motivates the workforce.

To evaluate management's passion and energy, top stock pickers look primarily at the number of hours that managers work. For instance, Shelby Davis and Peter Lynch were convinced they had found a passionate manager when they found him doing overtime – especially on weekends and holidays. Another indication of management's passion and energy is the way they speak about their business and their job.

## C.IV The board of directors

> *"The requisites for board membership should be business savvy, interest in the job, and owner-orientation. Too often, directors are selected simply because they are prominent or add diversity to the board. That practice is a mistake. Furthermore, mistakes in selecting directors are particularly serious because appointments are so hard to undo: The pleasant but vacuous director need never worry about job security."*
>
> **Warren Buffett, 1993 letter to the shareholders of Berkshire Hathaway**

It is the task of the board of directors to defend the interests of shareholders and, in some countries, also the interests of other stakeholders (e.g., employees). In this capacity, the board is responsible for the selection of top management, the nomination of board members, executive compensation, the review of strategic decisions (e.g., acquisitions), and internal oversight and control (in collaboration with the auditors).

Unfortunately, not too many boards perform these duties well. The most common problems with board members are that they don't have the proper experience and competence, they keep silent when they should speak up, they are afraid to challenge underperforming managers, and they provide management with compensation packages that are far too generous or too much focused on the short term.

---

[128] Excellent leaders guard themselves against too much optimism because this can lead to complacency, excessive risk taking and inappropriate responses to competition.

As a final step in due diligence, top investors screen the board of directors. It is important that this screening happens after evaluation of the business and management. The reason is that the power of boards is limited. They cannot turn a poor business around and their power versus smart and dishonest managers is usually restricted. Nevertheless, it is worthwhile to check out the boards of companies in good businesses with fair to excellent management. Top investors are trying to find out whether the board is able and willing to defend the interests of shareholders and they therefore look at:

1. The **background of directors**: in the most effective boards, every single director has business savvy, unique expertise and knowledge (e.g., in law, audit, finances, the company's industry), and experience. As far as the latter is concerned, Anthony Bolton prefers directors with tenures that include at least one full business cycle.

2. The **independence of directors**: effective boards are made up of individuals that are independent in the sense that they are demanding on management. Excellent board members have the courage to criticise underperforming managers. They insist on fair compensation packages. And they challenge poor management decisions. As company insiders are less likely to exhibit this kind of behaviour, many people have come to believe that independent board members should be outsiders to the firm. According to Warren Buffett, this is far too simplistic for two reasons. First, commercial independence is not the same as moral responsibility. Second, excluding insiders from boards also implies excluding people with rich experience and thorough knowledge of the business. Warren Buffett believes that the past dealings between the board and management are a better indication for the board's independence. Other subtle indications of (in)dependence are:

   - *Board size*: according to Warren Buffett, boards should be small (probably around seven people), because large boards can be a sign that members are on the board due to some kind of payback.

   - *Management compensation*: compensation packages that are outrageous and/or based on criteria that have little to do with the creation of shareholder value (e.g., compensation based on revenues and the size of the company), are clear signs that management, and not the board, is calling the shots.

   - *Director pay*: Buffett is concerned about the independence of directors whose board compensation is a high fraction of their annual income. The problem with such directors is that they are likely to avoid any type of confrontation with the CEO lest they may lose an important source of income.

   - *Family relationships*: family ties between members of the board and top executives definitely need further scrutiny.

   - *Chairman versus CEO*: Anthony Bolton does not want to see a chief executive as the chairman of the board, because this may imply that the CEO sets the agenda.

   - *Decision making*: the way the board takes decisions can have an important impact on its independence. For instance, independent boards avoid decisions where unanimous consensus is required and they organise meetings where the CEO is not supposed to be present. An example of how decisions should not be made is Quaker Oats, where board members received $1,000 each time they achieved a unanimous written consent.[129]

3. **Skin in the game**: one of the strongest incentives for directors to think like owners is to align their interests with those of the shareholders. The most straightforward way to achieve such alignment is for directors to have a large share of their personal wealth tied up in the company's stock. Ideally, the shares directors hold are worth much more than their annual salaries and they are preferably purchased with their own resources (i.e., not given by the company), such that they have invested their hard-earned money directly in the company. Another way to put skin in the game, as applied at Buffett's Berkshire Hathaway, is the absence of officer liability insurance. This exposes officers to great risk if they don't do their job well and is likely to put any director off who doesn't take his job seriously.

4. **Devotion of board members**: commitment implies that directors devote sufficient time to their function. To evaluate the devotion of individual directors one can look at the number of boards the director is on (more than three is a red flag), and the director's attendance at board meetings. To evaluate the devotion of the board as a whole, one should look at the number of annual board meetings.[130]

# C.V Sources of information

Investors who want to do a due diligence of a company, its industry, its board of directors and senior management based on the framework explained above will discover quickly that it is not easy to obtain the desired information. Gathering relevant and non-trivial information requires experience, a network of people to fall back on, and a knack of seeing important information inside the noise. Even then, serious company sleuths will have to work hard to obtain unique information.

On the other hand, since the majority of investment professionals limit their due diligence to a (quick) reading of the financial statements, the payoff to thorough research can be huge. As explained hereunder, there are basically two ways by which top investors try to obtain the information they want: public sources and scuttlebutt.

## C.V.1 Public information sources

Investors can read public information about a company and its key people (management, sales people, engineers, etc.) in various places, such as:

1. **Official documents produced by the firm**: publicly traded companies have to publish several reports and documents to satisfy regulatory requirements. When

---

[129] Staley, 1997.

[130] For instance, companies where the audit committee has no executive members and that meet at least twice a year are the least likely to restate earnings.

reading these documents, it is important to realise that they are written under supervision of management and possibly with the aid of public relations people. Although certain documents are subject to strict rules and regulations, they are inevitably coloured by management's beliefs, objectives and intentions. Therefore, investors should read these documents with a critical mindset.

In addition, it is always a good habit to read the documents that were issued over the past few years to see how well management delivered on its promises, to understand management's priorities, and to make an educated guess about what management is up to.[131] Red flags are unclear, complicated documents, documents that sound unrealistic, or inconsistencies between different documents. The most relevant documents that investors should take a look at are:

- *Annual and quarterly reports*: these are the most important sources of public information on a company's business, its management, its strategy, and its business model. One can peruse the financials in these reports. Or one can get an idea about the strategy and about management by reading the Letters to Shareholders over the past few years. It is important to realise that there are usually two versions of these reports: one official version submitted with the regulatory authorities (e.g., 10-K and 10-Q submitted to the SEC in the US), and another (usually more glossy) version distributed to shareholders or made available on the company's website.

  Many investors prefer the latter, as the official version is rather dry. Thorough investors, however, prefer the official reports. The reason is that official reports are subject to strict rules and regulations, whereas management has the freedom (due to the freedom of speech) to present what it deems desirable in the glossy version. As a result, official reports sometimes contain key information that is not reported in the glossy reports and the verbiage may be quite different.

- *Proxy statements*: although most investors don't read proxies, intelligent investors search these documents for examples of self-dealing and greed such as exuberant remuneration or excessive stock options to management.

- *Prospectuses*: these are filed by companies that go public. From the prospectus one can get a good idea about the business model. The first pages and in particular the 'Investment considerations' of the prospectus are definitely worth a closer look because these explain the risks and why the company might fail.

2. **Broker reports**: although Warren Buffett derides broker reports, other top investors (e.g., Michael Price, Kevin Daly and John Templeton) find them very useful to quickly gather background information on companies, the industry and management. Kevin Daly points out that especially the initiation reports (i.e., the

---

[131] In the experience of Russell Wilkins, for instance, past actions are a better predictor of future actions than management talk.

more extensive reports written at the initiation of coverage by an analyst) can be excellent sources of information.[132] On the other hand, John Templeton warns that broker reports should only be read for their information. The broker recommendations are better ignored, as information contained in these reports is probably discounted in the company's stock price.

3. **Company websites**: often, the websites of companies describe the business in detail, provide company presentations, allow investors to listen to earnings calls, and so on.

4. **Independent commercial services**: some commercial investment services (e.g., Thomson Reuters) aggregate information about companies, provide transcripts of earnings calls, bundle broker research, and so on. Other commercial services (e.g., the Value Line Survey) publish research reports or quick reads that summarise the main information about companies.

## C.V.2 Scuttlebutt

*Scuttlebutt* was coined by the late Philip Fisher and refers to the gathering of intelligence on a company by walking through stores, talking to management, talking to (ex-) employees, contacting customers and competitors, interviewing suppliers, and the like. Scuttlebutt can provide investors with subtle information from people who are close to the company.

It can, for instance, reveal some very specific problems that management doesn't want to talk about. Or it can refute the claims of senior management about competitors (e.g., have sales people the same opinions as management about competitors?), about processes (e.g., is there really no bureaucracy as management claims?), about innovation and R&D (e.g., are they really a priority as management claims or are they seen as a burden?), about HR (e.g., are people really valued in the company?), about the company's culture (e.g., are the values true and firmly established or are they fake and taken out of the management literature to impress outsiders?), etc.

It needs little explaining that investors who take the trouble to do a thorough scuttlebutt can gain a significant edge over those who base their investment decisions solely on public documents. In fact, for serious sleuths it can be *the* way to beat the market, as much of the public information – at least the easy stuff – is probably priced into the market. Scuttlebutt is therefore popular among short sellers (who usually do their homework more thoroughly than long investors) and among many top investors (e.g., Alex Roepers, Francisco García Paramés, Julian Robertson, etc.).[133]

However, as pointed out by Philip Fisher, it should be the final step of a due diligence as scuttlebutt messages are much easier to interpret correctly when one is well informed about the company and its industry. Hereunder I give an overview of the various ways

---

[132] Schwager, 2012.

[133] Although virtually all top investors acknowledge the value of scuttlebutt, not all of them believe that thorough sleuthing is an essential part of an effective investment process.

scuttlebutt can be applied. In a first section I discuss the potential sources of information. In a second section I explain how one can tap these sources in practice. In a third section I briefly discuss some unconventional sleuthing techniques.

## C.V.2.a Scuttlebutt sources

The best information sources that stock sleuths can consult to obtain unique and relevant information on a company and its management are:

1. **Personal experiences**: one can get impressions about a company by:
   - *Visiting the premises*: company visits can reveal what is really going on inside a company. One can check whether visitors are welcomed graciously by friendly receptionists, whether the toilets are clean (indicating respect for employees and visitors), and whether employees look happy. The location of the CEO's office and the decoration of that office can reveal a lot about what the CEO values most. Also important is to check out whether people in charge are proud of their business. One can look at the company's logo on the premises (is there a letter missing?), its parking lot (is it well maintained?), the gardens around headquarters (is it grass or is there a lot of weed?), and so on.
   - *Checking out the company's product and purchase experience*: most investors haven't seen, let alone touched, the products of companies in which they invest thousands (or even millions) of dollars or euro. Smart investors, by contrast, try to get their hands on the company's products to check out their value.

2. **First-hand sources**: next in line are people who have first-hand experience and information about the company under examination:
   - *(Ex-)employees and external consultants* know a lot about the working atmosphere inside the company (e.g., is there really a strong and effective culture and are the company's values really what the company claims they are?), private matters about management (e.g., is the CEO involved in a difficult divorce?; how does the CEO behave versus subordinates?), potential risks, looming disasters, and the like. Talking with executives is an essential part of scuttlebutt. Executives are definitely not the only employees that can provide valuable information though. People on the lower corporate rungs often know equally well (or even better) the negatives and buried skeletons, and they are usually more honest and open about problems inside the company.
   - *Competitors*: as explained in Chapter B, many executives know their competition well. Indeed, management (and also the sales reps) of any company have to keep track of their competitors if they want to beat them. They also have a vested interest in being able to identify and explain the weaknesses of their competitors. For this reason, management and sales people of competing firms are good places to get information about the strengths and weaknesses of a company and its offerings. They can also tell you why the company will take or lose market share. Especially interesting is to know whether customers have defected from or to the company's products, and why.

- *Creditors and bankers* that have lent money to the company keep track of its performance to ensure that the loans will be serviced. They therefore are excellent sources to get information about the company's creditworthiness. Note, however, that in certain countries it may be illegal to trade a company's shares based on input of credit departments of banks as they may have access to non-public information.

- *Customers and ex-customers* can tell you why they buy the company's product, whether they like doing business with the firm, or why they abandoned the firm for another.

- *Suppliers* (of raw materials or other inputs, packaging manufacturers, etc.) can tell you whether the company is a tough negotiator and a reliable partner. Even more importantly, they can say whether the company is hungry for supplies (which may indicate a booming business) or not. Provided that the supplier's sales to the company are a large share of its business, a look at the financial statements of the supplier may give indications about how the company under examination is doing.

3. **Third parties**: finally, there are several types of people who know something about the firm and/or its management, and who can shed another light on the company's investment merits. For instance, the CEO's friends and acquaintances, people from the CEO's community, and ex-colleagues of the CEO may tell you something relevant about his past and his personality. Reporters and journalists may also know something more than what is written in public documents. Finally, the following two types of professionals are also worth consulting:

   - *Investment professionals*: security analysts who keep track of the company and institutional investors who have large stakes in the business may be intimately acquainted with what's going on in the firm.

   - *Industry experts* of the company's industry and Chambers of Commerce are also well positioned to have professional knowledge about the firm. In the same vein, some sleuths go to conferences to check out how the company's product is positioned versus that of its competitors and monitor how a company's sales pitch changes over time.

## C.V.2.b Practical aspects of scuttlebutt

Although all investors can benefit from scuttlebutt, not all will be as good at each particular scuttlebutt technique. Some people are not good at reading other people's minds. Others don't get much valuable information out of conversations. Scuttlebutt can also be very time-consuming and it can take years to develop scuttlebutt skills or to build a network of contacts.

What can complicate scuttlebutt even more nowadays are the many regulations that prohibit insiders from distributing sensitive information about their corporation. Furthermore, some scuttlebutt techniques (e.g., meeting people in person) will only be feasible for companies with activities that are geographically close to the investor. Here is an overview of the most important scuttlebutt practices:

1. **Company visits** can give impressions about the company's culture, the way operations are managed (e.g., how is capacity met when business booms?), what management values, etc. As said above, during company visits, one has to pay attention to how one is welcomed, look for corporate excesses (e.g., expensive art, special perks for executives), and check out the cleanliness of the rest rooms (which is directly proportional to the value the firm assigns to its workforce). Company visits are also the perfect occasion to grill the company's investor relations officer, to get more information about customers and competitors, and to ask about the different parts and physical details of the company's products (e.g., where are they made?, what are they meant to do? etc.).

2. **Turning oneself into a customer**: as explained above, smart investors want to touch the company's product. They try it out. They see whether it looks attractive (versus that of competitors). They evaluate the marketing. And they go through the entire purchasing experience (always presenting themselves as customers and not as investors). A definite red flag is a bad first customer experience.

3. **Conversations**: one can strike up conversations with key people in the firm, suppliers, employees, customers, etc.[134] When sleuthing, it is important to remain critical and to double check when possible. One should also keep the gathered information to oneself in order not to build a reputation that shies away future informants. Furthermore, to get the most out of a conversation one should convey interest in the person, establish trust (e.g., one should not go straight to the question), and create a feeling of reciprocity where possible. The latter is especially important with key people.[135] Conversations can take two forms:

   • *Face-to-face conversations*: some top investors like to meet people – in particular management – in person. Personal encounters can be enlightening, especially if the investor is asking the right questions. For instance, one of Chuck Akre's favourite questions for management is how they measure their success. Another excellent question to get insight into the capital allocation skills of management is to ask how they allocate capital and why. There is one caveat about personal encounters, though. CEOs often get to their position thanks to their persuasive and/or charismatic personality. Hence, there is a risk that management can bias an investor's opinion during such meetings. As a protection against this investors are advised to go well prepared to meetings with management.

   • *Phone calls*: this can be a fast way to speak to many people. Moreover, some people may say more over the phone than when they talk face-to-face.

---

[134] One can get information about customers, employees, suppliers, etc. from the sales department, competitors, examination of the packaging, etc.

[135] For instance, one can start a conversation with a CEO by giving some information that was gathered during the investigation about client problems and competitor moves. In this way, the CEO may feel forced to give something back in the form of valuable information.

4. **Annual meetings**: one can encounter valuable information about management during annual meetings. For instance, one can see how well the CEO and CFO know their business and how they answer questions.

5. **Internet searches**: one can go to the website of the company and try to find out what the firm really values. Is the website customer-friendly (which is a sign of being close to the customer)? Is it easy to apply for a job (i.e., are there effective HR policies?) or do applicants have to go through numerous clicks before they can find information? And so on. Also user groups, where clients explain what they value in the company's product, can be an excellent source of information.

## C.V.2.c Unconventional sleuthing techniques

Although few top investors mention them, it is useful to briefly say something about the more unconventional sleuthing techniques.[136] When applying any of the following, it is advised to take precautions (by taking notes, taking time-stamped pictures, having witnesses and informing legal advisors) to avoid suspicions of inside trading:

1. **Observations**: investors can benefit from observations of all sorts of activities:

   - One can wait in front of warehouses and see when supplies are being stocked.

   - One can wait in front of plants[137] and examine the activities. Bullish signs are people who do overtime, new work shifts that are being introduced and a parking lot that is full of cars until midnight. Plant observations can also be used to verify the numbers if one suspects fraud. In *The Sleuth Investor* Mandelman gives the example of a sleuth who counted the number of trucks that left the plant of the company Bramble during a period of two weeks. Based on a calculation of the number of pavement stones that could be stacked on each truck, he managed to estimate the company's sales. This confirmed his suspicion that the company's reported sales were fabricated.

   - One can get wind of important deals ahead of the crowd by looking at who comes in and out of a company's headquarters or an investment bank. To be successful at this kind of observation, one has to know important deal makers and take pictures that can be analysed afterwards.

2. **Involving third parties**: one can get information on how a company is doing by cooperation with third parties. For instance, suppose that a supplier of champagne delivers champagne to a company each time it throws a party thanks to a new contract. One can get information about new contracts by striking a deal with that supplier to tip you off each time the company places an order with the supplier.

---

[136] See (Mandelman, 2007) for a discussion of these techniques.

[137] If the company farms out some activities to another firm, watching activity at that other firm can also give clues. One can obtain information on such third parties during company visits, by asking about how the company deals with capacity shortfalls, etc.

# C.VI Putting the pieces together

Fundamental analysis can point an investor in the direction of businesses with high intrinsic quality, but businesses of high quality that are recognised by the market as such are seldom good investments.

Therefore, in an effective investment approach one first tries to identify businesses that are likely to be undervalued (based on the bargain ideas of Chapter B) and one tries to obtain a rough, back-of-the-envelope valuation of the stock (e.g., based on multiples as explained in Chapter D) before making a detailed fundamental analysis or full valuation.

The intelligent investor only starts digging deeper and performs a full fundamental analysis (based on Chapter C) and a thorough valuation (based on Chapter D, and with the help of what was found in the full fundamental analysis) when there are indications that the stock may be an interesting idea.

In fundamental analysis, the analytic framework presented in Chapter C can be extremely valuable. Although it is not comprehensive it focuses on the most important angles from which top investors evaluate companies. Certain corporations may require extra due diligence (e.g., because they are relatively complex) and certain industries may require attention to very specific business aspects, but the golden rule is always that it is best to keep the analysis as simple as possible. Therefore, the presented framework should be sufficient for most investments. To conclude, I recapitulate the main themes of this chapter and discuss the use of checklists for investments.

## C.VI.1 Summary of evaluation themes

Figure 13 gives a schematic overview of the four themes that investors need to examine in potential investments:

1. **Quantitative analysis**: this entails a thorough scrutiny of the financial statements to see whether the numbers add up:

    - *Income statement*: one must definitely look at the track record in earnings and dividends, and examine the evolution and absolute level (especially compared with competitors) of profit margins and return on investment (ROIC, ROA, and ROE).

    - *Balance sheet*: it is important to know whether the company is financially healthy by examining its solvency (debt ratios) and liquidity (current ratio, working capital, type of debt, etc.). In addition, it is worthwhile to evaluate the risk of distress through the Altman Z-score and the H-score.

    - *Cash flow statements*: one has to examine operating cash flows and free cash flows on an absolute basis and compared with competitors.

2. **Qualitative business analysis**: investors who do a qualitative check of the business can gain a clear edge in the market as the majority of investors pay little attention to the following aspects:

- *Industry*: the most attractive businesses are often (but not always) to be found in industries that have little to fear from substitutes, that have high barriers to entry, and that exhibit little internal competition. The most compelling industries also require little capital and do not suffer from a high rate of change (i.e., they are typically considered boring).

- *Business models*: strong business models are simple and scalable. To avoid the risk of unproven businesses, investors are also advised to stick with business models that have excellent track records.

- *Competitive position*: the best companies have a sustainable moat around their business that results from their industry, from their position within the industry, and/or from company-specific strengths. Excellent businesses are in a strong bargaining position versus their customers (e.g., through their products, service, switching costs, etc.) and their suppliers. They are also in a powerful position versus direct competitors (e.g., through a leadership position).

  In addition, the best companies pay a lot of attention to the development of the pillars of their competitive strength, such as the corporate culture (look for integrity, excellence, action, candid communication, respect, innovation, ownership), HR (look for respect and consideration for the workforce), processes (e.g., little bureaucracy), the organisational and management structures (e.g., lean management structure and decentralisation), innovation (e.g., focus on opportunities, R&D, demos), marketing (e.g., brand management, excellent sales, close contact with customers), and operations (e.g., unique operations based on excellence).

- *Control over destiny*: even a company that scores high on virtually all important business aspects can suffer a tremendous blow if it loses control over its own destiny. Therefore, one should be wary of companies that are vulnerable to government intervention, that depend too much on R&D, that are fashion-related, that frequently have to make critical decisions, that are too highly (financially, operationally or geographically) leveraged, and that are too dependent on weather conditions or the macro environment (business cycle, inflation, commodity prices, interest rates).

- *Growth prospects*: attractive long-term investments have excellent growth prospects in terms of sales and earnings. The most interesting high-growth companies are not the pioneering businesses but the moderate-to-fast growing companies with solid track records (i.e., companies with strong and high-quality profit growth over a long period that includes at least one business cycle) and a strong (and sustainable) competitive position. The best growth companies also manage their growth consciously and introduce appropriate processes and HR practices to cope with the expansion of their organisation. Finally, it is important for investors to anticipate growth saturation of a fast grower because the saturation stage can be disastrous for stock returns.

3. **Management evaluation**: investors cannot ignore management. Although the impact of individual managers is often overrated, there is no doubt that bad managers can bring a so-so business to ruin, and that extraordinary managers can leverage the performance of intrinsically good businesses. The points that deserve most attention in management evaluation are:

- *Personality*: excellent managers show a high degree of integrity (e.g., they talk straight, they take responsibility for failures and they avoid related-party transactions), they usually remain down-to-earth and modest (e.g., they admit to mistakes, listen to others, ask for feedback and keep their ego in check), they feel uneasy with the status-quo, and they have the courage to ignore the corporate imperative.

- *Experience and skills*: the managers that inspire most confidence have successful track records, allocate capital in an efficient way (e.g., they run a tight ship, focus on opportunities, think long-term, avoid leverage and have no interest in value-destroying empire building), and think out a unique strategy that hinges on the company's core competencies.

- *Value management*: managers should be ambassadors of the company's core values. They should promote the values, enforce strict compliance and be perfect role models.

- *Ownership and allegiance to stakeholders*: excellent managers feel responsible to all of the company's stakeholders. They therefore make the company self-sustaining, have high shareholder ownership, have long tenures, avoid favouritism, think long-term and pursue fair compensation.

- *Energy and passion*: excellent managers love their job. They are fascinated by their industry, and feel motivated by the challenge of their task (and not by their compensation). As a logical consequence, they usually work long hours.

4. **The board of directors**: good and efficient boards of directors consist of directors that:

- Have the necessary *skills, business savvy and experience.*

- Are *independent and willing to challenge management*: look for small boards, reasonable management compensation, absence of family ties, director pay that is small as compared to their wealth and board meetings without the CEO.

- Have *skin in the game*, i.e, significant shareholder ownership versus their wealth.

- Are *devoted*: directors that feel responsible attend all board meetings and avoid sitting on too many different boards.

Finally, as part of a quantitative, qualitative, management and board evaluation, one has to:

1. carefully read the footnotes,

2. keep track of insider purchases and sales,

3. be on guard against typical red flags such as late filings, auditor turnover and the resignation of key people, and

4. look for earnings management (e.g., perfect figures, anomalies between the balance sheet and the income statement, improper capitalisations, complicated accounting and a track record of manipulation).

**Figure 13: Fundamental business analysis**

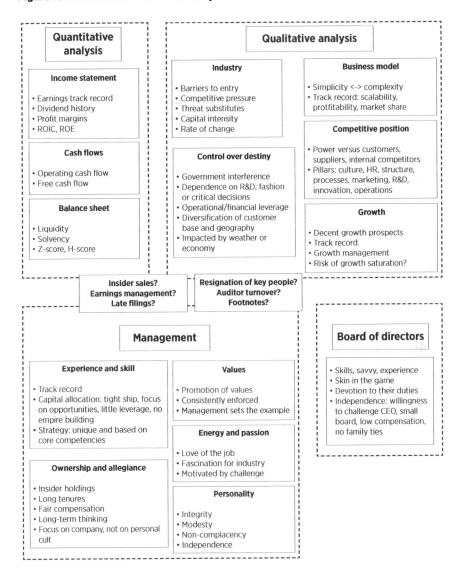

## C.VI.2 Final check-list

In the aviation and medical sector, checklists are used by professionals before takeoff and before operations respectively to reduce the number of errors, to avoid pitfalls and to prevent overlooking important elements. Inspired by this practice, Mohnish Pabrai promotes the use of checklists in the evaluation of investments. A checklist can consist of two parts:

1. **Fixed checklist**: this consists of a number of questions that should be asked about every investment. The questions can be based on the fundamental analysis discussed in this chapter, on advice from top investors, or on mistakes that the investor (or other investors) made in the past. Here are some examples:

   - Does the company have a sustainable moat around its business?

   - Why does the market misprice the stock and why is the consensus wrong?

   - What are the strongest bearish arguments for the stock? Anthony Bolton likes to confront his own view with that of brokers who disagree. He then tries to find out why he does not share their view.

   - What are the risks and weaknesses and why (or how) could competitors beat the company?

   - What are the strongest bull arguments for the investment?

   - Is the company great and why?

   - Are there management issues?

   - Is there enough information to evaluate a sufficiently long track record of the company and its management, and is this track record satisfactory?

   - Do I really understand the investment? Is the company sufficiently simple to fully grasp, and is it in my circle of competence?

   - What do credit and bond investors think about the investment?

   - Is business momentum positive or negative? For instance, Anthony Bolton always checks whether expectations among analysts are improving or deteriorating.

2. **Variable checklist**: investors should not only use a fixed checklist but also must look for a limited number of factors (say, four or five) that are most pertinent to the company's success, and monitor them closely over time.

---

*"I never like to work too hard to understand an investment. So if a potential investment is too complicated or difficult to understand, I'd rather skip it and find something easier to figure out."*

**Joel Greenblatt (Greenblatt, 1997)**

---

# CHAPTER D

## VALUATION

"If I were running a business school I would only have two courses. The first would obviously be an investing class about how to value a business. The second would be how to think about the stock market and how to deal with the volatility."

WARREN BUFFETT (WWW.THEBUFFETT.COM/QUOTES/VALUATION.HTML)

THE MOST CHALLENGING step in fundamental analysis is valuation, i.e., the computation of a stock's intrinsic value. The problem is that business valuation is more of an art than an exact science. It requires a lot of estimates, projections, qualitative and quantitative considerations, and so on. Indeed, the value of a business depends on its future cash flows, which, in theory, have to be estimated based on a thorough fundamental business analysis (see Chapter C). Hereunder I first give an overview of the most common valuation methods. Subsequently, in section D.II there is a summary of advice from top investors on the proper use of valuation methods in the investment process.

## D.I Valuation methods: an overview

There are many methods by which investors can value businesses, ranging from the mathematically rigorous discounted cash flow (DCF) model, to the calculation of replacement value, and down to simple multiples. This section gives an overview of the most popular methods used to value stocks. It is assumed that the reader has some basic accounting knowledge.[138]

---

[138] Recommended further reading for those who lack basic accounting knowledge can be found in (Epstein, 2005), (Friedlob, 2001), (Bernstein, 2000) and (Bragg, 2007).

## D.I.1 Valuation by means of the discounted cash flow model

In the DCF model, the Intrinsic Value (IV) of a stock is estimated as:

$$\widehat{IV} = c + \sum_{q=0}^{+\infty} \frac{\widehat{fcf}_q}{(1+\alpha)^q}$$

where $\widehat{IV}$, $\widehat{fcf}_q$, c, and $\alpha$ are respectively the estimated intrinsic value, the estimated annual free cash flow to equity per share generated q years from now, the cash (cash + cash equivalents) per share, and the return the investor requires from the stock given its risk profile.

The DCF model assumes that:

1. all debt is rolled over in perpetuity (such that only interest is paid to creditors),
2. all free cash flows are either distributed to shareholders at the moment they are generated or are reinvested in the business at a return $\alpha$, and
3. c is reinvested in the business at a return $\alpha$.

The following is restricted to some practical remarks about the application of the model.[139]

Although the DCF model is undoubtedly one of the most appealing theoretical valuation models around, its usefulness is limited. First of all, the DCF model should only be used for companies about which the future cash flows can be estimated with relatively high reliability. The model is not suited for businesses with lumpy and highly unpredictable cash flows such as insurance companies or cyclical businesses.

Secondly, a DCF calculation needs cash flow estimates from now until eternity. In fact, the intrinsic value of a typical company is not determined by the cash flows produced in the next four to five years, but by the period beyond five years. The problem is that even the forecasting of cash flows of very stable businesses some years ahead is a formidable challenge. Experienced analysts who are fair will admit that nobody is able to make such bold forecasts.

The challenge appears to have become greater in recent decades as there seems to be an acceleration in the speed of business evolution.[140] In practice, one should take the estimated intrinsic value of a DCF model with a grain of salt. The model is probably only reliable to some extent for companies with very stable and predictable cash flows, such as utilities, toll roads or pharmaceutical companies.[141]

Given its limitations the DCF model is not popular among top investors. If they use it at all, they apply it sparingly and only for very predictable businesses. In addition, they heed the following practical rules:

---

[139] For a thorough discussion of how to find the inputs for the model refer to (Koller, 2005) and (Damodaran, 2006).

[140] Mauboussin, 2006.

[141] As a conservative valuation, Michael Price values pharmaceutical companies based on the drugs the company is selling, assuming a fixed profit margin (e.g., 85%), and the lifetime of the patent of each drug.

1. They examine the intrinsic value for **a set of growth scenarios** to avoid surprises due to unrealistic estimates. The corresponding range of fair values, combined with the estimated probability of each scenario, gives a better idea about the true fair value of the stock. It can also be useful to determine the growth rate that corresponds with the current stock price and examine whether this scenario looks realistic or not.

2. Application of a **margin of safety**: top investors like Benjamin Graham, Warren Buffett and John Templeton buy stocks only when they trade at a significant discount (of about 30%) to their conservatively computed fair value. A discount provides a margin of safety that serves as a protection against errors in the estimation of the future cash flows.

3. **Keeping it simple**: as the estimated intrinsic value should be based on educated estimates of the future free cash flows, it is best to limit the number of parameters that are used to forecast these cash flows. Since each parameter has some uncertainty, the risk of error propagation (where errors in one parameter magnify errors in other parameters) increases as the number of parameters grows.

   Likewise, making detailed projections of free cash flows too far into the future is more a sign of overconfidence than common sense. It is, for instance, often better to make simple assumptions about cash flows many years from now. One can assume, for example, that cash flows are constant or grow with GDP starting some years from now. The bottom line is that DCF practitioners must remember Warren Buffett's and Charlie Munger's advice that it is better to be *approximately right* than to be *precisely wrong*.

## D.I.2 Valuation by means of multiples

Multiples are popular and simple tools to determine whether a stock is cheap or expensive. The many multiples that are used throughout the investment world usually compare a market price and/or a balance sheet item with another balance sheet or income statement value. It is important, though, that when the multiple is calculated, one should not take the reported accounting figures at face value. It is often necessary to make proper adjustments to obtain consistent and relevant multiple values. Hereunder I briefly discuss the most popular valuation multiples.

### D.I.2.a Income and cash flow ratios

### 1. Price-to-earnings (P/E) ratio

The Price-to-Earnings (P/E) multiple (or its inverse the Earnings Yield) is without any doubt the most popular multiple. It is also broadly used by famous investors like John Neff and John Templeton. Its popularity can most probably be attributed to its (apparently) simple and straightforward calculation. However, many people don't calculate it or use it correctly. Hereunder I explain how P/E should be calculated, interpreted and used.

## Definition of P/E

The most commonly used definition of P/E is given as:

$$P/E = \frac{P}{earnings_{norm} / \text{number of shares}}$$

where P is the stock price and where:

1. earnings$_{norm}$ are the normalised net or operating earnings. In the *trailing* P/E, this term is the earnings that have been reported over the previous X months. For the *forward* P/E, this term is the earnings expected in the coming X months. Commonly investors use 12 for X, which means that they use the earnings over the trailing 12 months (for the trailing P/E) or the earnings expected over the next year (for the forward P/E). The normalisation can be done by judiciously carrying out the following set of adjustments:

   • The earnings should be as *recurring* as possible to avoid one-time anomalies that can distort the firm's true earnings power. One should correct for extraordinary and nonrecurring items, for all changes that are deemed unsustainable (e.g., exceptional – but temporary – margin expansions), or even for items that from a reasonable point of view should not be included in profits. For instance, investors can decide to capitalise R&D costs that are expensed in the financial statements as R&D should pay off over the long term.

   • If convertible bonds are included in the number of shares that are used to calculate P/E (see hereunder), one has to *add back the interest expense of these convertibles* to earnings since this expense will disappear upon conversion.

   • In order to obtain a multiple that is comparable with that of other companies, one should put the earnings of all companies on the same footing through proper *accounting adjustments*. For instance, one must make adjustments for differences in depreciation methods, inventory methods, etc.

   • Benjamin Graham and John Templeton used for X a much larger number than 12. They *averaged the earnings over the last four to five years* (i.e., X = 48 to 60) because this reduces distortions caused by the business cycle, by the profit margin cycle, by accounting practices and by extraordinary items.

2. Number of shares is the number of shares outstanding. If the company has convertible bonds, options and/or warrants outstanding, it is best to include those that are likely to be converted into common stock in the number of shares. Referring to the fact that the share base is likely to be diluted in the future due to this conversion, the resulting P/E is called the diluted P/E.

**The fair P/E of a stock** is determined by a number of factors:

1. **Expectations**: the fair P/E multiple is determined by the expectations about the

company's future. When a company's prospects are bleak and/or uncertain, the fair P/E is usually lower than when the prospects are bright and/or stable. Elements that play an important role in the evaluation of a company's prospects are:

- *Expected earnings (cash flow) growth*: all else being equal, companies with higher expected growth deserve a higher P/E than those with lower growth. Here are two ways to integrate the expected earnings growth into the evaluation of P/E ratios:

  (i) Peter Lynch and John Templeton use the PEG ratio to determine the fair (12-month trailing) P/E ($(P/E)_{trail}$) of a stock.[142] The PEG ratio compares $(P/E)_{trail}$ with the projected annual growth over the next five years:

$$PEG = \frac{(P/E)_{trail}}{\text{average annual compound earnings growth over the next five years}}$$

  A popular rule-of-thumb states that a stock is cheap, fairly valued or expensive when its PEG ratio is respectively lower than, equal to and higher than 1. Although it has been demonstrated that the universe of stocks with PEG < 1 outperforms the market, it is dangerous and simplistic to apply this rule to individual stocks.[143] The rule of thumb ignores other factors that have an impact on a stock's fair P/E (as described hereunder).

  In fact, the PEG ratio is deservedly higher for companies with high return on capital (because such firms create more value) or for companies with low earnings growth (as the denominator of PEG can be very small in that case). Likewise, the PEG ratio should be lower for risky stocks. In addition, smart investors know that growth projections for the coming five years must be taken with a grain of salt. As such, they know that the PEG ratio should be applied merely as one check (out of many) of the fair P/E.

  (ii) Instead of the simple one-year forward earnings expectations, one can use in the denominator of the P/E ratio the earnings expected a number of years in the future. For instance, John Templeton liked to buy stocks with:

  P/(earnings per share five years from now) < 5

- *Risk and uncertainty* of the business: all else being equal, companies with erratic performance, highly-leveraged companies, or businesses with significant operations in (risky) developing countries deserve a lower multiple than companies with reliable and stable earnings.

2. **Fair value of the market**: it is logical that the fair P/E of a stock should be lower when the fair P/E multiple of the entire market is lower.

---

[142] (Lynch, 1993) and (Lynch, 1989).

[143] See (Damodaran, 2004).

## How to use P/E

Studies have shown that over the long run the return of the universe of all stocks in the low-P/E deciles of the market exceeds the return of the universe in the highest P/E deciles.[144] This does not, however, imply that every low-P/E stock is attractive per se. The intelligent investor:

1. Looks for a **mismatch**: since undervalued stocks are likely to produce excess returns, investors should only purchase stocks that trade at a significantly lower P/E multiple than their estimated fair P/E multiple.

2. Takes **trailing P/E ratios** more seriously than forward P/Es. Trailing P/Es use results that have been delivered. Forward P/Es, by contrast, use projections. They can be very misleading as projections can be wide of the mark.

3. Realises the **limitations of P/E**: the P/E ratio is not suited for every type of stock. It should not be used, for instance, for companies that don't have (positive) earnings, for cyclical stocks (which are driven by business cycles instead of P/E), or for companies with dubious accounting.

## 2. Price-to-cash flow ratio

The price-to-cash flow metric is the ratio of a company's stock price to its Operating Cash Flow (P/OCF) or to its (adjusted) free cash flow (P/FCF). In the latter case, the most common expression is:

$$P/FCF = \frac{\text{stock price}}{FCF_{maintenance}/\text{number of shares}} = \frac{\text{stock price}}{(FCF + capex_{growth})/\text{number of shares}}$$

where:

1. $FCF_{maintenance}$ is the cash flow that is left over after payment of all maintenance expenses, but before payment of the capital expenditures $capex_{growth}$ that are earmarked for growth[145] (i.e., $capex_{growth}$ is added back to FCF). The reason we add back $capex_{growth}$ is that the P/FCF does not want to punish growth companies that plough back a lot of their cash into their business to fuel expansion. For very fast growing companies, one can replace FCF with the so-called *owner earnings run rate* to capture the impact of the very high (or accelerating) growth. In that case the denominator is twice the maintenance free cash flow over the last two quarters.

2. Similar to the P/E calculation, the number of shares can be the number of shares outstanding, or the diluted number of shares.

---

[144] For example, see (Damodaran, 2004).

[145] $Capex_{growth}$ must be determined through an educated guess of the portion of capital expenditures that is necessary for maintenance and the portion that supports growth. In the case of a mature company, it is fair to assume that $capex_{growth}$ is negligible.

The P/FCF and P/OCF metrics are most useful for mature companies because these multiples are easier to calculate for such companies. The ratio may be harder to interpret and calculate for young growth companies, since $capex_{growth}$ is often hard to estimate. David Dreman also mentions that these metrics are more useful than P/E for companies with large non-cash expenses, and for cyclical companies.[146]

### 3. Price-to-sales ratio

The price-to-sales ratio is defined as:

$$P/S = \frac{\text{market cap}}{\text{revenues over last 12 months}}$$

Analysts tend to use the P/S ratio for the valuation of companies that have little or no earnings, or for companies whose earnings are not reflective of the company's true earnings power due to temporary setbacks or circumstances (e.g., turnarounds and cyclical companies that have recently hit a rough patch). The use of the P/S ratio should not be limited to such companies, though. Price-to-sales actually turns out to be one of the most effective valuation metrics to identify bargains in the broader market.[147]

The strength of the P/S ratio is that it is much more stable than metrics like P/E and P/FCF. The P/S ratio is not impacted by fluctuations in profit margins or capital expenditures. It is also less sensitive to earnings manipulation.

A drawback of the P/S ratio is that, unlike other metrics, it does not take into account the capital structure of companies. Indeed, companies with very different levels of leverage can have similar P/S ratios even though lower leverage (and attendant lower risk) should usually be rewarded with a higher P/S. Therefore, some analysts prefer the EV/S ratio instead of the P/S (see hereunder). Furthermore, the P/S ratio can be a downright dangerous metric for pioneering companies that haven't turned a profit yet, because such companies may run out of cash before they even turn their first profit.

### 4. Ratios based on enterprise value

Very similar to the two ratios discussed above, there are a number of ratios that compare the company's enterprise value (EV = market cap + debt - cash) instead of its market cap with income, sales or cash flows. Ratios based on EV are especially popular as valuation tools for companies that hunt for acquisition targets. They are also popular with certain top investors (e.g., Jean-Marie Eveillard, Joel Greenblatt, and Chuck Royce) as ratios with EV in the numerator are conservative due to the inclusion of the debt structure in EV.

---

[146] Dreman, 1998.
[147] O'Shaughenessy, 2005.

## EV/EBIT

The ratio of enterprise value to earnings before interest and taxes (EV/EBIT) is championed by Joel Greenblatt in *The Little Book That Beats The Market*, and is defined as:

$$\frac{EV}{EBIT_{adj}} = \frac{\text{market cap} + (\text{debt \& debt equivalents - excess cash \& cash equivalents - equity stakes})_{prop}}{EBIT + \text{implied interest on debt equivalents} + \text{adjustment for majority equity holders}}$$

The enterprise value (EV) is the net amount an acquirer would have to pay for the company (if we ignore the premium shareholders would ask in exchange for tendering their shares) after retirement of all debt and the sale of all equity investments in which the company has a minority stake. It is the company's market capitalisation increased by all debt and debt equivalents (such as the present value of off-balance sheet operating leases), and reduced by the company's excess cash[148] (which the acquirer gets for free), and by the value of all minority equity investments (which the acquirer can sell in the market if it would want to).

Note that, as indicated by the *prop* subscript, in case the company has subsidiaries one should use the proportionate (and not the entire) share in the debt (equivalents), cash (equivalents) and equity stakes of these subsidiaries.

In the denominator we put the pre-tax earnings that the acquirer would get from the company when all debt is retired (i.e., when there is no interest expense left) and when all excess cash is used to pay for the acquisition (so there is no interest income). This is EBIT where the implied interest expense on operating leases is added back (because it is an interest expense that would no longer be there if the operating leases were settled), and where adjustments are made such that only the proportionate share of income of the majority holdings (and not the entire consolidated income) is included.

Assuming a constant growth rate g, a constant Return On Invested Capital (ROIC), and a constant Weighted Average Cost of Capital (WACC), it can be shown that the fair EV/EBIT is given as:[149]

$$\left(\frac{EV}{EBIT}\right)_{fair} = \frac{1-T}{ROIC} \times \frac{ROIC - g}{WACC - g}$$

where T is the tax rate.

This expression illustrates that the fair multiple increases with growth only if the growth is sufficiently profitable (i.e., when ROIC > WACC).[150]

---

[148] Although many analysts subtract total cash to calculate EV, it is better to subtract excess cash (i.e., cash the company does not need for its day-to-day operations). The reason is that cash that is required to run the business is not at the acquirer's discretion. Note that a second reason to subtract excess cash in the numerator is that the benefits of this cash are not included in the denominator of EV/EBIT.

[149] Koller, 2005.

[150] If we take the derivative to g in the expression above, we obtain: $\frac{\partial}{\partial g}\left(\frac{EV}{EBIT}\right)_{fair} = \frac{1-T}{ROIC} \times \frac{ROIC - WACC}{(WACC - g)^2}$. This derivative is positive (which implies that the fair multiple rises with rising g) if and only if ROIC > WACC.

### EV/EBITDA

This ratio is similar to EV/EBIT, but also excludes depreciation and amortisation in the denominator (i.e., EBITDA = EBIT + depreciation & amortisation). In this way, it puts companies with different depreciation/amortisation methods on the same footing. Nevertheless, one should be careful with this measure because companies that have higher depreciation and amortisation charges usually deserve a lower EV/EBITDA multiple.

### EV/FCF

The enterprise value to free cash flow (EV/FCF) metric tells you how many years of the company's current cash flow are needed to pay for the entire company. The inverse of a variant of this metric is called the *capitalisation rate* and is defined as:

$$\text{cap rate} = \frac{\text{EBITDA - capex}}{\text{EV}}$$

### EV/sales

The EV/sales ratio is supposed to be a somewhat better measure of value than the P/S multiple as it takes into account the capital structure of the company. Indeed, as mentioned in the discussion of P/S, one of the major drawbacks of the P/S ratio is that it fails to take into account the financial leverage of companies.

$$* \quad * \quad *$$

Similar to the P/E ratio, one can combine the above multiples with growth to obtain an adjusted PEG ratio. Two examples are:

$$PEG_{EBIT} = \frac{\text{EV/EBIT}}{\text{expected EBIT growth rate}}$$

$$PEG_{FCF} = \frac{\text{EV/FCF}}{\text{expected FCF growth rate}}$$

Similar to the PEG ratio based on P/E, there are no clear rules as to what constitutes a fair PEG ratio. The fair value is determined by the ROIC and the growth rate of the company.

## D.I.2.b Metrics based on balance sheet items

Three popular metrics compare a balance sheet value with the company's market cap to determine whether its stock is cheap or expensive:

    A.  price-to-book value,

    B.  price-to-liquidation value and

    C.  price-to-replacement value.

As we will see hereunder, whereas book value is straightforward, the calculation of liquidation value and replacement value can be quite complicated.

## 1. Price-to-book value

### Definition of Price-to-Book Value (P/BV)

Although many people define P/BV as the ratio of market cap to common equity $E_{common}$ (= paid-in capital - treasury stock + accumulated retained earnings), a comprehensive definition of P/BV involves several adjustments to the numerator and denominator:

$$P/BV = \frac{\text{market cap} + \text{stock price} \times \text{outstanding options}_{conv}}{E_{common} + RS + OA + \alpha.E_{preferred} + \beta.DT + \varepsilon.Exp - \delta.GW}$$

where:

1. outstanding options$_{conv}$ is the number of outstanding options that are likely to be converted into *new* stock (i.e., for which the company will issue new stock). As such, this option adjustment makes the numerator equal to the larger market cap that is likely upon conversion of the options. Note that this also requires an adjustment in the denominator (see hereunder, under OA).

2. RS is the repurchased stock: it is best to add back to equity shares that have been repurchased recently to avoid stock repurchases (which reduce $E_{common}$) artificially increasing P/BV. This adjustment will be more important if the repurchased stock was bought back at a price below the assumed fair value because in that case the ratio may punish companies that create value through share repurchases. Of course, upon retirement of the repurchased shares this adjustment can be removed as the market cap will also come down.

3. OA is the adjustment to equity due to options, and is given as:

   OA = outstanding options$_{conv}$ x average cash inflow per option upon conversion

   This adjustment to equity represents the cash that will be paid by option holders to the company when they convert their options into stock.

4. $\alpha.E_{preferred}$ is the portion $\alpha$ ($\leq 1$) of preferred equity $E_{preferred}$ that is more like equity than debt because it is likely to be converted into equity.

5. $\beta.DT$ is the portion $\beta$ ($\leq 1$) of deferred taxes DT that is unlikely to become payable in the foreseeable future and that therefore is more equity-like than debt-like.

6. $\varepsilon.Exp$ is the portion $\varepsilon$ ($\leq 1$) of (after-tax) expenses Exp that are better capitalised (instead of expensed) as they are expected to provide future benefits (e.g., R&D). Note that, strictly speaking, Exp should be the depreciated capitalised expense over all prior years (including the current year).

7. GW is goodwill, and $\delta = 1$ or $0$, depending on whether one is interested in the price to tangible or to total book value.

## Fair P/BV of a stock

Some investors argue that a stock's fair price is its book value since book value represents the value of all assets minus all liabilities. This is a misconception for two reasons. First of all, book value is an accounting figure that may differ significantly from the market value of the net assets. Second, for most companies investors should be more concerned about the going-concern value than the net asset value. Indeed, as we have seen above, a company's fair value is the discounted value of the cash flows it can earn on its (net) assets. These cash flows are determined by the way the company manages its assets.

One can show that the fair P/BV for a company with a constant earnings growth rate g, constant Return On Equity ROE and a cost of equity $C_{eq}$ (= the return equity investors expect given the company's risk profile) is given as:

$$(P/BV)_{fair} = \frac{ROE - g}{C_{eq} - g}$$

From this relationship, we see that the fair P/BV increases when the expected growth rate g increases (as this reduces the denominator) or when the firm is more efficient by earning a higher ROE (which increases the numerator). Conversely, the fair P/BV decreases when the risk of the firm gets higher (i.e., when $C_{eq}$ rises).

Put differently, the intrinsic value of a company does not only consist of the corporation's (accounting) book value, but also includes a contribution of intangible *economic goodwill or badwill*, resulting from respectively superior and inferior returns on the company's equity and assets (e.g., due to brand power, competitive barriers, etc.). Hence, while companies with high ROE and low risk deserve a P/BV in excess of 1, companies with inferior returns and/or high risk may be overvalued at P/BV = 1.

## How to use P/BV

Price-to-Book Value is a popular valuation metric among value investors. Benjamin Graham, for instance, was a fervent champion of this metric. There is also evidence that low P/BV stocks tend to outperform stocks with higher P/BV – especially during difficult markets.[151] This does not imply, however, that indiscriminate buying of low P/BV stocks is a smart strategy. Similar remarks apply as with other valuation metrics:

1. It only makes sense to buy stocks for which there is a **mismatch** (undervaluation) between the investor's estimated fair P/BV and that assigned by the market.
2. The P/BV ratio has its own **limitations**: it can be useful for asset-heavy businesses, such as financials (banks, insurance companies), real estate companies, and investment holdings since (tangible) assets of these companies are highly liquid and can easily be converted into cash. Also, P/BV is usually meaningful for companies in capital-heavy industries, as these companies have regular inflows of new assets, which implies that most assets on their books are close to current market prices. The value of P/BV is, however, quite restricted for companies that are not capital intensive and that have a lot of economic goodwill.

---

[151] (Damodaran, 2004) and (O'Shaughenessy, 2005).

## 2. Liquidation value

A company's liquidation value is the value that one would expect to collect upon the liquidation of the company through the sale of all assets and the settlement of all liabilities. It is relevant only for companies that are in decline and/or for companies that are likely to go out of business. It should not be used for businesses that are likely to stay in business for many years to come as assets in going concerns are usually more valuable. Moreover, unlike companies that are in very bad shape, going concerns also tend to have some economic goodwill that is not captured in the liquidation value.

For this reason it is better to value going concerns through their replacement value (see below). Hereunder I first describe the original version of liquidation value as proposed by Benjamin Graham many decades ago. Secondly, I present a modern version of liquidation value.

### Graham's Net-Nets

Benjamin Graham used a very conservative definition of liquidation value, which he termed "Net Current Asset Value (NCAV)" or simply "Net-Nets":

NCAV = (cash + cash equivalents + inventories + receivables) - (all liabilities + preferred stock)

NCAV assigns no value to intangibles and fixed or miscellaneous assets, as Graham argued that the value of these assets should not be taken too seriously. Moreover, ignoring the value of these assets compensates for the fact that it may be hard to sell certain inventories, or that certain receivables may remain uncollected.

Even though NCAV is a very conservative measure, Graham was even tougher in his hunt for bargains. He looked for companies with market caps of less than about two-thirds of NCAV. This means that he was looking for companies that were trading at a discount of at least 30% to their Net-Nets. In addition, to *avoid value traps* (i.e., to avoid companies that deserve a low valuation), such bargain issues needed to have a *satisfactory earnings record and decent earnings prospects*.

### Liquidation value as an adjusted book value

It is widely believed that Net-Nets is too conservative, because it underestimates the prices that are paid in a liquidation sale. The modern approach to liquidation value (LV) is therefore to start with *tangible* book value, and to bring the reported values of assets and liabilities closer to their liquidation value by means of three types of adjustments:[152]

1. **Adjustments due to accounting principles**: the following types of adjustments may be needed to offset accounting rules that produce an unrealistic value of certain assets:

---

[152] Accounting goodwill is assumed to be worthless as it merely represents the amount the company overpaid for companies it acquired. For the typical company that is valued through liquidation value (i.e., companies in decline or in poor financial shape), it is unlikely that there is much value in goodwill (and in other intangibles for that matter). See also (Jean-Jacques, 2003).

- *Adjustments to inventory*: if the company uses the Last In First Out (LIFO) inventory accounting method, the reported inventory should be increased by the LIFO reserve to obtain a more realistic value.

- *Marking to market*: some assets (e.g., long-lived assets like land and bonds) should be marked to market as they are reported at a historical cost that may significantly misstate their current value. Marking to market can become very important if inflation has been high since assets were purchased. Note that also the book value of debt should be replaced with its market value as a buyer would look in the first place to the market value of the liabilities.

- *Adjusting for unrealistic depreciation*: depending on the depreciation method and the asset, accounting depreciation may have little to do with economic depreciation. Therefore, proper adjustments are recommended to bring depreciated assets closer to their economic value. For instance, depreciation for real estate is usually meaningless as most real estate tends to appreciate rather than depreciate in value. Or an accelerated depreciation method may reduce an asset's book value to much below what it is really worth.

- *Adjustment for hidden and off-balance sheet assets*: although a conservative valuation assigns no value to goodwill and intangibles, it is sometimes recommended to add certain hidden or off-balance sheet assets to the liquidation value. For instance, there can be interest in a valuable brand or in R&D in a liquidation sale.

2. **Adjustments due to market conditions and selling pressure**: the market conditions (e.g., business cycle), competition among bidders (or lack thereof) and the pressure under which the assets have to be sold in a liquidation can have an important impact on the price that is ultimately paid for those assets. After adjustments due to accounting principles, it is therefore recommended to make the following (downward) adjustments to the estimated economic value of certain assets, based on an assessment of the conditions under which the assets are likely to be sold:

   - *Adjustments for sales under duress*: if a company has to sell its assets under duress (e.g., due to a high debt load that becomes due soon), the cash collected for the assets is bound to be much lower than when the company has the time to look for the best bidder.

   - *Adjustments for industry conditions*: the prices that will be paid in a liquidation sale depend on the supply of those assets in the marketplace. So, when several competitors are in trouble at the same time (and want to sell their assets), prices are likely to be under pressure.

   - *Adjustments for buyer interest and buyer competition*: interest of buyers in the assets is related to the business cycle (do interested buyers have the necessary resources?) and the versatility of the assets (are there many different applications for those assets?). The value of very specialised assets should be discounted heavily (e.g., by 50%), especially in the midst of a severe recession where there may only be interest close to scrap value. On the other hand, it is fair to assume that the liquidation value of assets that can easily be sold (e.g., commodities in inventory) is close to book value.

3. **Adjustments out of conservatism**: it is recommended to apply a haircut to assets that are hard to convert into cash. For instance, accounts receivable of a bankrupt company are unlikely to be recovered in full. The recoverable amount may be estimated at about 85% – provided that the company remains dedicated to the collection of the receivables.

## 3. Replacement value

As explained above, the liquidation value can seriously underestimate the true worth of a going concern. A more useful value estimate for companies that are likely to stay in business is the replacement value. This is the cost a competitor would incur if it would build a clone of the company from scratch. Although the replacement value is an improvement upon the liquidation value, it comes with its own limitations.

Replacement value only gives a fair estimate of the value of stable businesses. It should not be used for businesses that experience high growth or for companies with unique competitive advantages that are hard to replicate, as it does not adequately reflect the economic goodwill of such companies.

Another problem of the replacement value is that it can be hard to compute for investors who are not familiar with the company's industry and business. To avoid large valuation mistakes, investors are therefore recommended to stay within their circle of competence and/or to seek professional advice (from professional appraisers or industry experts) on the value of certain assets.

In essence, the replacement value can be expressed as the sum of three terms:

replacement value = reproduction cost of assets + excess assets - liabilities

Hereunder I give some rules of thumb that can be helpful in the calculation of these terms.[153]

### Reproduction cost of assets

The reproduction cost is the cost a competitor would face to acquire similar assets to those which the company holds, and to achieve a comparable competitive position. It starts with the book value of the tangible assets and adjustments are made to reflect the cost for a new entrant:

$$\text{reproduction value} = BV_{tangible} + Adj_{inventory} + Adj_{A/R} + Adj_{PPE} + Adj_{deferred\ taxes} + \text{intangibles}$$

---

[153] See also (Jean-Jacques, 2003) and (Greenwald, 2001).

where:

1. **Adj$_{inventory}$** are adjustments to the reported value of inventories to bring them closer to the required investment in inventories for a new entrant. Typical adjustments are:

   - *Adjustments due to accounting rules*: if accounting rules distort the true value of inventories one should make appropriate adjustments to the reported inventory value. For instance, with LIFO accounting it is recommended to add back the LIFO reserve to obtain the more realistic FIFO inventory value.

   - *Finished goods that are idle* for a long time can probably partly be avoided by a new entrant (e.g., because they are obsolete). Hence, if the inventory turnover of the company is much lower than that of competitors (indicating a high likelihood that many items are unlikely to be sold at book value), the value of inventory should be reduced.

   - *Supplier advantages/disadvantages*: when the company can acquire certain raw inventory goods at very favourable prices thanks to its good supplier relations or because of its excellent geographic location, it is reasonable to expect that a new entrant would not be able to buy these goods at comparable prices. In that case, an upward adjustment to the value of these goods is recommended.

2. **Adj$_{A/R}$** is an adjustment to the reported value of Accounts Receivable (A/R). As a new competitor would probably have to deal with more delinquent customers than the company (as the latter has more experience and more sophisticated systems than new entrants), it would have to invest more in A/R than established companies. As such, an upward adjustment to A/R (e.g., by adding back the bad debt allowance) is recommended to obtain the reproduction value.

3. **Adj$_{PPE}$**: the reproduction value of Property, Plant and Equipment (PPE) must reflect the cost to a new entrant to build PP&E that provides a similar competitive advantage. The value in excess of this reproduction value (which may, for example, be due to the fact that the company's office is built on an expensive location which offers no competitive advantage as compared to a cheaper location), should not be included in the reproduction cost but must be added to the excess assets (see below). Furthermore:

   - For *Plant and Property* significant adjustments to the depreciated value shown in the financial statements are often needed. One should adjust for inflation and for the fact that accounting depreciation often has little to do with the evolution of the economic value of PP&E.

   - Since *Equipment* is depreciated over its useful life, adjustments to the reported depreciated book value are usually less important. However, sometimes a downward adjustment may be necessary, such as when a new entrant would be able to buy similar (or even better) equipment at prices significantly below the historical cost of the company's (older) equipment.

4. **Adj$_{\text{deferred taxes}}$**: deferred tax assets should be converted to their Present Value (PV). Lacking knowledge about when these assets will be realised, one can use the following rule of thumb:

PV of deferred tax assets = deferred tax assets/(1 + discount rate for the firm)

5. **Intangibles**: a new entrant will have to invest to establish a brand and a reputation, build a culture, perform R&D, build customer relations, establish competitive advantages, acquire licences and patents, and so on. Therefore, it is necessary to include a certain amount of intangibles[154] in the replacement value. It takes some level of industry expertise to estimate the value of these intangibles. For growth companies or for companies with unique competitive moats it may be extremely hard – even for an expert – to estimate this value based on a simple formula (which explains why replacement value should not be used for such companies). For stable businesses one can use the following rule of thumb:

$$\text{intangibles} = \lambda \times \text{SG\&A} + \text{R\&D}_{\text{capitalised}} + \text{government licences}$$

where:

- The first term ($\lambda$.SG&A) represents all manner of non-R&D expenses a new entrant would have to incur to achieve a similar competitive position as the company under examination. Usually, it is fair to assume that this expense would be somewhere between one and three years of the company's Selling, General and Administrative expenses (SG&A), i.e., $1 < \lambda < 3$.

- R&D$_{\text{capitalised}}$ is an asset that represents the R&D efforts. For industries where R&D is important, one can assume that a new entrant would have to invest an amount equal to the R&D expenses of the company, capitalised and depreciated over, say, five years. With straight-line depreciation this would imply that the R&D expense for a new entrant is estimated as the R&D expense of the current year plus 80% of the R&D expense of the previous year plus 60% of the R&D expense of two years ago, and so on.

- Government licences are licences that give a company the right to operate in a certain region. Examples are licences for TV stations, or licences for mobile operators. The value of these licences can be estimated based on what they have sold for in the private market.

**Excess assets**

The reproduction cost merely represents the cost to build or acquire assets that provide a competitive advantage to a new entrant that is comparable to that of the firm's assets.

---

[154] These assets have nothing to do with goodwill or other intangible assets that appear on the balance sheet. The latter accounting intangibles are ignored in the calculation of replacement value because they usually bear little relationship to the true value of the intangibles the company has created over the years.

Of course, the value of the firm's assets can be higher, due to factors that offer no competitive advantage (e.g., the location for real estate).

To take this into account the replacement value also consists of a contribution due to the value of certain assets in excess of their strict reproduction value. Typical examples are excess cash (e.g., cash that is not needed to run the business), the excess value of certain PP&E, and the excess of the mark-to-market value of securities held for investment (and not for strategic reasons) over their book value.

### Liabilities

Finally, assuming that a clone would be able to take on the same amount of liabilities as the company, we have to subtract the value of the company's liabilities from the reproduction cost and the excess value. For most liabilities one can use the market value (if easy to calculate) or the reported book value, and keep in mind the following potential adjustments:

1. If the deferred tax assets were converted to their present value, one should also **convert the deferred tax liabilities to their present value**:

   PV of deferred tax liabilities = deferred tax liabilities/(1 + discount rate)

2. Some **off-balance sheet commitments** that must be settled prior to a distribution to shareholders (e.g., operating leases or certain claims) should be partly included in liabilities.

3. One can **increase reserves** that are not conservative enough.

## D.I.2.c Other valuation tools

As mentioned above, the classical DCF approach is not popular among top investors due to its strong sensitivity to uncertain parameters. Sophisticated investors usually favour multiples based on income, cash flows or balance sheet items. But these, in turn, may not always be easy to interpret. Indeed, the relevance and fair value of a multiple is very dependent on the company's industry, its specific operations, its growth ambitions, its strategy, and so on.

As we will see hereunder, top investors also use a number of other valuation tools. The first two methods (*value on a deal basis* and *sum of the parts*) are straightforward alternatives to DCF and multiples. The last two methods (*EPV* and *value of growth*) are extensions to the liquidation value and replacement value discussed above.

### 1. Value on a deal basis

Value on a deal basis attempts to determine what a knowledgeable and professional buyer (e.g., an acquirer) would pay for a business. Practitioners of this valuation tool (e.g., the legendary investors John Templeton, Michael Price, Bill Nygren and Mario Gabelli) keep extensive notebooks and databases with all possible details of previous mergers and acquisitions.[155] These notebooks give a good idea what multiple acquirers were willing to pay in prior takeovers for similar companies.

---

[155] Templeton, 2008.

From the notebooks and databases one can also identify the valuation multiple that is used the most – and is probably the most relevant – for certain businesses. Bill Nygren found, for instance, that P/S is the most relevant multiple in the auto parts sector. He also found that price-to-subscriber or price-to-cash flow are the most relevant multiples for cable TV companies.

In practice, to arrive at the relevant value on a deal basis one should *apply a discount* to the value one would expect an acquirer to pay for the business. The reason is that acquirers usually buy companies above their stand-alone value to deter competing bidders, and because they believe they can create extra value in the businesses they acquire (e.g., by firing incompetent management, changing the strategy, disposing of unproductive assets, creating synergies, and the like). In addition, buying at a discount also implies that the investor can capture the premium an acquirer is likely to pay if the company were to be taken over.

Investors who apply this valuation method must be careful for two reasons. First, it may not be easy to find companies that are sufficiently similar to the business under examination (in terms of business segments, geographical coverage, efficiency, etc.). In that case it is best to apply the value on a deal basis to the various parts of the business by identifying companies that are similar to certain business segments.

Second, the prices paid during acquisitive booms may overstate the true value of businesses. Acquirers tend to overpay for acquisitions during such times due to the higher competition and because they tend to be overly optimistic about the value they can extract from their acquisition targets. For this reason, the prices paid in mergers and acquisitions during acquisitive booms should be discounted even more heavily than during normal times.

## 2. Sum of the parts

In the sum-of-the-parts method a company's value is calculated as the sum of the values of the company's divisions. The challenge is to calculate the value of each division separately based on relevant valuation tools (e.g., DCF, value-on-a-deal-basis, multiples, value at which similar businesses are selling for in the market, etc.). It is most useful for companies that have various significant and different business units, such as diversified conglomerates and holding companies.

## 3. The Graham-and-Dodd approach

In the Graham-and-Dodd approach, introduced by Benjamin Graham and David Dodd, the investor values a company in three steps.[156] First, for companies with few competitive advantages, the fair value is assumed to be the Net Asset Value (NAV). This is the liquidation value (for businesses in serious decline) or the replacement value (for going concerns). Graham and Dodd adepts are very conservative and assume that only companies with competitive advantages can have a value that is higher than the NAV.

---

[156] The approach was updated in (Greenwald, 2001) and (Calandro, 2009).

For most companies with a franchise, the company value is called the *Earnings Power Value* (EPV), and the excess over NAV is called the *franchise value* (EPV - NAV). Companies that are likely to grow significantly within a franchise can be assigned an even higher value, as the value of growth is taken into account. In that case one obtains the *full growth value* by adding a growth premium to EPV.

**Earnings power value**
In the Graham-and-Dodd approach one makes the conservative assumption that most companies have little in the way of competitive advantages *unless proven otherwise*. By consequence, those following the Graham-and-Dodd approach assume that the fair value of most companies is simply their NAV (liquidation value or replacement value). They will only accept a value in excess of NAV if they can identify credible and sustainable competitive advantages.

The central assumption for companies with clear and sustainable franchises is that they can maintain a constant stream of earnings and cash flows in perpetuity. To remain conservative, though, it is assumed that this income stream does not grow, unless one has serious reasons to believe that income will grow substantially on a sustainable basis (in which case one should make a full growth valuation, see below). The challenge of an EPV valuation is to estimate the company's sustainable and distributable income, and to discount it to the present by means of the discount rate R:

$$\text{EPV} = \sum_{i=1}^{+\infty} \frac{\text{adjusted earnings}}{(1+R)^i} + (\text{excess cash - debt}) = \frac{\text{adjusted earnings}}{R} + (\text{excess cash - debt})$$

In this expression:

1. **Adjusted earnings** represents cash that the owners can extract each year from the business without hurting the company's operations if the company were to have no excess cash and no debt. It can be calculated as:

$$\text{adjusted earnings} = (1-T).\text{EBIT}_{\text{correct}} + (\text{D\&A - capex}_{\text{maintenance}}) + \text{RDSGA}_{\text{growth}}$$

   with:

   - $EBIT_{correct}$ being the smoothed earnings before interest and taxes (EBIT) corrected for unsustainable and/or nonrecurring items:

   $$\text{EBIT}_{\text{correct}} = \text{EBIT}_{\text{smoothed}} - \text{charge for recurrent "nonrecurring" expenses}$$

   As shown in this expression, two typical corrections to EBIT are:

   (i) *Correcting for cyclical effects*: since EBIT fluctuates due to cyclical effects (e.g., the business cycle), one has to smooth EBIT over the previous years to obtain a more relevant value. This can be done through the calculation of the average EBIT profit margin over the last couple of years, and applying this to current revenues:

$$\text{EBIT}_{\text{smoothed}} = \text{revenue} \times \text{average EBIT margin} = \text{revenue} \times \left( \frac{\sum_{i=0}^{4} \text{EBIT}_{-i}}{\sum_{i=0}^{4} \text{revenue}_{-i}} \right)$$

where $\text{EBIT}_{-i}$ and $\text{revenue}_{-i}$ are the EBIT and revenue $i$ years ago.

(ii) *Subtracting recurring "one-time" charges*: some companies exclude certain expenses from EBIT under the pretext that they are "exceptional" or "one-time" charges. But if these charges persist from year to year, they are recurring, and should be subtracted from EBIT. Therefore, one has to reduce EBIT proportionally by the average of these charges to the EBIT over the past few years. For instance, if $C_{-i}$ is the questionably "exceptional" charge $i$ years ago, we have to subtract the following charge from $\text{EBIT}_{\text{smoothed}}$ to obtain $\text{EBIT}_{\text{correct}}$:

$$\text{charge for recurring nonrecurrent charges} = \text{EBIT} \times \left( \frac{\sum_{i=0}^{4} C_{-i}}{\sum_{i=0}^{4} \text{EBIT}_{-i}} \right)$$

- $T$ is the average effective tax rate ((paid taxes + deferred taxes)/Earnings Before Taxes) over the past few years.

- *D&A - capex$_{\text{maintenance}}$*: Depreciation and Amortisation (D&A) includes investments for growth and is an accounting value that seldom represents the true amount of annual investments. Since adjusted earnings should be reduced by the amount the company needs to reinvest in its business to maintain its position (i.e., we ignore investments meant for growth), it is better to replace D&A with *maintenance* capital expenditures (i.e., capex$_{\text{maintenance}}$), by adding D&A back and subtracting:

$$\text{capex}_{\text{maintenance}} = \text{total capex} - \Delta\text{sales} \times \left( \frac{\sum_{i=0}^{4} \text{PPE}_{-i}}{\sum_{i=0}^{4} \text{sales}_{-i}} \right)$$

where $\text{PPE}_{-i}$, $\text{sales}_{-i}$, and $\Delta\text{sales}$ are respectively the Property, Plant and Equipment (PPE) (net of depreciation) $i$ years ago, the sales $i$ years ago, and the sales growth in the current year. This expression is derived from the fact that many companies have a relatively stable relationship between sales and PPE (net of depreciation), such that the amount subtracted from total capex is the capital expenditure for growth.

- *RDSGA$_{growth}$*: for most companies part of research and development (R&D) and selling, general and administrative (SGA) expenses is intended to support growth. Since we are only interested in the amount of R&D and SGA that is needed to protect the business against decline, we add back the R&D and SGA expenses RDSGA$_{growth}$ that are earmarked for growth. In the absence of indications about the value of RDSGA$_{growth}$ (such as a certain percentage of R&D + SGA), we can use the following rule of thumb:

$$RDSGA_{growth} = \Delta sales \times \left( \frac{\sum_{i=0}^{4} RDSGA_{capitalised,-i}}{\sum_{i=0}^{4} sales_{-i}} \right)$$

In this expression, RDSGA$_{capitalised,-i}$ is an asset of $i$ years ago that is obtained by capitalising (and depreciating) R&D and SGA over a number of years, and where sales$_{-i}$ are the sales $i$ years ago. This expression is motivated by the assumption that the amount of RDSGA$_{capitalised}$ required to produce a certain amount of sales is proportional to the amount of sales, such that RDSGA$_{growth}$ is the R&D and SGA expenses required for growth.

2. **Discount rate R**: this rate should reflect the risk of the firm and depends on the prospective returns of competing investments (e.g., bonds). For an average stock, one could take the long-term stock market return (e.g., R = 9% for US stocks). For a highly rated company, one could use a rule of thumb such as R = 1.25 x 10-year Treasury bond yields.

3. **Excess cash - debt**: the first term in EPV assumes that all of the company's capital is equity capital and that the firm has no debt (and no interest expenses) nor excess cash (so it also does not receive interest). To obtain the final EPV we have to subtract the company's debt and add the excess cash[157] (e.g., all cash in excess of 1% of sales).

To illustrate that only franchises with a protective moat have an EPV that exceeds their NAV, we can rewrite the above expression of EPV through the factorisation of adjusted earnings in the operating part of NAV (i.e., NAV$_{op}$ = NAV - (excess cash - debt)) and the return RONAV$_{op}$ the company earns on its operating assets:

$$EPV = \frac{NAV_{op} \times RONAV_{op}}{R} + (excess\ cash - debt) \longleftrightarrow NAV = NAV_{op} + (excess\ cash - debt)$$

From this expression we can see that EPV will only be higher than NAV if RONAV$_{op}$ > R. In other words, there will only be a franchise value (EPV - NAV) if the company

---

[157] By doing so one implicitly assumes that (cash - debt) will grow at rate R into perpetuity.

manages to earn a return on its operating assets in excess of its cost of capital. Translated into economic terms, EPV will be higher than NAV only if the company earns excess returns on its operating assets thanks to sustainable competitive advantages.

**Full growth value**

Graham-and-Dodd investors are very reluctant to assign value to growth. They are sceptical of above-average growth projections because they know that these expectations seldom materialise. For this reason, they do not assign value to growth in companies that lack a strong franchise. Even for franchises with significant growth, they will not pay full price for growth. As a rule of thumb, for the calculation of the full growth value one can use the following expression:

$$\text{full growth value} = \text{NAV} \times \left( \frac{\text{ROIC} - g}{R - g} \right)$$

where ROIC is the return on invested capital, and g is a conservative estimate of the earnings growth rate in perpetuity.

For companies with strong franchises (i.e., ROIC is relatively high) and good growth prospects (i.e., g is close to R), this full growth value will be higher than EPV, and we can express the above expression as:

$$\text{full growth value} = \text{NAV} + \text{franchise value} + \text{growth premium}$$

# D.II Valuation tenets championed by the masters

From the previous sections it should be clear that business valuation is not an exact science. Top investors acknowledge the difficulty of valuation and they realise that they inevitably will make many errors when they try to assess the value of businesses. To avoid as many mistakes as possible and to restrict the impact of valuation errors, they heed the following rules.

## D.II.1 Conservatism

The inherent uncertainty in valuation means top investors remain conservative in their fair value estimates. They basically adhere to the following guidelines:

1.  They apply a significant **margin of safety**. In practice, they only buy a stock when it trades at a discount of at least 25% to 30% to its conservatively estimated fair value.

2.  Templeton recommends **correcting for sudden performance improvements** (e.g., margin improvements) in the absence of convincing evidence that they are sustainable.[158] Conservative investors know the power of reversion to the mean and will give higher weight to historical performance than to temporary excellence.

---

[158] Templeton, 2008.

3. Graham-and-Dodd adepts preach **scepticism about growth**. They rely much more heavily on the balance sheet than the income statement when they value businesses.

## D.II.2 Simplicity

Top investors embrace the Keep It Simple Stupid (KISS) principle when they apply valuation measures. Few use the DCF methodology because of the inherent uncertainty about the parameters of the model. They also avoid valuation exercises of companies that are too risky. For instance, they typically steer clear of highly leveraged firms, as the valuation of such companies is extremely sensitive to small estimation errors.

Top investors focus on relatively stable businesses and they try to determine the most relevant valuation method for each business they examine. Often, they use simple multiples or models that depend on only a few (e.g., three to five) parameters. Warren Buffett's right-hand man in Berkshire Hathaway, Charlie Munger, stresses that for the relative valuation of stocks consistency of the valuation model is much more important than sophistication (e.g., six-dozen variables) as inaccuracies will be replicated through consistency.

## D.II.3 Triangulation

Given the fact that all valuation methods above have their limitations and uncertainties, investors must realise that it is unwise to determine a stock's fair value based on one single valuation metric. For this reason, top investors like Templeton recommend the practice of *triangulation*. This involves the use of a set of relevant valuation methods (e.g., DCF, P/E and P/BV) to determine a stock's fair value. Real bargains then stand out on all (or most) of the chosen valuation measures.

## D.II.4 Comparative valuation

Top investors pay special attention to how the valuation metrics hold up against:

1. **Peers**: one can compare the valuation metrics of a company with that of its competitors and try to find explanations for possible discrepancies. One must remain careful, though, because competitors are often only partially comparable with each other due to differences in business mix, strategy and the like.

2. **Historical values of the valuation metric**: top investors also sometimes compare the company's valuation metrics (e.g., typically multiples) with the range the stock commanded historically.[159] According to Anthony Bolton, one should compare metrics over a period of a minimum of ten years, and at least an entire business cycle. This is important because it reveals how the valuation changed over a period with a lot of variety in business conditions. On the other hand, historical valuation makes little sense if the company has changed dramatically compared with the past. For this reason, historical comparison is most useful with:

---

[159] Kobrick, 2006.

- *Cyclical stocks*: the valuation can be compared with that at comparable points in the business cycle.

- *Mature companies (moderate growers)*: such stocks have the habit of moving sideways or falling in price when they are priced higher than their historical P/E until they reach more reasonable valuations.[160]

- *Growth stocks*: in his search for bargains, T. Rowe Price looked for growth stocks with P/E ratios about 30% above the lowest P/E that was reached over previous business cycles.[161]

3. **Market**: When doing a comparative analysis investors must remain cautious because the multiples that are used as a reference may be unfairly high or low due to distorted market circumstances (e.g., boom and bust cycles), or due to the fact that an entire industrial sector has been in or out of favour at some moment in time.

## D.II.5 Prefer quality over "low price"

A common mistake among investors is to overpay for quality. The problem is that excellent businesses are usually recognised by the market as such. In a study in *Investment Fables*, Aswath Damodaran found that the market is quite good at pricing in strong corporate governance, strong business quality, etc. Hence, paying up for quality can lead to subpar returns.

An equally harmful mistake is to buy a fair or so-so business at a *cheap* price. Top investors like Warren Buffett and John Templeton are convinced that buying **good businesses at fair prices** usually pays off much better than buying fair businesses at good prices. Indeed:

1. The market sometimes underestimates the potential of good businesses, because there is a cap on the multiple (e.g., P/E ratio) the market can accept for any stock. In other words, the market has a hard time pricing in exceptional performance (e.g., consistent earnings growth of 40% to 50% like those seen with Microsoft and Dell in the 1990s). This is also illustrated in a comprehensive study that found that the best performing stocks of the last 50 years in the US had P/E ratios of around 20 to 50 (i.e., they were already rather expensive according to common market norms) before they made their big advance.[162]

2. The market often exaggerates the risks and uncertainties of good businesses and underestimates the risks/uncertainties of so-so businesses. In other words, whereas good businesses tend to surprise the market positively quarter after quarter (with a positive impact on the share price), fair or so-so businesses have the persistent habit of matching or falling short of expectations (with a negative impact on the share price).

---

[160] (Lynch, 1993) and (Lynch, 1989).

[161] (Train, 2000) and (Ross, 2000).

[162] O'Neil, 2002.

## D.II.6 Scepticism

There are a lot of smart people at work in the stock market, which leads to a high level of pricing efficiency. By consequence, when a stock looks cheap based on certain valuation metrics, chances are that the stock is cheap for a reason. Similarly, stocks with excellent prospects are likely to trade at relatively high multiples. Put another way, mismatches between stock prices and the most reliable intrinsic value estimates tend to be rare.

Knowing this, intelligent investors remain sceptical when they believe that they have discovered a bargain. Here are some recommendations:

1. Investors should recheck their investment thesis and search for weaknesses each time they believe they have discovered a bargain. This practice helps investors to identify elements they may have overlooked in their first valuation exercise. For instance, sometimes it may be well-advised to check the accounting methods (e.g., especially for foreign stocks) and see whether adjustments are needed to obtain more normalised valuation metrics.

2. Marty Whitman notes in *The Aggressive Conservative Investor* that investors must realise that even if a stock is genuinely undervalued there is no assurance that investors will make a profit on it. Some stocks can stay undervalued for a very long time. Or undervalued stocks can be taken private or acquired at a bargain price that offers little gain to the patient long-term shareholder.

3. As recommended by many top investors, people should stay as much as possible within their circle of competence. Within that circle their chances of success are higher as they should know much better than other market players how to recognise bargains. In any case, investors always have to determine whether they have sufficient knowledge of an industry or business to value it correctly. They should skip businesses they are unfamiliar with.

## D.III Summary

Figure 14 summarises the various valuation tools discussed in this chapter. As indicated in the figure, valuation is governed by six principles. First, one should keep the valuation model as simple as possible. This implies that one must restrict the number of parameters that are used in a DCF model. It also means that DCF valuation should be avoided when possible. Simple multiples are often at least as reliable as DCF values.

A second important principle is conservatism. When they value a business, investors must always apply a margin of safety as a protection against valuation errors. Conservative investors also prefer balance-sheet based multiples. If they use income or cash flow-based multiples, they make sure that they are based on normalised and trailing values. As they are sceptical of growth and competitive advantages, they don't take them into account unless they have very strong arguments to believe the opposite.

Finally, one can learn a lot about a company's fair value by making a comparison with peers and with historical multiples. One can also limit errors through the use of triangulation. One should look for quality at a fair price and one must always double check valuation results since the markets are not stupid.

As a concluding remark, it is always a good idea to check whether external signals (such as the ones discussed in Chapter B) confirm a valuation thesis. Although lack thereof should not be of concern, the presence of such signs makes the investment thesis even stronger. For instance, heavy insider buying by various insiders, or large stock repurchases, can confirm an investment thesis.

**Figure 14: Valuation tools and basic valuation principles**

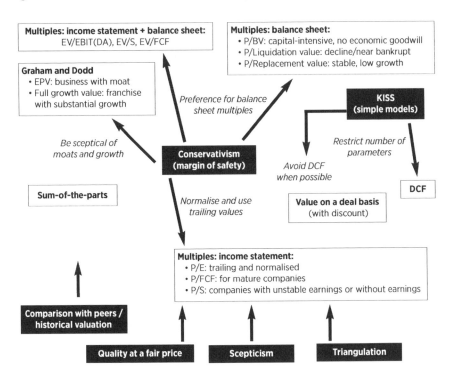

# CHAPTER E

## COMMON PROCESS MISTAKES AND HOW TO AVOID THEM

"Nothing sedates rationality like large doses of effortless money. After a heady experience of that kind, normally sensible people drift into behaviour akin to that of Cinderella at the ball. They know that overstaying the festivities – that is, continuing to speculate in companies that have gigantic valuations relative to the cash they are likely to generate in the future – will eventually bring on pumpkins and mice. But they nevertheless hate to miss a single minute of what is one hell of a party. Therefore, the giddy participants all plan to leave just seconds before midnight. There's a problem, though: They are dancing in a room in which the clocks have no hands."

WARREN BUFFETT, 2000 LETTER TO THE SHAREHOLDERS OF BERKSHIRE HATHAWAY

IN CHAPTERS B, C and D we have seen that a sound investment process consists of three elements: screening out potentially interesting stocks, fundamental analysis and valuation. Although this process looks straightforward, investors tend to make a number of common mistakes in each step of this process. They look in the wrong places for bargains. They perform a superficial or biased fundamental analysis. Or they take shortcuts in the valuation process. But first and foremost, many investors approach the market with a flawed investment process that is incoherent, ineffective and inconsistent.

This chapter looks at common mistakes made by investors. In a first section I give an overview of common process mistakes. In a second section I give advice on avoiding them.

## E.I Overview of common process mistakes

### E.I.1 Incoherent investment approach

The most common process mistake is probably not to have any process to speak of. Many people buy stocks they don't know anything about based on tips or headlines in the media. Another problem is that very few investors have a clear notion of what the investment philosophy (as discussed in Chapter A) stands for.

They pay lip service to the idea that stocks should be purchased when they are cheap and that they should be sold when they are expensive, but they have no clue what *cheap* and *expensive* really mean. As a result, they play the market through an investment approach that has little to do with investing.[163]

Frequently, playing the markets is further encouraged by overconfidence (e.g., one believes to have an edge because one has access to a lot of information) and the illusion of being in control (because investing looks easy and familiar). The worst thing that can happen to people who play the markets is to have a winning streak. Temporary success can bolster the conviction that one is doing great even though one's process and strategy offer no edge over the long term. This invites disaster further down the road.

As explained hereunder, the two most important examples of incoherent investment style are the confusion of investing with trading and with speculation.

> *"You have to know what you own, and why you own it. 'This baby is a cinch to go up!' doesn't count."*
>
> **Peter Lynch (www.youtube.com/watch?v=pnCLI1dCJfQ)**

## E.I.1.a Confusing investing with trading

Trading and investing are based on two very different philosophies. Investors purchase and sell when a stock deviates from its intrinsic value. Traders, on the other hand, take their cues from price action. Although there are a number of highly successful market players that combine trading and investment elements, virtually all of them ignore the fair value concept (so they are basically all traders).[164]

Problems arise when people integrate trading concepts in an investment approach. For instance, it makes no sense for pure value investors to:

1. **Use stop-loss orders for long positions**: stop-loss orders are automatic sell orders that are triggered when a stock falls below a predefined price target. Stop-losses make perfect sense for traders because they want to get out of positions if the price action disconfirms their trading thesis. For investors, however, stop-loss orders conflict with the basic investment philosophy. Warren Buffett, for instance, likens a stop-loss order with buying a house for $1 million dollar and instructing your broker to sell the house if he gets a bid for $800,000. Indeed, according to the investment philosophy price declines make a stock *more* (not less) attractive – provided that the intrinsic value stands firm. Hence, true investors see price declines as potential purchase opportunities rather than reasons for a sale.

---

[163] Note that, as discussed in the introduction of this book, the market can be beaten through styles that are very different from the investment style. The problem discussed here is that of people who are adrift, because they can't express their philosophy, style and market approach in a clear way, and because they can't even explain why they have an edge in the market.

[164] Some traders use fundamentals as a criterion for stock selection, but they buy and sell based exclusively on trading signals (and not on intrinsic value considerations). One example is William O'Neil who uses the so-called CANSLIM approach (O'Neil, 2002). He looks for fundamentally strong companies with excellent price action and he buys/sells these stocks through typical momentum signals.

2. **Pyramid up**: traders often buy more of a stock (i.e., they pyramid their position) when it goes up. This is consistent with the momentum trading philosophy, which states that strong price action is likely to continue. For investors, pyramiding makes little sense. Investors don't take their cues from price action. They analyse businesses fundamentally. For them, buying more of a rising stock is only warranted if the stock remains sufficiently undervalued at the higher price.

## E.I.1.b Speculation instead of investing

Investors must understand the difference between speculation and investing. Speculation can be defined as playing the markets based on hunches, rumours, hope and wishful thinking. Speculators don't care about the fair value concept. Their only goal is to unload their stocks on unwary buyers at a price above their own purchase price.

Speculators believe in the Bigger Fool Theory, which says that paying a foolish price for a stock (i.e., more than its fair value) makes sense if one can expect that someone else (a bigger fool) will later be willing to buy the stock at an even higher price. As such, speculators feel no qualms about buying fundamentally weak stocks if they can see a reason that someone else will later take the stock out of their hands at a higher price.

An example of a speculation would be the purchase of a stock in anticipation of a takeover (which may never come), or in the belief that management will do something special. Another example is the purchase of very expensive stocks during a market bubble.

Although speculation can be rewarding over short periods of time, it seldom pays off over the long term. Speculation becomes very dangerous once people begin to take it seriously. And it is at its most destructive when it looks easiest.

**Table 3: Investors versus speculators**

| | True investor | Speculator |
|---|---|---|
| **Strategy** | Buys when value > price; sells when value < price | Belief in the Bigger Fool Theory |
| **Attitude** | Strives for adequate and realistic returns over the long term; patient | Chases quick and extraordinary returns; Nervous; Sees daily price fluctuations as vital to his/her wealth |
| **Behaviour during bull markets** | Cautious; Selective buying; possibly net seller (with accumulation of cash) | Speculation is the name of the game; ridicules investors who lag behind; complacency: "I will get out before the crash" |
| **Behaviour during bear markets** | Holds on to high-quality stocks; buys when the bear market is in full force | Gets caught off guard and loses his/her shirt; panics near the bottom |
| **Investment process** | Screening + fundamental analysis + valuation | Hunches + rumours + hope + jumping on the bandwagon |

As Warren Buffett stated in the quote at the beginning of this chapter, the major problem with speculation during a market frenzy is that it is extremely difficult to know when to call it quits. Most speculators get caught in the downdraught when the bubble bursts. Even outside of market bubbles, speculation is outright dangerous, because it is not based on a sound philosophy and style. Warren Buffett is convinced that nobody is smart enough to make money from buying stocks one actually doesn't want with the aim to sell them to other people.

It should be clear by now that speculation has nothing in common with investing and that people should never delude themselves that they are investing when they are speculating. In fact, as illustrated in Table 3, the profile of a typical speculator is totally different from that of a true investor.

## E.I.2 Looking for bargains in the wrong places

Smart investors seek out ideas that deserve further scrutiny based on the framework explained in Chapter B. They don't waste their precious time on stocks that probably offer no excess return. Notwithstanding, the average investor does not consciously screen for potential bargains in a disciplined way; many investors analyse stocks they accidentally bump into.

As we have seen in the Chapters A and B, many investors even feel attracted to exactly the wrong stocks (e.g., hot stocks), due to herding behaviour, extrapolation, etc. Less known, but potentially equally harmful, are mistakes due to the familiarity and sympathy bias (see Chapter A). People often feel comfortable with stocks that have their headquarters close to where they live, that have excellent products, that are active in businesses they believe they are familiar with (e.g., one's employer), and so on.

## E.I.3 Mistakes in fundamental analysis

### E.I.3.a Lack of independence

Carrying out an independent due diligence is time-consuming, it requires effort and it can only be done by people with the appropriate expertise and experience. Independence also demands courage because it doesn't provide the comfort to hide behind the opinions of others. It is therefore understandable that many investors take their cues from professionals, follow the latest advice they overhear in the financial media, or take tips from friends and family. Admittedly, nothing is easier and more tempting than letting other people do the heavy lifting. Unfortunately, as explained here, it is seldom the road to success.

#### 1. The flaw in taking one's cues from professionals

In the field of investing, it is hard to find valuable and unbiased information from analysts, market gurus and economists. Study after study shows that the track records of these professionals are poor. Stock analysts don't do a particularly good job of predicting future earnings and the asset allocation skills of market gurus are questionable.[165] There are only

---

[165] (Dreman, 1998) and (Damodaran, 2004).

a few people who have managed to beat the market by following the advice of investment newsletters and economic forecasts are unreliable. This is illustrated in Figure 15, which compares the 1-year forward forecasts of economic analysts with the actual 1-year real GDP growth over the year following these forecasts since 1970. As we can see from this figure, economists don't recognise recessions and strong growth spurts until after the facts.

**Figure 15: Analyst forecast versus GDP**

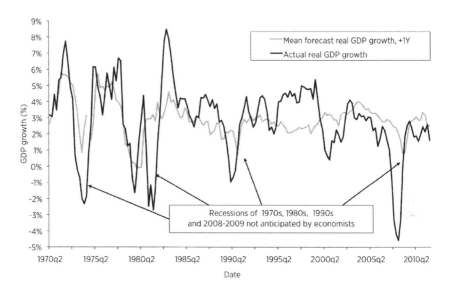

Sources: Federal Reserve of Philadelphia, Bureau of
Economic Analysis – US Department of Commerce

There are various reasons behind the poor showing of professionals. First of all, making forecasts about the economy or about a company's sales and earnings is extremely hard. What is more, experts with more professional knowledge turn out to be only slightly more successful at forecasting than those who know less.[166] In fact, forecasts by people with the most knowledge (who often also have the highest intelligence) are even less reliable than those of the average person. This can be explained by the fact that ego often gets in the way of common sense. Smart people are usually less willing to change their view and admit errors. Besides, smart people tend to overcomplicate forecasting models out of overconfidence.

A second reason for the poor track records of professionals is that a lot of the information in the investment world is biased. Sell side analysts and market gurus of investment banks, for instance, are supposed to generate business for the bank. They are paid to convince investors to turn their portfolio over in order to generate commissions for their employer. As a result, their story is often more of a sales pitch than a genuine expression of their conviction.

---

[166] Kahneman, 2011.

Making matters worse, it is hard for investors to benefit from valuable and unbiased professional advice due to an *implementation shortfall*. Acting on recommendations after they are made public inevitably implies acting on information that is probably already discounted in the stock market. The implementation shortfall is also present for private investment services like newsletters. There the problem is that most subscribers cannot buy or sell on the same terms as those used by the newsletter due to timing differences and/or because they lack the cash to take all recommendations.

Finally, following the moves or recommendations of highly successful investors also suffers from a serious implementation shortfall. Although mimicking legendary investors can pay off handsomely, it is very unlikely that copycats will match the return of these top investors for three major reasons. First, excellent investors pursue discretion to avoid competition from copycats. Therefore, one usually has to wait several weeks (or even months) before the moves of professional investors are made public.

Second, when a trade of a top investor gets out potential excess returns are quickly eliminated by the actions of imitators. Third, following single moves of top investors will result in a portfolio that is quite different from that of the top investor (in terms of stock weights, number of stocks, stock names, etc.). This also implies that there may be a weak relationship between the performance of the investor's portfolio and that of the top investor.

---

*"There are no highly predictable industries in which you can count on analysts' forecasts. Relying on these estimates will lead to trouble."*

**David Dreman (Dreman, 1998)**

---

## 2. The bad counsel of the financial press

The financial press is not in the business of providing valuable news on a complicated topic like investing. It is in the business of generating high viewer and reader ratings. To this end, the financial media (newspapers, financial press, television, etc.) like to feature mediagenic and outspoken investment professionals that generate sensational news of little substance. The media are also primarily preoccupied by the short term (because most viewers and readers are), and seldom provide news of interest to true investors with long time horizons.

Moreover, the financial media are focused on making – and not on preserving – money (as most viewers and readers are). Hence, the financial press will seldom recommend a defensive approach, not even when this would be the most appropriate action (e.g., in a speculative bubble or towards the end of a bull market).

## 3. Taking tips from friends and acquaintances

Taking tips from friends, family, or insiders is tempting, but it is not the road to riches.

In Chapter B I mentioned that intelligent investors don't take tips from family, friends, neighbours or acquaintances. Many of the greatest investors admit that they have fallen for tips early in their career, but they almost always had a bad experience that taught them not to rely on tips anymore. This is obvious. In all honesty, what should well-thinking investors expect of friends and acquaintances in a complicated field like investing?

> *"Vanity plays a great part in the willingness with which traders fall victim to supposed 'straight tips.' If, however, he will have the humility to believe that he may be the thousandth rather than the first or second to hear the bullish story, this lack of self-pride will probably be well rewarded. No one ever attained a fortune by seeking the advice of others."*
>
> **David Carret (Krass, 1999)**

## E.I.3.b Biased analysis

Doing a thorough company analysis is tough. Doing an objective analysis is even tougher. Investors often trip up when cognitive biases colour their opinions about companies (see also Chapter A). When this happens, they tend to be sloppy in their due diligence. Or they look for evidence that confirms their investment thesis and ignore disconfirming elements.

The fact that many of the greatest investors in the world have fallen prey to the following cognitive biases should serve as a warning that nobody can totally exclude their influence in a due diligence:

1. **Mindless extrapolation**: to many people it seems obvious that historical trends are likely to continue. Therefore investors are inclined to project financial performance as a simplistic continuation of the company's growth path. Although such mindless extrapolation is understandable, company earnings and sales seldom behave so predictably. Moreover, through extrapolation one will surely miss the really big swings above or below the growth path that have a large impact on a company's stock price.

2. **Cherry-picking of information**: people are selective in the information they use to make up their minds. They overweight information that is more recent, more emotionally charged and/or that is presented in the most appealing way. The consequence is that investors often feel comfortable with a superficial due diligence based on incomplete or anecdotal information. They may, for instance, be convinced that a company is excellent after a sensational presentation by a charismatic CEO. Or they may be impressed by a retail chain after a single excellent shopping experience (which may not be representative of the retail chain).

3. **Sympathy and home bias**: when people like a company for one reason or another, they often look for evidence that confirms their positive stance and they ignore

things that disconfirm their thesis. Even worse, they may forgo a serious due diligence altogether when they are convinced beforehand that the company is excellent. For instance, many investors are positively biased towards companies that make products they like, that have major operations close to their home, that have nice and/or familiar names, or that have accidental similarities to them (e.g., a ticker that matches their initials).[167] In *The Billion Dollar Mistake*, Stephen Weiss gave a good example of the destructive force of the sympathy bias. Kirk Kerkorian, a seasoned and highly successful investment veteran, lost a bundle when he invested in GM right before its bankruptcy. His problem was that he had been passionate about cars since boyhood. Hence, he did not think straight when he took a stake in GM at the worst possible time in its history.

4. **Illusion of familiarity**: people sometimes forgo a serious analysis because they feel familiar with a business for one reason or another. For instance, many people buy shares of their employer because they believe that they know what is going on at the firm. In reality, though, employees don't usually know much about the financials of the company they work for. Another excellent example of how the illusion of familiarity can affect even very successful investors was given by Stephen Weiss.[168] David Bonderman, one of the greatest private-equity investors in the world, lost his shirt when he invested in Washington Mutual (WM) right before its demise in 2008. He did not analyse the company (as he used to do with his private equity investments) because he had been on WM's board a few years before. His mistake was to believe that he was familiar with WM due to his previous board experience – he failed to acknowledge that the company had changed a lot since he had left.

## E.I.3.c Poor understanding of probabilities and randomness

A proper understanding of probability and randomness is hard because it is counterintuitive. Experiments have shown that even experts in statistics can't shut out their misleading intuition when they are faced with certain statistical problems. It is therefore understandable that people tend to make the following mistakes during a due diligence process:

1. Investors often draw conclusions from too few (i.e., a statistically insignificant number of) facts and events. This cognitive bias is also referred to as the **representative bias**. For instance, it is wrong to conclude from the poor sales at one particular shop of a retail chain that the entire chain is not doing well.

2. Investors have **problems with causality**. They often confuse correlation with causality, or they assume incorrectly that one factor causes another while in reality it is the other way around. For instance, there may be a correlation between the economy and the average length of female skirts but it would be absurd to make predictions about the economy and corporate profits based on the average length of skirts.

---

[167] Zweig, 2007.
[168] Weiss, 2010.

3. Some people **use averages** to predict future events. For instance, they may use the average length of past bear markets to predict when a new bear market will end. Or they use the average economic rebound from previous recessions as an indication for the strength by which the economy (and corporate profits) will rebound after a trough.

### E.I.3.d Attention to the wrong factors

Finally, many investors pay too much attention to elements that do not really matter in a due diligence. Typical distractions are:

1. **Focus on economic scenarios (for bottom-up investors)**: many bottom-up investors incorporate economic forecasts in their stock analysis. As said before, economic forecasting is extremely hard and investors who take their economic forecasts seriously should wonder whether they belong to the top-down or bottom-up camp. As a general rule, bottom-up investors pay scant attention to the economy. They focus instead on the analysis of individual companies, always trying to uncover value that will emerge irrespective of the economic climate.

2. **Short term considerations**: true investors focus on the long term and do not incorporate short-term elements in their analysis. True investors are not mesmerised by a company's results over the next quarter. They focus instead on how they see companies growing and prospering over the next couple of years.

> *"Charlie and I continue to believe that short-term market forecasts are poison and should be kept locked up in a safe place, away from children and also from grown-ups who behave in the market like children."*
>
> **Warren Buffett, 1992 letter to the shareholders of Berkshire Hathaway**

## E.I.4 Valuation mistakes

### E.I.4.a Price considerations in the valuation process

Some investors believe that the *price* (not the valuation) of a stock versus other stocks or versus its historical price range reveals something about the attractiveness of that stock. Here are the most common mistakes:

1. **Current stock price as a measure for value**: there is a persistent belief among inexperienced investors that stocks with a very low price (e.g., $3) must be cheap and that stocks with a high price (e.g., $400) must be expensive. These people are convinced that they can hardly lose anything on low-priced stocks and they believe that high-priced stocks are risky. They are also the ones that buy stocks (and

therefore push prices up) after stock splits, which is of course all too absurd.[169] Confusing price with value is a serious mistake. We know from Chapter D that the intrinsic value of a stock is determined by its future cash flows. Price does not have anything to do with this. Price is what you pay, value is what you get.

2. **Historical price as a measure for value**: an equally common valuation error is to compare the current stock price with the historical price. For one reason or another, most people look at a price chart over the past five to ten years before they buy a stock. When the price is high in a historical perspective, it is believed to be expensive and when it is at a low, it is believed the stock is due to go up. Likewise, when a stock has gone up and down in a trading range for some time, many people see that range as fair. So when the stock reaches the low end of the price range, they believe that the stock is attractive and when it climbs to the upper end of the price range, it is believed to be expensive.

    There are two major problems with this type of anchoring to historical prices. First of all, it assumes that the market priced the stock correctly in the past. Second, anchoring to historical prices ignores possible changes that may have happened at the company over the past few months or years. According to Philip Fisher, far too many people underestimate the impact that corporate changes can have on a company's intrinsic value over the course of only a few years.[170]

3. **Purchase price as an anchor for value**: another common mistake is to confuse a stock's value with the price at which it was purchased. Many people refuse to accept that a stock's fair value has fallen after they bought it. So, they are reluctant to sell below their purchase price.

4. **Price action as a factor in intrinsic value**: price movements have an impact on the fair value that investors assign to a stock. For instance, many investors get second thoughts when a stock drops suddenly below a price which they previously considered to be cheap. The mere fact that the stock falls raises doubts about the original investment thesis. This is understandable because selling pressure elicits the idea that the sellers know something the buyers don't. Although scepticism is healthy in investing, changing one's convictions due to price action is not. Seasoned investors are not swayed by market movements. Nevertheless, even the greatest investors seem to wrestle with the impact of price action. For instance, to guard himself against the inclination to defer purchases during bear markets, John Templeton entered buy orders for stocks at very low prices (which he believed were cheap) when the markets were doing well.

---

[169] Stock splits do not create value. Suppose that a company has shares outstanding at $10 each. After a split of the stock in ten, a shareholder will get ten new shares for each old one. So, the price of the stock will be $1. The shareholders will not have gained anything because nothing has changed with the value of the entire firm. Each new stock has one-tenth of the claim on the same company compared to the old stocks. In other words, the intrinsic value of the new shares is one-tenth the intrinsic value of the old ones. So the gap between the price and the intrinsic value (if there was any before the split) remains the same after the split.
[170] Fisher, 1996.

> *"The correct attitude of the security analyst toward the stock market might well be that of a man toward his wife. He shouldn't pay too much attention to what the lady says, but he can't afford to ignore it entirely."*
>
> **Benjamin Graham (Lowe, 1999)**

All of the mistakes above are due to cognitive biases (anchoring in particular) and the fact that many investors take shortcuts in the valuation process. It is tempting to use price as a proxy for value but it makes little sense to do so. Intrinsic value is the fair price of a stock based on its current cash assets and future cash flows. Price is what the market believes the intrinsic value to be.

The main lesson is that investors should pay less attention to the stock price. It is, for example, a good practice to start out an analysis without looking first at the historical stock price. And it is recommended not to change previous conclusions merely based on price action.

### E.I.4.b Too little attention to the valuation-quality trade-off

A second type of valuation mistake is to buy or sell stocks based on multiples, without proper attention to the underlying business' quality. Two common mistakes are:

1. **Buying "cheap" crap**: a stock is not a bargain because it has a rock-bottom multiple. Many low-multiple businesses deserve their low multiple and don't make for good long-term investments. After all, cheap crap is still crap.

2. **Overpaying for quality**: some investors buy high-quality businesses irrespective of their price in the assumption that there is a consistent connection between a company's business success and its stock price. Even though it is true that long-term investors are advised to invest in great businesses, they stand to incur serious losses when they forget to ask, "How much?" One must always keep in mind that it is very rare for medium to large companies to grow their intrinsic value over multi-decade periods at more than 15% per year. This should serve as a warning that the price at which a stock is bought constitutes a very important factor in the overall return of an investment. Hence, investors who hope to achieve returns in excess of about 15% per year over the long run have no other choice than to buy the shares of exceptional companies at significant discounts to their intrinsic value.

> *"Our goal is to find an outstanding business at a sensible price, not a mediocre business at a bargain price."*
>
> **Warren Buffett (Cunningham, 2001-A)**

# E.II Summary of process mistakes and how to deal with them

Table 4 shows the typical process mistakes discussed above and how investors can limit the impact of these errors or avoid them altogether.

**Table 4: Process mistakes and how to avoid them**

| Common process mistakes | | How to avoid process mistakes |
|---|---|---|
| Incoherent strategy (trading/speculation, no targeted search for bargains) | | Powerful investing philosophy; disciplined and consistent execution |
| Mistakes in fundamental analysis | Lack of independence | Proprietary knowledge through hard work; mental strength to go one's own way |
| | Biased analysis (extrapolation, cherry-picking, illusion of familiarity, home & sympathy bias) | Close attention to the bear case; selling stocks about which one is biased; thorough due diligence; check for unconscious biases |
| | Representative bias; poor vision on causality; use of averages | Gather as much information as possible and apply common sense |
| | Focus on economy and short term | Focus on bottom line and long term |
| Valuation mistakes | Price instead of value | Pay little attention to stock prices |
| | Too little attention to the valuation-quality trade-off | Pay attention to qualitative factors in fundamental analysis |

A first type of mistake is an incoherent strategy. Many investors have only a rudimentary idea of what investing is about. They don't actively look for bargains because they don't know where these can be found. Or they integrate trading and speculative elements in their strategy even though these elements are incompatible with investing.

The obvious way to counter such mistakes is through a powerful and well-articulated investment philosophy. In addition, the strategy (i.e., the implementation of the philosophy in practice) must be perfectly compatible with the philosophy. Equally important is that the strategy be applied consistently and irrespective of the market conditions. Indeed, strong discipline in the execution is of paramount importance because far too many investors are tempted to abandon their strategy (and philosophy) when they hit a rough patch only to find afterwards – perhaps a few years later – that they would have been better off if they had stuck with their original approach.

Among the mistakes in fundamental analysis, lack of independence is probably the most prevalent and persistent. Beating the market is almost impossible if one can't think for oneself, make one's own investment cases, take one's own decisions, and have the courage to go against the prevailing market opinion of the day.

To maintain their independence, top investors avoid the noise and rumours in the media, sometimes by moving physically to locations far away from the chatter.[171] They are not interested in inside information or tips. They ignore analyst recommendations. And they don't take their cues from gurus or the crowd. The keys to independence are proprietary knowledge through hard work (in order not to have to rely on external research) and mental strength (to go against the market).[172]

> "Knowledge brings confidence, and confidence is what keeps people in stocks that are undergoing price pressures yet continue to have great growth in earnings. Confidence is what helps successful investors to buy more shares when prices dip, while investors who do not know what they own become emotional and sell out of fear and lack of knowledge."
>
> **Frederick Kobrick (Kobrick, 2006)**

Another type of mistake in fundamental analysis is bias due to extrapolation, consistency, sympathy, familiarity, and the like. One way to counter these biases is to pay *special attention to the bear case of one's trades.* Many top investors try to find as many arguments as possible to kill their investment thesis, and see whether the thesis holds up against these counterarguments.

Another practice of some top investors is to sell stocks when they have the impression that their thinking about these stocks has become coloured. For instance, the legendary macro investor Michael Steinhardt fought the consistency, familiarity and sympathy biases by sporadically selling all his long positions and by covering all his short positions. In this way he could start over with a clean slate devoid of preconceptions.

A third practice that serves as a protection against cognitive biases is a thorough due diligence. By examining a stock from all angles, one can hope to acquire objective and unique insights about the investment. Finally, it is also a good habit for investors to deliberately check for unconscious biases that may influence one's opinion. For instance, one can look for similarities between the stock and other stocks, see whether previous personal experiences can be associated with the stock, or check whether one has the impression of being familiar with the company for one reason or another.

A further mistake in fundamental analysis is the improper understanding of probabilities, causalities and randomness due to the representative bias, the recency bias, and so on. To fight mistakes that result from fragmental data and to form a more reliable opinion one must gather as many facts as possible and interpret them through common sense.

---

[171] For instance, John Templeton moved to Nassau and Warren Buffett headquartered in Omaha. Bernard Baruch fled Wall Street when he realised that he lost his focus and discipline by being close to the action.
[172] Note that, according to Jim Chanos, being and staying independent is even tougher for short sellers than for long investors. The reason is that short selling usually means that one has to stay the course although one is constantly bombarded by the positive noise that is all too common in the media (e.g., positive analyst recommendations, bullish talk by management, positive chatter on TV, etc.).

Finally, referring to the bottom row in Table 4, investors must be on guard against valuation mistakes due to price considerations. To this end, they should try to limit their attention to (changes in) stock prices (e.g., by not checking prices on a daily and/or hourly basis). Not looking at short-term price movements helps to counter the inclination to seek patterns and serves as a protection against anchoring to historical prices.

# PART II

## BUYING, HOLDING AND SELLING

# CHAPTER F

## DIFFERENT TYPES OF STOCK

"Most bad companies stay bad, and most cheap stocks get cheaper. Once you realize that, then you're ready for investing in turnarounds situations."

CHARLES KIRK, THE KIRK REPORT

THERE ARE VARIOUS types of stocks on the market and each one of them should be approached in a different way. Every investor who wants to make money must know these stock categories, their particular behaviour and how they should be traded. Without trying to be exhaustive, this chapter discusses the following types of stocks that all investors should understand:

1. stocks in different growth phases: stocks of emerging companies, fast growers, and mature companies (including stalwarts and slow growers),

2. cyclicals,

3. turnarounds,

4. asset plays, and

5. special situation stocks.

For each type of stock I explain the challenges and compile the recommendations of top investors on how these stocks should be bought and sold.

### F.I Investing over the growth cycle

A popular model in business theory used to describe a company's or an industry's evolution is the product life cycle or the company growth cycle (see Figure 16).[173] According to this concept, new (or emerging) companies initially grow their sales slowly due to the natural reluctance of potential customers to do business with a new and small firm.

---

[173] Porter, 1980.

If the company survives the emerging phase, sales can pick up rapidly provided that the initial buyer inertia eases, and/or that the business expands geographically and over new types of customers. This is the growth phase of the company. After some time, the company's customer base saturates and maturity sets in. At that point, the firm serves such a large part of the market that business expansion slows down significantly. Finally, the company can get trapped in decline when sales drop due to competition or when the company's products become obsolete.

**Figure 16: Company growth cycle**

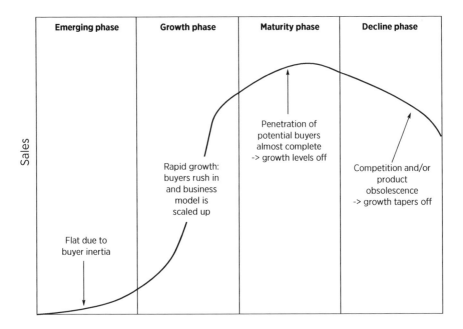

The company growth cycle is an attractively straightforward model, but it is far too simplistic. Not all companies go through the different phases of the growth cycle. Some companies never grow fast and go into decline before they even get started. Some new companies immediately reach maturity and turn into slow growers. Still others move almost immediately into the fast growth stage. For some companies (e.g., cyclical growers) fast growth is characterised by high sales volatility. And some companies manage to avoid the decline phase altogether through continuous innovation.

Nevertheless, the growth cycle is useful to explain the characteristics of stocks in different stages of growth and it helps us to understand how the market looks upon them. Following, there is a discussion of five types of stocks along the growth cycle. Emerging companies are companies that are in the very early stages of their lives. As we will see, they are very different from companies in the fast growth phase (fast growers) or from mature companies (stalwarts, slow growers or mature cyclicals).

## F.I.1 Emerging companies

Emerging companies are new companies with track records that are typically shorter than ten years. Some still haven't found a viable business model. Others have a solid business plan in place and predict ambitious sales growth. Some are growing in totally new industries, whereas others try to find a foothold in mature and established industries. As they are small and new all have in common that they have some aura of mystery around them. Many thrive on the hopes of investors who want to believe that they will be giants some day.

As we have seen in Chapter B, top investors are more down to earth about emerging companies than the average market participant. Their first problem is that emerging businesses don't have sufficiently long track records to evaluate management, their strategy and their business model. Related to this is the problem that emerging companies are very risky.

Management of these businesses is usually inexperienced, even though it has to face extraordinary challenges. Indeed, emerging companies have to go head to head with competitors which may be much more experienced and may have much deeper pockets than them. They must choose an appropriate strategy. They have to deal with growth pains. They must build out systems (e.g., HR). They have to convince customers to buy their product instead of the products they are used to. They have to deal with production problems. And so on.

More often than not, emerging companies fail because they cannot win over sufficient customers, because they become the victim of their own success (e.g., the company can't keep pace with the growth and the lack of organisation/experienced staff/accounting expertise, etc., throws the company into chaos), or because they are overtaken by smarter or better capitalised competitors that come from behind. For example, in the industries of hamburgers, running shoes and computer operating systems, first movers were beaten by companies such as McDonald's, Nike and Microsoft.

It bears repeating that sound advice for most people is to ignore the siren calls of emerging businesses. Such companies are not for the regular common stock investor, but for private equity experts.[174] Another question that one should ask before pouring one's money into a new venture is the following – given the fact that promising ventures can probably find private equity partners when they need cash, why would one invest in ventures that can't find such professional partners and that have to tap the stock market to fund their business? It's fair to assume that many publicly listed ventures are probably second-rank businesses that private equity investors have looked into and given a pass.

## F.I.2 Fast growers

Fast growers are companies that have successfully gone through the emerging phase. They have demonstrated that their business model works and that their successful formula can

---

[174] Professional private equity investors of the venture type buy shares in (usually non-listed) companies and support them operationally.

be duplicated to other customer groups and/or to other locations (e.g., a restaurant chain that successfully expands into new locations). They have overcome initial buyer inertia and are winning over new customers at a fast pace. They have also turned a profit. Even though emerging businesses can grow rapidly too, the big difference with fast growers is that the latter grow profits and cash flows, whereas fast growing emerging companies typically only grow sales (with negative profits and cash flows).

Fast growers are the growth investor's favourites. These stocks can enjoy ten to hundred-fold price increases over the course of several years. This is illustrated in Table 5, which shows the best returns of some very successful American growth companies over periods of 10 and 20 years.

**Table 5: Annual compound returns and total cumulative multiplier of the stock price of some very successful fast growers**

|  | Ten years ending | Annual return | Stock price multiplier |
|---|---|---|---|
| Dell | 23/12/1999 | 101% | x 1093 |
| Cisco | 31/8/2000 | 99% | x 964 |
| Wal-Mart | 21/8/1987 | 56% | x 87 |
| Microsoft | 30/3/1999 | 56% | x 87 |
| The Home Depot | 14/12/1995 | 45% | x 42 |
| Starbucks | 29/12/2004 | 36% | x 22 |
| Southwest Airlines | 21/11/2000 | 34% | x 19 |
|  | **Twenty years ending** | **Annual return** | **Stock price** |
| Wal-Mart | 22/9/1994 | 39% | x 764 |
| Cisco | 30/3/2010 | 34% | x 323 |
| Dell | 15/9/2009 | 33% | x 303 |
| Microsoft | 17/1/2006 | 30% | x 199 |
| The Home Depot | 22/7/2005 | 30% | x 180 |
| Starbucks | 2/5/2012 | 25% | x 86 |
| Southwest Airlines | 8/2/2000 | 23% | x 64 |
| McDonald's | 8/12/1999 | 21% | x 46 |

Source data: Yahoo Finance

As we can see from this table, tech companies like Dell and Cisco enjoyed a 1000 fold increase in their share price in the ten years leading up to the top of the tech bubble in early 2000 (but had to give back a lot of their gains thereafter). Also standing out are retailers like Wal-Mart and The Home Depot, which managed to grow their stock price by 30% to 40% a year over a period of 20 years. The most remarkable growth company in the list is probably Southwest Airlines. The stock of this airline managed to gain about 23% annually over a period of 20 years, even though it operated in one of the most competitive, least profitable and most cyclical industries around.

Table 5 can make people dream, but smart growth investors must remain down-to-earth. After all, investing in fast growers is riddled with pitfalls and challenges. Even Peter Lynch, one of the greatest growth investors in history, admitted that four out of five of his growth stocks did not work out.[175] To be successful at growth investing one needs to pay attention to two factors. First, purchases and sales of fast growers must be timed correctly. Second, it is important to be (very) selective in the choice of fast growers.

## F.I.2.a Timing purchases and sales of fast growers

Fast growers are ideal buy-and-hold investments, with one caveat. Bad timing of one's entry and exit can be costly, as explained in the following commentary and using Figure 17:

1. In phase A the company transitions from the emerging into the fast growth phase. Around that moment there may be a relief rally as the uncertainty about the company's business model diminishes. Depending on the valuation and on the clarity of the situation (is the company really transitioning into fast growth?), growth investors may start buying (an initial position) or wait for further confirmation.

2. In phase B the company grows rapidly and demonstrates that its business model works. The market expects strong growth going forward, and bids the stock price up such that multiples usually expand. This is the sweet spot for growth investors as the combination of high earnings growth and multiple expansion can yield phenomenal returns. It is here that the typical growth investor comes on board (even if valuations are already stretched), attracted by the fact that the uncertainty and doubts about the business are vanishing, and because the stock still has a lot of room left to run. Successful growth investors intend to hold on to the stock (often for many years) until phase C.

3. In phase C, the company has expanded so much that it can no longer sustain the high growth rates of the preceding years. Initially, the market doesn't realise that the room for growth isn't there anymore. Paradoxically, at that point investors and professionals expect more of the same, and analysts unanimously put a buy stamp on the stock. The company is hot and trades at a very high valuation. Institutional ownership peaks. The number of analysts that cover the stock hits a new high. This is a treacherous moment because profits and sales are about to slow down significantly. Moreover, there is a risk that sloppy operational execution, which was masked by prior high growth, may get exposed. Other potential problems are that the company may face overcapacity and that buyers get more sophisticated (so they

---

[175] He explained his success by the fact that the phenomenal returns of about 20% of his growth stocks more than made up for the mediocre to poor returns of the other 80%.

bargain harder and they are less likely to buy new versions of the company's products if they are only marginally better than the previous versions). In addition, lower growth also affects staff motivation due to the fact that there are fewer opportunities for promotion. Top performers may become frustrated and leave the company. The high valuation sets the stock up for a fall once the first signs of saturation emerge. Smart growth investors try to get out before the market realises its mistake.

4. In phase D, the market reigns in its expectations. Investors realise that the high growth rates of the past are over. Multiples come down and the stock drops or moves sideways for many years. Depending on the sustainable growth rate and the company's industry, the stock may turn into a stalwart, a slow grower, or a mature cyclical (see below for further explanation).

**Figure 17: Fast growers and basic buying/holding/selling rules**

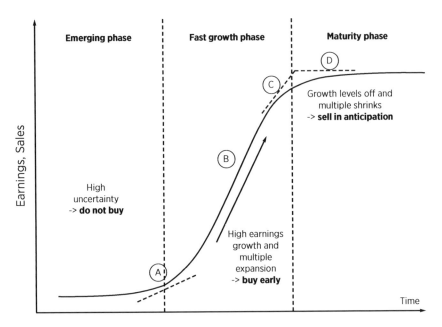

Figure 18 illustrates the timing issue for the growth stock Cisco. This tech company went public in the midst of its high growth phase in 1990. In the year of its IPO, the stock was rather expensive with trailing P/E ratios of about 25 to 30. Nevertheless, even at these valuations investors clearly underestimated the potential of Cisco. Earnings per share (EPS) actually grew at an annual rate of about 95% in the first four to five years that Cisco was a public company. In response to this exceptional growth the P/E gradually rose to about 50 between 1990 and 1993. True growth investors who believed in the story of Cisco would have accumulated positions in the stock (in spite of the lofty valuation) as the company was clearly in phase B.

**Figure 18: Cisco as an example of a fast grower, one data point per quarter**

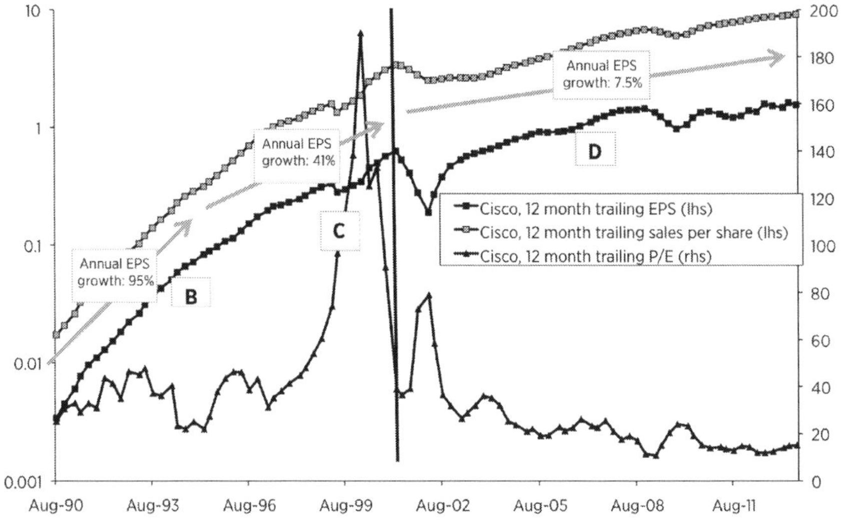

Source data: Bloomberg

Then, in spite of its strong earnings and sales momentum, investors suffered from a fear of heights. The stock's P/E ratio came down to the (still relatively high) low twenties in 1994 and 1995. Smart growth investors could have bought more of the stock at the lower multiple. As an aside, even shares that had been bought at the P/E peak in May 1993 would have posted a gain of more than 30% by March 1995.

From March 1995 onwards, the P/E gradually rose back to about 50 in the summer of 1998. At that time, the internet and technology frenzy were raging and Cisco had become very hot. It was on the buying list of numerous analysts and institutional investors were wild about it. Given the high valuation and the fact that the annual earnings growth rate had come down significantly to about 41%, cautious growth investors would have got cold feet by then.

Positions bought in May 1993 had risen ten times in five years and investors who had taken advantage of the stock's temporary weakness in March 1995 would have made 700% in three years. This illustrates that growth investors can make impressive returns on growth stocks by buying late (i.e., in the midst of phase B, and at relatively high valuations) and by selling early (close to phase C).

Between the summer of 1998 and March 2000, the stock really went through the roof. It actually rose from about $13 (in May 1998) to $80 in March 2000. As we can see in Figure 18, EPS could not keep up with the stock price and the P/E multiple expanded to an extremely high 190! At that point, many people saw the writing on the wall. The valuation had become ridiculous.

Cisco's growth rate of the late 1990s had been much lower than in the early 1990s and the company had become so big that even the lower growth rates of the late 1990s were not sustainable. Moreover, there were signs that the economy was not doing well. The stock sold off sharply and hit $13.63 on 6 April 2001. This came down to a huge loss of about 83% in around a one-year period. But the decline was not over. On 8 October 2002 the stock bottomed out at $8.6. This corresponds to a loss of about 89% compared with its top of March 2000.

As we can see on the figure, the market correctly anticipated the serious slowdown in earnings and sales growth. As a matter of fact, Cisco has clearly been in phase D since 2000, with a pedestrian annual EPS growth of about 7.5% between 2000 and 2013. As investors have reconciled themselves to this fact, P/E ratios have steadily declined to levels that correspond with a mature company.

### F.I.2.b Selection and follow-up

Fast growers can be found in any type of industry. Although many people naturally gravitate towards high-growth companies in popular, fancy and newfangled industries, these are not the favourites of top investors. Indeed, as mentioned in Chapter B, top investors usually steer clear of companies in the spotlight as *hot* often implies overvaluation and high competitive pressure. Many also give high-growth technology companies like Dell, Microsoft and Cisco a quick pass because the competitive landscape in technology is too unstable for their taste.

It may sound strange, but growth investors frequently look for fast growers that take market share in slow-growth industries. For instance, Peter Lynch took a special liking to retailers and restaurant chains. As we can see from Table 5, successful retailers (e.g., Wal-Mart, The Home Depot), restaurant chains (e.g., McDonald's) or even a coffee shop chain like Starbucks have demonstrated that they can reward investors with impressive long-term returns.

What retailers and restaurant (coffee shop) chains have going for them is that they can expand across wide areas and keep up high growth rates (e.g., of 20% a year) for many years or even decades, even if their overall industry is low growth. Moreover, if they have a unique formula competitive pressure tends to remain subdued as they cannot easily be challenged by new entrants from abroad.

Another similar type of low-growth industry where excellent execution can pay off handsomely is the hotel business. For example, the hotel chain Marriott managed to grow about 20% a year in the 1980s in the US, even though the hotel industry as a whole did not grow at more than 2% a year.

Growth in the fast growth stage is of course seldom as smooth[176] as in the Figures 17 and 18. Fast growers experience bumps along the growth trajectory from point A to C. This bumpy road reflects the threats and challenges that fast growers face. Common problems of fast growers are increased competition (e.g., due to the entrance of new competitors, or because existing competitors catch up with the company), and growing pains where the fast grower becomes a victim of its own success (see also Chapter C). Therefore, intelligent

---

[176] Some companies may even be so-called cyclical growers. These are businesses that experience fast growth in a cyclical industry. After each industry downturn they come out ahead and easily break through their prior peak earnings and peak sales.

growth investors closely monitor whether fast growers stay on track. They try to distinguish temporary setbacks from problems that can impair the company irreparably.

To conclude this section, here are some recommendations of very successful growth investors (e.g., Peter Lynch and T. Row Price) on the selection and the follow-up of growth stocks:

1. The most attractive growth stocks have **low gearing**. Little debt combined with substantial earnings power provides a cushion against the inevitable misfortunes that befall fast growers.

2. Successful fast growers are **disciplined growers**. They realise that fast growth is dangerous because it can be self-defeating (see also Chapter C). Successful fast growers do not overreach. They rather expand in a controlled way. As pointed out by Peter Lynch, disciplined growth is critical for retailers and restaurant chains because many fail in their rush for glory by picking poor locations, overpaying for real estate, paying too little attention to the training and hiring of people, etc. An example of how a fast grower should manage its growth is Starbucks. When it introduced Frappuccino in the supermarkets, it couldn't keep up with demand. To avoid frustration with customers Starbucks withdrew the product from the supermarkets and cancelled all marketing initiatives until the manufacturing capacity was increased.[177]

3. To make sure that one is still years away from the maturity phase, one should focus on companies that have **plenty of room for expansion**. Preferably, the company's market share is small and growing. Or the company targets new promising and substantial markets. A red flag is a company that announces new and unrealistic expansion plans that suggest management's desperation to maintain a high growth rate. An example would be a company that talks about expansion into emerging countries (probably because opportunities in the home market are drying up).

4. Excellent growth stocks **deliver on their promises**. The best of the pack even constantly beat analyst expectations. Beware of growth companies that systematically underperform and blame their poor performance on external factors such as weather conditions. Some red flags that indicate it may be time to move on are:

   • earnings shortfalls,

   • delays in the expansion plans,

   • sales growth deceleration, e.g., due to delayed orders, and

   • steadily falling profits margins and returns on investment, which indicate that the company is losing its edge in the market place.

5. It is best to limit investments to fast growers with **significant insider ownership**. Co-investment by senior leaders aligns management's interests with those of its shareholders. It also serves as a sign of strong personal commitment and credibility.

---

[177] Schultz, 1997.

6. One should look for fast growers with **stable senior management**. Poorly explained management turnover is often a sign that something bad is brewing at the company.

7. Peter Lynch had a soft spot for growth stocks that were still **under the radar** of professionals. He looked for growth stocks with little analyst coverage and low institutional ownership. The reason is that undiscovered growth stocks can get an extra boost the moment they are discovered by the professional community.

8. One must be **flexible on the valuation side**. Promising growth stocks deserve much higher multiples than deep value stocks. So intelligent growth investors know that they have to pay up to get on board. For instance, Cisco and Microsoft never were cheap on conventional earnings multiples in their high growth phase. On the other hand, smart growth investors stay realistic. As a rule of thumb, they avoid fast growers with a PEG ratio of more than one. They are also sceptical of stocks which discount growth rates in excess of 25% a year, as such high growth rates are rare and very hard to sustain.

## F.I.3 Mature companies

Fast growers enter the maturity phase when growth slows down irreversibly. At that point the business has to transform itself to adapt to the new reality. The transition from fast growth to maturity is a period of high uncertainty. It may even be unclear whether the company will move into the maturity phase or directly go into decline.

As said above, due to the poor price action investors are advised to stay away from companies in the transition phase. One can take another look once growth stabilises at a lower level, after the company has successfully implemented the required transformations, and when valuations are much lower than at previous peak levels (see also Figure 18 for the example of Cisco). Provided that growth rates are still positive the company will have turned into a moderate grower, a slow grower, or a cyclical.

From a risk-return perspective, it is safer to focus on the large caps among the mature companies. After all, the earnings and sales growth of small and big mature companies should be comparable and as we have seen in Chapter C, bigger companies are on average safer than smaller ones. Hence, unless there is a compelling difference in valuation, one can expect similar returns from big mature stocks as from small mature ones – and with lower risk. The discussion of cyclicals is left to section F.II. Here I discuss the big moderate growers (which are referred to as "stalwarts" by Peter Lynch) and the big slow growers.

### F.I.3.a Stalwarts

Stalwarts are multi-billion dollar companies with long and excellent track records that have nice, though not exceptional, growth prospects. Thanks to a strong competitive moat, they grow earnings and sales faster than the economy. Stalwarts tend to beat the market over the long term, typically by about 2% to 5% a year (including dividends), but they are no match for successful fast growers.[178] Some examples of stalwarts are Coca-Cola, Johnson & Johnson, Unilever, Danone and Procter & Gamble.

According to Peter Lynch all investors should have some stalwarts in their portfolio because they offer good protection during recessions. Stalwarts hold up well when the economy turns down thanks to their decent dividend yields and because the market knows that they will stay in business.

As far as selection is concerned, one should look for big companies that have superior track records over various business cycles, excellent management, and clear and sustainable competitive advantages. There is reason for concern with stalwarts that constantly yield market share, that bring few new products to the market (due to ineffective innovation), that branch out into businesses unrelated to their core business, or that take on too much debt.

The way to trade stalwarts depends on the investor's goals. People who are satisfied with returns of a few percentage points above the market's average can buy a strong stalwart at a fair price and hold it for many years. More ambitious investors who want to beat the market by a significant margin must trade stalwarts more actively. They should try to buy stalwarts at depressed multiples in order to capture the excess returns when multiples revert to normal levels. And they should not be greedy on the upside. For instance, Peter Lynch usually sold stalwarts that had risen 30% to 50% over a period of about a year.

## F.I.3.b Slow growers

Big mature companies that grow earnings and sales at a pace below that of the market are called slow growers. Examples are regulated utilities or companies that operate in a (over)saturated market (e.g., telecom players). Although Peter Lynch did invest in slow growers that had something special about them (e.g., utilities in distress, see Chapter B), he consistently avoided stable and safe slow growers.

The problem of slow growers is that they are sluggards that offer a stable albeit below-average return. It is definitely not the type of stock that investors should buy if they want to beat the market. If one invests in slow growers anyway one should be alerted by the same red flags as with stalwarts: loss of market share, lack of innovation, diworseification and an unhealthy balance sheet.

---

[178] A nice example is Coca-Cola. The stock returned about 26% a year in its high-growth phase between 1919 and 1938, and 12.4% between 1938 and 1993 in its maturity phase.

# F.II Investing in cyclicals

> *"Buying a cyclical after several years of record earnings and when the P/E ratio has hit a low point is a proven method for losing half your money in a short period of time."*
>
> **Peter Lynch (Lynch, 1993)**

Cyclicals are businesses that are very sensitive to the business cycle due to the elastic demand for their products. Examples of cyclical industries are car manufacturing, steel, airlines, paper and chemicals. Profits of cyclicals often rise spectacularly when the economy gathers steam but they tend to drop precipitously during recessions. The market tries to anticipate the volatile earnings movements of cyclicals by bidding up shares during downturns (in anticipation of the inevitable economic recovery), and by dumping them without mercy when they fear that the economy is becoming overheated.

As an illustration of a cyclical Figure 19 shows the earnings per share (EPS) and the share price of the German airline company Lufthansa from 2000 to 2013. We can see clearly that each time the economy turns down, EPS takes a dive. EPS even turned negative on three occasions over these 13 years. When the economy recovers, EPS grows, although it does not go much beyond previous earnings peaks. As such, EPS goes up and down on the waves of the economy but basically goes nowhere over the long term. We can clearly see that the share price anticipates the heavy swings in EPS – it goes down when earnings are on a peak and it starts to go up when earnings are bottoming out.

**Figure 19: Lufthansa as an example of a cyclical**

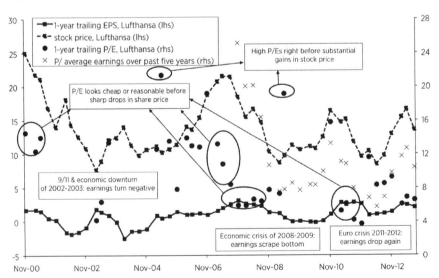

Source data: Bloomberg

Figure 19 demonstrates that investing in cyclicals is all about timing. Cyclicals are not safe buy-and-hold investments. Investors who are wrong in the timing of their entries and exits can easily lose 50% or more of their money over a short period of time. They then may have to wait many years to recoup their losses (if they are ever able to do so). To be successful one must be earlier than other market players in the anticipation of the yo-yo movements of these companies' stock prices. This can become tricky because it not only involves an anticipation of the cycles of the business (or of its industry), but also a factor of speculation about when the market will start to price in the expected earnings fluctuations.

Investing in cyclical stocks does not fit nicely into the investment philosophy. First of all, cyclical stocks should not be traded on intrinsic value considerations as their behaviour is largely determined by earnings cycles. Second, whereas many top investors try to avoid economic forecasts, one cannot afford to ignore the economy when one invests in cyclicals. And third, few investors feel comfortable speculating about when the market will react to certain (expected) economic developments. It should therefore not come as a surprise that cyclicals are not popular with top investors. Nevertheless, those who successfully invest in them give the following advice (see also Figure 20):

1. **Valuation issues:** inexperienced investors are often deceived by valuations when they trade cyclicals. Buying at low and selling at high multiples (which is very effective with other types of stocks) is actually a foolproof method to lose one's shirt. Cyclicals should be purchased when the situation looks desperate and earnings are awful, but some time (e.g., six to nine months) before the business improves again. Conversely, one should get out of cyclicals when earnings momentum is high and before the cycle turns down. Translated into valuation metrics, these rules imply that one should:

   - *Buy at high trailing P/E, sell at low trailing P/E.* It may sound paradoxical, but cyclicals are usually the best buys when their one-year trailing P/E is at a peak and they are the best sales when that P/E is scraping bottom. A high P/E indicates that the company is going through difficult times (earnings are very low), and that investors don't take the low earnings too seriously. A low P/E indicates that earnings are peaking and that the market is suspicious about the sustainability of these earnings. This can be seen very well on Figure 19 for Lufthansa. Close to peaks in the share price, trailing P/E ratios look reasonable or cheap. Around price bottoms, P/E ratios tend to be high (sometimes so high that they are off the chart).

   - *Buy when normalised earnings are at a low, and sell when normalised earnings are at a high.* In order to value cyclicals it is better to replace the trailing P/E with the ratio $P/E_{norm}$ of price (P) to normalised earnings ($E_{norm}$). Hereby, John Neff defines $E_{norm}$ as estimated earnings at a more fortuitous point in the business cycle. David Dreman uses for $E_{norm}$ the average of the earnings over a period of about five years that encompasses a business cycle. The rationale behind normalised earnings is that earnings are likely to revert to normal levels over the long run. So, one should buy when $P/E_{norm}$ is historically low, or sell when this ratio is at a historical high. Figure 19 illustrates the strength of $P/E_{norm}$ for Lufthansa, where we take the average earnings over the last five years as $E_{norm}$. As opposed to the 1-year trailing P/E, this multiple tends to be low around price bottoms and high around price tops. Hence, it is clearly a much more valuable valuation metric for Lufthansa than the 1-year trailing P/E. One potential pitfall of normalised earnings is that the circumstances after the recovery may not be the same as before the recession such that earnings do not go back to normal.

2. **Observation of the business (industry) cycle**: to be successful with a cyclical one must discern and anticipate turning points in the cyclical's industry faster than the market. Therefore, top investors understand the cyclical's industry better than other people. They stay in close contact with professionals of that industry and they closely monitor the following factors to determine when an industry cycle is about to turn:

   - *Capital expenditures*: Jim Rogers looks at capex or capex relative to accumulated depreciation as leading indicators for supply imbalances. Low capex or a low ratio of capex to accumulated deprectiation are positive signs as they are forerunners of a lack of supply in the industry. High capex/accumulated depreciation, on the other hand, is a red flag because it points to potential future oversupply.

   - *Inventories*: rising inventories are indicative of oversupply, whereas falling inventories often precede a recovery.

   - *Power of the unions*: wage concessions under pressure of the unions are worrying because they often indicate that the industry (company) is getting overheated after a long period of strong earnings. Conversely, union power is usually weakest around market bottoms.

   - *Cost discipline*: another typical phenomenon around business tops is that companies in the sector lose their discipline and get complacent. They may, for instance, start building new plants and fancy headquarters.

3. **Front running the market**: successful investors in cyclicals anticipate business (industry) fluctuations before the rest of the market. This is very difficult, though, and it requires:

   - *Contrarian thinking*: successful investors buy when everybody else is giving up on cyclicals, when the brokerage houses are unanimously advising their clients to wait and see. They sell when cyclicals are popular (usually around the peak of a business cycle), at the moment that all analysts that cover the sector issue a buy rating on the stock and the industry.

   - *No bottom fishing nor top picking*: given the difficulty of timing investors in cyclicals should not be greedy. They should not try to buy at the bottom or sell at the top. Cyclical investors survive and thrive by buying (often gradually) on the way down, and by selling into strength.

   - *Looking at insiders*: if insiders buy while earnings are still low, it may be time to join the insiders who, through their action, express the belief that the worst is over.

4. **Type of cyclical**: the safest cyclicals are big companies with strong balance sheets that have plenty of cash to wait out recessions. Such companies always come back, even after deep crises. On the other hand, it is possible to earn higher returns in smaller cyclicals but one has to realise that these stocks come with much higher risk.

5. **Red flags**: Peter Lynch was concerned especially about cyclicals that increased wages after significant pressure from the unions, cyclicals that wasted their money on prestigious projects with little added value (e.g., a fancy headquarters), cyclicals that had to face new competition (e.g., due to new entrants), or cyclicals that had tried but failed to improve their competitive position.

Figure 20 provides a summary of the recommendations for investing in cyclicals.

## Figure 20: Investing in cyclicals – summary of recommendations

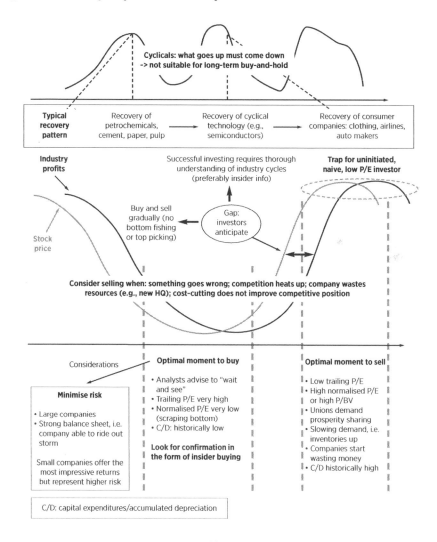

# F.III Investing in turnarounds

All companies – be it fast growers, stalwarts, cyclicals, or any other type of company – can suddenly be confronted with serious problems and challenges. They may lose a competitive advantage and rapidly give up market share to an aggressive competitor. A very important customer may leave or go bankrupt. New trends (e.g., demographic trends, substitutes) can make their product offerings obsolete. Or a recession can make a serious dent in the company's profits and cash flows.

When a company is faced with important challenges of this kind, it is bound to fall out of favour – in particular if the company is also highly leveraged (as leverage compounds its problems). Investors hate uncertainty and discount a dire outcome into the stock price of companies that reel on the verge of collapse.

This is often justified because many struggling businesses cannot work out their problems and see their stock price go from bad to worse. On the other hand, the stock of a company that manages to overcome its problems (these are known as *turnarounds*) can stage a spectacular recovery. Even more, the strong price action of a beaten-down turnaround that has resolved its issues is inevitable and will happen even in a weak market environment.

Figure 21 sketches the turnaround story of the English tour operator Thomas Cook Group, which will be used as an example in the following sections. In 2009 and 2010, a number of initiatives by its former CEO weakened the company's liquidity position. In 2011, all things turned against the business. The tour operator was hit by a shock slump in bookings caused by three unfortunate events that happened at about the same time.

**Figure 21: The turnaround of Thomas Cook Group**

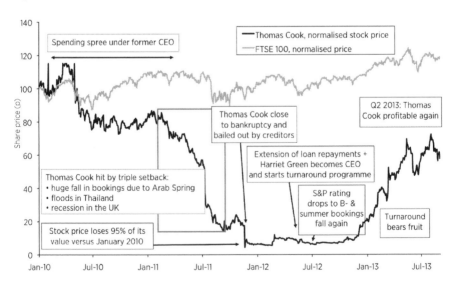

Source data: Yahoo Finance

First, bookings to Arab countries like Tunisia and Egypt plummeted due to the revolutions in these countries. Second, Asian bookings suffered from floods in Thailand. And third, the UK's recession had serious repercussions on discretionary holiday spending. The company's financial position deteriorated quickly and the CEO left. The problems escalated and the company came close to a default on its debt in November 2011.

By that time, the stock had lost about 95% of its value compared to January 2010. Thomas Cook was eventually bailed out twice by its creditors: through a boost of its credit facilities in November 2011 and by the extension of maturing loans in May 2012. Although this solved the immediate liquidity problems, the company still wasn't out of the woods – due to its financial difficulties customers were reluctant to book their holidays with Thomas Cook and as a result the tour operator lost market share to its arch rival TUI Travel.

To turn the business around, Thomas Cook hired a new CEO in May 2012. She managed to restore market confidence through a number of bold steps. Even though summer bookings were down again, the stock started to climb rapidly by the end of 2012. In the summer of 2013 the stock had rallied more than 1000% in just one year (compared to a gain of about 10% for the FTSE 100 over the same period) when it became clear that Thomas Cook had returned to profitability in the second quarter of 2013.

The example of Thomas Cook Group illustrates that, provided that the investor can separate the wheat from the chaff, investing in potential turnarounds can be very rewarding. It can even deliver excellent returns during bear markets. But it is not easy. Some top investors find turnaround investing too hard and they avoid such stocks altogether. Warren Buffett, for instance, states that "turnarounds seldom turn." Other great investors (e.g., Prem Watsa), however, love turnaround plays.

In the following sections I summarise the recommendations of some of the greatest turnaround investors. Before moving over to this, I would like to point out that turnaround investing has nothing to do with vulture investing. The turnaround investor buys *equity* and therefore ranks far behind creditors in case of a bankruptcy. This implies that almost all the upside of turnaround investments is tied to the survival and recovery of the underlying businesses. Turnaround investors are not interested in equity of companies that have gone bankrupt (except on very rare occasions)[179] and they steer clear of businesses that are unlikely to survive.

Vulture investors, by contrast, look explicitly for companies that are in bankruptcy proceedings, or that cannot avert bankruptcy. Vultures also seldom buy stock. They prefer the company's debt securities in order to be the first in line when the business emerges from bankruptcy or when it is liquidated. That's why vulture investing is also called distressed debt investing.

---

[179] An example would be the purchase of new stock issued by a bankrupt company through which the company can settle the creditors' demands and move on as a going concern.

## F.III.1 Attractive turnarounds

As stated above, many companies with serious problems deserve a low valuation. To be successful the turnaround investor must focus on the propositions where the odds favour a recovery. The following issues must be addressed by the due diligence of a turnaround play:

1. **Has the company sufficient liquidity?** If the company's liquidity situation is so bad that it won't buy the company enough time to work out its problems, bankruptcy will be extremely hard to avoid. Peter Lynch paid special attention to the amount of short-term debt, the nature of the debt (e.g., bank debt can be much worse than other types of debt if the bank can call in the loan), and the amount of cash on hand to cover normal expenses. In the case of Thomas Cook, liquidity was horrible in 2011 as the company came close to a default. Nevertheless, as we will see below, there were several reasons to expect that its creditors would bail the company out.

2. **Does the company have a decent core business?** Smart investors seldom invest in turnaround plays with a poor business. There is actually little hope that a company's business will bail the company out of trouble if it has no franchise (i.e., if it lacks competitive advantages) or if its business model is flawed. For a troubled and highly leveraged company with a poor business, the situation is usually desperate. If, on the other hand, the core business is healthy and operations throw off a lot of cash, the chances of survival are much higher. All else being equal, businesses with a strong franchise can survive much longer without defaulting on their debt (which buys them time to resolve their problems), they can count on more goodwill from their creditors, they can come back with a vengeance if external conditions (e.g., the economy) improve, and so on.

   When we look at the example of Thomas Cook, it was clear that the company had a good core business. Thomas Cook was one of the two market leaders in Europe for tour operations. It had a great brand that was very well known in several European countries. Although it suffered from low bookings when it was trying to sort out its financial problems (as customers want to avoid negative surprises with respect to their holidays), it was reasonable to expect that the business would come back if it managed to restore confidence.

3. **Does the company face (other) serious risks?** The last thing a company wishes for when it is trying to solve a difficult problem is to get a new major problem on its plate. Successful turnaround investors avoid turnaround plays that are exposed to other serious risks which can finish the company off. One concern, for instance, is customer concentration. If sales are concentrated heavily in a few customers, loss of business to one of these customers (e.g., because it is also suffering due to poor industry conditions, or because it switches to a more stable supplier) can be fatal.

4. **Can the company rally the necessary resources?** Companies in trouble often cannot turn things around by themselves. They need external support such as new management and new capital. Large companies are at a serious advantage here

over smaller ones. Experienced and skilled managers like the challenge and prestige of turning a big company more than messing around with a small and obscure business. Also, big sponsors – banks, creditors, private investors – have more confidence in large and established businesses, and are therefore more likely to provide them with emergency funds.

As far as Thomas Cook was concerned, there were several reasons to expect that its creditors would throw it a lifeline. First of all, Thomas Cook had about 20,000 employees in the UK. So, pressure from the UK government on the banking sector (which, after all, owed its own survival to the government bailouts of 2008-2009) to come up with a solution was high. Second, creditors realised that a liquidation of Thomas Cook would be anything but straightforward. It was, for instance, unclear who might have been interested in the assets of Thomas Cook as the only possible interested party (TUI) would most probably not be allowed to bid (since this would create a quasi-monopoly in the tour operating industry).

5.  **Is management up to the task?** Star activist investor Bill Ackman believes that one should never invest in turnarounds where one doesn't know management well. It is important to evaluate whether management is capable and trustworthy, and one must examine whether management is taking the right steps to turn things around (e.g., by cost cutting, by redirection of resources, by asset disposals, etc.).

    In the case of Thomas Cook, the CEO who had made the company vulnerable to a downturn had left in the summer of 2011. In May 2012, the new interim CEO was replaced by Harriet Green. She had a stellar track record managing a transformation at her previous firm Premier Farnell and she took the right steps to get the business back on track. She simplified the company, focused on a limited number of brands, sold unprofitable divisions, stripped costs, strengthened the management team and merged the airline activities.

6.  **Will there be anything left for shareholders if the company goes belly up?** Although they want to avoid being dragged into a bankruptcy adventure, turnaround investors try to build a margin of safety into their investments. They only buy turnarounds when they believe that they can recover something if the situation deteriorates. To this end, they compare the company's market cap with the (realisable) value of the assets that would be left over after all creditors are made whole.

7.  **How spectacular will the stock price recovery be if the business turns around?** Obviously, the return of a turnaround play is a function of the price at which the stock was purchased, and of the market conditions (one can expect a more spectacular recovery in a bull market than in a bear market). Less obvious is that the return is also determined by:
    *   *The company's profit margin*: star investors Peter Lynch, Philip Fisher and Marty Whitman point out that less efficient or less profitable companies (such as companies with high fixed costs) usually make for better turnarounds, albeit

with a higher risk. First of all, such companies are usually sold off more aggressively upon trouble as the market correctly believes that they are riskier than the average turnaround. Second, earnings of low margin businesses can recover more spectacularly than in high margin businesses when industry conditions improve. Indeed, even a small increase in the profit margin can give rise to an extraordinary increase in profit for a low-margin business. This can be seen from the following formula (assuming constant sales):

$$\text{profits} = \text{sales} \times \text{margin} \Rightarrow \frac{\Delta\text{profit}}{\text{profit}} = \frac{\text{sales} \times \Delta\text{margin}}{\text{sales} \times \text{margin}} = \frac{\Delta\text{margin}}{\text{margin}}$$

where $\Delta$profit and $\Delta$margin are respectively the change in profit and the change in profit margin. The lower the margin, the lower the denominator, and the higher the profit increase in percentage terms.

- *The presence of tax-loss carryforwards*: turnaround investors must pay special attention to tax loss carryforwards because these can give an extra boost to profits if the business recovers.

In summary, the safest turnaround plays are big companies that got themselves in trouble (e.g., through too much leverage), that have no immediate liquidity problems, that have solid operations and that have excellent management which can sort the problems out.

Experienced investors that are willing to take an extra risk in return for potentially higher rewards can try their chances on low-margin businesses. Turnaround plays that are to be avoided at all cost are small, overleveraged and liquidity-strapped businesses that barely generate cash flows (because they have no business), that have only a few customers, and that have management of questionable integrity and capability.

Finally, Peter Lynch also recommends staying away from tragedies about which the outcome is totally unpredictable. Turnaround investors must clearly identify and understand the problems. Then they must explain in a plausible way why the company will overcome its issues.

Glenn Greenberg also believes that turnaround investors should determine whether the company will make it on its own. Counting on the possibility that the ailing company will be acquired is pure speculation and has no place in sound turnaround investing. In fact, it is rare for turnaround plays to be taken over because selling out is rarely on the minds of turnaround managers. In addition, potential acquirers are unlikely to pay a decent price for a business that is in trouble. They may either negotiate a low takeover price or wait until the company goes bankrupt at which point they can buy its assets on the cheap in a fire sale.

## F.III.2 When and how to buy a turnaround

The aim of intelligent turnaround investors is to build a position in a potential turnaround at a price that discounts a dire outcome. Similar to investing in cyclicals, investing in turnarounds is contrarian because one must feel comfortable buying what others are avoiding. According to Anthony Bolton, because it is virtually impossible to identify the ideal entry point one should buy gradually and accept that the stock will probably go down after the purchase. Given the significant risk of turnarounds, one should also limit the weight of each particular position in one's portfolio. Finally, one or more of the following positive signs can serve as a catalyst to buy a turnaround:

1. **No dividend cuts**: David Dreman believes that steady dividends inspire trust and confidence.

2. **Insider buying**: Robert H. Heilbrunn likes to see insiders buying the company's stock as this is a confirmation that the stock has value.

3. **Confident bond markets**: Peter Lynch suggests looking at the price of outstanding bonds (if there are any) as a clue for whether conservative and balance-sheet oriented bond investors believe that the company will survive the crisis. However, one must realise that the bond market often gives the same signal as the stock market. In the case of Thomas Cook Group, for instance, the bond with a maturity date of October 2015 was trading at 100 in July 2011 (indicating no concern). Around the near-default (in November-December 2011), the bond traded down to around 37-38 (indicating high concern). The bond recovered to 64 in April 2012 but was back at 45 in July 2012. After that, it rallied in line with the stock market price of the company to reach 105 in August 2013.

4. **The market ignores further bad news**: when a stock stops plunging on additional bad news, it may be bottoming out. When we look at Thomas Cook Group, we can see in Figure 21 that the stock held its ground in the summer of 2012 in spite of a downgrade of S&P's credit rating to B-, in spite of declining summer bookings, and even though the company made serious losses. This suggested that investors were looking ahead and ignored the bad news.

5. **An experienced and skilled manager from a leading company takes the reins**: a manager with a strong reputation who leaves a well-paid job to join the company not only inspires confidence (as talent gets on board), but also can be seen as a strong sign that the new manager believes that the company can be turned around (if not, he or she would probably stay in their previous job). As discussed above, Harriet Green, who became the new CEO of Thomas Cook Group in May 2012, had an excellent track record at her former company. The fact that she decided to take the reins was definitely a positive sign.

## F.III.3 When to sell a turnaround

Turnaround investors must consider a sale in two possible scenarios:

1. **The company has solved its problems and everybody can see it**. At the moment that concern about the company's previous problems ebbs away, the stock will have rebounded (spectacularly) from its trough. For instance, concerns about the survival of the Thomas Cook Group were all but gone by the summer of 2013, as the stock was back to its pre-crisis levels and because the bonds were no longer pricing in distress. At that point, the turnaround investor should look at the fundamental picture. If the company has all the required characteristics of an attractive long-term investment, one can hold on to the stock. For not-so-excellent businesses (e.g., companies with below average profit margins), it may be wiser to take profits off the table and move on to another turnaround play. Similar to buying, since it is almost impossible to pinpoint the best exit point it is often better to sell gradually, spreading sales in time.

2. **The company doesn't seem to get a grip on its problems**. When there are indications that the turnaround derails or that the company plunges into turmoil a few years after the initial problems, it may be recommended to slip out of the stock – even if this involves taking a (serious) loss. According to Peter Lynch, red flags that can trigger a sale are: the company's deleveraging, which was on track in previous years, reverses (i.e., debt suddenly rises again); inventories are growing much harder than sales; and turnover in senior management (especially in the operating divisions) – which is normal in the first phase of a turnaround as underperforming managers are removed – continues even two to three years after the company began to tackle its problems.

## F.III.4 Summary

Figure 22 summarises the recommendations discussed above. Turnaround investing revolves around the question of whether the company will be able solve its problems. The most important piece of advice is to avoid ailing companies if one can't make a convincing case that the company will make it.

For instance, it would have been perfectly reasonable not to buy the stock of Thomas Cook Group until the greatest uncertainties around the company were resolved. This would have meant waiting until the summer of 2012 (after the bailouts and after the arrival of a new first-class manager) before accumulating the stock. If the company has liquidity problems, if it can't generate decent cash flows (because it has no business), if it is exposed to other major risks (e.g., customer concentration), if management does not inspire trust, and if it is unlikely that the company can find external support to solve its problems, it is probably safer to give the stock a miss.

If the company does not have these issues, one can take a chance on the turnaround play. This will especially be the case when the stock price is compelling, and if there are encouraging signs such as a stable dividend and insider buying. Conservative turnaround investors stick with sound businesses that have able management and that encounter a hard but temporary problem. More aggressive turnaround investors can try to reap higher rewards through low-margin turnaround plays.

Once the stock is bought, one should monitor closely if the turnaround stays on track. Some years after the problems started, there is reason for concern if there is still no stability in the ranks of senior management, if debt reduction is not on track, or if inventories get out of control. If the turnaround succeeds, one should either sell the stock (if one has little trust in the company's long-term prospects), or hold on to it (if the company makes for an excellent long-term play).

**Figure 22: How top investors proceed in turnaround investing**

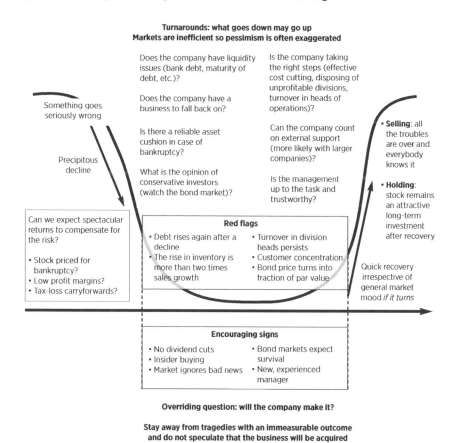

## F.IV Investing in asset plays

Asset plays are companies with assets whose value is not fully recognised in the stock price for one reason or another. Sometimes the assets in question are hidden and can only be discovered by diligent investigators. For instance, John Templeton invested in the

Japanese company Hitachi when he discovered that its earnings did not reflect the earnings of all the companies Hitachi owned. When the earnings of the subsidiaries were taken into account, the price/earnings ratio dropped from 16 to about 6.[180] Likewise, Peter Cundill made excellent profits in the 1980s on a number of German blue chip companies when he discovered an accounting anomaly by which German companies vastly overstated their liabilities.[181]

On other occasions, the value of the assets is hard to determine. For example, it may not always be easy to estimate the value of real estate that is on the books at the historical purchase price of decades ago. Assets may also not be recognised by the market when there is an overall belief that their value will never be reflected in the stock price. This can happen, for instance, in businesses with incompetent management or with managers that have a poor track record of asset allocation. In that case investors often fear that the company would rather squander the asset than realise its value.

Finally, the market sometimes does not recognise assets when their value is unlikely to be realised any time soon. This can be the case, for instance, with tax loss carryforwards.

Investors in asset plays bet that the value of the unrecognised assets will be reflected in the stock price in the near future. They look for catalysts that can unlock the asset's value such as a sale of the assets, an acquisition of the company (with recognition of the assets), or the fact that the market will find out about the existence of the assets (if they are still hidden). Nevertheless, investing in asset plays is an art. Successful asset play investors are able to answer the following questions to a good degree of accuracy:

1. **What is the value of the asset?** It makes no sense to invest in an asset play if one can't estimate the value of the asset with some degree of reliability. So, first of all one must make an educated guess of the realistic value of the asset and examine whether its value is reflected in the stock price.

2. **What is the risk that the value of the asset will decline before it is discounted in the stock price?** A danger that asset play investors have to deal with is the possibility that the value of the asset erodes before it is recognised in the stock price. An important risk factor in this respect is management and its objectives. For instance, a common concern is that management could sell the asset far below its fair value. Or a strategic shift could undermine the value of the asset. Other risk factors are external developments, such as changing trends, the economy and the tax code. For example, a recession or a change in the tax code can make it less likely that a company will realise the full value of a tax loss carryforward.

3. **Are there reasons to believe that the value of the asset will soon be recognised by the market?** Some hidden assets are ignored by the market for decades. So, a major risk of an asset play is that it will take years before the market recognises the value of the asset. Due to the opportunity cost of waiting, it makes no sense to wait too long for the recognition of the asset's value. Successful asset play investors

---

[180] Templeton, 2008.
[181] Risso-Gill, 2011.

therefore look for catalysts that are likely to expose the value of the asset to the market. Activist investors may even take action against management as a way to realise and/or reveal the value of the asset. On the other hand, smart investors sell an asset play when it becomes apparent that the realisation of the value has become less likely, or when they are dissatisfied with the progress of the process.

4. **Is management capable and trustworthy?** We have already seen that management can have an impact on the asset's value but there is still another reason why the evaluation of management is so important with asset plays. It usually takes time (from one year to a few years) for an asset to be recognised in the stock price. If management destroys value in the meantime, the investment is unlikely to pay off – even if the asset is recognised eventually. Asset plays that are managed by people with a poor track record, with doubtful capital allocation skills (especially in the presence of a large cash pool that can be squandered), or with questionable integrity are therefore seldom good investments.

As far as selling is concerned, the same considerations apply as with turnarounds. Once the asset's value is discounted in the stock price, the investor should turn his or her attention to the long-term merits of the company. If the stock was bought for the asset and if the business is only so-so, it is logical to sell the stock and move on. If the company is an excellent business that trades at a cheap to fair price, one can hold the stock for a longer time.

## F.V Investing in special situation stocks

A final category of stocks is that of the special situations. As explained in Chapter B, special situations are stocks with a special corporate event that causes a temporary pricing anomaly. Refer to Chapter B for a thorough discussion of these types of stocks and for advice on when to buy them.

The decision to sell depends on the company. If you buy a special situation stock solely because of a special corporate event, but you don't like the business, be prepared to sell once the market rectifies its error. If the business is excellent intrinsically, one can hold the stock even after the special attributes are reflected in the stock price.

## F.VI Summary and conclusions

The most important lesson of this chapter is that different types of stocks must be traded differently. Fast growers are ideal buy-and-hold investments, provided that they stay on track. With cyclicals the buy-and-hold approach is to be avoided. Stalwarts can be buy-and-hold or shorter term plays depending on the investor's objectives. Turnarounds, asset plays and special situation stocks should all be bought in anticipation of a specific event. After the event has taken place, the investor's attention should turn to the intrinsic long-term qualities of the business.

A second lesson is that investors don't have to dabble in every type of stock. It's probably better to pick one's fights carefully. One can specialise in a few types of stocks with which one feels comfortable, and which fit well within one's personal style and philosophy. Many top investors do just that. They focus on certain stock types and they avoid others. For instance, Glenn Greenberg is not fond of cyclicals and turnarounds and Warren Buffett is not a great fan of turnarounds either, due to his bad experience with such companies.

A third lesson is that there are no free lunches. No stock is easy to trade and for all stock types it is indispensable to have deep knowledge and to perform a thorough due diligence. Fast growers and turnarounds cannot be bought without a clear understanding of their industry and their intrinsic strengths and weaknesses. Investing in cyclicals requires a good understanding of industry dynamics. And the discovery of asset plays and special situation stocks depends in large part on the amount of time one is willing to spend on the scrutiny of financial statements or other types of key documents.

Furthermore, even after the stock is bought, the investor must keep a close track of the evolution of the firm. In addition, successful investors display a healthy dose of mental fortitude to go against the crowd and exercise patience. People who are afraid to be contrarian will never be successful with cyclicals and turnarounds. Those who buy stocks for short-term gains are unlikely to make a lot of money on asset plays, special situation stocks, fast growers or stalwarts.

Finally, a recurring theme among the trading strategies for all stock types is to buy and sell gradually. Top investors are unanimously positive about the merits of this practice and they apply it with almost any type of stock. The rationale behind the gradual accumulation or reduction of stock positions and other general recommendations about buying and selling are the topic of the next chapter.

# CHAPTER G

## BUYING AND SELLING CONSIDERATIONS

"We believe that according the name 'investors' to institutions and individuals that trade actively is like calling someone who repeatedly engages in one-night stands a romantic."

WARREN BUFFETT, 1991 LETTER TO THE SHAREHOLDERS OF BERKSHIRE HATHAWAY

IN THE PREVIOUS chapter we looked at a number of rules that top investors recommend when they buy and sell particular types of stocks. This chapter takes a broader approach and looks at rules irrespective of the stock type. Once again, a thorough study of the approaches of the world's top investors shows that there is a great similarity in their activities. Although the way they buy and sell varies depending on personality and style, they almost all share and champion a common set of intelligent trading rules.

## G.I Buying

A buying process consists of two steps. First, one has to select attractive purchase candidates. Second, one has to pick the right moment to buy the stock. Stock selection and the attendant due diligence were discussed in-depth in the Chapters B and C. Here I briefly recapitulate the main points of attention in the selection process and give some advice on the actual purchase process.

### G.I.1 Selection of purchase candidates

Carrying out a correct due diligence process is hard and time-consuming. Laziness, a poor understanding of what a value-added due diligence process entails, and a lack of time are some of the major reasons why only very few investors (professionals and non-professionals alike) do their homework according to the frameworks discussed in the Chapters B and C. Most investors are far too eager to buy everything that comes their way with an appealing story and/or with a strong endorsement stamp from analysts and brokers.

Top investors distinguish themselves through their thorough and serious due diligence. They try to do as much as possible by themselves (and ignore the advice of other professionals), in order to form an independent opinion. They question their own opinion by checking all that could go wrong. They know that they buy from a seller who may be very sophisticated, or may even be better informed than themselves (e.g., an insider). And they realise that the vast majority of cheap stocks are cheap for a reason. Therefore, they give serious attention to the bear case.

In addition, top investors don't just buy anything that looks attractive at first blush. They are very selective. They know that investment success depends to a large extent on being picky and avoiding losing stocks. They also have no interest in speculative bets, unproven businesses or stocks that are effectively lottery tickets. Since they know that the investment world is very competitive and efficient, they realise that consistently finding truly outstanding stocks requires a competitive advantage, such as hard work, or a focus on one's circle of competence. Finally, to mitigate the impact of mistakes, they buy at a compelling price that offers a serious margin of safety.

---

*"The number of truly attractive companies is fairly small."*

**Philip Fisher (Fisher, 1996)**

---

*"If you limit your investments to those situations where you are knowledgeable and confident, and only those situations, your success rate will be very high."*

**Joel Greenblatt (Greenblatt, 1997)**

---

## G.I.2 The purchase process

When it comes to the actual purchase of stocks, top investors apply the following guidelines:

1. **Patience:** intelligent investors don't compromise when it comes to their investment criteria. They exercise patience and they are not afraid to hold serious cash balances if they can't find stocks that meet their stringent criteria. They don't sacrifice returns by relaxing their target price and discount requirements just to be invested all the time. For instance, between 2000 and 2008, Warren Buffett held a very high cash stash because he couldn't find attractive stocks. During the crisis of 2008-2009 he put that cash to work at very attractive prices. And Peter Lynch asked those who worked at his dealing desk to be price-sensitive and not to chase prices when a stock got away.

2. **Gradual buying**: top investors accumulate positions over time. They seldom buy large positions overnight. The rationale is simple: a stock's fair value is noisy (i.e., it is hard to pinpoint a precise value), and it is almost impossible to call the bottom of a stock. So it makes perfect sense to spread one's purchases over a period of time. Another advantage of gradual buying is that it helps to protect against frustration and attendant ill-considered purchases in case the stock gets away. On the other hand, gradual buying can be psychologically difficult because it implies that the investor may have to buy more stock at a price above the initial purchase price. Although top investors like Philip Fisher, Peter Lynch and Frederick Kobrick applied gradual buying with every type of stock, they used it even more frequently with:

- *Lower conviction ideas*: sometimes, a stock may not be a compelling bargain, even though it has something exceptional about it. In such cases, investors can cut the stock some slack given that the valuation process is full of uncertainties. So, the investor can take an initial limited position to which he/she can add later on when the stock goes down and/or when he/she gets to know the company better.

- *Riskier stocks*: for stocks that represent an above-average risk (e.g., fast growers and turnarounds), gradual buying is highly recommended. Taking small initial positions also allows the investor to diversify among different companies and add to those that work (while selling those that don't).

3. **Averaging down**: closely related to gradual buying is the practice of buying more of a stock when it declines in price, provided that the original investment thesis remains valid. In this way, one can buy an even more attractive stock on its way down.

## G.II Selling

Buying at the right moment is difficult. Knowing when to sell is even harder. In theory, intelligent investors should constantly monitor their holdings to see if they remain sound investments. According to the investment philosophy, they should sell when the stock price increases beyond its intrinsic value, or when the estimated intrinsic value falls below the current stock price.

However, the high uncertainty of the valuation process makes it hard to apply this theory in practice. Selling is hard because numerous emotional factors constantly interfere in the decision process. Indeed, surprises and the uncertainty about a stock's intrinsic value constantly put the shareholder's convictions and beliefs to the test. Sell decisions are also complicated by the fact that buying tends to be more enjoyable than selling because the former is more optimistic (i.e., looking forward to potential gains) than the latter (i.e., saying goodbye to a profitable stock or selling a stock with a loss).[182]

Due to all of these problems, most people base their sell decisions on instincts, feel, rumours, and the like. To force themselves to stay rational and logical in their sales

---

[182] Heins, 2013.

decisions, top investors, by contrast, adhere to solid exit strategies. Similar to the purchase process, they often sell gradually. They sell out of a position step by step because they don't want to guess where the stock price will go over the short term. By selling gradually they also deal with the fact that valuation is no exact science and that one might sell too cheap. Finally, gradual selling also mitigates regret that one might have if one sells a stock position in full before a new rally in the stock price. The time span over which the stock is sold can vary from relatively short to long depending on the price and the investor's convictions.

As far as the reasons for a sale are concerned, top investors know that it is a mistake to sell a stock on a hunch. Before selling, they always reassess the situation to determine if they have all the elements to make the decision. Some top investors even ask someone who was not involved in the original purchase decision (e.g., an analyst who did not look into the company before) to re-evaluate the situation in order to get an unbiased view on the matter. Once the picture is clear, they sell the stock under four circumstances:

1. they have lost confidence in their original investment thesis,
2. they realise that they don't understand the company as well as they thought they did,
3. the price is getting (far) ahead of the intrinsic value, and
4. the stock can be replaced with a better bargain.

## G.II.1 The original investment thesis is invalidated

When one buys a stock, one should know what to expect from it. Intelligent investors like Mohnish Pabrai write down their investment thesis before they buy a stock and they regularly recheck these expectations.[183] They get out of stocks that fall short or for which the original investment thesis is invalidated – even if they trade (far) below the price at which they were bought. Here are two examples of broken investment theses:

1. Peter Lynch usually sold a stock when its **catalyst** (the event that was expected to move the stock price) **disappeared**.[184] For example, he would buy a cyclical stock in anticipation of a strong economy, but if economic conditions weakened instead of improving, he would sell the stock.

2. A **deteriorating outlook for free cash flows**: since lower free cash flows automatically lead to a lower intrinsic value, it can be recommended to slip out of a stock when one or more of the following red flags pop up:

   • *Deteriorating fundamentals* (taking into account the current state of the business cycle), such as declining profit margins, a shrinking return on equity or capital, slackening sales growth, loss of market share, plummeting cash flows, a saturating customer base (i.e., little opportunity for new customers), and/or a worsening balance sheet.[185]

---

[183] Tier, 2005.
[184] Train, 2000.
[185] Kobrick, 2006.

- *A weakening competitive position*, due to intensified internal competition, a weakening industry position (e.g., caused by new inventions), new legislation, and the like. To anticipate these kinds of problems and to stay informed about important industry changes, Peter Lynch had a conversation with a representative of every important industry once a month.

- *Management problems*: this can refer to poor capital allocation decisions (e.g., mergers or acquisitions that make no sense), strategic blunders, weak leadership (e.g., complacent top managers), greedy management (e.g., excessive management compensation), high management turnover, and changes at the highest management levels.[186]

Selling a stock when one realises that a mistake was made seems straightforward. In reality, though, it is not easy. It is human to look for new reasons to hold on to a stock when the original investment thesis is broken. Also, ego often interferes with sell decisions. Many people would rather incur an increasing loss by holding on to a losing and worsening position than admit that they were wrong. What complicates matters even more is that certain cognitive biases tempt investors not to sell a losing stock (see also Chapter A). For instance, due to the asymmetric loss aversion many people prefer to hang on to a losing stock in the hope that they will get back to even.

Intelligent investors don't struggle with ego problems and they don't change their investment rationale to justify the status quo. They realise that they are in the business of making money, not in the business of being right, and they try to fight cognitive biases by staying as rational as possible about every trading decision. They sell when they realise that they have made a mistake, regardless of the price at which they bought the stock. In this way, they contain the damage.

> "We try not to have many investing rules, but there is one that has served us well: If we decide we were wrong about something, in terms of why we did it, we exit, period. We never invent new reasons to continue with a position when the original reasons are no longer available."
>
> **David Einhorn (Heins, 2013)**

## G.II.2 Poor understanding of the business

Sometimes investors are surprised by certain developments at a company, whether positive or negative, because they don't understand the company well. That's something top investors try to avoid. They don't want to be shareholder of a business they don't understand because this would be more like a gamble than a true investment. In this vein,

---

[186] Kobrick, 2006.

they get out of a position if they come to the conclusion that they actually don't understand it as well as they would like to. For example, many great investors sold their bank stocks during the credit crisis of 2008-2009 because they felt they didn't understand what was going on and where these companies were headed.

Typically, investors find out that their understanding of a company is poor after more thorough scrutiny or after they have monitored the business for some time. The financial statements may suddenly seem far more complex than thought initially, or certain dynamics in the business may puzzle the investor.

A further subtle indication that one probably doesn't understand the stock is unsatisfactory price performance. One practice among a number of top investors is to revisit the investment thesis (to decide either to sell or to buy more) if a stock is down about 15% to 25% since purchase on an absolute basis or relative to the overall market.

A related practice of some top investors (e.g., Mohnish Pabrai, Philip Fisher, John Templeton, Joel Greenblatt) is to automatically sell a stock when it underperforms the market three to four years after purchase. The rationale behind these rules is simple. Although patience is a virtue, market efficiency ensures that undervalued stocks rarely remain hidden for a long time. So, when a stock (consistently) underperforms, the market is actually saying that very few bargain hunters (including the smart ones) are showing interest in the stock. A humble investor will see this as a sign that he/she may have missed something essential about the company.

## G.II.3 The price reaches fair value or is too far above fair value

When the stock price rises above a company's intrinsic value the expected return drops below the investor's discount rate. When this happens the stock's appreciation potential is lower than the investor's target. A recurring theme among top investors is that they sell a stock somewhat before it achieves full value (e.g., when it reaches about 90% of its fair value).

The reason is that the last 10% of the valuation gap closes the slowest. So, waiting for the gap to close completely involves an expensive opportunity cost. In addition, when the valuation gap falls below 10% it becomes harder to sell the stock as the incentive for buyers to take the merchandise off the investor's hands is far from compelling.[187] Intelligent investors therefore focus on the juiciest part of the ride. They buy at 50% to 60% of fair value and get out at 90%.

Obviously, intrinsic value is not clear-cut, it always remains somewhat elusive. For this reason, the investor clearly has to weigh two possible outcomes to decide whether to sell or hold on to a stock. The first possibility is that the investor underestimates the potential of a winning stock and sells too soon. This can happen with a truly exceptional company that has unique prospects. Such stocks deserve high multiples, and can deliver outstanding returns as they grow their business value at a much higher pace than normal

---

[187] This problem is more relevant for professional investors who manage large portfolios. They usually have to spread the sale of significant positions over a certain period of time because the number of shares they have may be much higher than the average daily trading volume of that stock in the market.

discount rates, and/or because their multiple keeps expanding. The other possibility is that the investor does not sell and hangs on to an underperforming stock. How investors deal with this dilemma depends on:

1. **Style (growth versus value)**: growth investors, who by definition look for spectacular growth stories, pay less attention to pure intrinsic value considerations. They are therefore more likely to hold on to outstanding businesses. Deep value investors, on the other hand, are very critical of growth. They sell automatically when a conservative valuation gap has closed. Many other investors who lie on the spectrum between growth and deep value will give more or less leeway to a stock depending on its characteristics.

2. **Market type**: stock markets tend to move in short and long bull and bear cycles.[188] In so-called range-bound markets, stocks go nowhere for periods of one to two decades and valuations come down from high levels. In such markets, the buy-and-hold strategy is not effective and it is better to trade actively by selling stocks before they reach fair value. In secular bull markets, where stocks go up over a period of one to two decades and valuations expand, buy-and-hold works. In such markets it pays off to give stocks more leeway on the upside, and to sell only when a stock rises above its fair value.

## G.II.4 There are much better bargains

A fourth reason for a sale is that the stock can be replaced with a better bargain. Top stock pickers do this all the time. They point out that this strategy is most rewarding during bear markets where one can prune out the least attractive stocks and replace them with the most appealing beaten-down stocks. At the same time, they warn that such swap operations are difficult. For instance, John Templeton, one of the greatest investors the world has known, admitted that when he advised clients to replace one stock with another, about one-third of the time they would have been better off sticking with the original stock.

A first problem with replacements is that the investor usually has to give up thorough knowledge (about the stock that will be sold, gathered over the holding period) in favour of less knowledge (about the new stock). Second, the investor may underestimate the fair value of the stock that is sold and overestimate the value of the purchased stock. Due to these problems, John Templeton suggests that one should restrict replacements only to situations where the new stock is a compelling bargain as compared to the old one (e.g., when there is a 50% difference in estimated value between the two).[189]

---

[188] (Easterling, 2005), (Katsenelson, 2007) and (Schiller, 2005).
[189] Templeton, 2008.

# G.III Short selling

Apart from conventional buying and selling, investors can also sell stocks short. Short selling refers to the practice where an investor sells a stock he/she doesn't own, in the hope of buying it back at a lower price in the future.[190] In other words, the short seller borrows a stock and sells it in the market. Later on he will *cover his short*, by repurchasing the stock and giving it back to the rightful owner. If the short seller can cover his short below the price at which it was shorted, he will make a profit. If the price at which the stock is bought back is higher than the price at which it was shorted, the short seller incurs a loss.

In practice, short sellers borrow from brokers that have inventories of stocks available for short operations. Brokers hedge themselves against short sellers by demanding collateral (the difference between the current value of the stock and the value at which the stock was sold short) that must be replenished on a daily basis. In addition, the short seller must pay the dividends on the borrowed stock to the owner, as well as a compensation for the use of the short inventory.

Short selling is very different from regular buying and selling. First of all, the ability to sell short depends on access to brokers with large inventories of shortable stock. Even more important is that short selling is substantially riskier than normal buying and selling – it has a loss-return pattern that is the opposite of that of purchases. The maximum profit from a short sale is capped by the amount of stock that is sold short. With a long position, by contrast, there is no cap on the potential profit. Conversely, when the short seller is wrong, there is no cap on the loss he/she may incur as there is no cap on how high a stock can rise. With a long position, the maximum loss is limited to the amount invested in the stock. A consequence of this profit-loss pattern is that short sales that go awry become a larger part of the portfolio. In other words, risk increases when a short sale goes against the investor.

As if this were not enough, there is still another risk short sellers have to cope with. The owner of a shorted stock can ask for his/her stock back at any time. This exposes the short seller to the risk that he or she may have to cover their position at an unfavourable moment in time.

Given the idiosyncratic nature of short selling, it should not come as a surprise that many of the greatest investors avoid it altogether. Some tried but failed.[191] Others believe that it is much easier to restrict one's operations to long positions and to simply avoid the bad stocks. They are also concerned about the fact that time does not necessarily favour short sales if the investor is right on the fundamentals. Indeed, short sellers may suffer disastrous or even fatal losses due to irrational price fluctuations before the bad fundamentals finally dawn on the market.

---

[190] This is similar to a car salesman who sells a car that must be ordered with a car manufacturer. The vendor is short the car when the client signs the purchase contract.

[191] For instance, Benjamin Graham admitted that he was not successful at shorting due to the fact that one out of four of his shorted stocks were run up to the skies by overenthusiastic market players.

That being said, there are a number of excellent investors who are successful short sellers. Examples are Robert Wilson, Julian Robertson, Jim Chanos and David Einhorn. Some top investors even argue that all investors should at least try to short stocks to get a more balanced view on the markets. They say that short selling helps to counter the positive market bias that is too common among long-only investors. Hereunder I summarise the advice of some of the most successful short sellers in the world.

# G.III.1 Sound advice on short selling

## G.III.1.a The right mindset

Short selling puts very specific demands on the investor. People who intend to sell short first have to look inside and determine whether they have the right mental make-up to be successful on the short side. It is important to realise that many successful long-only investors are not cut out to be good short sellers, because they don't have that demanding mindset. To see whether one stands a chance as a short seller, one must answer the following questions:

1. **Can I stand the stress?** Ordinary investing can be stressful, but short selling is more so. As said above, positions that go against the short seller become larger the further they go in that direction. As such, short sales constantly test the investor's resolve. In addition, unlike long-only investors short sellers cannot afford to take their eyes off the stock screens (let alone go on a holiday with a short position on). They must closely follow all price movements to avoid a runaway stock ruining their portfolio.

2. **Do I feel comfortable as a contrarian?** I have said repeatedly that successful investors have the courage to go against the crowd. They beat the market because they buy stocks that other people ignore or avoid. With short selling, the contrarian mindset is even more important. In fact, it is fair to say that true short sellers feel comfortable with contrarian positions. Success as a short seller is almost impossible without emotional detachment from the crowd and the conviction of one's ideas.

   The problem is that short sellers have to face much more disconfirming noise than long-only investors. After all, the investment world has a positive bias. Buy recommendations, optimistic CEOs and bullish talk are much more common than negative reports and downbeat statements. As such, short sellers are constantly slapped in the face with the message that they are wrong. Making matters worse, short sellers must be early to sell a stock short. They have to anticipate the bad news and establish their position when everything seems fine (and few other people agree that something is wrong).

3. **Can I live with the fact that rewards come on discrete moments?** Jim Chanos, a renowned short seller, points out that many short ideas work out quickly at some discrete moment (typically with the release of some news). This implies that short sellers have to sustain long periods where they don't make money on an idea. When interest rates are low, these long periods will be even more painful as the short seller cannot earn much on the cash he/she received from the short sale.

## G.III.1.b Proper risk management

Since short selling has an unfavourable risk-reward payoff, one cannot afford to sell stocks short without proper risk management. One of the biggest mistakes of short sellers is to underestimate the insanity of the public. Market irrationality can kill short sellers with inappropriate risk management as the market can stay irrational for much longer than many short sellers can stay solvent.

Some businesses with flawed business models manage to attract new (dumb) money again and again. And some good companies can trade at ludicrous valuations for many years before rationality finally sets in. Even more, irrationality can keep an ailing business alive until it is bailed out by changing market or business conditions (e.g., a sudden improvement in the economy). In sum, short sellers who do not apply proper risk management are unlikely to survive. Here are two essential risk management tools for short sellers:

1. To limit the damage that any single position can inflict on one's portfolio, stop-losses make perfect sense. With stop-losses – a popular tool with traders that is seldom used by the most successful long-only investors – one selects a price point at which one will get out of a position no matter what. Stop-losses cap the maximum possible loss of a position. The legendary investor John Templeton, for instance, used stop-losses for his short ideas. Jim Chanos, on the other hand, is not a fan of stop-losses because he believes that they make it hard to re-enter a position.

2. Although many great investors like to focus their long portfolio on a limited number of their best ideas, focus is not so wise in short portfolios. In fact, a high level of diversification is recommended to limit the impact of positions that do not work out. For instance, David Einhorn sizes his shorts half as large as his longs. Jim Chanos does not put more than 5% of his capital at risk in any single short idea – whenever one of his shorts goes above 5% it is automatically cut back to 4.5%. And Warren Buffett recommends investors to go short the entire market (or a very diversified basket of stocks) rather than individual stocks.

## G.III.1.c Selectivity

Finally, short sellers must be very selective in the choice of their short sales. It is probably harder to find good short candidates than good long ideas due to the stock market's tendency to move up over time. Smart short sellers carry out a thorough due diligence and limit themselves to stocks which they expect to decline substantially (e.g., by at least 50%). They don't waste their energy and money on less compelling ideas.

As explained in Chapter B, the most attractive short candidates are non-technology companies with poor fundamentals (i.e., companies with management issues, a weak financial position, a flawed business model or saturating growth) that trade at an overinflated price and that enjoy high popularity among professionals.

To avoid accidents due to a lack of liquidity (e.g., a short squeeze) the stock should have a high float and its short interest should be moderate. Preferably, there are some triggers that can ignite the stock's collapse, such as insider sales, the resignation of key managers, auditor turnover, persistent rumours that something is wrong, or late filings.

## G.IV Summary

In this chapter I have discussed some general trading rules of top investors for individual stocks. Given the inherent uncertainty about a stock's intrinsic value, it is often recommended to buy and sell gradually. Closely related to this, averaging down is a sensible investment approach that allows buyers to reduce their average purchase price.

A second point of attention is that purchases and sales must be prepared adequately. In general, to be a successful buyer one should perform an independent and unbiased due diligence, insist on a margin of safety, remain within one's circle of competence and work hard to understand the business better than other investors. All this implies that successful investors are selective and patient. They jump only on exceptional investments.

As far as selling is concerned, it is fair to sell stocks when the investment thesis is proved incorrect, when one realises that one doesn't understand the business well, when the price is above the intrinsic value, or when the stock can be replaced with a better bargain. Finally, short selling is hard, requires proper risk management and puts high mental demands on investors.

# CHAPTER H

## THE BOOM-BUST CYCLE

"It is the emotional nonprofessional investor who sends the price of a stock up or down in sharp, sporadic and more or less short-lived spurts. The professional investor has no choice but to sit by quietly while the mob has its day, until the enthusiasm or the panic of the speculators and nonprofessionals have been spent."

J. PAUL GETTY (KRASS, 1999)

THE STOCK MARKETS move in cycles that typically last a few years. Each cycle consists of a *bull phase* (where the market rises by at least 20% from a previous market bottom), and a *bear phase* (where the market loses at least 20% from a previous market top). Even within these bull and bear markets, stocks seldom move in one straight direction. Bulls and bears are actually often interrupted by corrections (in bulls) and rallies (in bears), where the market temporarily moves against the longer-term trend.

The cyclical behaviour of the stock market is illustrated in Figure 23, which shows successive bull and bear markets of the S&P 500 stock market index from 1963 to 1992. As one can see, over that period the S&P 500 experienced about five bull-bear cycles. We can also see a wide variation in the intensity and duration of these cycles. The bear market of 1973 to 1974 was vicious as the market lost almost 50% of its value over less than two years. The bull market of 1987 to 2000, on the other hand, was extraordinarily long and strong with a duration of more than 12 years and a gain of almost 600%. The bear market of 1987 was something special as it included a steep drop over a very short period of time (i.e., a crash).

Superimposed on the bull-bear cycles, the stock market moves in cycles that usually last between one and two decades. This is illustrated in Figure 24 for the S&P index. These supercycles encompass various bull-bear cycles, and are referred to as *secular bull, secular bear* or *range-bound* markets.

In secular bull markets (e.g., from 1951 to 1966), stocks move higher and multiples expand from low to depressed levels to high levels. Also, tops of new bull phases in secular bulls usually pierce the tops of previous bulls, whereas the bottoms of new bears are typically above the bottoms of previous bears. In range-bound markets (e.g., 1966 to 1982) multiples contract while the market moves sideways. Finally, stock prices and multiples decline during secular bear markets (e.g., from 1929 to 1932).

From time to time, and especially towards the end of secular bull markets, the investing crowd loses its senses and a mania develops. This is then invariably followed by a merciless implosion (e.g., in 1929).

**Figure 23: Bull and bear markets 1963 to 1992**

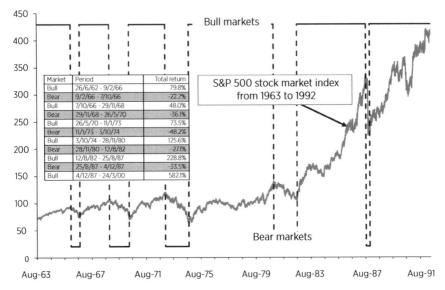

Source data: Yahoo Finance

**Figure 24: Secular markets in the S&P between 1871 and 2013**

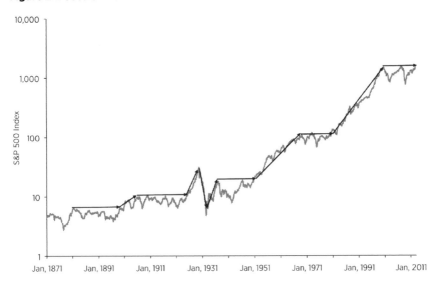

Source data: www.irrationalexuberance.com

The fact that the stock market moves in secular cycles and in shorter bull and bear cycles is no coincidence. In fact, one can identify a large number of factors that drive this market behaviour, like the economy, perceptions and feelings about stocks, emotions among shareholders, and so on.[192]

With regards to investing over market cycles, it is obvious that it would be extremely rewarding if one could make timely entries and exits into the market by anticipating its short-term and long-term movements. Unfortunately since numerous investors try to do just that, this is an incredibly hard task. In this chapter I take a closer look at how some of the best investors try to capitalise on market movements.

A first observation is that **none** of the top investors attempts to forecast the market's behaviour. They actually unanimously decry crystal ball gazing as an exercise in futility. They also seldom try to make profits from short-term market swings. Instead, the top investors anticipate long-term movements and position themselves accordingly.

Indeed, since investors focus on the disparity between value and price, they see market cycles as opportunities to buy cheap and sell expensive. More precisely, smart investors see the bottoms of bear phases – in particular those towards the end of range-bound or secular bear markets – as compelling buying opportunities because then many stocks are trading far below their intrinsic value.

Conversely, they are cautious around the tops of bull phases – especially those towards the ends of secular bulls – as stocks usually trade far above their intrinsic value at those moments. Although the idea of buying close to market bottoms and postponing purchases close to market tops seems absurdly simple and obvious, the vast majority of investors seem to be unable to put this into practice. Most people do just the opposite: they buy close to market tops and sell (or refuse to buy) close to market bottoms.

The major reasons for this behaviour are that the average investor does not recognise tops and bottoms, and that he does not have the required mental setup to follow through with this strategy. The following sections give a comprehensive overview of how great investors deal with market cycles. First I give an overview of some of the tip-offs used by top investors to detect market tops and bottoms. A second section discusses the strategies adopted by top investors to capitalise on market cycles.

## H.1 Indicators for market tops and bottoms

As explained above, top investors don't try short-term market timing. They merely try to take advantage of medium to long-term market dislocations. To be successful, they resort to a number of indicators that tell them when the market looks attractive, and when it is wiser to play defence.

These indicators are not foolproof, and they require a high degree of subjective judgment. They are also not intended to give the accurate moment in time where markets

---

[192] For a thorough discussion of market cycles refer to the following excellent books on the topic: (Easterling, 2005), (Katsenelson, 2007), (Schiller, 2005), (Smithers, 2009) and (Napier, 2009).

are likely to bottom out or top out. They rather give an indication about whether a patient and contrarian investor should get on board or not. Bearing in mind these caveats and because every single one of these indicators in isolation may not be reliable, it is advisable to always look at various indicators. The indicators that are most closely watched by top investors are market sentiment, valuations, imbalances, insider transactions, and catalysts for inclination points.

## H.I.1 Indicator 1: Market sentiment

As explained in Chapter A, investor sentiment turns from negative (i.e., pessimistic) to positive (i.e., optimistic) over the course of bull markets. The opposite occurs over bear markets. Over secular cycles there is a fundamental shift in perception about the stock market among investors and in society. During secular bull markets, sentiment about stocks evolves from disinterest and apathy to strong interest and wide media coverage. During range-bound markets, sentiment moves in the opposite direction.

The logic behind these sentiment cycles is simple. Bull markets end when most investors are fully invested (i.e., they have no money left to push prices higher) due to a high level of optimism about future returns. Bear markets end when the last pessimist throws in the towel. Likewise, growing disinterest in stocks over range-bound markets is a consequence of the fact that many people get disillusioned about their stock returns and leave the scene. Growing interest over secular bull markets is the result of excitement and extrapolation of past returns.

Based on the inevitable and close connection between sentiment and market cycles top investors pay special attention to trends in sentiment to anticipate market movements. They prefer to take the opposite side of the prevailing sentiment of the moment. They see a high level of optimism or high interest in the stock markets as warning signs for a nearing top. Conversely, they argue that a high level of pessimism among investors, or widespread disinterest about the stock market in society, signals a potentially rewarding opportunity for investors.

This contrarian indicator is sometimes very subtle. Sentiment can, for instance, still be bullish after a severe market collapse. This can happen when a majority of stock advisors recommend taking advantage of the decline, or when a lot of market observers claim that the market has capitulated. Investors should realise, though, that these bullish sounds bode ill for the market. As long as positive news dominates the media, stock prices are likely to go even lower.

Conversely, a widespread conviction that a rally off a market bottom is a sucker rally is a bullish indicator because this suggests that investors are bearish. For instance, Anthony Bolton correctly predicted that the stock market rebound from the March 2009 lows was likely to be sustained, since the dominant market conviction at that time was that the stock market was going to double dip.

Prevailing sentiment can help to assess the likely future direction of the market, but when it comes to turning points top investors look for extremes in sentiment. The most reliable signs that a market top or bottom is close are extremes in pessimism/optimism (among investors) or interest/apathy (among the general public). In order to gauge prevailing sentiment, top investors use both *subjective impressions* and *objective metrics*:

1. **Subjective impressions**: telling signs are:

   - *Level of speculation*: close to market tops, it is common to see irrationally strong price action in IPOs, in speculative stocks and in low-quality businesses. Also, around tops investment advisors, market gurus and (sell side) analysts typically recommend the most aggressive investments because these performed the best in the preceding years (or months).

   - *General interest in the stock market*: this refers to the attention of the media and the general public for the stock market. A nice example of the latter is Peter Lynch's cocktail theory.[193] In his experience, close to market bottoms people at cocktail parties are not interested in the ideas of investment professionals. When the market rises, people ask for advice. At the extreme, close to market tops, people are no longer interested in advice but actually tell the professionals what *they* should buy.

   - *Occasional stories*: top investors closely follow stories about capitulation among experienced investors, because these tend to coincide with tops and bottoms. John Templeton believed that when the most hardened investors throw in the towel in a bear market, the bottom is usually near because there are few sellers left. Conversely, when experienced investors abandon their discipline and principles to join a bull market, one may be close to a top as all bulls are fully invested.

2. **Objective metrics**:

   - *Bullish versus bearish market advisors*: when bullish investment advisors significantly outnumber bearish advisors, markets may be close to a high, and vice versa. In practice, David Dreman recommends looking for a majority of about 70% or more of bulls as a bearish signal, and more than 70% of bears as a bullish signal.[194]

   - *Put/call ratio*: Anthony Bolton pays close attention to the number of put options versus the number of call options in the market. An exceptionally high put/call ratio suggests a very high level of pessimism and is therefore bullish. An exceptionally low put/call ratio is bearish since it indicates optimism and a high level of complacency. To avoid confusion caused by daily fluctuations in the put/call ratio, it is better to look at the trend of a smoothed version of the daily put/call ratio (e.g., a trailing monthly average).

   - *Cash positions of mutual funds*: Anthony Bolton closely monitors the cash balances (as a percentage of the total portfolio) of mutual funds. Historically low cash positions are bearish as they indicate optimism. High cash positions, by contrast, often precede a strong market.

---

[193] Lynch, 1989.
[194] Dreman, 1998.

- *Advertisements*: this can include:

    (i) The percentage of space devoted to mutual-fund adverts in important investment magazines (in absolute terms or relative to the space devoted to alternative investments such as bonds), bullish ads, etc. Obviously, when bullish adds and mutual fund adds peak, one may be close to a market peak, and vice versa.

    (ii) The percentage of mutual fund adverts that emphasise recent performance: close to market tops, a high percentage of mutual funds tend to boast of their strong short-term track record. Close to market bottoms, ads remain silent about prior performance and the emphasis shifts more to corporate puffery.

- *Credit conditions*: a common characteristic of market bubbles is that credit conditions become too lax. Andrew Smithers points out in *Wall Street Revalued* that a valuable metric to measure credit conditions is the price of liquidity. When the price for illiquidity drops to historical lows, it can be taken as an indicator that there is insufficient risk aversion and that credit conditions have been eased dangerously. Conversely, very tight credit conditions can indicate that risk aversion and pessimism is too high.

- *New stock offerings*: towards the end of bull markets the number of IPOs typically peaks. This is logical because entrepreneurs are eager to IPO their business at the very high price that investors are willing to pay late in bull markets.

- *Members of advisory services and investment clubs*: the membership of advisory services and investment clubs is usually highest after a period of strong market performance, and lowest after a severe bear market. Hence, a bearish sign for the market is a high membership, whereas a low membership is bullish.

## H.I.2 Indicator 2: Valuations

Not surprisingly, the overall valuation of the stock market is an indispensable market indicator for top investors. It must be stressed, however, that although the discrepancy between (estimated) fair value and stock price is a good predictor of returns over the long term (decades), valuation metrics are not particularly useful to forecast short-to-medium term market movements.[195] To determine turning points, valuation metrics should always be used in combination with other indicators such as sentiment.

In order to value the stock market, top investors keep track of the divergence of certain valuation metrics from their historical averages. They argue that effective metrics inevitably revert to their mean over time. Owing to the limitations of each individual metric they usually observe several metrics at the same time. Here are the most common valuation metrics and their merits:

---

[195] It may seem paradoxical but the fact that valuation metrics are not that reliable over the short term makes them more effective over the long term. Indeed, metrics that would be good predictors of short-term movements would quickly become (very) popular and therefore lose their power.

1. **Fed Model**: this model argues that the stock market is cheap when its earnings yield (earnings/price) is higher than risk-free long-term interest rates and vice versa. The rationale behind this model is that stocks and risk-free Treasuries compete for the investor's money and that stocks should always deliver a somewhat higher prospective return than risk-free investments. This would imply that investors are willing to accept lower future stock returns (i.e., higher multiples and lower earnings yields) when interest rates are low, whereas they would demand higher stock returns when interest rates are high.

   Although the Fed Model looks plausible at first blush, it is far too simplistic. It also has a poor track record in predicting long-term stock market returns. Nevertheless, some top investors use it to gauge the short to medium-term market outlook. The Fed model can indeed be useful as a predictor for market movements in the presence of anomalies between stock valuations and interest rates, provided that the investor realises the following asymmetry:

   - *When long-term interest rates are high, stock valuations must be low.* This is just common sense. High interest rates imply that investors can earn a high risk-free return over the long term. Smart investors will not accept the risk of equity unless the prospective returns on stocks are higher than interest rates, so elevated valuations are not sustainable when interest rates are high. Based on this knowledge, star hedge fund manager Eddie Lampert correctly warned for a crash in 1987 because he felt very uncomfortable with rising stock valuations in a climate of high long-term interest rates.

   - *It is doubtful that low interest rates can sustain high stock valuations.* The problem is that history has shown that periods with low interest rates are invariably followed by periods with higher interest rates. So, assuming that stocks are cheap at high valuation multiples when interest rates are low is absurd. In addition, using the Fed model as a predictor of short-to-medium term market direction in an environment with low interest rates is dangerous, because what looks cheap (based on the Fed model) can become expensive overnight (if interest rates suddenly rise).[196]

2. **Price-to-book value (P/BV)**: Anthony Bolton and John Templeton like the P/BV of the market as a valuation measure. Nevertheless, it is not the most popular metric among many other top investors. The problem with P/BV is that book value does not accurately represent the true underlying value of a business's equity. Accounting conventions, the fact that book value does not adequately reflect economic goodwill and the impact of inflation all imply that investors should not rely blindly on P/BV when they assess the market level.

3. **Price-to-replacement value**: this should be superior to P/BV, because it compares the price of the stock market to the current cost of the market's net assets.

---

[196] Warren Buffett pointed out in the late 1990s that valuations were not expensive, provided that the prevailing interest rates of that time were to continue indefinitely. Since the latter assumption was unreasonable based on historical experience, stocks were highly overvalued.

Replacement value takes into account the impact of inflation and strips away distortions caused by accounting. The most popular metric of price-to-replacement is the q-ratio introduced by James Tobin. This ratio appears to be one of the best predictors of long-term market returns for the US stock market. Nevertheless, Warren Buffett is sceptical about its merits. The problem is that the theoretical replacement value of assets can vastly overstate the price that knowledgeable people would be willing to pay for those assets (as Warren Buffett experienced firsthand during the liquidation of his textile business in the 1980s).

4. **Price-to-sales** or **Market cap-to-Gross National Product (market cap-to-GNP)**: Warren Buffett and Prem Watsa consider the ratio of the market's total capitalisation to GNP as one of the most relevant metrics to evaluate where the market stands in terms of valuation. According to Buffett, stocks are fairly valued when P/GNP is about 70% to 80%.

5. **Dividend yield**: dividend yield only gives an indication about the expensiveness of the market. One must be careful not to use its absolute value as a strict valuation metric, because dividends are also determined by the payout ratio. For the S&P, for instance, the ten-year averaged payout ratio (i.e., average ten-year trailing real dividends/ten-year trailing real earnings) has steadily declined from about 83% in 1940 to 37% in 2007. Hence, investors who use the dividend yield as an indication for valuation must take into account trends in the payout ratio.

6. **Population of value screens**: an alternative way to gauge the level of the stock market is to count the number (or aggregate market capitalisation) of stocks that pass rigorous value screens. When that number is historically high the stock market is probably undervalued. When it is low, the market is overvalued.

7. **Price-to-earnings (P/E)** and **price-to-free cash flow (P/FCF)**: these multiples are the most popular in the investment community, but they are also the least understood. The denominator of these multiples should **not** be the value over the preceding year because earnings and free cash flows over one particular year are not representative of the true earnings power of the market.

Even worse are P/E and P/FCF values where the expected earnings and free cash flows over the next year are used in the denominator. In that case one introduces an extra element of uncertainty – will the expectations be true or not? – which makes the value even harder to interpret. In fact, the E and FCF should be the fair earnings and fair free cash flows, based on long-term trends in sales (or GDP) growth and profit margins. They should be values where earnings or cash flow fluctuations are averaged out.[197] The most popular metric in this respect is the Schiller P/E, defined as:[198]

---

[197] Valuation based on trend lines of FCF, GDP or earnings are not that useful for stock markets in economies with volatile growth (e.g., unstable countries) or unsustainably high growth (e.g., emerging economies like China), as it is very dangerous to extrapolate the past growth rates into the future for these types of countries. In such cases, valuations based on underlying assets (P/BV or P/replacement value) are more appropriate.

[198] Schiller, 2005.

$$P/E_{Shiller} = P / \left( \frac{1}{10} \sum_{i=1}^{120} \frac{CPI_{current}}{CPI_i} \times E_i \right)$$

with $CPI_{current}$ and $CPI_i$ the current Consumer Price Index (CPI) and the CPI $i$ months ago, and with $E_i$ the one-year trailing earnings of all companies in the stock market $i$ months ago. In $P/E_{Shiller}$ the denominator is an average of the *real* earnings over the past ten years.[199] Real earnings are used instead of nominal earnings to eliminate the effect of inflation. This is recommended as inflation can bias the averaging towards the most recent earnings if it was significant over the ten-year period.

## H.I.3 Indicator 3: Imbalances

Similar to valuation imbalances there are a number of other imbalances that can persist for quite some time although they tend to normalise over the long run. Imbalances are useful indicators for future market direction over time horizons of several years, but they are less useful to determine turning points. For shorter-term movements they should be used in conjunction with other indicators. Here are some examples of imbalances that many top investors closely watch:

1. **Imbalances in sector weights**: as pointed out by Jeremy Siegel in *The Future For Investors*, when the weight of a particular sector in the stock market is seriously above its historical average after a steep rise, that sector is bound to collapse. What is more, if that sector represents an important part of the stock market it may even drag the entire market along in its fall. The reason for the latter is that the collapse of a sector leads to massive redemptions with institutional investors who then often prefer to sell the stocks that held up well (because these stocks look expensive versus the stocks that collapsed). An example was the technology bubble of the late 1990s, where the technology sector commanded a historically excessive 30% of the value of the S&P 500. During the collapse of the technology sector in the early 2000s, many other stocks that were unrelated to technology fell in sympathy and the S&P 500 suffered a bear market.

2. **Imbalances in profit margins**: historically high profit margins in a particular sector or in the entire economy are unsustainable as competition forces profit margins to revert to their mean. Indeed, when profit margins are exceptionally high, all manner of new competitors will show up (attracted by the high returns on invested capital), and existing players will be tempted to grab market share from each other (as they have room to slash prices). The intensified competition will lead to falling profit margins sooner or later. Conversely, historically low profit margins will lead to above-average profit growth in subsequent years as competition tends to ease in

---

[199] *Real* refers to the value of the earnings in current money. Put another way, real earnings correspond to the real value (i.e., with the true purchasing power) of the earnings at the moment they were earned.

such an environment. If stock prices do not reflect this inevitability, the market stands to suffer a serious hit. For instance, top mutual fund manager Stephen Yacktman asserts that he was out of financial stocks before the collapse in 2008 largely because profit margins in that sector had peaked in 2007.

3. **Economic imbalances**: although economic views are seldom part of the toolkit of bottom-up investors, some basic knowledge about reversion to the mean in GDP growth and inflation can be useful:

   - Extraordinarily strong economic growth can be a reason for caution if the stock market discounts a continuation of this growth in perpetuity.

   - Conversely, troughs in the economic cycle (i.e., during recessions, when the economic situation looks bleak) are often exceptionally rewarding periods for investors with the guts to 'load up the truck.' According to Russell Napier in *Anatomy of the Bear* this may be especially true around economic bottoms of range-bound or secular bear bottoms. At these moments investors are slow to react to green shoots in the economy like a return to price stability in commodities (in particular metal prices, including those for copper), a reluctance to sell products forward, increasing demand for durable goods (e.g., cars), and historically low inventory levels.

## H.I.4 Indicator 4: Insider and corporate transactions

Another way to gain insight into the level of the market is to observe the actions of corporate leaders. Obviously, corporate leaders are human beings that can make mistakes but they are more knowledgeable about business conditions and the fair value of their business than the average investor (see also Chapter B). Two types of transactions can be monitored to evaluate the opinion of corporate leaders on the stock market:

1. **Insider transactions**: when insider buying is stronger than insider selling, it is fair to assume that insiders are bullish, and vice versa. The overall insider transactions can be monitored through the ratio of insider sales to total insider transactions (sales + purchases) for a large universe of stocks.[200] Alternatively, Josef Lakonishok and Inmoo Lee found that the net purchase ratio (NPR) is the most informative insider indicator for market movements:

$$\text{Net purchase ratio} = \frac{IP_{-6M} - IS_{-6M}}{IP_{-6M} + IS_{-6M}}$$

In this expression, $IP_{-6M}$ and $IS_{-6M}$ are respectively the number of insider purchases and insider sales over the previous six months. Exceptionally low values in the NPR are bearish whereas high ratios are bullish. Note also that insider

---

[200] An example is the Brooks ratio, which is based on 2500 companies. When the Brooks Ratio is lower than 40% (indicating much more insider buys than sales), the market outlook is bullish. Above 60%, the outlook is bearish.

indicators are more reliable for small companies and when they are computed only from the insider transactions of managers (i.e., excluding transactions of less informed insiders).

2. **Corporate transactions**: to get an idea about the future direction of the stock market, John Templeton watched the number of corporate takeovers, the premiums at which these takeovers occurred and the number of companies that repurchased their shares. Many corporate takeovers at high premiums above the market price (e.g., 50%) and a high number of repurchases – or better yet, delistings where companies repurchase all of their shares – indicate that corporate leaders are convinced that there is value in the stock market.

   Investors must be wary though, as corporate transactions are less reliable than insider transactions for the simple reason that the latter involve private cash (which directly affects the insider's personal financial position), while the former are done with corporate cash (which only affects the company's financial position). What is more, repurchases have become all the rage in the last 10 to 20 years, and many repurchase programmes appear to have little to do with increasing shareholder value. The limited relevance of the repurchase indicator was on display in the market crash of 2008. Right before the collapse in 2008, there were a lot of repurchases at very high price levels but the amount of repurchases dropped to spectacularly low levels around the market bottom in 2009.

## H.I.5 Indicator 5: Potential catalysts

Finally, some top investors look for catalysts that may trigger a change in the direction of the stock market. Although a powerful catalyst can be helpful to determine a potential turning point more accurately, it is usually very difficult to find reliable ones. In addition, even the most effective catalysts are unreliable when no other indicator confirms the change of direction. Therefore, top investors don't typically look for catalysts. Those who do look for:

1. **Expectations of heavy selling**: John Templeton correctly pinpointed the collapse of the technology bubble in 2000. He calculated the moment when many lock-up periods (typically six months) for the sale of stocks of hot techno-IPOs by insiders expired. Knowing all too well that their technology stocks were vastly overvalued, Templeton expected that insiders would sell massively as soon as they were allowed to do so. He expected that this wave of selling would trigger the implosion of the techno mania.

2. **Duration**: Anthony Bolton and Jim Rogers closely observe the duration and strength of bull and bear markets to determine turning points. It must be said that this is quite tricky because there can be a wide spread on the duration and strength of bull-bear cycles.

3. **Cash on the sidelines**: John Templeton closely observed the *cash on the sidelines*. He believed that an excessively high amount of money parked in cash accounts represents latent firepower that can push a depressed market higher.

Apart from the indicators suggested by top investors, investment professionals have come up with numerous other indicators to anticipate market movements. Examples are the evolution of oil prices, short-term interest rates, currency rates, federal budget deficits, inverted yield curves, the economic picture, and the behaviour of the bond market.

Investors are advised to restrict the number of indicators they monitor to those that really matter (the ones mentioned above), and to ignore unproven fancy indicators. It has been found, for instance, that oil prices, currency rates and budget deficits of a nation have little to do with stock market movements.[201] Besides, it is worth stressing once more that sentiment, valuations, imbalances and corporate/insider transactions are **not** reliable methods for anticipating turning points (or even short to medium-term movements) in the stock market. They should be used all together. And one should only pay attention to extremes in these indicators.

Even then, there is no assurance that they will help to accurately identify turning points. Indeed, as the late 1990s and the late 1970s have shown, valuations, market sentiment and imbalances can remain at *dangerous* or *attractive* levels for several years on end.

In summary, the above indicators must be used only as guidelines to assess the long-term potential of the stock market. Top investors position their portfolios based on their interpretation of these indicators but they realise that they may be wrong in the short-to-medium term. In the next section I explain how they deal with market cycles in practice.

## H.II Investing over the boom-bust cycle in practice

### H.II.1 Strategic aspects

Keeping to the basic investing philosophy, top investors remain focused on the value-price disparity over market cycles. They are humble enough to admit that they are regularly wrong in their fair value assessment and they realise that market trends can remain irrational for a long time. For this reason, top investors tread cautiously when they interpret market signals. They also do not attempt to time the market, even openly admitting that their market timing skills are poor.

Top investors gradually change their bias to buying or selling depending on the attractiveness of the markets according to the indicators discussed in H.I. Their strategy is determined to a large extent by their style and their level of comfort with the interpretation of the facts. Here is an overview of some of their tactics:

1.  They start buying (sometimes aggressively) in bear markets when valuations have come down sufficiently. As they realise it is virtually impossible to pinpoint the bottom of a bear market, they **buy gradually in the midst of a bear market and on the way down**. This implies, as Seth Klarman points out, that smart investors buy when things look really bad and they accept the fact that the bargains they purchased probably will go down even more before they recover.

---

[201] Fisher, 2007.

2. Their actions around **market tops** or in **overheated markets** are much more diverse. From a value perspective, one should stay out of overvalued markets. Top investors would rather wait on the sidelines when a market is overvalued, even though this may lead to consistent underperformance over several years. Indeed, because markets can remain irrational for a long time, staying out of overvalued markets can be costly as long as the market rallies. In the end, though, the patient and disciplined investor comes out well ahead.

On the other hand, it is not always necessary to abandon the stock market during the late stages of bull markets. More often than not, certain pockets of the market are ignored (and stay undervalued) when valuations of the broader market are out of whack. What top investors tend to do in expensive markets depends in large measure on their personality, and on what they feel comfortable with. Here are four types of possible actions:

- *Defensive actions*: some money masters like Benjamin Graham, John Templeton and Philip Carret recommend *easing out of stocks* and *moving partially into cash* when things heat up. At the very least, they didn't buy (and stuck to their cash) when they couldn't find value opportunities. The shift from stocks to cash is not only attractive to cushion the impact of a downturn, but also ensures that the investor has a lot of dry powder to buy stocks at bargain prices during the subsequent bear market.[202] As mentioned by Anthony Bolton in *Investing Against the Tide*, selling should be done gradually though (to avoid market timing), and first in those issues that are most overpriced and/or riskiest. Top investors mention two procedures that can be used to change the weight of cash in a stock portfolio:

  (i) Benjamin Graham recommends the use of a mechanical method to vary the proportion of stocks in one's portfolio. For instance, one can pursue a fixed percentage of stocks, irrespective of market conditions. In this way, stocks are sold in bull markets (when they become more expensive), and they are purchased during bear markets (when they are cheaper).

  (ii) Many top investors vary the weight of cash based on the ease by which they can find stocks with attractive expected forward returns. They would rather stay in cash and wait for a market downturn than settling for poor forward returns. For instance, Prem Watsa had only 6% of the investment portfolio of Fairfax Financial Holdings in stocks at the top of the techno bubble in 2000. Similarly, the Yacktmans and Robert Rodriguez held unusual amounts of cash around the market top of 2007.

- *Offensive actions* like hedging and shorting are difficult, risky, and require a lot of courage and conviction. Moreover, they should be balanced since we

---

[202] Warren Buffett, for instance, sees cash as a call option on every asset class with no strike price and no expiration date.

know that top investors avoid market timing. Owing to all of this, many top investors avoid offensive actions and prefer to remain invested on the long side (including going into cash) under all market conditions. In that case they are willing to take the up and down movements of the market in their stride. Others feel more confident when they protect their gains, but restrict their offensive actions to exceptional situations. Finally, offensive actions are part and parcel of the strategy of hedge fund managers, because these people are focused on delivering positive returns, irrespective of market conditions. Here are the two most important types of offensive actions:

(i) *Hedging* is applied by top investors like Prem Watsa, David Einhorn and Seth Klarman. It consists of buying some market hedges (e.g., puts on an index) or hedges on baskets of particularly vulnerable stocks (e.g., puts on technology stocks during the techno bubble). These hedges offer protection or excellent returns when the market turns down. The drawback of hedging is that it costs money. It can therefore be a drag on one's returns.

For instance, Seth Klarman hedged his portfolio between 1996 and 2000. These hedges were a drag on his portfolio for four years before they really paid off. Prem Watsa had a similar experience during the bull market between 2002 and 2007, but was rewarded lavishly for his patience in 2008. Another example is Peter Cundill who incurred huge losses on his Nikkei puts between 1987 and 1990 before he made back all of his losses and then a whole lot more in 1990.[203] On the positive side, hedging can be relatively inexpensive at the moment that it is most attractive. Indeed, during times of euphoria few people expect a market collapse, making hedges rather cheap.[204]

(ii) *Shorting*: here investors sell borrowed stock in the hope of purchasing the stock later in the market at a lower price before they return it to the owner. As said before (see Chapter G), short selling is risky because it can theoretically lead to unlimited losses if it is applied without proper risk management. Even though some famous investors like Julian Robertson, George Soros, David Einhorn and John Templeton were/are very successful at it, shorting is not commonly practiced by top investors. Benjamin Graham got burnt by his short activities and many others (e.g., Seth Klarman) don't do it because they don't like its risk-return profile. Warren Buffett's advice on short selling is to avoid it altogether because the stock market can remain irrational longer than the short seller can remain solvent.

Nevertheless, Buffett says that those who really want to give it a try during bubbles should go short the entire market or a diversified and

---

[203] Risso-Gill, 2011.

[204] Hence, the price of options can also be used as an indicator of market sentiment. Expensive put options imply fear (a bullish sign), whereas cheap put options imply complacency and optimism (a bearish sign).

representative set of overpriced stocks[205] rather than individual stocks (because sustained irrationality is less likely in a large set of stocks than in individual stocks).

- *Shifting to undervalued pockets of the market*: a stock index like the S&P 500 only represents the major part – but not all – of the market's capitalisation. In reality, stock markets can be very heterogeneous and stock indices may not be representative of the situation in certain pockets of the market. In addition, the performance of an index can be distorted by the exceptional performance of some particular sector(s) or due to some type(s) of stock (e.g., megacaps and technology stocks in the late 1990s). This implies that it is not uncommon for certain pockets of the stock market to be undervalued when aggregate valuations in the market index are excessively high.

What is more, during strong bull markets or manias, undervalued stocks may become even cheaper as disenchanted shareholders of these stocks capitulate and flock to the hot stocks du jour. Selling stocks in the hot pockets of the market and shifting the proceeds into stocks of undervalued pockets is therefore the easiest and most logical course of action for investors. It actually means *going where the value is*. This method is not foolproof as a protection against bear markets, however, due to the fact that about 80% of stocks follow the market's cycles. This means that undervalued issues may become even more undervalued during major bear markets (or when a bubble bursts), because they can be dragged down with the collapsing stock market. Therefore, it is advisable to combine this strategy with the defensive and/or offensive actions described above. Here are some examples:

(i) During the technology mania of the late 1990s, Seth Klarman focused his investments in undervalued small and medium caps. This was a smart move because small caps vastly outperformed the S&P 500 during the collapse of the techno bubble in the early 2000s.

(ii) Peter Lynch recommends the use of a quasi-mechanical method to take advantage of cycles in different pockets of the market. He recommends getting out of small caps and moving into large caps when the P/E ratio of small caps (e.g., represented by the Russell 2000 or Russell 3000 index) is about twice the P/E of the S&P 500. When the P/E ratio of small caps is below 1.2 times the P/E of the S&P, he recommends moving into small caps.

(iii) In *Active Value Investing*, Vitaliy Katsenelson points out that deep value stocks enjoyed a bull rally with almost 15% annual returns over the vicious

---

[205] Even then, timing is crucial. Julian Robertson and George Soros shorted *new economy* stocks in the late 1990s. Due to the fact that the bubble lasted for almost five years they suffered major losses. John Templeton, on the other hand, was successful because he looked for a catalyst. In 2000 Templeton went short a basket of technology stocks that had increased three times over their IPO price shortly before the lockup period for these issues was due to expire. He reasoned that these stocks were particularly vulnerable because he expected massive insider sales once the insiders were allowed to unload their extremely expensive shares.

range-bound market between the late 1960s and 1982. A study even found that a strategy focused on deep value stocks that were selected based on Benjamin Graham's criterion of Net Current Asset Value (see Chapter D) delivered almost 30% annually between 1970 and 1983. A recent result found that the ten lowest-P/E stocks with market caps of at least $500 million and more equity than debt had bull-like annual returns of almost 17% a year over the range-bound market between 2000 and 2009. Hence, there are clearly opportunities for value-oriented investors around the peaks of secular bulls.

(iv) According to Philip Fisher and Richard Bernstein there seems to be an alternating cycle between value (i.e., stocks with low multiples) and growth (i.e., stocks with high multiples). In essence, value and growth alternately tend to outperform each other depending on three factors:

a) *Profit growth momentum*: when corporate profits decelerate, growth becomes scarce. So, companies with above-average growth become more popular. As a consequence, growth stocks tend to outperform value stocks. Conversely, when corporate profits accelerate, value tends to outperform growth as growth becomes a commodity.

b) *Long-term interest rate movements*: growth stocks seldom pay a dividend and reward investors through price appreciation over the long term. So, investors are inclined to identify them with long-term bonds. Many value stocks, on the other hand, pay high dividends and are held for a shorter period of time. So the market associates them more with short-term bonds. The implication is that, as long-term bonds outperform small-term bonds when interest rates fall, growth stocks tend to outperform value stocks in that situation. The opposite occurs when interest rates rise.

c) *Spread on the global yield curve*: when the global yield curve steepens, value companies (which typically borrow more than growth companies) can find easier access to financing as banks can make a decent profit on the loans. So, value companies thrive and their shares tend to outperform growth stocks. When the yield curve flattens value companies will find it harder to finance themselves than growth companies, and the latter tend to outperform.

- *Shifting into better value assets*: closely related to a shift into cash or into undervalued pockets of the stock market, investors can consider alternative types of assets that may be better value for their money. Evidently, only those assets where the investor has relevant expertise are acceptable alternatives.

Macro investors like George Soros typically have expertise in many different types of assets (e.g., commodities, derivatives, interest rate instruments, currencies, stocks, real estate, etc.) and therefore have a lot of latitude to shift into other asset classes when stocks look expensive. For stock-focused investors, bonds are usually the natural alternative.

John Templeton, for instance, invested in zero-coupon bonds with a yield of 6.3% in March 2000 (right at the top of the techno bubble) because he reasoned that stocks would offer far lower returns in the decade thereafter, and because he expected interest rates to come down as the Fed would have to fend off a recession once the bubble would burst. Likewise, Warren Buffett invested a significant amount in junk bonds in 2002 because he believed that stocks were still unattractive (in spite of the bear market between 2000 and 2002), and because he was convinced that dire business conditions were priced into these bonds. Similarly, according to Steven Romick, high-yield bonds offered much better value than stocks in the midst of the credit crisis of 2008-2009 as they, unlike stocks, priced in a depression.

## H.II.2 Mental requirements and attitudes

> "*The most common cause of low prices is pessimism – sometimes pervasive, sometimes specific to a company or industry. We want to do business in such an environment, not because we like pessimism but because we like the prices it produces. It's optimism that is the enemy of the rational buyer.*"
>
> **Warren Buffett, 1990 letter to the shareholders of Berkshire Hathaway**

> "*The time of maximum pessimism is the best time to buy, and the time of maximum optimism is the best time to sell.*"
>
> **John Templeton (Krass, 1999)**

> "*When I see hysteria, I usually like to take a look to see if I shouldn't be going the other way. Just about every time you go against panic, you will be right if you can stick it out.*"
>
> **Jim Rogers (Schwager, 2006)**

We saw in Chapter A that the human brain is wired against successful investing over market cycles. Almost all top investors therefore urge investors to control their emotions, to act rationally and to gather the courage to do things that feel uncomfortable. They point out that the most important psychological requisites to succeed as an investor over market cycles are:

1. **Mental fortitude to go against the herd**: the fact that market tops are characterised by a high level of optimism and that pessimism is high around market bottoms implies that selling at tops and buying at bottoms goes squarely against the prevailing market sentiment. Being contrarian is hard because most people feel very uncomfortable when they don't follow the herd. Here are a number of ideas of some top investors on going against the herd:

    - Benjamin Graham described the stock market with the metaphor of *Mr. Market*.[206] In his view, Mr. Market is a manic-depressive person who is mostly either too euphoric (corresponding to market optimism, when the market sees only a rosy future) or too depressed (corresponding to market pessimism, when the market sees nothing but trouble ahead). When Mr. Market is depressed, he is willing to sell companies at cheap prices. When he is in a euphoric mood investors have to pay up. According to Graham, intelligent investors are unaffected by the mood swings of Mr. Market. In fact, intelligent investors are realists who sell to Mr. Market when he is in an optimistic mood and who buy from him when he is downbeat.

    - Warren Buffett says that investors should be greedy when others are fearful and vice versa. He believes that investors must see volatility as their friend (to snap up shares on the cheap), and that they should stay far away from market folly.

2. **Patience and discipline**: top investors are patient and disciplined in sticking to their strategy, even if this leads to temporary underperformance versus the market. Patience and discipline are essential to withstand the siren call of long periods of irrationality (on the upside and on the downside), but they require a high level of confidence and faith. Intelligent investors are happy to wait during times of irrational exuberance until the market comes to its senses.[207] Absent this, investors are prone to follow the herd, chase returns in manias and defer purchases near bear bottoms.

3. **Independence and critical stance**: top investors are seldom impressed by the latest fashions in economics and finance. They don't buy theories about new eras and new fundamentals, which are common during market manias and towards the end of secular bulls. They also steer clear of doomsday prophets who forecast the end of the stock market and even the world as we know it around deep market bottoms. Furthermore, sudden panics in the stock market due to crises such as terrorist attacks (e.g., 9/11 or the 1993 WTC bombing) or political murders (e.g., assassination of JFK in 1963) do not throw top investors off balance. As Templeton points out, these events seldom have an important impact on the economy. In short, top investors ignore the current headlines in the media and form their own opinion based on facts, history, fundamentals and the price-value gap.

---

[206] Graham, 2003.

[207] For instance, as mentioned before, Seth Klarman had to endure several years of underperformance in the late 1990s (because he refused to participate in the bubble) and reaped the profits of his discipline only after the bubble burst in the early 2000s.

4. **Humility**: top investors are humble because they know that greed and hubris are fatal when dealing with market cycles. More specifically:

- They seldom try to forecast short-to-medium term market movements and they ignore economic predictions (to some extent, see above). Jim Rogers, for instance, openly admits in the financial media that he's not smart enough to predict how the markets will behave in the near future.

- They remain humble about the gains they can earn in the stock market. People who extrapolate an exceptionally profitable or unprofitable spell, by contrast, are likely to lose their discipline and independence, and seldom can muster the energy to go against the crowd.

- They stress the importance of luck. This also means that they do not equate making a gain with being right, or making a loss with being wrong. After all, each investment is an educated bet where successful investors manage to tilt the odds in their favour. And it is a matter of statistics that not all bets work out.[208]

5. **Tolerance for losses**: people who can't accept the occasional depreciation of their stock portfolio with equanimity should not be in the stock market. Those who can't tolerate losses will never be able to exhibit the psychological requirements discussed above (i.e., going against the herd, being patient and remaining independent). Stock investing is not for everyone, and Warren Buffett warns that one should stay away from stocks if one can't stand losing about 50% of one's investment.

---

> "We simply attempt to be fearful when others are greedy and to be greedy only when others are fearful."
>
> **Warren Buffett (Cunningham, 2001-A)**

---

> "In 2007, a major U.S. bank CEO famously said 'as long as the music is playing you have to get up and dance.' After the Lehman bankruptcy in 2008, this same bank needed $45 billion from the U.S. government to continue in business. Expensive dance! We prefer to wait for the music to stop and not depend on the kindness of strangers to be in business. From the distant past comes the warning of our mentor, Ben Graham, whom I have quoted before: 'Only 1 in 100 survived the 1929-32 debacle if one was not bearish in 1925.' "
>
> **Prem Watsa, 2012 letter to the shareholder of Fairfax Financial Holdings**

---

[208] This is similar to a game of poker. Excellent poker players can calculate (through probability theory) which choices and steps are most likely to be profitable. In spite of the superior process that these people use, they cannot expect to win every single game, but they can expect good results over the long term if the process is applied consistently.

# H.III Summary and further remarks

Figure 25 summarises the main lessons of this chapter. First, investors must realise that stock markets move up and down in bull/bear cycles of a few years, and in secular supercycles that typically last one to two decades. To maximise returns, top investors try to exploit phases of irrational pricing over these cylces.

**Figure 25: How top investors deal with market cycles**

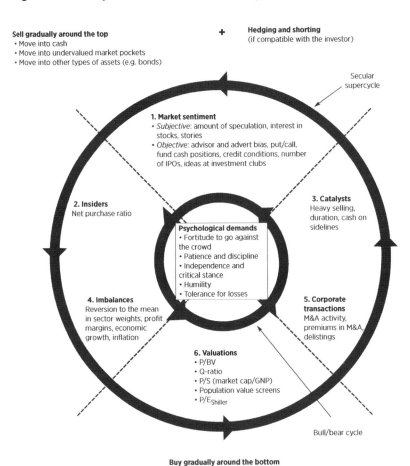

Buy gradually around the bottom

There are a number of indicators that can be used as guideposts. These indicators are not reliable timing tools but they can give rough signals of turning points in bull/bear cycles when they are combined and when they reach extreme levels. Or they can be used as signals to start making slow and gradual changes to one's long-term asset allocation (when a turning point in the secular cycles is expected).

For investors, the first and foremost indicator is the market's valuation in terms of P/BV,

Tobin's q, market cap/GNP, $P/E_{Shiller}$, and the number of bargains that can be found. Closely related to valuation are imbalances that are likely to mean-revert, such as excessive sector weights, unsustainably high or low profit margins, and economic imbalances. Another important indicator is market sentiment. Subjective impressions (the amount of speculation, general interest in the stock market) as well as objective impressions (advisor bias, put/call ratio, cash positions in mutual funds, bias in the ads, credit conditions, number of IPOs, popularity of advisory services and investment clubs) can give clues about whether the majority of market players are complacent and optimistic or downright pessimistic.

Another useful indicator is the number of insider transactions (insider purchases and sales) and corporate transactions (M&A, share buybacks (delistings in particular), etc.). Finally, cash on the sidelines, the duration of a bull or bear market and other subjective assessments can be seen as potential catalysts.

The strategy of top investors during market cycles reflects their reluctance for market timing and their sense of realism about their ability to profit from these cycles. They typically buy and sell gradually. Depending on their style, their approach in overvalued markets can be to go (partially) into cash or other asset classes, to hedge their positions, or to shift to undervalued pockets of the market.

Profiting from market cycles also puts rigorous demands on the investor's attitude and mental makeup. Little reward awaits people who can't stray from the crowd, who seek advice from third parties, who lack the patience and discipline to stay the course, who can't stand losses, and who are complacent or arrogant. Intelligent investors are contrarian, do their own homework, stick with their strategy through thick and thin, have tolerance for losses and always remember that beating the market is hard.

# CHAPTER I

## COMMON BUYING AND SELLING MISTAKES

"Inactivity strikes us as intelligent behaviour. We are quite content to hold any security indefinitely, so long as the prospective return on equity capital of the underlying business is satisfactory, management is competent and honest, and the market does not overvalue the business."

WARREN BUFFETT (CUNNINGHAM, 2001-A)

IN THE PREVIOUS chapters I have discussed three important trading aspects of investing championed by top investors. First I explained how to trade different types of individual stocks. A second chapter was about general aspects of how to buy, hold and sell individual stocks. And finally, I looked into smart trading strategies over market cycles. All of these trading rules are pretty straightforward and will undoubtedly appeal to many people.

Unfortunately, the vast majority of investors will find it hard to put the sound trading advice of the previous chapters into practice. This is at the same time one of the reasons why these trading rules are so powerful. The main problem is that buying, holding and selling based on considerations that fit into the investment philosophy are incompatible with most people's gut feel, their intuition, their basic instincts (see also Chapter A), and their understanding of investing.

Less successful investors trade incoherently and based on impulses that have nothing to do with the fair value concept. They also try things that top investors consider impossible or unwise. As I explain in this chapter, common trading errors of the average investor are the result of a poor understanding of the stock market, the lack of a coherent or well-thought out strategy and philosophy, and the impact of psychological biases.

### I.I Error 1: Picking tops and bottoms

Many investors believe that they can buy a stock at a price bottom and sell at a price top. Bottom fishing refers to the practice where one defers a stock purchase *until the stock price hits bottom*. Top picking is the practice where one tries to squeeze the last cents out of a stock before selling.

A first reason for the popularity of bottom fishing and top picking is overconfidence.

Modern behavioural finance has found that the average investor has too much confidence in his abilities to time purchases and sales. This is caused mainly by the fact that, even though investing is extremely hard and complex, it looks familiar and easy. After all, one only needs a computer and a broker account to trade. So, people are too confident that finding a bottom or top is feasible with a little technical analysis, through chart reading, or by observation of market movements.

A second reason for the popularity of bottom fishing and top picking is pattern seeking. People believe that predictable and understandable patterns can be found in everything, even in noise. So, due to their conviction that stock prices move in predictable price patterns, many investors find it logical that tops and bottoms can be recognised by people who can *read* these patterns.

Top investors unanimously reject bottom fishing and top picking. They don't believe that anyone can reliably call the bottom or top of a stock, because stock price movements are far too random.[209] They see bottom fishers and top pickers as reckless and overconfident speculators. Even more, they warn people against the dangers of these practices. Bottom fishers are likely to miss attractive stocks on the way down since they wait too long before they buy. If they missed an opportunity and a stock bounces off a bottom, they are reluctant to buy the stock on its way up as they fail to acknowledge the upward movement (or because they don't like buying a stock above the bottom). The end result is a missed opportunity. Likewise, those who try to pick tops are apt to hang on to stocks way too long. They usually miss the top and then they are reluctant to sell below that top. More often than not, they get trapped in the downdraft after the top.

The main lesson for investors is that one should not aim for the best possible price to buy or sell. John Templeton says that although one should not expect to buy or sell a stock within 10% of a top or bottom, most of the money can still can be made in the remaining 80%. Smart investors base their decisions on fair value considerations and common sense, and they take random price movements in their stride. They accept that a stock can and probably will go lower after a purchase, or move higher after a sale. Therefore, they usually buy gradually at attractive valuations. They then sell in steps when a stock reaches full value. Thanks to the accumulation and gradual reduction of positions, they welcome random price fluctuations.

---

*"Postponing an attractive purchase because of fear of what the market might do will, over the years, prove very costly. This is because the investor is ignoring a powerful influence about which he has positive knowledge through fear of a less powerful force about which, in the present state of human knowledge, he and everyone else is largely guessing."*

**Philip Fisher (Fisher, 1996)**

---

[209] Maybe to the surprise of many readers, the world's greatest technical traders say exactly the same.

## I.II Error 2: Selling a winning stock and buying it back at a lower price

Numerous investors have tried to squeeze an extra profit out of a strong stock by selling it with the aim to buy it back later at a cheaper price. Few people realise how hard it is to successfully pull such a trade off. Selling a star performer after a rally and picking it back up as the price comes off its highs looks straightforward and feasible on paper but in reality chances are high that the *sell high, repurchase low* investor will get burned, or will be pushed out of the stock permanently. The flaw of this strategy is that it can only be successful if two speculative bets work out:

1. First, the investor must time his sale around a temporary top of the stock. In other words, he/she must pick a top correctly. If the investor is wrong, and sells before a top, the stock may get away (permanently) as most investors are reluctant to repurchase at a higher price.

2. Second, if the stock was sold around a top, the investor still has to time his repurchase correctly around a temporary bottom. In other words, he/she must be good at bottom fishing. The big problem here is that investors usually overestimate the decline of a strong stock. They wait too long and therefore miss out on the opportunity to buy the stock back.[210] Once the stock recovers from its temporary weakness and rises above the price at which it was sold, investors are reluctant to buy.

## I.III Error 3: Selling winners and hanging on to losers

It is natural for people to sell winning stocks and to hang on to (or even buy more of) stocks on which they have incurred a significant loss. There are several explanations for this behaviour. First of all, investors tend to use the stock price before a serious price movement as an anchor. To the financially untrained, it is hard to imagine that a stock that has advanced a lot over a short period of time can go any higher, or that a stock that has lost a lot can go any lower. Many people believe that a winning stock has exhausted its upside potential, and should be replaced with something that hasn't gone up that much. Likewise, it seems logical that a losing stock is due for a bounce. So in people's minds it makes little sense to part ways with such stock.

A second reason is pressure and the avoidance of regret. Shareholders of winning stocks are concerned that they may lose their gain and people around them do their best to reinforce this concern. Financial advisors encourage them to sell their star performers and conventional wisdom says "You can't go broke taking a profit," "Take profits as long as you can," or "A sure gain is better than a possible loss." With underperforming stocks, investors would rather wait and see than take an action (i.e., selling) they may regret.

A third reason for the fact that investors prefer to hang on to losers is asymmetric loss aversion combined with mental accounting (see Chapter A). As a financial loss hurts twice as much as an equally large gain is enjoyable, people are reluctant to take a real cash

---

[210] Fisher, 1996.

loss. As long as the stock is not sold, they only see the paper loss (which feels very different from a cash loss), and they hope that they eventually will be able to *break even* when it bounces back.

Both selling a winning stock and holding on to a losing stock are misguided steps if they are based only on price action. After all, a spectacular rally or a steep drop in a company's stock price may well be vindicated by changes in the company's intrinsic value. Many top investors therefore denounce the conventional belief that stocks that double should be sold, and that stocks that lose half of their value should be kept. In fact, Peter Lynch likens this behaviour to "pulling out the flowers and watering the weeds."[211] Here are their problems with these practices:

1. It is often a **mistake to take a profit on a star performer** because investors frequently underestimate the potential (fair value) of excellent companies. The stock price of outstanding companies should exhibit strong performance. Such companies deserve high multiples. What is more, many excellent companies keep on surprising the market and continue their strong price performance much longer than most people can imagine. Smart investors therefore cut star performers some slack on the upside. They don't sell automatically after they have doubled their money on a great business and they ridicule the "You can't go broke taking a profit" talk.[212] They rather embrace the adages "Let your winners ride," "Be reluctant to take profits," and "It's better to sell a winning stock too late than too soon."

2. According to top investors, **holding on to losing stocks in the hope to get out even** is probably the costliest mistake in the investment world. Stocks of poorly run businesses that don't produce positive cash flows and have management of questionable integrity should get hammered in efficient markets and don't deserve high multiples. Intelligent investors swiftly get rid of shares when they lose faith in the company, even if this means taking a serious loss.

# I.IV Error 4: Overtrading

Many investors are hyperactive and relentlessly churn their portfolios in a quest for profit. A major cause for this high level of trading is that people are too confident in their abilities to determine turning points in the market and in individual stocks. A second reason is that many people believe that *hard work in the market* is necessary to make a decent profit. Then there is lack of patience and thirst for action. Few investors can resist the latest hot stocks of the day and therefore replace their old stocks with stocks that are in vogue.

---

[211] Lynch, 1993.

[212] Warren Buffett wonders: "Can you imagine a CEO using this phrase to urge his board to sell a star subsidiary?" (Cunningham, 2001-A) As an aside, many leveraged traders and investors have actually gone broke by taking profits on their winners. Each trader and investor has winners and losers in his or her portfolio. The excellent track records of many of the most successful traders and investors are to a large extent determined by a limited number of winners that were held for a long time. By consistently selling one's winners one can rest assured that one limits one's upside, and that the return of one's portfolio will move into the direction of the subpar results from the losers. This can lead to disastrous results if one is leveraged.

Finally, few people realise the underlying cost of trading because the transaction costs of each single trade (bid-ask spread, broker commissions and fees, taxes, etc.) are small compared to the amount sold or purchased. So, they don't feel the need to restrict the number of transactions.

Unfortunately, the track records of active market players are unenviable. Numerous studies have shown that the long-term performance of the average active investor is horrible as compared with that of more passive investors.[213] Top stock pickers know that the quick turnover game doesn't pay off. Their average holding periods are usually around two to five years. They regularly keep stocks in their portfolio for more than a decade. And they openly praise low-turnover strategies.

The low-turnover approach of intelligent investors makes perfect sense. In fact, active trading is inconsistent with the investment philosophy. Smart investors don't buy and sell based on hunches or the latest hot news. They only trade when their well-defined buying and selling criteria are met. Intrinsic values and under or overvaluations do not change often enough to justify more than some moderate amount of turnover.

In addition, intelligent investors know that people who trade frequently operate with a handicap, due to friction costs (transaction costs) and taxes. Although transaction costs may look trivial for single trades, they can add up quickly when investors buy or sell frenetically. The tax burden can even be more of an issue.

**Figure 26: After-tax returns as a function of the buy-and-hold period**

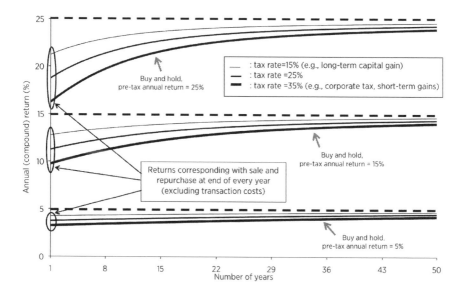

This is illustrated in Figure 26, which shows the annual after-tax return earned by a buy-and-hold investor as a function of the holding period in nine possible scenarios. The

---

[213] Mauboussin, 2006.

upper three lines show the annual after-tax return (as a function of the holding period) of an investor who earns 25% a year before tax. The upper and lowest line of these three show the returns if the tax rate is respectively 15% and 35%. The other lines in Figure 26 show the annual after-tax returns when the pre-tax annual return is 15% and 5%.

We can clearly see that the annual after-tax return increases significantly if the portfolio is held (without sale) for one to two decades compared with only a single year. The returns of investors who turn their portfolio over every year (these are the returns when the value on the x-axis – the number of years – is 1) are seriously impacted by taxes. Making matters worse, in many countries short-term trades are taxed at higher rates than long-term trades.

> *"If you aren't willing to own a stock for ten years, don't even think about owning it for ten minutes."*
>
> **Warren Buffett, 1996 letter to the shareholders of Berkshire Hathaway**

## I.V Error 5: Buy-and-forget

Some investors take the admonitions of Warren Buffett about buy-and-hold far too literally. They mindlessly apply a buy-and-hold strategy and stick for too many years with the same stocks. Their strategy can be described as *buy-and-forget*.

A convenient advantage of the buy-and-forget approach is that it relieves investors of the burden of keeping track of their stock holdings. The problem is that buy-and-forget is unlikely to beat the market over the long term. Indeed, companies that manage to grow their intrinsic value per share at more than about 12% to 15% annually over a couple of decades are few and far between.[214]

So, even in the very optimistic situation where one has identified the strongest stocks for future decades, annual returns of about 12% to 15% are the best one can hope for in a buy-and-forget approach. In a more realistic buy-and-forget portfolio, with winners and losers, one should probably not expect returns much higher than 10%.

How then do top investors who champion the buy-and-hold approach manage to beat the market by a large margin? When we study the operations of top investors, it is striking to see the way in which they apply the buy-and-hold strategy. For instance, John Templeton had an average holding period of four years.[215] Warren Buffett turns his private portfolio (which he manages independently of Berkshire Hathaway) over rather frequently. For his part, Peter Lynch is convinced that his relatively high turnover would have been even higher if he had done his job better.[216]

---

[214] Siegel, 2005.
[215] Templeton, 2008.
[216] Train, 2000.

It appears as if top investors – like Shelby Davis, Peter Lynch, Warren Buffett, Philip Fisher and John Neff – earned high returns by holding on to a **limited** number of stocks over the long term, i.e. many years and decades. Charlie Munger and Warren Buffett even state that Berkshire Hathaway owes its superior track record to no more than about 15 stocks that were held for a very long time.

Apparently, the buy-and-hold strategy practiced by top investors is far more subtle than buy-and-forget. If we take a closer look at the recommendations of top investors, one can see what they really mean. The claim of Warren Buffett that his "**favourite** holding period is forever," is preceded by the qualification that this should be "When we own portions of outstanding businesses with outstanding management."[217] Unfortunately, most investments are not outstanding in terms of business and management. In other words, buy-and-hold is a powerful strategy if it is applied to exceptional companies.

As we saw in Chapter B, good candidates for a buy-and-hold approach would be fast growers or exceptional stalwarts. On the other hand, some stock types like cyclicals and turnarounds *should* be traded actively. In addition, buy-and-hold can never be an excuse to overrule the basic selling rules, such as deteriorating fundamentals or irrational valuations.

# I.VI Error 6: Emotional trades

> "*While enthusiasm may be necessary for great accomplishments elsewhere, on Wall Street it almost invariably leads to disaster.*"
>
> **Benjamin Graham (Graham, 2003)**

Investing can get very emotional. People tend to overreact to surprises, especially when these surprises are negative. They can build a cosy bond with a stock, or they may find it unbearable to exercise patience. While intelligent investors postpone transactions when emotions are running high in order to shut emotions out of the decision process, the average investor gets him or herself in trouble through emotional trades, such as:

1. **Impatient trades**: people sometimes think that they must buy a stock quickly before the window of opportunity closes. Or they start buying (after they avoided stocks for a long time) when a bull market is about to top out. Alternatively, in Peter Lynch's experience, many people sell when it takes too long before something happens. According to Peter Lynch, trades driven by impatience often lead to grief. Instant action is seldom required for real opportunities and it is a mistake to throw in the towel after a long wait. In investing, one should always remember that patience is a virtue.

2. **Buying immediately after good news/selling immediately after bad news**: many people are tempted to buy a stock when it releases good news. Or they sell when

---

[217] Cunningham, 2001-A.

a company announces bad news. However, taking action immediately on news is unwise. First of all, Peter Lynch and Benjamin Graham believe that such trades are too impulsive. The emotions of the moment cloud one's judgment, and lead to a bias in the way the investor processes the (good or bad) news.

Secondly, David Einhorn points out yet another problem with such trades. When the news comes out, many other people feel the same way about the news. As a result, the market often overreacts in the hours and days after the news, which makes for a bad moment to put on a trade. For instance, if management does something that angers you, numerous other people are likely to be angry too. So, many will sell the stock in exasperation, which may cause a (temporary) exaggerated price drop. The wise investor sits down after news has broken and reevaluates the situation thoroughly before taking action. He/she also knows that most of the time there are better moments to buy or sell a stock than when emotions overwhelm the market.

3. **Selling in panic**: sales in a fit of panic are common in the stock market. Panic can happen after/during a market crash, or towards the end of a bear market. Panicky sales are also common after a series of disappointments. The driving forces behind such sales are crowd behaviour and asymmetric loss aversion. People feel comfortable following the herd when they are faced with a vague and complex problem (such as investing), especially when they are emotionally strained. So, it feels safe to sell when everyone else is giving up on a stock (or the market). Furthermore, people often sell near a bottom because they want to get rid of the pain of a loss. Intelligent investors always remind themselves that panic is a bad teacher. Sales should be prompted by value versus price considerations, not by crowd behaviour, or the feeling that the market has rendered a definitive verdict on the fair value of a stock or the market.

4. **Desperately trying to recoup losses**: investment losses can cause a lot of emotional stress when the investor can't afford to lose. This can happen, for instance, when the investor had set himself a financial goal (e.g., to buy a car or to pay for the tuition of a child), or when he or she is leveraged to the hilt. It is evident that such people are under enormous pressure to make up for the losing trades as soon as possible. Realising that it won't be easy to recover the losses in a conventional way, they automatically begin to take more risk (e.g., they invest in speculative stocks) or take desperate gambles (e.g., through derivatives). The end result is often a total catastrophe. Investors should never forget that loss of discipline and the departure from a sound investment strategy seldom pay off.

5. **Falling in love with a stock**: people can develop emotional connections with stocks. This happens frequently with stocks that have performed extremely well. Alternatively, investors may have a special bond with a company because they like its products, because its headquarters is in their hometown, or because it is regularly in the news.

The problem with falling in love with a stock is that it leads to complacency and a loss of objectivity. People that feel an emotional bond with a stock won't be as critical about the company as about other businesses. They tend to overlook negative information, try to find confirmation of their positive view in the media and in analyst reports, and buy or hold on to the stock even in the presence of a negative news flow. Some top investors (e.g., John Neff and Robert Wilson) protect themselves against the love bias by selling every stock that gives them *the warm fuzzies*, or about which they feel like bragging. Others avoid complacency by showing *tough love* to stocks that have been good to them.

> *"It is obvious that the inner warm glow that results from having held a winner last year is of no importance in making a decision as to whether it belongs in an optimum portfolio this year."*
>
> **Warren Buffett, letter to the shareholders of**
> **Buffett's private partnership, January 1965**

## I.VII Error 7: Holding on to a stock out of the need to be right

Ego problems are ubiquitous in the investment world. Many investors just want to be right. They are reluctant to give up their view because they see an admission of error as a defeat. Smart investors, on the other hand, know that they are not in the business of being right. They are in the business of making money. They don't have large egos. They stay humble vis-à-vis the market. And they change their views when the facts indicate that they should. George Soros, one of the most successful macro traders of the past 40 years, admits that he is rich in spite of numerous wrong market calls because he acknowledges his mistakes quickly.

> *"To survive in the financial markets sometimes means beating a hasty retreat."*
>
> **George Soros (Tier, 2005)**

## I.VIII Error 8: Waiting for a catalyst before buying a stock

Due to their short-term focus, it is popular among investment professionals to look for catalysts that can boost a company's stock price in the immediate future (e.g., M&A activity, corporate events, etc.). It is even a common practice among analysts not to recommend attractively priced stocks when they can't identify a catalyst. Anthony Bolton warns investors that the focus on catalysts is misguided. The problem is that catalysts are priced into the share price the moment they become clear to the market, thus leaving little opportunity for people who wait for such a catalyst. As always, one should buy based on the fundamental story, be patient, and forget about short-term catalysts.

## I.IX Error 9: Trading based on tax considerations

Some investors let tax considerations interfere too much with their stock operations. They try to minimise taxes by deferring the realisation of gains (to benefit from the lower tax rate on long-term gains), by selling losing stocks too quickly (to benefit from the higher tax deductions on short-term losses), or by selling losing stocks to offset the gains made on winning stocks.

Warren Buffett and Charlie Munger warn that this kind of behaviour is dangerous. They stress that what matters to investors is the after-tax rate of return, not the amount of taxes paid. Minimising taxes should never be the objective. Maximising the after-tax rate of return should. Star investor Kevin Daly also admits that he missed out on a lot of profits by paying too much attention to tax considerations.[218] He is now convinced that investors must stay true to their investment process. They must base their decisions on fair value grounds and give minor thought to tax issues.

## I.X Error 10: Buying a laggard when a winner gets away

Out of frustration over missing a strong stock (which they consider too expensive), investors often buy a second-tier competitor of that successful company. Their idea is that laggards still have room to run and will eventually catch up with the star performer. According to Peter Lynch, this is naïve. More often than not, there are good reasons why a second-tier company lags a star performer. It may, for instance, lose market share, use too much leverage, have poor management, and so on. In the end, investors who let a winner get away and then chase it through a cheaper, lower-quality laggard are likely to compound their error.

## I.XI Error 11: Quibbling about tens and quarters

When they try to time a purchase, investors have a tendency to fixate on a certain purchase price. They are reluctant to buy as long as the stock stays above their threshold. These investors quibble about eights and quarters of a point when the stock gets close to their price target. In the process, they risk missing the stock even if it stays only marginally above their target price.[219] Intelligent investors know that fair value is always a ballpark estimate. They try to buy on the cheap and realise that quarters and tens are insignificant as compared to the long-range potential that attractive stocks should have.

---

[218] Schwager, 2012.

[219] Fisher, 1996.

## I.XII Error 12: Selling quickly after a takeover announcement

When a company launches a takeover bid on a target company, many shareholders of the target are tempted to sell the stock in the market. Their reaction is understandable. The stock price usually trades close to the offering price upon an acquisition announcement. So why wait for the acquisition to close, sitting on dead money in the meantime, if the cash can be put to work in other stocks?

Star fund manager Anthony Bolton disagrees. Unless one sees a reason for the deal to go south, there are two reasons why it is usually better to wait for the consummation of the deal. First, the final offering price may be higher if another interested buyer enters the scene. Second, if no competing bidder shows up, the difference between the offering price and the current trading price often presents an attractive return – even if the stock price is close to the offering price – because the period until the completion of the deal can be short.

## I.XIII Error 13: Acting on what is generally known

Making money on something that is well known and processed by most other investors is extremely hard. One should always remember that markets are very efficient, as market players quickly price in every new piece of information. This also explains why markets often do not behave in the way laymen expect. For instance, the stock market will ignore bad news about the economy when most investors already expect a recession. Or stocks may start rallying on the outbreak of an impending war, when most people already saw the war as inevitable.

Intelligent investors ignore old news. They look for what may surprise the market. Surprise can come from events that are totally ignored by the market (e.g., an economic contraction when the market is upbeat about the economy), or from the market's miscalculation of the intensity of an expected event (e.g., the underestimation of the depth of an economic crisis). Smart investors therefore try to determine the scenario that the market currently discounts (by watching and listening to the news, looking at analyst expectations, etc.), and painstakingly compare it with their own expectations and concerns.

## I.XIV Error 14: Trading in the belief that 'this time is different'

John Templeton stresses that the four most dangerous words in investing are *this time is different*. It's a big mistake for investors to buy or sell based on new era theories that invariably accompany asset bubbles or depressions. Intelligent investors do not believe in new eras where the economic laws of the past would no longer be valid. Their critical stance seems to be vindicated by Carmen Reinhart who shows in her book *This Time is Different: Eight Centuries of Financial Folly* that *this time is different* has been used time and again over the past eight centuries to justify asset bubbles before they popped.[220]

---

[220] Reinhart, 2009.

# I.XV Error 15: Too much attention to the economy

Many people believe that one should have a view on the economy to invest successfully. They are convinced that strong economic views are indispensable to time one's entries into or exits out of the market correctly. Or they select stocks that fit neatly into their economic picture (e.g., they buy defensive food companies in anticipation of a recession).

Top investors argue that this is a mistake. Peter Lynch, for instance, asserts that when he was a mutual fund manager he spent about 15 minutes *a year* thinking about the economy. The rationale behind this is that the economy is so complex and so hard to predict that it is a waste of time trying to predict it. Even if an investor were to be right about the economy, he may have trouble capitalising on this because there can be a marked disconnect between the economic reality and the behaviour of the stock market.

Making matters even more complicated, Ray Dalio warns that central bank interventions may push the stock market in a direction opposite to what one might expect based on one's economic scenario. In addition, according to Warren Buffett, focus on the economy invites high portfolio turnover which is costly (see also above in the discussion of overtrading).

The idea that investors should pay less attention to the economy in their investment strategy is championed by true bottom-up investors. But it must be said that this view is definitely not shared by macro investors, who actually take positions based on perceived bubbles and economic dislocations. Even prominent investors, such as Prem Watsa, do build their strategy around their economic views – at least when they expect major dislocations.

Even more remarkable, some top investors (e.g., David Einhorn and Warren Buffett) admitted after the market collapse of 2008-2009 that it was a mistake to pay scant attention to the impact of the housing bubble on the economy. It can be concluded from this that bottom-up investors don't have to pay too much attention to the normal economic cycles, but that the impact of major bubbles on the economy should not be ignored.

> *"The way you lose money in the stock market is to start off with an economic picture. All these great heavy-thinking deals kill you."*
>
> **Peter Lynch (Train, 2000)**

> *"We will continue to ignore political and economic forecasts, which are an expensive distraction for many investors and businessmen."*
>
> **Warren Buffett, 1994 letter to the shareholders of Berkshire Hathaway**

# PART III
## RISK VERSUS RETURN

# CHAPTER J

## RISK MANAGEMENT

"To invest successfully, you need not understand beta, efficient markets, modern portfolio theory, option pricing or emerging markets. You may, in fact, be better off knowing nothing of these."

WARREN BUFFETT, 1996 LETTER TO THE SHAREHOLDERS OF BERKSHIRE HATHAWAY

ALL INVESTORS HAVE to manage their risk exposure if they want to survive in the market. According to conventional wisdom, risk management means making a trade-off between risk and return. High returns are supposedly only achieved by taking on higher risk and people who want to sleep well at night would have to settle with low returns. The academic view on risk is very similar. In addition, proponents of the efficient market theory actually believe that the concept of risk can easily be captured in a few simple mathematical numbers and formulas.

As described hereunder, top investors disagree. They reject the idea that there is a clear inverse relationship between risk and return. They manage the risk in their portfolios through practices that are completely at odds with conventional theories of risk.

### J.I The academic view on risk

#### J.I.1 The Capital Asset Pricing Model

Modern portfolio management has an elegant and simple theory on risk and return. Based on the assumption that stock markets are perfectly efficient all of the time, risk can be modelled through the clean and simple Capital Asset Pricing Model (CAPM). More specifically, CAPM posits that the realised return R on an individual stock can be broken down into three terms:

$$R = R_f + R_s + e \quad \text{with} \quad R_s = \beta \times [R_m - R_f]$$

where:

1. $R_f$ is the risk-free rate of return, i.e., the return of risk-free bonds such as US Treasuries or German government bonds.

2. $R_S$ is the return investors earn by exposing themselves to the so-called **systematic risk**. Systematic risk is the risk of a stock caused by its correlation to the overall market. The drivers behind this correlation are factors that impact virtually all stocks such as the uncertainty about the economy, interest rates, inflation, etc. As indicated in the formula above, $R_s$ is the product of $\beta$ (a measure of the (historical) volatility of the stock versus the overall market) and the excess return of the overall market (with $R_m$ the market return) over the risk-free rate of return $R_f$. According to modern portfolio theory, systematic risk cannot be eliminated.

3. e is the abnormal return that is earned by taking on **non-systematic risk**. Non-systematic risk is the company-specific risk caused by uncertainties with respect to the firm. This abnormal return is assumed to be random (with zero mean), and can be eliminated through diversification. Due to market efficiency, CAPM assumes that it is impossible to estimate the value of e for any particular firm.

CAPM has a number of interesting consequences.

1. First of all, according to CAPM the systematic risk of a stock is determined exclusively by the historical volatility of its stock price, i.e., its $\beta$. In fact, CAPM states that the higher a stock's volatility versus the market the riskier the stock is.

2. A second remarkable consequence is that investors are compensated for taking on higher systematic risk, provided that the stock market outperforms the risk-free rate of return. Indeed, the higher $\beta$, the higher $R_s$ when $R_m > R_f$.

3. Thirdly, the same applies to stock portfolios consisting of many stocks: the higher a portfolio's $\beta$ (= weighted average of the betas of all stocks in the portfolio), the higher its risk and the higher its return.

4. Finally, as said above, according to CAPM adepts it makes no sense to invest in individual stocks, as these exhibit non-systematic risk that is beyond the investor's control, and for which he/she is not compensated. The logical conclusion is therefore that investors should diversify their portfolios as much as possible in order to eliminate the abnormal return.

Intuitively, CAPM makes a lot of sense. Most people find it logical that investors have to take on more risk if they want to earn more and the idea that volatility is an important measure of risk is definitely correct for a number of reasons.

First of all, when a stock has gone up and down more heavily than the market it indicates that investors had problems determining the stock's intrinsic value in the past. Hence, given the market's problems in determining a stock's fair value, it is not far-fetched to consider stocks with high price volatility as more unpredictable or riskier.

Second, for investors and traders who use a lot of leverage volatility is a primary concern because even small movements can wipe them out. Also short-term oriented investors who see short-term gains and losses as permanent should pay special attention to volatility. Heavy price swings are undoubtedly also relevant for investors who do not plan to invest for the long term, but who need to convert their investments in cash in the near to medium term (e.g., to purchase a house).

Volatility is also a good measure of risk for investors/traders who cannot deal with huge losses (i.e., people who bail out after huge losses, making the loss permanent) or with huge gains (e.g., people who become so enthusiastic that they buy more stocks at market tops and sustain major losses afterwards). And finally, volatility is an important issue for professional money managers who may see major redemptions in the funds they manage when volatility is too high. Nevertheless, as I describe in the next section, I believe CAPM oversimplifies reality.

## J.I.2 Criticism of CAPM

As the saying goes, "when something looks too good to be true it probably is." The fact that CAPM purports to describe the very complex process of asset management in a very simple mathematical formula that makes life easier on academics looks suspicious. One weakness of the model is that its validity is critically dependent on the assumption that markets are always efficient. This is a hypothesis with which I definitely take issue (see also Chapter A). A second weakness is that the model uses a value for historical volatility ($\beta$) which may not give a reliable indication for future volatility.

The main problem for CAPM, though, is that the validity of the model can easily be verified due to its simplicity. Unfortunately for CAPM adepts, studies have shown no relationship between $\beta$ and return. What is more, there are even no indications that high-$\beta$ stocks outperform low-$\beta$ stocks over the long term.

Also the fact that price volatility would be the one and only measure of risk is preposterous. We have already seen that volatility is a major risk for certain investors and traders, but it is definitely not that relevant for non-leveraged market operators who have a long-term investment horizon, who apply sound risk management policies, and who are able to maintain their discipline when the going gets tough.

In reality, risk should be defined as the probability of a *permanent* loss of capital. From this perspective, volatility is just one aspect of risk. It can be important for some people, but less so for others. As we will see in the next section, the way top investors see risk is also totally different from the perception of risk preached by CAPM believers.

---

*"Graham & Dodd investors, needless to say, do not discuss beta, the capital asset pricing model, or covariance in returns among securities. These are not subjects of any interest to them. In fact, most of them would have difficulty defining those terms. The investors simply focus on two variables: price and value."*

**Warren Buffett, The Super investors of Graham-and-Doddsville (Graham, 2003)**

---

# J.II Risk management in the investment philosophy

## J.II.1 How investors see risk

It should not come as a surprise that the investment philosophy is incompatible with CAPM – and with any mathematical risk model for that matter.[221] Nothing in CAPM comes close to the intrinsic value concept as the model makes no allowance for business fundamentals and new company developments. What is more, for smart investors volatility is not risk but opportunity. Indeed, true investors buy stocks that trade below their intrinsic value and sell when they trade above that value.

Now, volatility gives investors the opportunity to buy and sell businesses at irrational prices (both cheap and expensive). As noticed by Warren Buffett, provided that the intrinsic value of a business remains the same, it would be silly for an investor to assume that a stock that has lost half of its value would be riskier at the much lower price (because of the higher volatility due to the previous price drop) than at twice that price (before the price drop).

> *"Basically, price fluctuations have only one significant meaning for the true investor. They provide him with an opportunity to buy wisely when prices fall sharply and to sell wisely when they advance a great deal. At other times, he will do better if he forgets about the stock market and pays attention to his dividend returns and to the operating results of his companies."*
>
> **Benjamin Graham (Graham, 2003)**

In fact, within the investment philosophy risk (defined as the probability of permanent loss) does not come from volatility, but from an incorrect assessment of the gap between price and intrinsic value. More specifically, investors have to cope with two types of risk:

1. **Risk of misjudging the true value** of a business: investors stand to overpay for the stock of a business when their appraisal of management and/or the business characteristics is deficient, or when they have a poor understanding of the company's financials. According to top investors, this risk can be mitigated through:

   - *Thorough due diligence*: by acquiring deep knowledge one can limit the risk of overestimating a company's value. Also, investors who know more about a company are less likely to make ill-considered sales by which they lock in a loss due to a lack of conviction in the position.

   - *A focus on one's circle of competence*: investors who focus on companies within a field of expertise about which they have superior knowledge (versus other investors) compete in the market with an edge.

---

[221] Top investors don't believe that risk can reliably be captured in sophisticated risk models. Due to the fact that the markets are dominated by human behaviour, they are convinced that risk should be assessed in real-time by people (and not by computers).

- *A margin of safety*: as explained in Chapter D one can reduce valuation errors by only buying companies that trade at a significant discount to their estimated intrinsic value.

2. **Risk from unexpected outside factors**, such as government interference, poor stock market action (at a moment that the investor wants to sell), economic downturns, inflation, terrorism, etc. As explained in the Chapters B and C top investors try to protect themselves against this type of risk by being tough on certain types of businesses, such as companies dependent on weather conditions, companies that are too dependent on a single customer, companies without pricing power, etc.

---

*"Risk comes from not knowing what you're doing."*

**Warren Buffett (Tier, 2005)**

---

Not unlike other market participants, investors try to maximise returns while keeping external and misvaluation risk in check. Their primary concern is to avoid disasters. The problem of disastrous trades is that they are very hard to make up for,[222] and that they can wreak havoc on stock portfolios, sometimes even permanently. As explained hereunder, to deal with the risk-return trade-off and to avoid outright disasters, top investors usually pursue portfolio management techniques that appear unconventional, but that fit perfectly into their view on risk.

---

*"The first rule in investing is to never lose money. The second rule is to never forget rule number one."*

**Warren Buffett (Clark, 2006)**

---

## J.II.2 Risk management techniques of top investors

### J.II.2.a Discipline

As capital preservation is the first priority of top investors, they see discipline as critical to investment success. Intelligent investors don't chase profits. They avoid hot stocks or industries that are popular. They insist on a serious margin of safety in every trade. They are selective and only buy when they have a true conviction. They don't get carried away by the market waves of the moment. They don't set up trades that could wipe them out if

---

[222] For instance, a 50% loss requires a 100% gain, and a 90% loss requires a 1000% gain just to break even.

there is even a remote chance that something can go wrong. And they don't switch strategy due to temporary underperformance or due to external or internal pressure. Their goal is consistent performance that beats the market over the long term.

## J.II.2.b Portfolio concentration

Top investors reject the popular idea that a high level of diversification is necessary to limit risk. Their tenet is that "Diversification leads to mediocrity, whereas concentration leads to excellence." Many master investors take large positions in a very restricted number of stocks. Philip Fisher had most of the time three or four companies that accounted for about 75% of his portfolio. Joel Greenblatt usually put about 80% of his funds in no more than eight stocks. Eddie Lampert holds about eight major positions at a time. And Glenn Greenberg has a rule that he will not buy a stock if he is not willing to put at least 5% of his assets in it.

Even a very cautious and conservative star performer like Warren Buffett champions the idea of strong concentration. He states that for relatively small portfolios (< $200 million), he would put about 80% of his portfolio in five stocks. He is also not afraid to bet big on ideas about which he is extremely confident. In portfolios that he manages on behalf of others he would consider a single position of up to 40% of the portfolio, but (obviously) only on very rare occasions.[223] In his private portfolio he is even willing to go up to 75% in one single stock. In 2009, he even said that if he would have been allowed by the regulators going "all in" on Wells Fargo would have made a lot of sense to him.

The rationale behind portfolio concentration is straightforward. First of all, truly exceptional opportunities are rare. By focusing on one's best ideas, one can take full advantage of these ideas and avoid dilution by second tier ideas. Secondly, as investors can only know a limited number of stocks in-depth, concentration leads to knowledge, whereas diversification leads to ignorance. From this perspective, intelligent portfolio concentration is less risky than diversification. Warren Buffett sees diversification as a protection against ignorance and Marty Whitman believes it is a poor surrogate for knowledge. Diversification makes no sense for an investor who knows what he's doing, as it dilutes overall returns, knowledge about the portfolio, and the comfort level with the investment merits of every stock in portfolio.

> *"While one can know all there is to know about a few issues, one cannot possibly know all one needs to know about a great many issues."*
>
> **Bernard Baruch (Tier, 2005)**

Nevertheless, one must understand what smart portfolio concentration really means. Great investors don't bet the farm on any single idea. They realise that on average, they are right on a stock no more than about 60% of the time. So they better have extremely

---

[223] He believes that clients should be warned in advance. For instance, in 1964 he put 40% of his portfolio in American Express but before doing so he gave investors in his partnership the opportunity to pull out their money if they wanted to.

good insight and a strong conviction that the odds are overwhelmingly in their favour when they bet big (i.e., when they invest more than 20% of their portfolio in a single stock). They know that some amount of diversification (in number of stocks and in sectors and industries) is needed to prevent disaster.[224]

It is common for focused stock pickers to spread some percentage of their portfolio (e.g., 20% to 40%) over a large number of stocks where each position represents a small part of the portfolio. Peter Lynch, for instance, sometimes had more than 1000 stocks in his portfolio (which offered him *skin in the game* in certain riskier stocks), although he had large positions in his best ideas. Also, a higher level of diversification is recommended when managing money of clients, because concentration typically leads to higher volatility (which clients hate). For instance, John Templeton did not concentrate his portfolio too much when he managed money for others but in his private account he frequently focused on a few of his best ideas.

Finally, portfolio concentration obviously only makes sense for true stock pickers. It does not make sense, for instance, for quantitatively driven investors (i.e., investors who base investments purely on data of the financial statements) as these investors usually focus on groups of stocks with certain quantitative characteristics (e.g., stocks with low price-to-book value).

## J.II.2.c Position sizing based on stock type

Although the risk that the value of a business is estimated incorrectly can drastically be reduced through knowledge and an unrelenting drive to stay informed about the evolution of the business, it can never be eliminated entirely. The weight of a stock in a portfolio should obviously be determined by the conviction of the investor in the investment thesis. But logic also says that investors must take smaller positions in businesses that are harder to evaluate, that are less stable, that still have to prove a lot, or that are exposed to more outside risk. In other words, companies with high visibility deserve a higher weight in a portfolio than those with poor visibility. Hence, given the same amount of information and knowledge, intelligent investors size stock positions based on factors such as:

1.  **Stock category** (see also Chapter F):
    *   *Emerging businesses* are very risky, and should be avoided by most people. If one decides to buy this type of stock anyway, the position should never be more than a small percentage of one's portfolio. According to Philip Fisher, it is unwise to put more than about 5% of one's funds into small companies with staggering potential but corresponding risk.
    *   It can be very rewarding to invest in companies that face a very hard problem or that are very dependent on the business cycle but it usually entails a high degree of risk. Due to this risk, it is recommended to keep positions in *turnarounds or cyclicals* small.

---

[224] One can make an exception in industry diversification when one has a deep level of expertise in a particular industry. For instance, Shelby Davis invested mainly in insurance companies as he was extremely familiar with the insurance industry.

- Although *fast growers* offer a much better risk-reward trade-off than emerging companies, turnarounds or cyclicals, they remain riskier than more established firms. In the experience of Peter Lynch, only one out of five fast growers works out excellently. This means that for each phenomenally strong growth stock he had to accept a poor to mediocre return of four others. This illustrates that diversification is also indispensable in this universe. Small fast growers with relatively short track records should never be more than a few per cents of one's portfolio (at purchase). Higher weights are acceptable for bigger fast growers that have already proven something. For instance, Philip Fisher recommends putting a cap of about 8% to 10% on the weight of fast growing stocks of moderate size that have excellent track records.

- *Stalwarts and slow growers of high quality* are typically among the safest stocks around. According to Philip Fisher, one can afford to invest up to 20% of one's portfolio in properly selected large and stable stalwarts or slow growers. He believes that one can leave positions in such companies undisturbed as long as they keep on delivering – even if the position grows (on its own steam) to about 40% of the portfolio.

2. **Company size**: in general, although small companies have more room for growth than large ones, they are riskier. Small companies still have to scale their business model and they can suffer from severe growing pains. They are usually more sensitive to changing business conditions. They rely on a smaller pool of human talent. Management is often not that experienced. Structures (business units, management hierarchies, etc.) are not well established. And they have seldom built a lot of goodwill with other parties (e.g., financiers, etc.). Hence, as a rule positions in small companies should be smaller than in large companies.

   The corollary is that investors who invest mainly in small caps are likely to end up with a high number of stocks. But since the analysis of small caps is usually much more straightforward than that of large companies (thanks to the lower number of business units), keeping track of a small cap portfolio with a high number of positions (say, 100) should not be more labour-intensive than keeping track of a large cap portfolio with a much lower number of positions (say, 20).

3. **Financial position**: many top investors admit that the biggest mistake in their careers was to invest in highly leveraged businesses. The problem of companies with poor balance sheets is that they have little control over their own destiny. Due to their high debt burden, they are very sensitive to, and can easily be brought down by, recessions, poor strategic moves, changes in interest rates, credit scarcity, etc. Investors are forewarned: one must tread with extreme caution with highly indebted businesses. Such businesses should never be more than a small position of one's portfolio.

4. **Intrinsic business diversity**: the risk of companies with a high degree of diversification is definitely lower than in single-business companies. Provided that

the various business activities are not too well correlated, downturns in one area of operation may be compensated by the other business activities. Hence, it is acceptable to take larger positions in excellently run conglomerates (e.g., General Electric) or investment holding companies (e.g., Berkshire Hathaway) than in single-line businesses.

## J.II.2.d The use of decoupled sub-portfolios

Nobody disputes that portfolios should be balanced between different industries and stock types. Concentration in a particular industry or in a particular type of stock leads to higher volatility as all stocks in the portfolio are closely correlated to each other. What is more, it is risky because a large part of the portfolio will be impacted by a very limited number of factors that the investor may assess incorrectly.

For instance, a portfolio where bank stocks account for about 80% of the portfolio exposes the investor to a high level of risk as events that have an important impact on the banking sector (e.g., a credit crisis like the one in 2008-2009) can cause a permanent and devastating loss of capital. Likewise, a portfolio that is focused heavily on cyclicals is extremely dependent on the correct assessment of the economic cycle. All told, strong sector focus or strong focus on a particular type of stock is dangerous. Therefore, Benjamin Graham and Philip Carret urge investors to focus the bulk of their portfolio on no less than about five different industries.

To reduce volatility and to have the flexibility to take advantage of the opportunities of the moment, many of the greatest investors (especially hedge fund managers) take the diversification principle to a higher level. They trade in a number of securities that have limited correlation with one another. We have already seen in Chapter F that special situation stocks, turnarounds and distressed debt can offer excellent diversification as they are event-driven and therefore less correlated with the overall market. Arbitrage positions also produce stable returns that are not that much impacted by overall market movements. Real Estate Investment Trusts (REITs) tend to track real estate prices and are therefore yet another type of stock that can offer returns that are to some extent independent of the stock market.[225]

Investors who manage large portfolios can even look for stability in still another type of investment. In the investment partnership that Warren Buffett managed during the 1950s and 1960s, his portfolio was divided between public stocks, arbitrage positions and so-called *control situations*. In the latter type of investment, Buffett tried to gain control of companies with the aim of influencing company policies. Provided that one can force significant changes upon the firm, control situations can provide excellent returns in bear markets.

There are some caveats to the pursuit of decoupled portfolios, though. First of all, one must realise that two types of very different securities can be highly correlated. For instance, even though private equity investments are very different from publicly traded stocks, they

---

[225] REITs are portfolios of houses, apartments, commercial property or shopping malls that are managed by real estate operators.

are positively correlated with the stock market. Indeed, the price at which ventures can be bought and brought to the market depends on the prevailing market conditions.

Secondly, it is a mistake to examine correlations over short periods of time (ranging from a few months to a few years). A serious correlation study should examine relationships over very long periods of time – preferably over several decades. To exclude the factor of coincidence, one should always look for a logical explanation behind this relationship. Thirdly, even if there is a clear historical correlation between certain securities, one must realise that correlations are not stable. They may actually change drastically during crises precisely at the moment that their correlation (or lack thereof) is of the greatest concern.

One reason for this is that when panic strikes and people need money they will sell everything that is sufficiently liquid irrespective of price and investment merits. For instance, arbitrage positions can fall in sympathy with the stock market during a market crash. Distressed debt may also get hit during a severe market crash if the crash is related to an economic malaise, because the worsening economic conditions can depress deeply distressed debt even more.

Ray Dalio also points out that in an environment where the economy slows down stocks and bonds can be expected to be negatively correlated, as stock prices and interest rates usually decline.[226] When inflation is high, by contrast, stocks and bonds tend to be positively correlated as interest rates will go up and stocks often go down. Another example of positive correlation is quantitative easing during balance sheet recessions (as done by Central Banks in recent years), which seems to benefit both bonds and stocks.

## J.II.2.e Strategic use of cash balances

> "The wise ones bet heavily when the world offers them that opportunity. They bet big when they have the odds. And the rest of the time, they don't. It's just that simple."
>
> **Charlie Munger (Munger, 1994)**

> "Never invest all of your funds. By maintaining a large cash reserve, I have also been in a position to take advantage of unforeseen opportunities as they developed."
>
> **Bernard Baruch (Baruch, 1957)**

---

[226] Schwager, 2012.

When disaster strikes, people say that cash is king. During market crises people that hold a lot of cash can limit their drawdown. Cash also enables people to buy beaten down stocks on the cheap in the midst of market turmoil. In other words, cash is most valuable when the stock market is in a tailspin and nobody else has it.

The big problem of cash is that it is expensive. Cash is a drag on returns in bull markets and can therefore cause serious underperformance versus the market. That's also the reason why most investors don't see cash as a strategic asset class and why they don't manage their cash balance actively. The top investors, on the other hand, do give cash the respect it deserves. They hold cash in the safest cash accounts and in the safest and most liquid bonds around.[227] They deliberately manage the amount of cash in their portfolio under all market conditions:

1.  They **only invest when they see opportunities**. In the absence of opportunities, they prefer to keep (part of) their funds in cash. This also implies that they usually grow their cash balances as a bull market gets overstretched.

2.  Some top investors **constantly hold significant amounts of cash** at all times in order to reduce volatility, and to have dry powder when something bad happens in the market. Benjamin Graham recommended keeping at least 25% to 50% of one's assets in cash, depending on the market level.

3.  They have the courage to **move a significant part of their portfolio into cash** when they don't trust the markets. They stick to their guns even if the cash drags their performance down for several years in a row.

## J.II.2.f Intelligent foreign investments

Many investors avoid foreign stocks because they assume that such stocks are riskier than stocks of their home country. It is true that investing in foreign stocks, even those of foreign developed countries, is more involved than investing in domestic stocks. It requires familiarity with and keeping track of changes in foreign accounting practices, customs (e.g., in terms of corporate governance), regulations and laws. It requires an assessment of the foreign company's operating environment. It requires an understanding of other cultural elements (e.g., shareholder orientation is often not a priority in Japanese companies). And so on.

The higher level of required due diligence and follow-up is the main reason why some of the greatest investors (e.g., Warren Buffett) prefer to stay close to home. Nevertheless, there are a number of top investors who have proven that investing in foreign stocks can be very profitable if it is done in the right way. Legendary investors – John Templeton and Mark Lightbown, for instance – achieved impressive returns by exploiting market folly all around the world. Intelligent investors in foreign stocks heed the following cautions:

---

[227] According to Seth Klarman, for cash one should never accept principal risk (risk that the value of cash falls in nominal terms) or liquidity risk (risk that the cash is not readily available). Cash should be stored in bank accounts of the safest banks in the world. Or it should be invested in highly liquid bonds of the highest grade which automatically have the lowest yields in the market. Fixed income investments that offer a decent yield are probably not the ones you want to have during periods of market stress.

1. One should only invest in stocks about which one can **acquire the necessary reliable knowledge**. With foreign stocks, this implies getting acquainted with other accounting rules, overcoming language barriers, finding ways to obtain access to relevant and reliable information sources, etc.

2. In **emerging countries**, one must be aware that **risks are higher** than in developed countries. Expropriations, government interference, shareholder unfriendly behaviour, fraud, and the like, are all much more common in developing countries than in developed countries. Refer to Chapter B for more on this subject.

3. For foreign stocks denominated in a foreign currency, one has to accept **currency risk**. Nevertheless, this risk must be seen in the right perspective:

   - Long-term investors who intend to keep their money invested in stocks in the foreign currency for ten years or more don't have to be concerned that much about currency risk. There is strong evidence that currency movements are cancelled out by the movements of foreign stocks.[228] This can be explained by the fact that over the long run relative currency movements are compensated by movements in the relative inflation between the countries. Since stock returns include inflation over the long run, stock returns compensate for currency movements.

   - Investors with a short time horizon are advised to protect themselves against unfavourable currency movements. They can hedge themselves against unfavourable currency movements through hedging strategies or by focusing on companies with significant business in countries where exports are much higher than imports (which tends to support the foreign currencies).[229]

## J.II.2.g The use of hedges

Some top investors use hedges to protect themselves against market turbulence. Similar to cash, hedges are expensive during bull markets because they reduce returns. However, they pay off handsomely when the tide turns. Since market timing is extremely hard, intelligent investors know that they should only use hedges if they have the courage to stay the course and if they can accept prolonged periods of below-average market performance. For instance, Seth Klarman lagged the stock market several years on end in the 1990s due to his market hedges but in the early 2000s these hedges more than paid back their previous cost.

## J.II.2.h Position size depending on transaction type

It is obvious that in smart risk management one should restrict the weight of the riskiest positions in a stock portfolio. This implies that on average leveraged positions should be

---

[228] (Siegel, 2005), (Fisher, 2007) and (Browne, 2007).
[229] Templeton, 2008.

smaller than non-leveraged positions. Similarly, the average short sale should remain smaller than the average long position. For instance, David Einhorn sizes his shorts half as large as his longs.

### J.II.2.i Playing defence in valuation

As explained in Chapter D, top investors protect themselves against negative surprises by insisting on a bargain price. Many are conservative in the sense that they first look at the balance sheet (and steer clear of businesses with poor balance sheets) before they size up future earnings and returns. And they always try to buy a stock at a steep discount to its intrinsic value. Even the practice of selling right before a stock reaches full value is defensive as it ensures that the shares of the investor are never overvalued.

## J.III Common errors in risk management

Time and again investors commit the same recurring errors against appropriate risk management. Loss of discipline in bull and bear markets (e.g., chasing profits around a market top and capitulation around a market bottom), putting all one's eggs in one basket (e.g., investing almost exclusively in the stock of the company at which one is employed), inappropriate position sizes for certain types of stocks and stock transactions, and investing without knowledge are just a few of the obvious – and far too common – errors. Hereunder I discuss some less obvious errors that can do just as much harm.

### J.III.1 Error 1: Distorted perception of risk due to changing risk tolerance

It is generally known that one's tolerance for risk is a function of one's personality, one's financial position, one's objectives, one's gender (women are less risk tolerant than men), one's age (risk tolerance declines as people grow older), and so on. What is less known is that risk tolerance is not static – it is determined by one's perception of risk. This perception is unconsciously influenced by a number of factors:

1. First of all, **past experiences** have an important impact on a person's perception of risk – especially when those experiences are fresh in mind and/or when they made a big impression. For instance, people tend to see investing as less risky when they have made a decent profit of late. Or they exaggerate the risk of stocks after a market crash.

2. Second, the **potential reward** influences how risk is perceived. People are willing to take a risk when the potential reward is high, irrespective of the probability of that reward. This explains why people take part in lotteries in spite of the infinitesimal chance of hitting the jackpot.

3. A third factor is the **pressure to make money**. People who desperately need money are usually willing to take more risk than those who are under less strain.

4.  Finally, the perception of risk is also influenced by **cognitive biases** such as herding behaviour (what other people do feels comfortable and therefore seems less risky), asymmetric loss aversion (after a significant loss people get scared and they become more risk averse), overconfidence (overconfidence and the illusion of being in control tempts people to take more risk than they can bear), and the familiarity and/or sympathy bias (stocks that seem familiar or to which one is positively disposed foster confidence, such that people let their guard down).

The constant flux in the perception of risk gets many people in trouble as it constantly swings their emotions between three states: concern (moderate risk tolerance), complacency (high risk tolerance), and capitulation (very low risk tolerance). People who do not critically question their changing perception of risk are bound to make a number of mistakes, such as:

1.  **Fleeing the market when things go bad or joining a market that is doing well**: when things go bad, investors who used to be aggressive suddenly turn cautious due to the recent experience and because of their asymmetric loss aversion. Conversely, when the market is doing extremely well, all kinds of conservative people who should know better join the party. This can be explained by herding behaviour (many other people buy too), extrapolation of the recent positive experience, and the flawed perception that investing is easy. Going with the stream is of course completely at odds with sound risk management as it implies that people buy high and sell low.

2.  **Taking more risk after a successful streak**: people who made a lot of money in their recent market operations may lose sight of the risks as they extrapolate their past experience, and/or because their confidence catches fire.

3.  **Taking more risk after a series of losses**: people who suffered significant losses may be willing to take more risks as pressure builds to get back to even.

4.  **Investing in speculative stocks**: lured by the prospect of huge potential gains or due to overconfidence, many investors forget that investing in speculative stocks is very risky.

5.  **Inadequate diversification**: due to the familiarity or sympathy bias people may concentrate their portfolios too much in large familiar companies, the firm they work at, or companies in a particular region. If overconcentration goes together with poor knowledge, the investor may unknowingly run a huge risk.

6.  **Little attention to price**: believing that high returns of familiar stocks are a sure thing, people frequently overpay for blue chips or other familiar names.

## J.III.2 Error 2: Not knowing one's risk profile

Each person has their own tolerance for risk – each investor can be located somewhere on the continuum between *defensive* and *entrepreneurial*. Defensive investors eschew risk and are satisfied with low returns, as long as they preserve their capital. Entrepreneurial investors, by contrast, chase high returns and take higher risk in their stride. The problem is that, due to the variability of a person's risk perception (see above), only few people realise what type of investor they really are. Their fluctuating tolerance for risk (caused by cognitive biases, past experiences, etc.) masks their true risk appetite (the equilibrium around which their risk tolerance fluctuates), which leads to inappropriate risk management.

To avoid investment strategies that are incompatible with themselves, smart investors try to determine their true risk profile before they tread in the stock market. Understanding one's risk profile is pivotal in the decision about diversification, the types of stocks one invests in, and so on. It is important to realise that stock investing is not for everyone, since it inevitably involves risk. People who absolutely cannot stomach temporary losses should avoid stocks altogether. Another practical rule that is championed by top investors (e.g., Bernard Baruch) to determine the acceptable percentage of stocks in someone's portfolio is to *sell to the sleeping point,* i.e., sell to the point where one no longer has sleepless nights due to one's stock positions.

## J.III.3 Error 3: Underestimation of price shocks and black swans

Lack of knowledge about financial market history is prevalent in the investment industry. A couple of decades after the end of protracted bear markets, severe market crises or spectacular price shocks, very few people in the investment industry have lived through such dramatic events and many of the new professionals can't imagine what they mean for investors.

A direct consequence is that some years after serious market crises most people (including professionals) underestimate the frequency and magnitude of price shocks (e.g., severe stock crashes) or rare events (e.g., a worldwide crisis).[230] They also don't realise that correlations between asset classes may suddenly become very high on such occasions. As a result, almost no one anticipates such events, let alone prepares for them.

## J.III.4 Error 4: Too much leverage

Leverage refers to the use of debt (e.g., margin accounts), derivatives, or other financial instruments that magnify price changes by the time they hit the bottom line. Leverage can work wonders when it works in one's favour, which is also the reason why it can be addictive. Few people can abandon leverage once they have enjoyed the miracles it can work.

The problem of leverage is that it works two ways. It magnifies both success and failure. Too many investors are attracted to leverage because of the former, with few acknowledging the latter. Leverage can wipe investors out when they are on the wrong

---

[230] Hedge fund manager Nassim Nicholas Taleb is a promoter of the idea that one can reap huge rewards through the purchase of securities and instruments that insure against very rare events. These instruments are virtually always significantly undervalued due to the fact that most people do not believe that rare events like a default of an emerging country (e.g., Russia in 1998), or a full-blown credit crisis (e.g., the financial turmoil in 2008) can happen (Taleb, 2007).

side of the market during price shocks. Leveraged positions should also never be left unattended as they can grow (sometimes rapidly) out of proportion. Another danger of leverage is that it can turn against the investor even if he or she is right. Whereas non-leveraged investors can afford to wait until they are proven right, leveraged investors typically do not have that luxury when the market temporarily moves against them.

Due to its inherent dangers, top investors use leverage sparingly. If they do use it, they make sure that their leveraged positions remain sufficiently small, through the use of stop-losses or by unwinding leverage quickly when markets behave in a strange way. They warn that most investors would be better off without leverage. Warren Buffett refers to derivatives as "arms of mass destruction" and he recommends people avoid leverage. As an example, Buffett refers to the story of Rick Guerin who managed Berkshire together with him and Charlie Munger in the 1970s. Rick was in a hurry to get rich and therefore leveraged himself. In the 1973-1974 stock market downturn he got margin calls and he was forced to sell his Berkshire shares to Buffett.

---

*"If your actions are sensible, you are certain to get good results; in most cases, leverage just moves things along faster."*

**Warren Buffett, 1989 letter to the shareholders of Berkshire Hathaway**

---

## J.III.5 Error 5: Cash of low quality

As explained in J.II, cash accounts deserve a place in stock portfolios as a protection against market malaise and to have firepower ready when the market throws bargains around. It is a mistake, though, to reach for yield in one's cash account.

Some investors store their cash in illiquid or subordinated bonds. Others put their cash in bank accounts of less creditworthy financial institutions that offer higher interest rates. And some even buy cash-like exotic instruments that they don't fully understand.[231] This is a mistake. When a catastrophe strikes, liquidity in all but the safest bonds tends to dry up, subordinated bonds may collapse, and financial institutions of questionable creditworthiness can go under (along with the customer's deposits).

It bears repeating that cash which is meant to be a protection against catastrophes must be stored in the safest bonds, money-market instruments or bank accounts. Safety should not be measured only on the basis of credit ratings (e.g., ratings were totally wrong with CDOs), but on common sense. Anything different from very low yielding plain and simple instruments or bank accounts should raise suspicion.

---

[231] A nice example was the Collateralised Debt Obligations (CDOs) which were popular in the years leading up to the financial crisis of 2008-2009. CDOs were marketed as cash instruments (usually with the highest possible credit ratings) that had a somewhat higher yield than classical money market securities. During the crisis of 2008-2009 they went down significantly due to the collapse of the housing market in the US.

## J.IV Summary

Figure 27 summarises the main points of this chapter. First, according to the popular academic theory CAPM, risk can be reduced to one single factor: volatility. In addition, CAPM states that investors who pick individual stocks take a risk for which they are not compensated.

Top investors totally disagree. They don't see volatility as risk but rather as an opportunity to buy and sell at attractive prices. They also reject the idea that a high amount of diversification is required to limit risk. They rather believe that diversification is a protection against ignorance.

In their opinion, to keep risk in check it is crucial to have knowledge and to remain disciplined. With knowledge and discipline, concentration on the best ideas makes more sense than diversification. They also point out that position sizing and a sound approach to foreign investments are important to keep risk under control. Moreover, many use hedges, cash accounts and decoupled sub-portfolios to reduce volatility and to avoid deep drawdowns during market turbulence.

Finally, a number of warnings are in order. Intelligent investors manage their portfolios based on their true tolerance for risk, and they protect themselves against (temporary) distortions of their risk perception. They keep in mind that price shocks, protracted bear markets and crashes are much more common than most people realise. They use debt sparingly and store their cash in the safest places that exist. They also acknowledge that volatility is just one of many measures of risk. They admit that volatility and diversification become more important the less an investor knows about his holdings.

**Figure 27: Different perspectives on risk management**

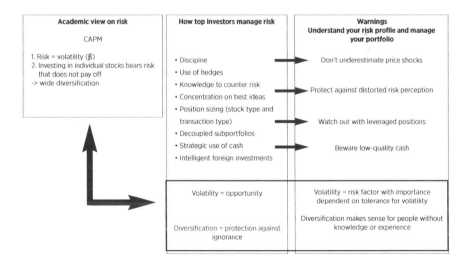

# PART IV
## THE INTELLIGENT INVESTOR

# CHAPTER K

## THE INTELLIGENT INVESTOR

"There is a persistent overall tendency for equity to flow from the many to the few. In the long run, the majority loses. The implication for the trader is that to win you have to act like the minority. If you bring normal human habits and tendencies to trading, you'll gravitate toward the majority and inevitably lose."

WILLIAM ECKHARDT (SCHWAGER, 1992)

THROUGHOUT THIS BOOK it has been stressed on several occasions that investors face a number of huge challenges. Beating the market is hard because pricing in the stock markets tends to be quite efficient. To succeed one definitely needs an edge. In the previous chapters I have identified a number of soft skills that, according to top investors, are indispensable parts of a strong edge.

It is fair to see these elements as factors that together define *investor intelligence*. In other words, only people who score excellently on these behavioural and processional requirements can be considered intelligent investors. And only intelligent investors stand a reasonable chance of beating the market.

The factors that are strongly endorsed by virtually all top investors (and even by all top traders[232]) can be divided into three pillars (see Figure 28).

First, investors need a unique and discretionary investment strategy that is applied in a consistent way and with strong discipline. The strategy should consist of an effective philosophy that identifies market inefficiencies and a (preferably proprietary and flexible) method through which one can take advantage of these inefficiencies. Furthermore, the strategy will usually have a much stronger edge when the investor stays within his/her circle of competence.

Second, when they apply their strategy intelligent investors pursue a process characterised by independence, hard work, eternal study, discretion and knowledge.

---

[232] Note that top traders and top investors identify the same set of soft skills that are critical for success in the stock market. For the reader's reference, excellent books written by or about top traders are (Boik, 2004), (Boik, 2006), (Schwager, 2006), (Schwager, 1992), (Covel, 2007), (Darvas, 2007), (Faith, 2007), (Lefevere, 2006), (Livermore, 2001), (Loeb, 2007), (O'Neil, 2002), (Ross, 2000), (Sperandeo, 1997), and (Morales, 2010).

Third, on the highest level the entire process of intelligent investors is supported by a set of indispensable attitudes, namely modesty, passion for the job, patience, emotional detachment and the courage to go against the crowd.

The aim of this chapter is to provide a clear synthesis of the three pillars of investor intelligence and their components. At the end of the chapter, I examine the role of experience, talent and classical intelligence, and provide a summary.

**Figure 28: The intelligent investor: strategy, process requirements and attitude**

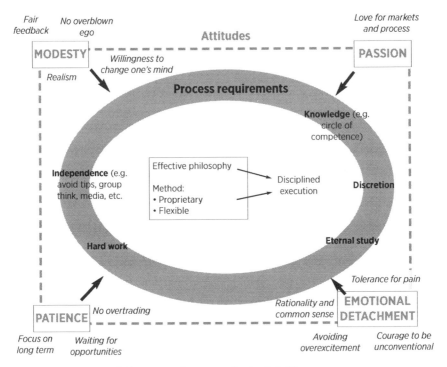

Other: experience + talent + intelligence

# K.I Effective investment strategy

Given the strong competition in the stock market and the power of cognitive biases, investors need a strategy. An investment strategy can be described as an approach to the market consisting of two elements:

1. a market philosophy, and

2. an execution method.

Without a clearly articulated investment strategy the investor competes without an edge over other market players, he is bound to take shortcuts, he is very sensitive to rumours and tips of any kind, and he is very likely to succumb to the insidious temptations of his inner voice (see also Chapter A). In the following sections I explain how a strategy is effective in helping an investor avoid these things and how intelligent investors select an appropriate strategy.

## K.I.1 Market philosophy

The first indispensable element of a strategy is a philosophy that describes the drivers behind the stock market and explains how these drivers create pricing inefficiencies. In other words, a philosophy guides market players to stocks that are temporarily mispriced. Needless to say, effective market philosophies make perfect sense (i.e., the theory about the drivers is sound), and are time-tested (e.g., there are many successful practitioners). Various philosophies have proven their merit in the stock market, with investing and trading the most prominent ones. For a thorough discussion of the investing philosophy refer to Chapter A.

> *"Choosing individual stocks without any idea of what you're looking for is like running through a dynamite factory with a burning match. You may live, but you're still an idiot."*
>
> **Joel Greenblatt (Greenblatt, 2006)**

## K.I.2 Execution method

A market philosophy is only one part of the equation. A strategy also requires an execution method that enables the investor to spot opportunities, and to time purchases and sales correctly. It is striking that the execution methods of different top investors with identical philosophies can be quite different.

The reason is that, as pointed out by these top investors, the execution method has to be **compatible with one's personality and experience**. In other words, successful investors have a discretionary method with which they feel comfortable. This is important because in the absence of a high level of comfort, the investor is bound to override his/her system in times of emotional stress. There are various dimensions to an execution method, such as:

1. The **type of stock**: different investors prefer different types of stocks. I have already mentioned on several occasions that some investors focus on (low-multiple) value stocks, whereas others look for growth. Some investors focus on distressed debt. Others, like Carl Icahn, want to be activists. And some specialise in arbitrage.

2. **Long side versus short side**: some investors only feel comfortable when they buy attractive stocks. Others feel comfortable both at the long and at the short side. And still others (e.g., Jim Chanos) prefer short sales over longs. As said in previous

chapters, the profit pattern of long positions is the opposite of that of short sales. Shorts are not for everyone as they cause higher emotional stress and because they require another type of risk management.

3. **Leverage versus being unleveraged**: leverage (e.g., taking on debt or buying leveraged derivatives) can magnify success in the market. The downside is that it magnifies failure. Due to its inherent risks many top investors (e.g., Warren Buffett) shun leverage. Other investors have thrived thanks to their leverage. Either way, all stress that in order to survive with a leveraged portfolio strict and appropriate risk management is indispensable.

4. **Short term versus long term**: short-term investors try to keep the time between purchases and sales short. Long-term investors prefer sitting on positions for a long time (as long as the stock remains attractive). The vast majority of top investors argue that a long-term orientation makes the most sense, because extraordinary opportunities are scarce and because a short-term orientation eats into one's returns (through transaction costs and taxes). Warren Buffett, for instance, has been known to sit on positions for several years or decades. Nevertheless, there are some excellent investors (e.g., Peter Lynch) who built extraordinary track records even though they regularly switched part of their portfolio in and out of stocks – sometimes holding stocks for no more than a few months.

## K.I.3 Strategy and the intelligent investor

I don't know of any successful investor who approaches the market without strict adherence to an effective and well articulated investment strategy. This is self-evident because due to the cutthroat competition in the market people can only survive if they develop and adopt their own discretionary market strategy.

Unfortunately, there is no single strategy that holds the promise of success for everyone. Every investor has to look for a market-beating strategy that fits him or her well. In addition, it is indispensable for investors to have sufficient confidence in their strategy such that they can hang on to it when things do not work out as planned.

### K.I.3.a Choice of strategy

Finding an appropriate investment philosophy and method requires introspection. Investors must know themselves in order to understand what strategy matches their personality and interests. Intelligent investors therefore closely monitor their feelings and actions over several market cycles. They also study effective market strategies and they do some trial-and-error in a learning process. More precisely, according to the best investors in the world, good strategies are:

1. **Effective**: valuable strategies have many successful practitioners and they are based on philosophies that explain the workings of the markets in a logical way. A recurring theme among top investors is their belief that the simplest and most

focused strategies are the most effective. The reason is that investing in the future is highly uncertain. Therefore, too many variables or complicated financial models (such as when estimating a stock's intrinsic value) do more harm than good due to error propagation (i.e., one wrong parameter estimate can have a huge impact on the end result) and a loss of focus on what really matters.

2. **Broad, flexible and dynamic**: the strategy must be sufficiently dynamic and flexible to deal with a world where inefficiencies come and go. For instance, an approach based on specialisation in one particular sector (e.g., technology) is ineffective because it limits the playing field considerably and because it subjects the investor to the whims of the market in that particular sector.

3. **Compatible with the investor**: the strategy must be compatible with the investor's personality, skills, tastes and interests. This also implies that – although one can find inspiration with successful investors – the servile and thoughtless imitation of the strategy of a great investor is seldom a good idea (unless that strategy fits the investor like a glove). Here are two reasons why compatibility between strategy and investor are so important:

   - Compatibility leads to *stronger adherence to the strategy*. When a strategy does not fit an investor's personality, skills and tastes, he will be inclined to override his system each time he encounters a rough patch.

   - It leads to *higher motivation*. If the strategy does not fit the investor's interests, abilities and tastes, he will find it hard to motivate himself to put in the effort required to beat the market.

## K.I.3.b Discipline

Choosing an appropriate investment strategy is one thing. Of equal importance is the discipline to stick with it when things don't work out as anticipated. When the selected strategy is effective, flexible and compatible with the investor, discipline will be easier to achieve for three reasons. First, an effective strategy does not let the investor down too much. Second, when a strategy is sufficiently broad and dynamic it is easier to deal with a new environment without violating the fundamental tenets of the style. And third, a strategy that is compatible with the investor is less likely to be questioned by that investor.

Notwithstanding, even investors with a well-chosen strategy often feel compelled to change tack when the heat is on or when fashions change. Common examples are value investors who abandon their conservative approach during market booms and bubbles in favour of trading or speculation.[233] Other examples are investors who turn greedy and lever up after significant gains. Investors without discipline usually come to grief (or even blow up) when the market turns.

The very best investors stick to their guns when times are hard. They use an effective system that is flexible enough to deal with a changing world and with changing market

---

[233] See also (Chancellor, 2000), (Kindleberger, 2005), (MacKay, 2008) and (Reinhart, 2009).

conditions. Confidence in their system gives them the courage to go against the crowd, to question conventional wisdom and to look at situations from another perspective. However, experienced investors are human after all and sometimes they find it necessary to consciously revisit their investment strategy during difficult periods to maintain their discipline. For instance, Bernard Baruch reminded himself regularly of his strategy and of everything he needed to maintain his discipline – especially during the most challenging times in the market.

> "The unpredictability of Mr. Market's moods and the pressure of competing with other money managers can make it really hard to stick with a strategy that hasn't worked for years."
>
> **Joel Greenblatt (Greenblatt, 2006)**

## K.II Process requirements

### K.II.1 Knowledge

> "In no field is the old maxim more valid – that a little knowledge is a dangerous thing – than in investing."
>
> **Bernard Baruch (Baruch, 1957)**

Great investors tend to agree that thorough knowledge of one's strategy (philosophy + method) and about every position in one's portfolio is indispensable to be successful in the stock market. As an example, in the hedge fund managed by Tiger Cub Lee Ainslie every investment professional is responsible for no more than about three investment positions while research that precedes every new position typically takes a few months.[234] This kind of focus provides for a very high level of knowledge on every idea.

The importance of knowledge is easy to understand. First of all, knowledge provides a competitive advantage over less informed market players. Investors who do their homework thoroughly easily outmatch lazy investors who rely on the latest tip or analyst recommendation. Second, knowledge is a very powerful ally in difficult markets. Knowledge helps to maintain discipline, because it serves as a counterweight to gut feelings caused by cognitive biases. Finally, knowledge reduces the risk borne by the investor. Through deep knowledge intelligent investors are able to identify high-probability events and avoid positions that are not worth the risk. Top investors develop a knowledge advantage through a combination of:

---

[234] Weiss, 2012.

1.  **Hard work**: intelligent investors work hard to get intimately acquainted with their investments. They ask "Why?" very often. They painstakingly examine the two sides of each trade. And they resort to unconventional (and time-consuming) sources of information. In the same vein, they expect an equally strong commitment and dedication from their team members, characterised by little tolerance for lazy colleagues who take shortcuts.

2.  **Thorough understanding of the tools**: intelligent investors gain the understanding required to apply their investment strategy. For instance, intelligent investors build sufficient accounting and business knowledge which enables them to determine the fair value of companies.

3.  **Focus on their circle of competence**: a frequently encountered conviction among great investors is that to have superior knowledge one should restrict one's attention to one's circle of competence. They recommend investors to look for bargains in industries and companies within their area of expertise.[235] In this way the investor competes with an edge versus market participants who are not that familiar with the industry. For instance, Warren Buffett has said that he shies away from technology companies because he admits that he is unable to evaluate the technology industry properly.

4.  **Experience**: top investors become better as they gain experience. A great deal of experience can even lead to a level of unconscious competence (knowledge on a subconscious level), where the investor understands a situation quickly, where he develops some intuition (automatic recognition), and where spotting bargains becomes second nature. For instance, George Soros regularly gets a headache when his subconscious tries to tell him that he has made a mistake.

---

> *"A skilled operator in any field acquires an almost instinctive 'feel' which enables him to sense many things even without being able to explain them."*
>
> **Bernard Baruch (Baruch, 1957)**

---

> *"My point is that to be successful in this business, you don't have to be better than everybody everywhere, just better than everybody in the league in which you play."*
>
> **Julian Robertson (Heins, 2013)**

---

[235] Surprisingly, this concept is very poorly understood by most investors. For example, it is common among doctors to trade flashy technology stocks, while ignoring stocks in the healthcare sector.

## K.II.2 Independence

For many investors, due diligence does not go beyond the reading of broker research, tracking of analyst recommendations, listening to the sales pitch on the latest hot IPO, or chatting with insiders, neighbours or cocktail-party acquaintances. People also like to listen to the financial media and crave for the market prophets of the moment, because they have an exciting story to tell, or because they feel lost in the financial markets. They can hardly be blamed. Taking advice from people who seem to be knowledgeable is an obvious choice for all those who don't have the time and energy – let alone expertise – to analyse stocks. Besides, following the advice of others conveniently allows the market operator to put the blame on others if things don't work out as expected.

> *"I go cold when someone tips me on a company. I like to start with a clean slate: no one's word. No givens. I'd prefer not to know what the analysts think or to hear any inside information. It clouds one's judgment – I'd rather be dispassionate. All I really need is a company's published reports and records; that plus a sharp pencil, a pocket calculator, and patience."*
>
> **Peter Cundill (Risso-Gill, 2011)**

Unfortunately, as we have seen many times over in previous chapters, the best opportunities in the market are rarely found in places that many others have already identified as attractive. Making matters worse, reliance on others makes the market operator extremely vulnerable to all kinds of external stimuli that can throw him off course. Therefore, in the field of investing, reliance on the opinions, feelings and recommendations of others is likely to lead to grief. *In the stock market, there is no surrogate for independence.* More specifically, intelligent investors are iconoclasts who demonstrate their independence through:

1.  **Thorough proprietary knowledge** and **hard work**: relying on others is easy; independence, by contrast, demands effort, is time-consuming and cannot be achieved without the appropriate knowledge.

2.  **Avoidance of exposure to tips of any kind**: because they realise that it is hard for almost everyone (including themselves) to resist the temptation of compelling tips, many top investors try to avoid exposure to tips. For instance:

    *   Intelligent investors *don't ask for tips*. They may talk to other investors (especially to people they respect), but they always avoid getting overly influenced by their opinions.

    *   Several top investors *moved (physically) to places far away from the chatter* and noise that is so common close to the scene. For instance, John Templeton and Warren Buffett deliberately decided to headquarter far away from Wall Street.

    *   Many of the greatest investors *cut themselves off from sources of chatter*. Intelligent investors sort out the information sources that provide the most

relevant (and unbiased) information they need. They restrict their exposure to the media, chat platforms and the like because these are usually expensive distractions that may (subconsciously) bias their ideas and opinions. For instance, Seth Klarman, Warren Buffett and Mohnish Pabrai don't have a Bloomberg terminal on their desk because they don't believe that this can help them to generate investment ideas.

3. **Scepticism about what is generally accepted and known**: intelligent investors always question the conventional wisdoms and accepted facts of the day. They know that things that are generally known are already (over)discounted in the stock market. Therefore, they look for unique information that can make a difference.

## K.II.3 Hard work

> *"Curiosity is the engine of civilization. If I were to elaborate it would be to say read, read, read, and don't forget to talk to people, really talk, listening with attention and having conversations, on whatever topic, that are an exchange of thoughts."*
>
> **Peter Cundill (Risso-Gill, 2011)**

It is hard to grasp for most amateurs, but people with only a few spare hours a month earmarked to investing are no match for sophisticated professionals. The markets are so competitive that only people who devote a generous amount of their time to their investments stand a reasonable chance of beating the market.

Hard work is indispensable because it leads to deeper knowledge, and because it builds confidence in one's own point of view. In addition, people who work hard are much more likely to chance upon the occasional golden nugget that is often well hidden in the market. Needless to say, hard work requires:

1. **Passion for the markets**: people who are not passionate about their investment activities are unlikely to keep up the hard work. People who lack passion also tend to take shortcuts in their decision process.

2. **Intellectual curiosity**: the best investors are curious about new products, companies, investment styles, market studies, etc. They are not afraid to ask questions. And they constantly try to find out everything they can about things they don't understand completely.

3. **Full-time occupation**: a full-time occupation is necessary to gain an edge over other full-time professionals. Hard work – defined as the number of hours put into the activity – is, of course, not a sufficient condition for success. The best investors also use their time very effectively. They constantly try to learn, only focus on the most relevant information, assimilate large amounts of information quickly, apply thorough feedback, examine different scenarios, ignore noise, and

read the small print that is ignored by most other investors. For instance, Warren Buffett spends several hours a day reading newspapers and annual reports, while he only sporadically looks at price charts.

## K.II.4 Eternal study

To develop and fine-tune an effective market strategy, to cope with the dynamics of the market, to gain experience, and to build expertise, investors have to make study an eternal endeavour. Permanent study is critical to gain and maintain a powerful edge over other market players in a constantly changing world. Warren Buffett's business partner Charlie Munger emphasises that Buffett's success has much to do with the fact that he is an amazing "learning machine."

Although it is obvious that learning is important in every area of activity, there are several reasons why most people underestimate its importance in the field of investing. First of all, people seldom examine their investment mistakes – let alone learn from them – because they prefer to put the blame on someone or something else. Second, appropriate feedback is impeded by the fact that people are wired against feedback due to cognitive biases such as overconfidence (and the belief in one's own superiority), the hindsight bias, and the tendency to seek patterns. Finally, investing is a highly probabilistic process. It is, for instance, equally hard to find stocks that will underperform as stocks that will outperform the market. The probabilistic nature of investing makes it extremely hard for most people to judge whether their process is right or whether their success or failure is caused by (bad) luck.

Due to the numerous impediments that people encounter when they try to learn from their personal experiences, the capacity to learn correctly from the past is a considerable asset in the stock market. A prerequisite for effective eternal study is to have the appropriate attitudes like *modesty, humility and responsibility*. These are essential because people who blame others or people who believe that they know all they need to know are unlikely to learn anything at all. Apart from this, to make the most of past experiences intelligent investors fervently pursue:

1. **Effective feedback**: intelligent investors examine how they achieved their results to improve their future market operations – they try to find out what they are good and bad at so they can focus on what works best for them. Amongst other things, effective feedback consists of:

   - *Focus on the long-term performance*: intelligent investors ignore short-term fluctuations because these tend to be random. They look almost exclusively at how they perform over the long term, i.e., over periods of many years. The importance of a long-term focus is illustrated in:

     (i) Table 6: this shows the annual returns of some exceptional investors from 1965 to 2004.[236] Highlighted in black are years where the investors underperformed the S&P 500, and highlighted in grey are the years where they outperformed the S&P 500 by more than 10%.

---

[236] Sources for the data in the table were the annual letters to shareholders of Berkshire Hathaway, (Graham, 2003), and (Greenblatt, 1997). S&P 500 figures are with dividends reinvested.

## Table 6: Annual returns of a number of highly successful investors

| | S&P, div included | Walter Schloss | Warren Buffett | Charles Munger | Rick Guerin | Tom Knapp | Bill Ruane | Joel Greenblatt | Lou Simpson |
|---|---|---|---|---|---|---|---|---|---|
| 1956 | 7.5% | 6.8% | | | | | | | |
| 1957 | -10.5% | -4.7% | 10.4% | | | | | | |
| 1958 | 42.1% | 54.6% | 40.9% | | | | | | |
| 1959 | 12.7% | 23.3% | 25.9% | | | | | | |
| 1960 | -1.6% | 9.3% | 22.8% | | | | | | |
| 1961 | 26.4% | 28.8% | 45.9% | | | | | | |
| 1962 | -10.2% | 11.1% | 13.9% | 30.1% | | | | | |
| 1963 | 23.3% | 20.1% | 38.7% | 71.7% | | | | | |
| 1964 | 16.5% | 22.8% | 27.8% | 49.7% | | | | | |
| 1965 | 13.1% | 35.7% | 47.2% | 8.4% | 32.0% | | | | |
| 1966 | -10.4% | 0.7% | 20.4% | 12.4% | 36.7% | | | | |
| 1967 | 26.8% | 34.4% | 35.9% | 56.2% | 180.1% | | | | |
| 1968 | 10.6% | 35.5% | 58.8% | 40.4% | 171.9% | 27.6% | | | |
| 1969 | -7.5% | -9.0% | 16.2% | 28.3% | 97.1% | 12.7% | | | |
| 1970 | 2.4% | -8.2% | 12.0% | -0.1% | -7.2% | -1.3% | 12.1% | | |
| 1971 | 14.9% | 28.3% | 16.4% | 25.4% | 16.4% | 20.9% | 13.5% | | |
| 1972 | 19.8% | 15.5% | 21.7% | 8.3% | 17.1% | 14.6% | 3.7% | | |
| 1973 | -14.8% | -8.0% | 4.7% | -31.9% | -42.1% | 8.3% | -24.0% | | |
| 1974 | -26.6% | -6.2% | 5.5% | -31.5% | -34.4% | 1.5% | -15.7% | | |
| 1975 | 36.9% | 52.2% | 21.9% | 73.2% | 31.2% | 28.8% | 60.5% | | |
| 1976 | 22.4% | 39.2% | 59.3% | | 127.8% | 40.2% | 72.3% | | |
| 1977 | -8.6% | 34.4% | 31.9% | | 27.1% | 23.4% | 19.9% | | |
| 1978 | 7.0% | 48.8% | 24.0% | | 37.9% | 41.0% | 23.9% | | |
| 1979 | 17.6% | 39.7% | 35.7% | | 48.2% | 25.5% | 12.1% | | |
| 1980 | 32.1% | 31.1% | 19.3% | | 24.1% | 21.4% | 12.6% | | 23.7% |
| 1981 | 6.7% | 24.5% | 31.4% | | 8.0% | 14.4% | 21.5% | | 5.4% |
| 1982 | 20.2% | 32.1% | 40.0% | | 32.0% | 10.2% | 31.2% | | 45.8% |
| 1983 | 22.8% | 51.2% | 32.2% | | 24.8% | 35.0% | 27.3% | | 36.0% |
| 1984 | 6.1% | | 13.6% | | | | | | 21.8% |
| 1985 | 31.6% | | 48.2% | | | | | 70.4% | 45.8% |
| 1986 | 18.6% | | 26.1% | | | | | 53.6% | 38.7% |
| 1987 | 5.1% | | 19.5% | | | | | 29.4% | -10.0% |
| 1988 | 16.6% | | 20.1% | | | | | 64.4% | 30.0% |
| 1989 | 31.7% | | 44.4% | | | | | 31.9% | 36.1% |
| 1990 | -3.1% | | 7.4% | | | | | 31.6% | -9.9% |
| 1991 | 30.5% | | 39.6% | | | | | 28.5% | 56.5% |
| 1992 | 7.6% | | 20.3% | | | | | 30.6% | 10.8% |
| 1993 | 10.1% | | 14.3% | | | | | 115.2% | 4.6% |
| 1994 | 1.3% | | 13.9% | | | | | 48.9% | 13.4% |
| 1995 | 37.6% | | 43.1% | | | | | | 39.8% |
| 1996 | 23.0% | | 31.8% | | | | | | 29.2% |
| 1997 | 33.4% | | 34.1% | | | | | | 24.6% |
| 1998 | 28.6% | | 48.3% | | | | | | 18.6% |
| 1999 | 21.0% | | 0.5% | | | | | | 7.2% |
| 2000 | -9.1% | | 6.5% | | | | | | 20.9% |
| 2001 | -11.9% | | -6.2% | | | | | | 5.2% |
| 2002 | -22.1% | | 10.0% | | | | | | -8.1% |
| 2003 | 28.7% | | 21.0% | | | | | | 38.3% |
| 2004 | 10.9% | | 10.5% | | | | | | 16.9% |

It is striking to see that *all* of them underperformed the stock market in one year or another. Five of the eight investors even underperformed the S&P in three or four consecutive years. Walter Schloss underperformed the S&P 500 in 6 out of 28 years, and Lou Simpson failed to beat the market in 8 out of 24 years. Warren Buffett underperformed the market in six years, with a staggering underperformance of more than 10% in two of these six years.

Finally, Joel Greenblatt owes his remarkable track record to eight out of ten years as he underperformed the S&P 500 in one year and performed in line with the S&P 500 in another. This illustrates that even the brightest investors regularly lag behind the market – sometimes even in several consecutive years.

(ii) Figure 29: this shows the annual return of the investors of Table 6 over trailing ten-year periods. As one can see, all of these investors outperformed the S&P 500 by impressive margins over long-term periods, in spite of their occasional underperformance.

**Figure 29: Annual returns of top investors over rolling, trailing ten-year periods**

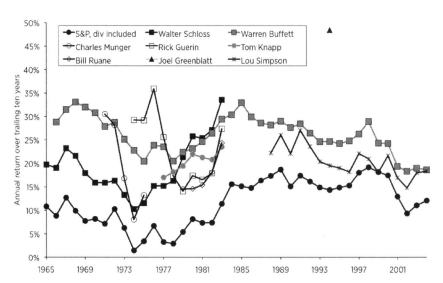

- *Focus on the process*: intelligent investors focus on their process and closely monitor when they override it. Every trade that does not fit into their strategy is considered a mistake – irrespective of its outcome. For instance, a good trade with a bad process (e.g., selling a winning stock right before it turns down without a proper reason for the sale) is considered a mistake – irrespective of the gains.

- *Examination of alternative actions*: intelligent investors not only track the performance of their portfolio but also examine what would have happened if they would have taken alternative actions. For instance, it is a common practice among successful investors to keep track of the price action of the stocks they sold or rejected for investment. Monitoring of these types of stocks can teach investors how they can perfect their investment method.

- *Keeping written notes*: top investors keep a log of what they did right and wrong. Also a written log of every action and each investment thesis at the moment it is initiated (as applied by hedge fund manager Ray Dalio) is helpful, because this can serve as a protection against cognitive biases (in particular, the hindsight bias) that interfere with effective feedback.

2. **Learning from mistakes**: top investors do post-mortems. They spend a lot of time analysing their mistakes (as well as those of others) and feed this knowledge back into their strategy and process. What is more, they embrace their mistakes as learning opportunities and see the money they lost due to these mistakes as a tuition fee.

3. **Eternal study of the markets**: top investors are avid students of the markets. They examine the past, analyse the present and draw appropriate conclusions to support their future actions.

## K.II.5 Discretion

Finally, whereas the average investor itches to give his or her opinion and advice to anyone who is willing to listen, top investors usually keep their trades and opinions to themselves. They cherish discretion for a number of reasons. First, telling everyone about one's trades and opinions creates the undesirable pressure to hang on to these ideas and positions to avoid losing face. Second, disclosure of positions can lead to undesirable market movements (if the investor is well respected), which can hamper the operations of the investor in question. For instance, it was not uncommon in the past for a stock to rally once the news was out that Warren Buffett was a heavy buyer. As a result, further accumulation of the position became more expensive for Buffett. And third, because intelligent investors are humble (see below), they don't feel the need to brag about their results and their ideas.

# K.III Required attitudes

## K.III.1 Modesty

There are many reasons why ego and arrogance are problematic for asset managers. For starters, arrogance fosters overconfidence and greed, which often lead to fatal mistakes (e.g., not taking a loss, picking tops, not learning from mistakes, etc.). Second, investors who lack humility often have unrealistic expectations. They therefore chase performance and overreach – which is a standard recipe for underperformance. Third, arrogance blurs the perception of what is going on in the markets. For instance, people who are convinced that they perfectly understand what is going on tend to take oversized risk in optimistic markets and undersized risk in pessimistic markets.

Due to this, virtually all great investors believe in the old saying "Pride goes before a fall." When we analyse top investors, one can see that they invariably exhibit a high amount of modesty about their abilities and skills. This is also illustrated by the fact that – unlike the popular market gurus of the day – the best investors try to keep a low profile.[237] They are relatively unknown (even in the investment world), and can be described as "the great investor you probably never heard about."

In essence, intelligent investors are humble in the sense that they typically display a healthy blend of:

1. **Realism about expectations**: intelligent investors have modest and realistic expectations. This keeps them from frenetically chasing unrealistic returns. More specifically, great investors are realistic about:

   - *Achievable long-term annual returns*: smart investors know that since stocks tend to return about 7% to 10% annually over the very long run, it is extremely difficult for anyone to achieve average annual compound returns of 15% to 20% or more. Many excellent investors therefore aim for multi-decade average annual returns from 12% to 15% (although they often beat that target).

   - *Gain/loss ratios in their portfolio*: a surprisingly high percentage (sometimes as high as 50% to 60%) of the positions of the best investors do not work out as expected. As a rule, great investors make the bulk of their market-beating returns on only a small percentage (sometimes as low as 10% to 20%) of their positions. For this reason, intelligent investors accept the fact that a significant number of their investments will disappoint.

   - *Consistency of their returns*: intelligent investors do **not** see it as their goal to beat their benchmark in every single year. If we look at the track records of the best investors (see Table 6 above), one can see that all had down years and that they lost out to the S&P 500 from time to time.

2. **Self-criticism and self-questioning**: top investors honestly recognise their limitations, because they realise that they have to compete against many smart and effective market players. Intelligent investors don't see themselves as market geniuses. They are not wedded to any particular idea. And they actually don't care about whether they are right or wrong. In fact, they change course when everything indicates that they are wrong. Practically speaking, intelligent investors:

---

[237] It is a common belief that top investors owe their nice track records in part to their public announcements by which they move markets in their favour. The truth is that smart investors shun the media. The nicest example is that of short sellers. Most people hate short sellers because they are believed to drag markets down by convincing everyone of their case. In reality, though, smart short sellers shy away from publicity and disclosures, because this can cause problems for their trades (e.g., it can lead to buy-ins).

- *Admit to their mistakes*: intelligent investors have no problem admitting when they have made a mistake.

- *Accept that they don't know everything*: smart investors remain within their circle of competence and are very cautious about where the market is going. When asked about their short-term market outlook, they invariably say that they are not smart enough to make that kind of prediction.

- *Invariably look at their ideas from different angles*: intelligent investors constantly question themselves and remain critical of everything they do. They exercise caution when things go exceptionally well because that is often the moment that ego and overconfidence catch fire. Here are two basic exercises that some of the greatest investors apply consistently:

  (i) They examine the bear case of every trade they are contemplating. Warren Buffett's sidekick Charlie Munger states that investors must try to kill their best ideas. To get a better idea of the bear case, some of the greatest investors talk with people who disagree (e.g., especially people who short the stock they would like to buy). They probe for disconfirming evidence. Another advantage of attention to the bear case is that once one is aware of the bear arguments one will find it easier to get out of a position if the investment doesn't work out as expected.

  (ii) Many successful investors try to understand their edge over the market in every trade they make. If they can't find any, they do not invest.

- *Are sufficiently open-minded to reverse field*: smart investors are willing to embrace positions that challenge their previous ideas when this is vindicated by new facts. This also comes naturally to top investors, because they, unlike most other market players, usually consider a range of possible scenarios before they enter a position. Open-mindedness has to be contrasted with the mentality of so-called *perma-bears* and *perma-bulls*. These people are regarded as *specialists* who stick with a bear or bull view no matter what.[238]

- *Take responsibility for their actions*: when a trade doesn't work out intelligent investors don't try to put the blame on others or on external elements. They realise that they – and they alone – are responsible for their trades.

3. **Well-calibrated confidence**: modesty and humility do not exclude confidence. In fact, intelligent investors *do* display well-calibrated (i.e., sufficient but not excessive) confidence. Confidence is important to think independently, and to have the courage to go against the crowd and conventional wisdom. Well-calibrated confidence is indispensable in particular when emotions are running high in the marketplace.

---

[238] These investment strategists or economists rarely manage money. If they do, they are seldom successful. They are popular in the press and give a lot of speeches during periods when their theories appear to be right.

> "My sense of insecurity keeps me alert, always ready to correct my errors. To others, being wrong is a source of shame; to me, recognizing my mistakes is a source of pride."
>
> **George Soros (Soros, 1995)**

> "We regard investing as an arrogant act; an investor who buys is effectively saying that he or she knows more than the seller and the same or more than other prospective buyers. We counter this necessary arrogance (for indeed, a good investor must pull confidently on the trigger) with an offsetting dose of humility, always asking whether we have an apparent advantage over other market participants in any potential investment. If the answer is negative, we do not invest."
>
> **Seth Klarman, letter to shareholders, 1996**

> "If there is no natural sceptic on an investment maybe it would be wise to appoint one of the team to play Devil's Advocate anyway."
>
> **Peter Cundill (Risso-Gill, 2011)**

## K.III.2 Passion

Great investors are passionate about the investment process. They are not primarily motivated by the prospect of money, but feel challenged by and excited about the stock market. Passionate investors are motivated and dedicated. They work hard and go the extra mile (e.g., they read some more and look for more detailed information). They also tend to be creative in their approach to the market and always look for ways to do things better and more efficiently.

People who are motivated by the money and not by the process, by contrast, are unlikely to put in that much effort. They primarily look for shortcuts that save them the effort of slugging through annual reports or talking to people. In sum, passionate investors are much more likely to apply a more effective investment process and therefore operate with a competitive advantage over their less passionate colleagues.

## K.III.3 Emotional detachment

Investing in stocks can be very emotional because it involves coping with financial losses and gains, making hard decisions (e.g., to buy or sell), and so on. Most people are not wired correctly to deal with this flow of emotions. They are overcome on and off by fear, greed, pessimism and optimism. They are therefore bound to make all manner of costly mistakes.

Intelligent investors are definitely not immune to the mood swings caused by stock price movements. What separates them from the crowd, though, is that they actively and consciously try to detach their emotions from their activities. They display tolerance for pain, remain rational under difficult circumstances and they do not let emotions affect their decisions. Above all, they don't lose control. In fact, it is hard to tell from their face whether they had a profitable day or not. The typical master investor remains emotionally detached by:

1. **Not being in the market for emotional satisfaction**: people who invest for emotional satisfaction stand little chance in the market. After all, what feels good is seldom the right thing to do. According to Warren Buffett, not playing for emotional satisfaction also means feeling equally comfortable taking positions with the crowd or against the crowd.

---

*"To buy when others are despondently selling and to sell when others are greedily buying requires the greatest fortitude, even while offering the greatest reward."*

**John Templeton (Krass, 1999)**

---

2. **Being very wary of feelings one way or another**: intelligent investors fight feelings of excessive optimism or pessimism, because they know that these feelings get people into trouble. They don't let themselves get carried away by a particular loss or gain, but always move on to the next trade. In other words, smart investors try to remain even-tempered day in and day out.

3. **Avoiding emotional attachment to positions**: intelligent investors acknowledge that they, just like any other human being, can get emotionally attached to certain stocks. They realise that it is useless to ignore this fact and they try to live with it by always trying to look at the facts in an unbiased way. Some top investors deal with emotional attachment by selling a stock when they feel that their thinking about the stock is getting blurred by their sympathy for the stock (e.g., after a very decent gain).

4. **Not playing for the money**: master investors stress that one should not focus on the money aspect, as playing for the money leads to an overwhelming emotional involvement. A corollary of this is that top investors strongly advise against investing when one has to win (e.g., to recoup previous losses, to pay for tuition, etc.).

5. **Limiting attention to changes in stock prices**: intelligent investors don't check stock prices every hour. They know that most price fluctuations are random. Constant confrontation with price changes can drain emotions as the investor constantly has to deal with losses and gains. Sporadic monitoring of stock prices, on the other hand, reduces the risk that the investor will make rash decisions due to overreaction or the asymmetric loss aversion.

## K.III.4 Patience

> "One of the best rules anybody can learn about investing is to do nothing, absolutely nothing, unless there is something to do."
>
> **Jim Rogers (Schwager, 2006)**

In a world dominated by short-term thinking and the chase for the quick and easy buck, patience is a virtue that represents a very powerful competitive advantage. In fact, the stock market is a place where money is transferred from the active to the patient. Patient people can take advantage of market dislocations caused by short-term oriented market players, such as crashes, bubbles, and the cheap prices of ignored and not-so-hot stocks. Besides, patient investors incur less in transaction costs and taxes than their impatient fellows. And they have more time to do their homework on every single idea.

It is therefore logical that virtually all top investors exhibit an inordinate amount of patience. They even don't relinquish that patience under the pressure of short-term focused clients, shareholders or the press (e.g., during a period of temporary underperformance). The highly respected investor Philip Carret claimed at the end of his life that patience was the most important lesson of his 75-year career. Here are some of the requirements to maintain patience over the years:

1. Having the discipline to **wait for opportunities:** intelligent investors wait patiently for (compelling) opportunities. Investors like Warren Buffett and Prem Watsa, for instance, have regularly waited on the sidelines for several years on end when the markets did not offer value for their money. Not buying when one can't find bargains not only avoids disappointments but also enables the investor to have enough dry powder when bargains abound.

2. Having the mental fortitude and **courage to maintain one's cool during market swings**: intelligent investors remain disciplined and patient no matter what the market does. Charles Munger once said that investors who can't stand watching their stock holdings decline 50% without becoming panic-stricken will get the results they deserve.

> "The seasoned investor does not allow temporary fluctuations in stock-market prices to influence his decisions to any great extent. Usually he waits until prices return to approximately the levels at which he wants to buy or sell. He is not impatient, nor is he even in a very great hurry, for he is an investor – not a gambler nor a speculator."
>
> **J. Paul Getty (Krass, 1999)**

3. **Avoiding unnecessary trading (overtrading)**: intelligent investors look at the long-term potential of every position. They therefore don't see why they should trade frequently.

4. **Understanding the power of compounding**: intelligent investors know that exceptional annual returns are not necessary to build exceptional wealth over the long term. It is believed that Albert Einstein once said that compounding was the most fabulous force in the universe. Indeed, even with a return of 12%, a portfolio doubles about every six to seven years, which amounts to about 30 times the original amount in 30 years. With 15%, 20% and 25%, the original amount turns into respectively 66, 237 and 808 times the original amount after 30 years.[239]

> *"If a situation is moving so fast that a couple of hours or days make a difference, it's probably not for you."*
>
> **Joel Greenblatt (Greenblatt, 1997)**

> *"The most important attribute for success in value investing is patience, patience, and more patience. The majority of investors do not possess this characteristic."*
>
> **Peter Cundill (Risso-Gill, 2011)**

# K.IV The role of experience, talent and intelligence

To conclude, it is worth reflecting on the role of experience, talent and intelligence in the success of top investors.

## K.IV.1 Experience

As in all activities of life, experience can be a huge asset for investors. There is one caveat, though. Experience will only benefit an investor provided that he or she learns from it. Investors who accumulate experience and who incorporate these experiences into their strategy eventually internalise their style, and develop some kind of market intuition.

---

[239] The power of compounding can be understood by a very simple and practical rule of thumb, the *rule of 70*. This rule gives the number of years L required for an amount of money to double at a certain rate of return $r_\%$ (expressed in %) as $L = 70/r_\%$. This is obtained by solving the following equation for L: $(1+0.01.r_\%)^L = 2$, which with $\ln(1+0.01.r_\%) \approx r_\%/100$, gives as a result: $L = 100.\ln(2)/r_\% \approx 70/r_\%$. The rule of 70 implies that one needs about 14 years, 7 years, 4.5 years, 3.5 years, 3 years and 2.5 years to double one's money at returns of respectively 5%, 10%, 15%, 20%, 25% and 30%.

## K.IV.2 Talent

The idea that everyone can be successful in the stock market is probably as absurd as the assumption that everyone can become a medical doctor, an MBA basketball player, or a rocket scientist. Although effective investing strategies can be taught, it is naïve to expect that all students will *get it*, or that all will be successful in the execution. Hence, only people with the right talents will be able to beat the market over the long term.

## K.IV.3 Intelligence

Since investing is rather an art than a science it is to be expected that intelligence in and of itself is not essential for success. The greatest investors agree. They are convinced that average to good intelligence is sufficient, but that exceptional intelligence is not necessarily an advantage. The fact that plenty of highly intelligent people have failed miserably in the stock market supports the thesis that the correlation between market success and intelligence is not that strong.

A famous example of this was Isaac Newton. Although he was without any doubt one of the greatest geniuses in mathematics and physics the world has ever known, Newton lost a (time-adjusted) capital of $3 million when he followed the mad crowd in the infamous English South Sea bubble.[240]

> *"Success in investing doesn't correlate with IQ once you're above the level of 125. Once you have ordinary intelligence, what you need is the temperament to control the urges that get other people into trouble in investing."*
>
> **Warren Buffett (www.businessweek.com/1999/99_27/b3636006.htm)**

To understand why a high amount of intelligence is not necessarily an advantage in the market, one has to realise that it can actually work against the investor. High intelligence can lead to a predilection for unnecessary complexity, arrogance (i.e., the idea of knowing better), and an unwillingness to learn from past mistakes (because one already assumes to know everything).

Having said that, intelligent people that also exhibit the characteristics of investment intelligence (e.g., modesty, accumulation of learning experience, emotional detachment, discipline, simple strategy, etc.) are clearly at an advantage over their less intelligent colleagues. People with extraordinary intelligence are able to analyse complex situations that other people avoid and they can typically process information and accumulate experiences much faster.

Warren Buffett is probably one of the best examples. He owes without any doubt his exceptional investing prowess to a combination of exceptional investment intelligence and extraordinary intellectual intelligence. The overall conclusion is that although most

---

[240] See, e.g., (MacKay, 2008).

successful investors do have an above-average IQ[241], too much of it can be harmful if it is not kept in check by a healthy dose of investment intelligence.

> *"Let me emphasize that it does not take a genius or even superior talent to be successful as a value analyst. What it needs first is, reasonable good intelligence; second, sound principles of operation; third, and most important, firmness of character."*
>
> **Benjamin Graham (Heins, 2013)**

## K.V Summary

To conclude this chapter Figure 30 presents the basic requirements of intelligent investors. This figure shows the interdependence between various process requirements, attitudes and the strategy.

The most important connections are:

1. First of all, excellent investors have the talent to beat the market by means of a particular strategy.

2. Second, intelligent investors execute their strategy in a very disciplined way. This can only be achieved through:

   - sufficient knowledge and experience,

   - independence,

   - emotional detachment, and

   - patience.

   Moreover, maintaining discipline will be easier if the strategy is flexible, effective and compatible with the investor.

3. Knowledge takes a central position, because it enables the investor to be independent and to maintain discipline through conviction. Knowledge is built through the accumulation of and conscious reflection on experiences, through eternal study and through hard work. In addition, it is easier for the investor to acquire knowledge in a time-effective way if he or she is more intelligent.

4. The basic pillars that support knowledge and independence are hard work and eternal study. These, in turn, have to be supported by modesty, as well as passion and interest in the markets and in the investment process. Passion supplies the energy and motivation to keep the hard work (and eternal study) up. Modesty is

---

[241] In Buffett's quote on page 302, he mentioned that an IQ of 125 is sufficient. Note that this IQ is significantly higher than the average human IQ of 100. Hence, through this statement Buffett indirectly acknowledges that an above-average IQ is necessary for success.

necessary to realise that hard work and eternal study are indispensable to succeed in the market.

5. Finally, modesty is not only necessary to convince investors that hard work is necessary, but also helps the investor to maintain discretion (because there is no urge to brag or talk about one's positions), and to focus on his/her circle of competence (where his/her knowledge is superior to that of the crowd).

**Figure 30: Interplay between process requirements, attitudes, strategy and experience, talent and intelligence for the intelligent investor**

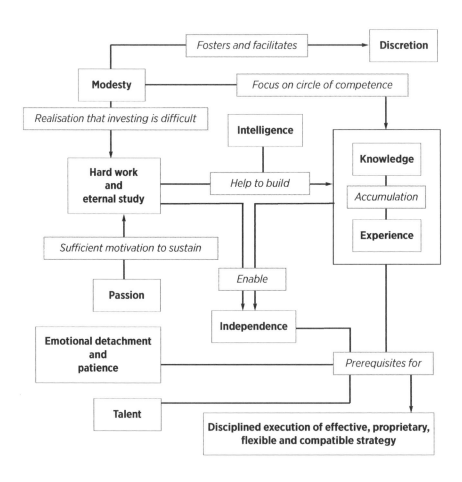

# GLOSSARY

**Active investing** is every type of investing where a portfolio manager tries to beat the market. This should be contrasted with passive investing, where the aim is to match the performance of an index before costs and expenses.

The **annual compound return** X of an investment is the geometric average of the annual returns over the considered period:

$$X = \sqrt[N]{(1 + r_1) \times (1 + r_2) \times (1 + r_3) \times \dots \times (1 + r_N)} - 1$$

where N is the number of years of the period, and where $r_i$ is the return in year i.

**Averaging down** is the practice where an investor buys more shares of a company he or she already owns when its price falls with the aim of reducing the average purchase price.

A **bear market** is a period in which a stock market loses at least 20% versus a previous market top.

The **Bigger Fool mentality/theory** is the idea that it makes sense to pay a "foolish" price (i.e., a price far above a stock's fair value) as it is often possible to find even greater "fools" who are willing to buy the stock at a higher price. Adherents of the Bigger Fool theory speculate that they can make money from momentum and crowd behaviour irrespective of the stock's intrinsic value.

**Blue chips** are the stocks with the highest market capitalisation of a stock market.

**Bottom fishing** refers to the practice where an investor tries to time the purchase of a stock around an absolute price bottom.

**Bottom-up investing** is an investment style where the investor looks primarily to the fundamentals of companies and where scant attention is paid to the economic picture and outlook.

A **bull market** is a period during which a stock market gains at least 20% versus a previous market bottom.

The **Capital Asset Pricing Model (CAPM)** is an elegant theory that posits that stock returns and risks can be captured through a simple mathematical model, based on the assumption that stock markets are efficient.

**Capitulation** is the event where investors throw in the towel and sell shares to get rid of the pain caused by the losses of these shares.

The **circle of competence** refers to the business areas, industries, or sectors about which someone has superior knowledge thanks to one's job, because one has built specific expertise in the past within that sector, and the like.

A **competitive moat** is the whole set of defences that make up a company's franchise. It protects a company against competitors, against demanding customers and suppliers, against threats like substitutes, and so on. A competitive moat includes barriers to entry, differentiation of the product/service, competitive advantages versus peers (e.g., scale), etc.

**Contrarian investing** is a mindset where an investor tries to beat the market by going against the prevailing market sentiment. Contrarian investors look for bargains among stocks that are out of favour, they see hot stocks as short candidates, they usually increase their purchases during bear markets, and they may reduce their stock positions during bull markets.

The **corporate imperative** is a term coined by Warren Buffett which refers to the irresistible propensity of managers to copy the behaviour of other corporate leaders. The corporate imperative is, for instance, responsible for flurries of acquisition activity in certain industries, management fads (that are mindlessly adopted in different companies), and the like.

A **credit rating** is a rating assigned to a company by a rating agency that reflects the companies' creditworthiness. The top three credit rating agencies are S&P, Moody's and Fitch and the following table gives a rough overview of the credit ratings they can assign to a company:

| S&P, Fitch | Moody's | Comment |
|---|---|---|
| AAA | Aaa | Extremely high creditworthiness (risk free) |
| AA+/AA/AA- | Aa1/Aa2/Aa3 | Excellent creditworthiness |
| A+/A/A- | A1/A2/A3 | High creditworthiness |
| BBB+/BBB/BBB- | Baa1/Baa2/Baa3 | Good creditworthiness |
| BB+/BB/BB- | Ba1/Ba2/Ba3 | Sub-investment grade (junk) with deteriorating creditworthiness when one moves down the scale from BB (Ba) to B to CCC (Caa) to CC (Ca) and to C |
| B+/B/B- | B1/B2/B3 | |
| CCC+/CCC/CCC- | Caa1/Caa2/Caa3 | |
| CC+/CC/CC- | Ca1/Ca2/Ca3 | |
| C+/C/C- | C1/C2/C3 | |

The **discounted cash flow (DCF) model** is used to determine an asset's fair value based on the future cash flows that the asset will generate. The fair value is basically the sum of the present values of all the cash flows that will accrue to the owner of the asset over the time the asset is held by the owner:

$$\text{fair value} = \sum_{i=1}^{K} \frac{(\text{cash flow})_i}{(1 + r_i)^{R(i)}}$$

In this expression, $(\text{cash flow})_i$ is the cash flow the asset throws off in year i, K is the number of cash flows that are received over the holding period, $r_i$ is the discount rate applicable to $(\text{cash flow})_i$, and R(i) is the number of years until $(\text{cash flow})_i$ will be received.

**Diworseification** is a term coined by Peter Lynch which refers to the common practice of companies to enter new types of businesses (typically through acquisitions) in an attempt to spur growth. Although "diversification" efforts seem sensible at first sight, the fact that companies typically lose the focus on their core business and their lack of familiarity with the new business(es) often leads to disappointing results.

**Earnings management** is the manipulation of the financial statements with the aim of presenting another (usually better) picture of the company's financials.

**Economic goodwill** is the value of a company's assets in excess of their book value that is not reflected in the balance sheet (as opposed to accounting goodwill). Economic goodwill derives from the superior returns that certain companies can extract from their assets due to brand power, their competitive position, excellent cost control, execution, etc.

The **Efficient Market Hypothesis (EMH)** is the assumption that stock markets are efficient in the sense that there is no opportunity for any investor to beat the market. Adherents of the EMH claim that rational and clever market operators eliminate immediately any potential mispricing, such that all stocks are priced correctly at all times in the market.

**Emerging markets** are countries with GDP per capita that is currently substantially below that of developed countries, but which are expected to grow faster than developed countries such that they are likely to become developed countries over the medium to long term.

**Fair value**: see "intrinsic value".

The **Fed model** is a valuation model for the entire stock market, which compares the market's earnings yield with the risk-free long-term interest rate.

**Float** is the amount of shares of a company that are freely tradable on a stock exchange. It is the number of shares outstanding minus all restricted shares.

**Free cash flow to equity (FCFE)** is the cash flow that accrues to the shareholders of the company. FCFE is discretionary cash that can be distributed to the shareholders, or that can be reinvested in the business. The most common definition of FCFE is:

FCFE = operating cash flow - capital expenditures

It is related in the following way to the so-called "free cash flow to the firm" FCFF, which is the cash flow that accrues to all shareholders and creditors of the company:

$$FCFE = FCFF - (1 - tax\ rate)\ x\ interest\ paid$$

**Growth investing** is an investment style that focuses on companies with high growth potential. As opposed to deep value investors, who are sceptical of growth, growth investors are willing to pay up for high growth companies.

An **initial public offering (IPO)** is an operation by which a company goes public. Before an IPO, brokers and the company try to determine the price at which they will sell the shares to the public based on the market circumstances and on the feedback they get when they sound the market for potential interest. As part of the IPO the company that brings its stock to the market has to publish certain documents (e.g., a prospectus) with financial data, a description of the company (including its risks), and the like.

The **intrinsic value** (or fair value) of a stock is the present value of the cash flows that will accrue to the shareholders in the future. Although the intrinsic value should be calculated based on the DCF model (see above), the many uncertainties and estimates that must be put into the DCF model mean that other valuation methods (e.g., based on multiples, replacement value, book value, etc.) are often more reliable to determine a stock's intrinsic value than the value that comes out of a DCF valuation.

A **large cap** is a stock with a market capitalisation that is large compared to other stocks in the market. As a rule of thumb, stocks with market caps above ten billion dollars or euro are considered large caps.

**Leverage** refers to the use of debt (e.g., margin accounts), derivatives, or other financial instruments to magnify price changes in an investment. The aim is to increase the potential return of an investment, but leverage also increases the potential loss.

A **long position** is the position an investor is in when he or she purchases a particular security with the aim to profit from its upside.

**Macro investing** is a type of top-down investing where the investor (usually) has the latitude to invest in any type of asset in (almost) every country in the world.

A **margin of safety** is the discount of the stock price versus its (estimated) fair value. Many investors apply a margin of safety (e.g., of about 30%) when they buy a stock, which provides a cushion against errors in the calculation of the fair value.

A **margin call** is the demand of a broker to an investor to provide more collateral for margin loans or short positions the investor has with the broker. If the investor ignores the margin call, the broker will sell the underlying securities to eliminate the risk to which he or she is exposed.

A **micro cap** is a stock with a market capitalisation that is tiny compared to other stocks in the market. As a rule of thumb, stocks with market caps below 100 million dollars or euro are considered micro caps. In general, micro caps are much riskier than stocks with larger capitalisations as these companies are still in the early stages of growth. In addition, liquidity in these stocks tends to be low, making it sometimes hard to buy and sell positions at a fair price.

A **mid cap** is a stock with a market capitalisation that is neither small nor big compared to other stocks in the market. As a rule of thumb, stocks with market caps between about five and ten billion dollars or euro are considered mid caps.

**Momentum** is the tendency of stock prices (or other assets) to move in the same direction as they did in the recent past.

**Passive investing** is every type of investing where one tries to match the performance of an index before fees and expenses.

The **PEG ratio** is the ratio of a stock's price-to-earnings multiple to its expected (annual) earnings growth rate over the next few years. It is a popular valuation metric among growth investors.

**Pipeline fill** is the event where the distribution channels of a company's product are saturated as all possible retailers have the product on their shelves. After a pipeline fill, the growth in sales drops to the rate of consumer consumption.

**Private equity** is a specific type of investing that is usually done through private equity partnerships that have a limited lifetime. Some private equity partnerships invest in early-stage companies with high growth potential, whereas others specialise in the buyout of stable and cash-generating businesses.

The **put/call ratio** is defined as the number of put options divided by the number of call options in the market.

**Pyramiding** is the practice where momentum traders buy more of a stock as it goes up, based on the idea that strong stock price action is likely to continue.

A **range-bound market** is a secular market cycle (see below) where stock prices move sideways and where valuations come down.

A **rating agency** is a company that rates the creditworthiness and that determines the probability of default of a company. The three biggest rating agencies are S&P, Moody's and Fitch. See also *credit rating*.

**Real earnings** are the earnings with purchasing power at the moment they were earned.

**Scuttlebutt** refers to the gathering of information on a company through first-hand experiences (e.g., one's personal customer experience) or through sources that are very close to the company such as employees, customers, suppliers, competitors, stakeholders, etc.

**Secular market cycles** are price cycles (of certain assets) that stretch over many years (typically decades). One can distinguish secular bull, secular bear and secular range-bound cycles. During a secular cycle asset prices usually move up and down in much shorter cycles of typically only a few years.

The **short interest ratio** is the number of shares that are sold short in the market relative to the total number of outstanding and tradable shares of that company.

**Short selling (shorting)** refers to the practice where an investor borrows shares from another investor to sell them in the market. The short seller bets on the decline of the share price and tries to make money by buying the shares back at a lower price (after which they are returned to the rightful owner).

A **short squeeze** is a sudden price increase caused by panic among short sellers who desperately want to cover their short positions.

A **small cap** is a stock with a relatively small market capitalisation compared to other stocks in the market. It is common to define small caps as all stocks with market caps between about 100 million and five billion dollars or euro. This has to be contrasted with micro caps, mid caps and large caps.

**Speculation** can be defined as playing the markets based on hunches, rumours, hope and wishful thinking.

**Stalwarts** are large and established companies that grow earnings and sales somewhat faster than the economy thanks to their strong competitive position.

**Stop-loss** orders are automatic sell orders that are triggered when a stock falls below (or rises above) a predefined price target. They are an indispensable part of the toolkit of traders and short sellers.

A **ten bagger** is a company that goes up ten-fold within a period of a few years.

**Top picking** is the attempt of many investors to sell a stock at its top.

**Top-down investing** refers to each investment style where the investor determines his or her market positions based on what he/she sees ahead in the economy.

The **trailing average annual return** is the average annual compound return over the past few years. For instance, the five-year trailing average annual return is the average annual compound return over the past five years.

**Triangulation** is the common practice of many top investors to value a stock by means of a number of different valuation methods in order to get a better idea of its true fair value (which may be distorted or error-prone in any single method).

**Value creation** is the task of corporate leaders to increase the value of their business through the strong management of the business and by reinvesting retained cash in projects that throw off sufficient cash.

**Value investing** is an investment style where one tries to buy stocks that are very cheap on a number of valuation multiples. As opposed to growth investors, value investors are sceptical of and don't want to pay up for growth.

A **value trap** is a stock that looks cheap at first sight but that has some important issues that are overlooked by many bargain hunters. Value traps tend to blow up in the face of those who didn't do a proper due diligence.

# REFERENCES

| | |
|---|---|
| (Baruch, 1957) | Baruch, B. M., *My Own Story*, Buccaneer Books, 1957. |
| (Bedbury, 2002) | Bedbury, S., *A New Brand World*, Penguin Books, 2002. |
| (Belsky, 1999) | Belsky, G. and Gilovich, T., *Why Smart People Make Big Money Mistakes and How To Correct Them*, Simon & Schuster, 1999. |
| (Berkun, 2007) | Berkun, S., *The Myths of Innovation*, O'Reilly, 2007. |
| (Bernstein, 2000) | Bernstein, L. A. and Wild, J. J., *Analysis of Financial Statements*, McGraw-Hill, 2000. |
| (Bernstein, 2001) | Bernstein, R., *Navigating the Noise*, Wiley & Sons, 2001. |
| (Blanchard, 1998) | Blanchard, K. and Bowles, S., *Gung Ho!*, William Morrow and Company, 1998. |
| (Boik, 2004) | Boik, J., *Lessons from the Greatest Stock Traders of All Time*, McGraw-Hill, 2004. |
| (Boik, 2006) | Boik, J., *How Legendary Traders Made Millions*, McGraw-Hill, 2006. |
| (Bolton, 2009) | Bolton, A., *Investing Against the Tide*, Financial Times Prentice Hall, 2009. |
| (Bragg, 2007) | Bragg, S. M., *Business Ratios and Formulas: A Comprehensive Guide*, John Wiley & Sons, 2007. |
| (Branson, 1998) | Branson, R., *Losing My Virginity*, Three Rivers Press, 1998. |
| (Browne, 2007) | Browne, C. H., *The Little Book of Value Investing*, John Wiley & Sons, 2007. |
| (Buckingham, 1999) | Buckingham, M. and Coffman, C., *First, Break All The Rules*, Simon & Schuster, 1999. |
| (Buffett, 1977-) | Buffett, W., annual letters of Berkshire Hathaway to shareholders, 1977 to present. |
| (Calandro, 2009) | Calandro, J., *Applied Value Investing*, McGraw-Hill, 2009. |
| (Chancellor, 2000) | Chancellor, E., *Devil Take The Hindmost*, Plume, 2000. |
| (Christensen, 2003) | Christensen, C. M. and Raynor, M. E., *The Innovator's Solution: Creating and Sustaining Successful Growth*, Harvard Business School Publishing, 2003. |
| (Cialdini, 2009) | Cialdini, R. B., *Influence*, Pearson Education, 2009. |
| (Collins, 2001) | Collins, J., *Good To Great*, HarperCollins, 2001. |
| (Collins, 2002) | Collins, J. and Porras, J. I., *Built To Last*, Collins Business Essentials, 2002. |
| (Covel, 2007) | Covel, M. W., *The Complete Turtle Trader*, New York: HarperCollins, 2007. |

(Cunningham, 2001-A)  Cunningham, L. A., *The Essays of Warren Buffett: Lessons for Corporate America*.

(Cunningham, 2001-B)  Cunningham L. A., *How to Think Like Benjamin Graham and Invest Like Warren Buffett*, McGraw-Hill, 2001.

(Damodaran, 2004)  Damodaran, A., *Investment Fables*, Prentice Hall, 2004.

(Damodaran, 2006)  Damodaran, A., *Damodaran on Valuation: Security Analysis for Investment and Corporate Finance*, John Wiley & Sons, 2006.

(Darvas, 2007)  Darvas, N., *How I Made $2,000,000 in the Stock Market*, Harriman House, 2007.

(Dreman, 1998)  Dreman, D., *Contrarian Investment Strategies*, Simon & Schuster, 1998.

(Drobny, 2009)  Drobny, S., *Inside the House of Money*, John Wiley & Sons, 2009.

(Drucker, 1993)  Drucker, P. F., *Innovation and Entrepreneurship*, HarperBusiness, 1993.

(Drucker, 2006)  Drucker, P. F., *The Effective Executive*, HarperCollins, 2006.

(Easterling, 2005)  Easterling, E., *Unexpected Returns: Understanding Secular Stock Market Cycles*, Cypress House, 2005.

(Einhorn, 2008)  Einhorn, D., *Fooling Some of the People All of the Time*, John Wiley & Sons, 2008.

(Epstein, 2005)  Epstein, L., *Reading Financial Reports for Dummies*, Wiley Publishing, 2005.

(Faith, 2007)  Faith, C., *Way of the Turtle*, New York: McGraw-Hill, 2007.

(Fisher, 1996)  Fisher, P. A., *Common Stocks and Uncommon Profits*, John Wiley & Sons, 1996.

(Fisher, 2007)  Fisher, K., *The Only Three Questions That Count*, John Wiley & Sons, 2007.

(Flamholtz, 2007)  Flamholtz, E. G. and Randle, Y., *Growing Pains*, Jossey-Bass, 2007.

(Fraser-Sampson, 2007)  Fraser-Sampson, G., *Private Equity as an Asset Class*, John Wiley & Sons, 2007.

(Freiberg, 1996)  Freiberg, K., *Nuts!*, Broadway Books, 1996.

(Friedlob, 2001)  Friedlob, G. T. and Welton, R. E., *Keys to Reading an Annual Report*, Barron's, 2001.

(Fridson, 2002)  Fridson, M. and Alvarez, F., *Financial Statement Analysis: A Practitioner's Guide*, John Wiley & Sons, 2002.

(George, 2003)  George B., *Authentic Leadership*, Jossey-Bass, 2003.

(Gerstner, 2003)  Gerstner, L. V., *Who Says Elephants Can't Dance?*, HarperCollins, 2003.

(Gladwell, 2002)  Gladwell, M., *The Tipping Point*, Brown and Company, 2002.

(Godin, 2003)  Godin, S., *Purple Cow*, Portfolio, 2003.

(Graham, 2003)  Graham, B., *The Intelligent Investor*, Collins Business Essentials, 2003.

(Greenblatt, 1997)  Greenblatt, J., *You Can be a Stock Market Genius*, Fireside, 1997.

(Greenblatt, 2006)  Greenblatt, J., *The Little Book That Beats The Market*, John Wiley & Sons, 2006.

(Greenwald, 2001)  Greenwald, B. C. N., Kahn, J., Sonkin, P. D., and Van Biema, M., *Value Investing: From Graham to Buffett and Beyond*, John Wiley & Sons, 2001.

(Hagstrom, 2005)      Hagstrom, R. G., *The Warren Buffett Way*, John Wiley & Sons, 2005.

(Hamel, 1996)      Hamel, G. and Prahalad, C. K., *Competing for the Future*, Harvard Business School Press, 1996.

(Harrison, 2007)      Harrison S., *The Manager's Book of Decencies*, McGraw-Hill, 2007.

(Heins, 2013)      Heins, J. and Tilson, W., *The Art of Value Investing*, John Wiley & Sons, 2013.

(Heiserman, 2004)      Heiserman, H., *It's Earnings That Count*, McGraw-Hill, 2004.

(Jean-Jacques, 2003)      Jean-Jacques, J. D., *The 5 Keys to Value Investing*, McGraw-Hill, 2003.

(Kahneman, 2011)      Kahneman, D., *Thinking, Fast and Slow*, Penguin Books Ltd, 2011.

(Katsenelson, 2007)      Katsenelson, V. N., *Active Value Investing*, John Wiley & Sons, 2007.

(Kelly, 2001)      Kelly, T. and Littman, J., *The Art of Innovation: Lessons in Creativity from IDEO, America's Leading Design Firm*, Doubleday, 2001.

(Kim, 2005)      Kim, W. C. and Mauborgne, R., *Blue Ocean Strategy*, Harvard Business School Press, 2005.

(Kindleberger, 2005)      Kindleberger, C. P. and Aliber, R., *Manias, Panics, and Crashes*, John Wiley & Sons, 2005.

(Klarman, 1991)      Klarman S., *Margin of Safety*, HarperCollins, 1991.

(Kobrick, 2006)      Kobrick, F. R., *The Big Money*, Simon & Schuster, 2006.

(Koller, 2005)      Koller, T., Goedhart, M. and Wessels, D., *Valuation: Measuring and Managing the Value of Companies*, John Wiley & Sons, 2005.

(Kouzes, 2007)      Kouzes, J. M. and Posner, B. Z., *The Leadership Challenge*, John Wiley & Sons, 2007.

(Krass, 1999)      Krass, P., *The Book of Investing Wisdom*, John Wiley & Sons, 1999.

(Lefèvre, 2006)      Lefevere, E., *Reminiscences of a Stock Operator*, John Wiley & Sons, 2006.

(Livermore, 2001)      Livermore, J., *How To Trade In Stocks*, McGraw-Hill, 2001.

(Loeb, 2007)      Loeb, G. M., *The Battle For Investment Survival*, BN Publishing, 2007.

(Lowe, 1999)      Lowe, J., *The Rediscovered Benjamin Graham*, John Wiley & Sons, 1999.

(Lowenstein, 1995)      Lowenstein, R., *Buffett: The Making of an American Capitalist*, Broadway Books, 1995.

(Lynch, 1989)      Lynch, P., *One Up on Wall Street*, Simon & Schuster, 1989.

(Lynch, 1993)      Lynch, P., *Beating the Street*, Simon & Schuster, 1993.

(MacKay, 2003)      MacKay, C., *Extraordinary Popular Delusions and the Madness of Crowds*, Harriman House, 2003.

(Mahar, 2004)      Mahar, M., *Bull! A History Of The Boom And Bust*, 1982-2004, HarperBusiness, 2004.

(Malkiel, 2007)      Malkiel, B. G., *A Random Walk Down Wall Street*, W. W. Norton & Company, 2007.

(Mandelman, 2007)      Mandelman, A., *The Sleuth Investor*, McGraw-Hill, 2007.

(Mauboussin, 2006)      Mauboussin, M. J., *More Than You Know*, Columbia University Press, 2006.

| (Miles, 2002) | Miles, R. P., *The Warren Buffett CEO*, John Wiley & Sons, 2002. |
|---|---|
| (Montier, 2010) | Montier, J., *The Little Book of Behavioural Investing*, John Wiley & Sons, 2010. |
| (Moore, 2005) | Moore, G. A., *Inside the Tornado*, Collins Business Essentials, 2005. |
| (Moore, 2006) | Moore, G. A., *Crossing the Chasm*, Collins Business Essentials, 2006. |
| (Morales, 2010) | Morales, G. and Karcher C., *Trade Like an O'Neil Disciple*, John Wiley & Sons, 2010. |
| (Moyer, 2005) | Moyer, S. G., *Distressed Debt Analysis*, J. Ross Publishing, 2005. |
| (Mulford, 2002) | Mulford, C. W. and Comiskey, E. E., *The Financial Numbers Game*, John Wiley & Sons, 2002. |
| (Munger, 1994) | Munger, C., 'A Lesson on Elementary, Worldly Wisdom As It Relates To Investment Management & Business', USC Business School, 1994. |
| (Napier, 2009) | Napier, R., *Anatomy of the Bear*, Harriman House Ltd, 2009. |
| (Neff, 1999) | Neff, J., *John Neff on Investing*, John Wiley & Sons, 1999. |
| (O'Glove, 1987) | O'Glove, T. L., *Quality of Earnings*, The Free Press, 1987. |
| (O'Neil, 2002) | O'Neil, W. J., *How to Make Money in Stocks*, McGraw-Hill, 2002. |
| (O'Shaughenessy, 2005) | O'Shaughenessy, J. P., *What Works on Wall Street*, McGraw-Hill, 2005. |
| (Pabrai, 2007) | Pabrai, M., *The Dhandho Investor*, John Wiley & Sons, 2007. |
| (Peters, 1994) | Peters, T., *The Pursuit of Wow!*, Vintage Books, 1994. |
| (Peters, 2003) | Peters, T., *Re-imagine!*, Dorling Kindersley, 2003. |
| (Peters, 2006) | Peters, T. J. and Waterman, R. H., *In Search of Excellence*, Collins Business Essentials, 2006. |
| (Pfeffer, 2000) | Pfeffer, J. and Sutton, R. I., *The Knowing-Doing Gap*, Harvard Business School Press, 2000. |
| (Pfeffer, 2006) | Pfeffer, J. and Sutton, R. I., *Hard Facts, Dangerous Half-Truths and Total Nonsense*, Harvard Business School Press, 2006. |
| (Pfeffer, 2007) | Pfeffer, J., *What Were They Thinking?*, Harvard Business School Press, 2007. |
| (Pine, 1999) | Pine, B. J. and Gilmore, J. H., *The Experience Economy*, Harvard Business School Press, 1999. |
| (Porter, 1980) | Porter, M. E., *Competitive Strategy*, The Free Press, 1980. |
| (Porter, 1985) | Porter, M. E., *Competitive Advantage*, The Free Press, 1985. |
| (Reinhart, 2009) | Reinhart, C. M. and Rogoff, K., *This Time is Different: Eight Centuries of Financial Folly*, Princeton University Press, 2009. |
| (Ries, 1996) | Ries, A., *Focus: The Future of Your Company Depends on it*, HarperBusiness Publishers, 1996. |
| (Risso-Gill, 2011) | Risso-Gill, C., *There's Always Something to Do*, McGill-Queen's University Press, 2011. |
| (Rogers, 2003) | Rogers, E. M., *Diffusion of Innovations*, Free Press, 2003. |
| (Rogers, 2007) | Rogers, J., *Hot Commodities*, Random House Trade, 2007. |

(Rosenberg, 2000)       Rosenberg, H., *The Vulture Investors*, John Wiley & Sons, 2000.

(Ross, 2000)            Ross, N., *Lessons from the Legends of Wall Street*, Dearborn, 2000.

(Rothchild, 2001)       Rothchild, J., *The Davis Dynasty*, John Wiley & Sons, 2001.

(Sartain, 2003)         Sartain, L., *HR From The Heart*, Amacom, 2003.

(Schilit, 2002)         Schilit, H., *Financial Shenanigans*, McGraw-Hill, 2002.

(Schiller, 2005)        Schiller, R. J., *Irrational Exuberance*, Doubleday, 2005.

(Schrage, 2000)         Schrage, M., *Serious Play*, Harvard Business School Press, 2000.

(Schultz, 1997)         Schultz, H. and Yang, D. J., *Pour Your Heart Into It*, Hyperion, 1997.

(Schwager, 1992)        Schwager, J. D., *The New Market Wizards*, John Wiley & Sons, 1992.

(Schwager, 2006)        Schwager, J. D., *Market Wizards*, Marketplace Books, 2006.

(Schwager, 2012)        Schwager, J. D., *Hedge Fund Market Wizards*, John Wiley & Sons, 2012.

(Siegel, 2005)          Siegel, J. J., *The Future For Investors*, Crown Business, 2005.

(Smithers, 2009)        Smithers, A., *Wall Street Revalued*, John Wiley & Sons, 2009.

(Soros, 1995)           Soros, G., *Soros on Soros*, John Wiley & Sons, 1995.

(Sperandeo, 1997)       Sperandeo, V., *Trader Vic II: Principles of Professional Speculation*, John Wiley & Sons, 1997.

(Staley, 1997)          Staley, K. F., *The Art of Short Selling*, John Wiley & Sons, 1997.

(Swensen, 2005)         Swensen, D. F., *Unconventional Success*, Free Press, 2005.

(Taleb, 2007)           Taleb, N. N., *The Black Swan*, Random House Trade Paperback, 2007.

(Taylor, 2006)          Taylor, W. C. and LaBarre, P., *Mavericks at Work*, William Morrow, 2006.

(Templeton, 2008)       Templeton, L. C., *Investing the Templeton Way*, McGraw-Hill, 2008.

(Tier, 2005)            Tier, M., *The Winning Habits of Warren Buffett and George Soros*, Truman Talley Books, 2005.

(Train, 2000)           Train, J., *Money Masters of Our Time*, HarperCollins, 2000.

(Utterback, 1994)       Utterback, J. M., *Mastering the Dynamics of Innovation*, Harvard Business School Press, 1994.

(Walton, 1992)          Walton, S., *Made in America*, Bantam Books, 1992.

(Welch, 2005)           Welch, J., *Winning*, HarperBusiness, 2005.

(Weiss, 2010)           Weiss, S. L., *The Billion Dollar Mistake*, John Wiley & Sons, 2010.

(Weiss, 2012)           Weiss, S. L., *The Big Win*, John Wiley & Sons, 2012.

(White, 2003)           White, G. I., Sondhi, A. C., and Fried, D., *The Analysis and Use of Financial Statements*, John Wiley & Sons, 2003.

(Whitman, 1979)         Whitman, M. J. and Shubik, M., *The Aggressive Conservative Investor*, John Wiley & Sons, 1979.

(Whitman, 2009)         Whitman, M. J. and Diz, F., *Distress Investing*, John Wiley & Sons, 2009.

(Zweig, 2007)           Zweig, J., *Your Money and Your Brain*, Simon & Schuster, 2007.

# INDEX

38625374R00186

Made in the USA
Lexington, KY
17 January 2015